Island Studies Series

Series Editor
Lino Briguglio

Mediterranean Islands and
Sustainable Tourism Development

Island Studies Series

Series Editor
Lino Briguglio
Islands and Small States Institute, Foundation for International Studies, University of Malta

The Island Studies series focuses on issues which particularly affect small inhabited islands, with special reference to politically independent ones.

The study of islands, as distinct from other geographical entities, is developing as a special area of interest because islands tend to face special problems associated with smallness, insularity, fragile eco-systems and proneness to natural disasters, which render them very vulnerable in the face of forces outside their control. This condition sometimes threatens their very economic viability.

Small island states also offer unique perspectives for study, especially in the areas of tourism and leisure, geography, anthropology, sociology, economics, the environment and sustainable development in general.

The volumes in this series include studies of a general nature and case studies, aimed at scholars and practitioners engaged in the study and in the management of small islands.

Also published in the same series:

Sustainable Tourism in Islands and Small States: Issues and Policies
Edited by Lino Briguglio, Brian Archer, Jafar Jafari and Geoffrey Wall

Sustainable Tourism in Islands and Small States: Case Studies
Edited by Lino Briguglio, Richard Butler, David Harrison and Walter Leal Filho

Banking and Finance in Islands and Small States
Edited by Michael Bowe, Lino Briguglio and James W. Dean

Insularity and Development: International Perspectives on Islands
Edited by Emilio Biagini and Brian Hoyle

Mediterranean Islands and Sustainable Tourism Development

Practices, management and policies

Edited by
Dimitri Ioannides,
Yorghos Apostolopoulos
and Sevil Sonmez

CONTINUUM
London and New York

Continuum

Tower Building
11 York Road
London SE1 7NX

370 Lexington Avenue
New York
NY 10017-6503

First published 2001

British Library Cataloguing-in-Publication Data
A catalogue record for this book is available from the British Library.

ISBN 0-8264-5146-2 (hardback)

Typeset by BookEns Ltd, Royston, Herts.
Printed and bound in Great Britain by The Cromwell Press, Trowbridge, Wilts.

Contents

Illustrations

Plates

Figures

Tables

Contributors

Yorghos Apostolopoulos is a Research Associate Professor of Sociology at Arizona State University in Tempe, Arizona, USA. His work delves into the epidemiological and public health repercussions of tourist migration and subsequent effects on sustainable development. His publications appear in social science and health journals. He is also the senior editor of four books on development and tourism.

Esteban Bardolet is an economist specializing in tourism marketing. His experience includes 15 years as Professor of Marketing at the School of Tourism at the University of the Balearic Islands and 30 years as a banker with a local bank. Bardolet now works as chief economist at the Chamber of Commerce of Majorca and Ibiza and as a Senior Researcher at the University of the Balearic Islands focusing on tourism marketing and sustainability projects for the government of the Balearic Islands. He is editor-in-chief of the *Annals of Tourism Research in Spanish* (edited since 1999 by the University of the Balearic Islands in agreement with Elsevier Science Ltd. and Jafar Jafari).

Inmaculada Benito is a PhD student and lecturer in the School of Tourism at the University of the Balearic Islands in Majorca, Spain.

Dimitrios Buhalis is a Senior Lecturer in Tourism in the University of Surrey. He also is an Adjunct Professor in the MBA Programme in Hospitality Management at the Institut de Management Hôtelier International in Paris. Buhalis regularly works as an advisor for international organizations such as the European Commission and the World Tourism Organization on the subject of information technology impacts on tourism. He also serves on the editorial board of several journals. He has co-edited the *Encyclopedia of Tourism,* and a number of books on topics such as alliance management in the hospitality industry and the role of information technologies in tourism.

Richard Butler is Professor of Tourism at the University of Surrey. He has a PhD in Geography from the University of Glasgow and has researched extensively on the development of tourism destinations in a wide variety of settings. His particular interests include capacity and seasonality issues. He also has a long-standing interest in islands.

Keith Debbage obtained his PhD in Geography at the University of Georgia in 1988 and is currently an Associate Professor in the Department of Geography at the University of North Carolina at Greensboro, USA. He is the author of numerous research articles in scientific journals including *Regional Studies, Journal of Transport Geography, Journal of Air Transport Management, Transportation Quarterly, Policy Studies Review, Annals of Tourism Research, Tourism Management, Geotimes,* and the *Geographical Bulletin.* Professor Debbage recently completed his first co-edited book *The Economic Geography of the Tourist Industry: A Supply-side Analysis* (Routledge, 1998). His most recent research work has been in two fields, namely the evolution of airline hub networks and its impact on regional economic development, and urban-economic restructuring within US metropolitan areas.

Dimitrios Diamantis is Head of the Tourism and Hospitality Research Centre in Les Roches Management School in Switzerland. Prior to this he worked in the International Centre for Tourism and Hospitality Research in Bournemouth University, as a researcher for the Millennium Vision Policy for the World Travel and Tourism Council. Alongside his research activities he teaches graduate and postgraduate students and coordinates a discussion group for the development of tourism in UNESCO's biosphere reserves. He has a degree in Hotel Management from South Bank University, a Masters in Tourism Marketing from Surrey University, a Diploma in Marketing from the Chartered Institute of Marketing, and a PhD from Bournemouth University.

Giovanni Giavelli is a biologist and ecologist who has been working since 1981 as a researcher and educator in the Department of Environmental Sciences at the University of Parma in Italy. His current work focuses on qualitative approaches to ecological relationships in natural communities, on the trade-offs between (eco)tourism and the environment, and on renewable energy and waste recycling.

Briavel Holcomb is a Professor in the Department of Urban Studies and Community Health at Rutgers University, USA. She has written extensively on urban regeneration and gender issues. In the last few years her research has included the marketing of the Caribbean to US tourists, gay tourism in the United States, and gender and the heritage industry. Holcomb co-authored *Revitalizing Cities* (Association of American Geographers, 1981) and co-edited *Women's Lives and Public Policy: The International Experience* (Greenwood, 1993). She has also published a number of articles and book chapters on tourism-related issues.

Sinisa Horak holds a PhD in transportation engineering. Currently, he is a senior research fellow at the Institute for Tourism (Zagreb, Croatia) where he also serves as director of the ITT Consulting enterprise. He has worked for seven years on transportation planning issues at the Institute for Transport Sciences (Zagreb, Croatia) and has 14 years' experience in the travel and tourism field. He has conducted numerous studies and projects concerning transportation, tourism development, and travel-related investments and market analysis. Dr Horak has published research articles in various journals and has authored several book chapters.

Dimitri Ioannides is an Associate Professor of Community and Regional Planning in the Department of Geography, Geology, and Planning at Southwest Missouri State University, USA where he also serves as the Coordinator of the Undergraduate Program in Community and Regional Planning. His research focus is on the supply side of tourism, tourism planning, and issues relating to sustainable development. Along with Keith Debbage he is co-editor of *The Economic Geography of the Tourist Industry* (Routledge, 1998). He co-edits, with Gareth Shaw, the Tourism, Retailing, and Consumption series for I.B. Tauris and Co. Ltd. and serves as North American editor of the international journal *Tourism*. He is currently chair of the Recreation, Tourism, and Sports (RTS) specialty group of the American Association of Geographers.

Maria Kousis is a University of Michigan (Ann Arbor) graduate, and is currently Professor in the Department of Sociology, School of Social Sciences, the University of Crete, Gallos Campus, in Rethimno, Greece. Her recent research interests include environmental movements and justice, and rural development and change.

Vesna Mikacic PhD is a scientific advisor at the Institute for Tourism (Zagreb, Croatia). As a geographer she has extensive experience in researching spatial and ecological aspects of tourism as well as problems of island and domestic tourism. Dr Mikacic has authored or co-authored conference papers and research articles in various journals. She serves on the

Editorial Board of the *Journal of the Croatian Geographical Society* and she is a member of EADI (European Association of the Development Research and Training Institute) and the Croatian Geographical Union.

Francesc Sastre is a Professor and Director of the School of Tourism at the University of the Balearics in Majorca, Spain.

Julie Scott is Research Fellow in the Centre for Leisure and Tourism Studies at the University of North London. Apart from gender and development issues, her current research interests include heritage, identity and representation in tourism, and the impact of gambling-related tourism in the eastern Mediterranean.

Tom Selänniemi is a cultural anthropologist specializing in the anthropology of tourists and, particularly, mass travellers. His major research has been on Finnish package holidaymakers to the Canary Islands and the Mediterranean. One of his interests is the relation between mass tourism and sustainability. He currently works as the Manager for Sustainable Tourism at Finnair Travel Services and lectures at the Finnish University Network for Tourism Studies.

Tom Selwyn is Professor of the Anthropology of Tourism at the University of North London. He has published widely on tourism, particularly tourism development and tourism images and myths. His present research is focused on tourism in post-conflict landscapes.

Sevil Sonmez is Assistant Professor of Tourism Management at Arizona State University, Tempe, Arizona, USA. Her research focuses primarily on terrorism/political instability and public health risks associated with international tourism. Her work appears in the *Annals of Tourism Research, Journal of Travel Research, Tourism Management,* and *Thunderbird International Business Review.*

Eleni Stiakaki is a native of Crete. Before undertaking postgraduate research in tourism at the University of Surrey she worked in the tourism industry in Greece. Her research interests include island development and management of tourism destinations. She is currently working in the tourism field in Crete.

José Fernando Vera Rebollo is Chair and Professor of Geography as well as Director of the Higher Studies in Tourism programme and of the Tourism Planning Research Group at the University of Alicante, Spain. He is a member of the Management Board of the Spanish Association of Scientific Experts in Tourism. His research focus is on environmental and territorial tourism analysis and planning. He is the author and co-author of many books and articles at a national and international level. Among his publications is *Análisis Territorial del Turismo* (Ariel, 1997). He is also an international consultant for the World Tourism Organization. His current research focuses on sustainable tourism management in a European Union co-funded project.

Sanda Weber PhD is senior research fellow at the Institute for Tourism (Zagreb, Croatia). Her research interests include tourism research methodology, and behaviour and travel patterns of tourists. She is also engaged in developing marketing concepts for tourism destinations. Dr Weber has published research articles in various journals and has authored several book chapters. She is editor of the international journal *Tourism* and also serves on the editorial boards of two international journals. She is national representative of ESOMAR (European Society for Marketing and Opinion Research) in Croatia and a member of AIEST (International Association of Scientific Experts in Tourism) and TRC (Tourist Research Centre).

Foreword

At the tender age of twelve years old, my parents decided to leave northeastern England for the azure-blue waters of the Bahama Islands. As a teenager, I therefore witnessed at first hand the radical socio-economic and ecological impacts that can dramatically transform an idyllic island setting into an internationally renowned mass-market resort destination for the jet set. During the 1970s, the Bahamas island-based economy became one where international tourism expenditures accounted for two-thirds of the national economy and annual tourist arrivals outnumbered the island population by a factor of 5 to 1!

Through the eyes of a young impressionable adult, many of these titanic changes seemed to be for the better – more nightclubs, more swimming pools, more parasailing and water-skiing opportunities, better retailing, and more restaurants. Nevertheless, the roads were always intolerably crowded and in a perpetual state of disrepair and the tiny Nassau International Airport terminal seemed to be dwarfed by large wide-bodied jets, which arrived every day from Europe and America. The resident population also began to endure frequent power 'brown-outs' and our water supply was in such short supply that sometimes it had to be barged in from a neighbouring island. Given these conditions, it is not surprising that some residents began to resent the high-spending, affluent lifestyles of the 'Ugly American (and European) Tourist'. Some of the local islanders even began questioning the wisdom of the tourism monoculture that had slowly begun to develop in the Bahamas.

In the late 1970s, I began my college career and proceeded to develop a natural interest in the study of tourism planning and development. However,

I was dismayed by the 'boosterish' nature of the literature that seemed to proliferate at the time. Much of this literature frequently extolled the various virtues of international tourism as the 'next great, smokeless industry'. In the intervening two decades, the academic literature on tourism seems to have matured and researchers appear to have developed a heightened sensitivity to the costs and externalities associated with the rapidly growing international tourist industry. The relentless geographic expansion of the pleasure periphery by Turner and Ash's (1975) *Golden Hordes* led many tourism academics to ask more penetrating research questions about the overall sustainability of a tourism-led economic development strategy. Although some critics may argue that sustainability is not a scientific word, the tourism literature of the 1990s became increasingly concerned with sustainability and 'limits-to-growth' type issues. While much of this literature is well developed in terms of island tourism, it has traditionally focused on the growth pressures experienced in the Caribbean and South Pacific islands rather than the Mediterranean. Given the proximity of islands like Cyprus, Malta and the Greek archipelago to the major tourist-generating countries of northern Europe, it is surprising that more research has not focused on this region. This book will help to address this obvious deficit.

Reference

Turner, L. and Ash, J. (1975) *The Golden Hordes: International Tourism and the Pleasure Periphery*. London: Constable.

Keith G. Debbage
Associate Professor of Geography
University of North Carolina at Greensboro

Preface

Over the past 50 years the Mediterranean has emerged as one of the most popular international tourist destinations worldwide. Within this region, islands such as Malta, Mykonos, Rhodes and Djerba have been turned into tourist meccas for sun-seeking northern Europeans. Despite the evidence of tourism's economic benefits to many islands of the Mediterranean, undoubtedly the sector has also caused a plethora of sociocultural and environmental problems. In many coastal areas tourism-induced urbanization has spread its tentacles, rapidly consuming pristine open spaces and valuable agricultural land, and often causing irreparable damage to the rich architectural and cultural heritage of existing settlements. Because of tourism, rapid and uncontrolled development has often put a strain on the existing infrastructure. Inadequate sewage treatment facilities have commonly led to seawater contamination and have polluted groundwater supplies. Moreover, the large numbers of tourists who descend on many of these islands each year place a heavy strain on water resources, a precious commodity in these semi-arid environments.

It is our first-hand observation of such events that inspired us to propose an edited book about tourism development on Mediterranean islands. Our mutual feeling has been that the Mediterranean as a whole has rarely attracted the attention of tourism researchers, despite the existence of plenty of case studies examining specific archipelagos or individual islands within the region. We have been particularly surprised about the absence of cross-Mediterranean comparative studies examining the dynamics of tourism development and the relationship of the sector to overall sustainable development on a par with investigations of the Caribbean and more recently the Pacific Ocean. We strongly believe that an edited collection with contributions from authors representing the Mediterranean's many archipelagos and islands will go a long way towards rectifying this research lacuna.

We would like to extend our thanks to Veronica Higgs and later Dr David Barker of Continuum Publishers for believing in our project and supporting it from the outset. We are very grateful to the publishers for patiently allowing us to extend our deadline twice and for providing encouragement throughout. We also would like to extend our gratitude to all participating authors from places such as Croatia, Greece, Italy, Spain, Finland, the United Kingdom, as well as the United States. Without their contributions this project would not have materialized. We have learned a lot from their research experiences and hope that their insights will be beneficial to all those policy-makers and academics who have an interest in enhancing sustainability in the insular Mediterranean.

Jeff Ikard provided invaluable help in preparing many of the maps that have gone into this volume. John Kotthenbeutel and Jennifer Connell, both graduate students at Southwest Missouri State University, gave us much appreciated assistance in terms of preparing the manuscript while Deana Gibson proved her true worth once more by helping us deal with computer viruses and other glitches that plague our computer-dependent world.

Last, but certainly not least, we extend a great thank you to Mara Cohen Ioannides who once more took time from her busy teaching and research schedule and her responsibilities as a mother to aid in the final production of this volume. She deserves our thanks for diligently checking the book's massive bibliography and ensuring that every reference was cited.

Dimitri Ioannides
Springfield, MO
Yorghos Apostolopoulos and Sevil Sonmez,
Tempe, AZ
June 2000

For Sasha and Anthony

Prologue

Perspectives on Mediterranean Island Tourism and Sustainability

Searching for Sustainable Tourism Development in the Insular Mediterranean

Dimitri Ioannides, Yorghos Apostolopoulos and Sevil Sonmez

The Greeks named this the stream of Ocean. It circled the earth at which they were privileged to live at the center, its precise location at Delphi, where a stone like a toadstool marked the Navel of the World. Mediterranean, after all, means 'middle of the earth.'

(Theroux, 1995: 3)

Introduction

In recent years a vast body of literature has been produced on the topic of sustainable tourism. This phenomenon is not altogether surprising considering the increasing attention that has been paid to the broader concept of sustainable development since the release of *Our Common Future*, the well-cited report produced by the World Commission on the Environment and Development (WCED, 1987).

The WCED document, better known as the Brundtland Report, has led to the widespread embrace of the principle of sustainable development. Campbell (1996) argues that this acceptance of sustainable development is inevitable because the alternative (i.e., non-sustainability) is unthinkable. What developers, after all, would ever admit that their project might lead to serious environmental damage or cause social problems? It is hardly astonishing, therefore, that the term 'sustainability' has entered the everyday vocabulary of various groups and individuals, regardless of their ideology or political affiliation. Considering that sustainable development aims to reconcile economic, environmental and societal objectives, it is unremarkable that tourism researchers have also embraced the concept (Bosselman *et al.*, 1999; Butler, 1999; Mowforth and Munt, 1998; Wall, 1997; Williams and Montanari, 1999).

Nevertheless, despite the popularity of sustainability both overall and in the context of tourism, its implementation has remained elusive. Perhaps the most important hurdle, barring the transformation of sustainable development into action, derives from the fact that there is no consensus as to the term's precise definition (Butler, 1999; Hall and Lew, 1998; McCool, 1995). Analysts generally agree that while the concept has merit as a long-term principle for ensuring that a society does not live beyond its means, it is impossible to achieve, given that it remains unclear what needs to be sustained and how (McCool and Stankey, 1999).

Tourism academics have grappled for some time with definitional issues relating to sustainable development. For instance, Butler (1999) questions the single-sector focus of the term sustainable tourism that prevails in so many writings. Both he and Wall (1997) agree that when talking about sustainability, it is problematic to focus solely on tourism given that this is a multifaceted sector that affects numerous businesses, institutions, and individuals.

Others have dismissed sustainable tourism and related terms such as alternative tourism or ecotourism as oxymora (Pigram and Wahab, 1997). Mowforth and Munt (1998) pessimistically argue that the so-called new forms of sustainable tourism (e.g., ecotourism or agrotourism) are not likely to change the uneven balance of power that finds such players as transnational tour operators, hotel chains, and airlines controlling the industry's fortunes in most destinations. Their comments contradict the views of people like Poon (1993) who believe that, compared to mass travel, more flexible forms of tourism can enhance the benefits to destination-based enterprises and individuals (cf. Milne and Gill, 1998). To emphasize their point, Mowforth and Munt maintain that 'the industry is unlikely to change its spots or its modus operandi. There seems no prospect of changes to the dominant imperatives of capitalism and capital growth' (1998: 327).

Critiques and debates such as these will undoubtedly continue in the foreseeable future. However, the problem with engaging in endless, and some may even say meaningless, academic battles over definitional issues is that in the long run they do not help us accomplish very much on the practical side. Surely, the true worth of the term 'sustainability', since it was made popular by the Bruntland Report, is that a variety of actors spanning the public and private domains are at least now familiar with the concept. If nothing more, sustainable development is useful as a 'guiding fiction'. It brings to the centre-stage 'precepts that cannot be proven or measured, but which act to create a sense of community, and purpose, and which serve necessary and useful social and political functions — such as organizing discourse, unifying diverse interests, and instigating action' (McCool and Stankey, 1999: 5).

The concept of sustainable development appears to have particular merit in areas that have become major foci of tourist destinations. This is because there is a growing realization that for tourism to continue to flourish there is a need to protect the very resources (e.g., the natural environment and cultural settings) that attract visitors in the first place. Thus, a variety of actors including governments, non-governmental organizations (NGOs), and industry representatives have embraced the term as a necessity. These actors recognize that more balanced development forms than uncontrolled mass tourism-oriented growth will in the long run serve to protect the destination's resources and, thus, enhance its competitiveness while also improving the quality of life of its inhabitants (Wall, 1997).

Areas where issues of sustainability have risen to the fore in recent years are the Mediterranean's littoral and insular regions, which have emerged among the premier tourist destinations in the world. This edited collection applies the concept of sustainable development to the islands of the Mediterranean, many of which have become important venues for tourism development over the past 40 years or so. Specifically, it offers a comparative perspective of the dynamics of tourism development in the Mediterranean insular region and highlights the problems that have emerged in many of its destinations following years of uncontrolled growth. Even though historical and geographical contingencies undoubtedly account for differences in the form of tourism growth witnessed from island to island, it is clear that, overall, the mass tourism model that predominates throughout much of the region is far removed from the vision of sustainable development. Given this alarming state of affairs, we hope that the lessons learned from the 13 chapters that follow will be of use to all those academics and practitioners who have been searching for realistic paths towards achieving a long-term vision of balanced development on the Mediterranean islands.

Insular Tourism

Islands commonly face a number of structural handicaps arising from their isolated and peripheral location, and their smallness in terms of population and area. Among the most serious problems characterizing many of these environments are their limited resource base, tiny domestic markets, diseconomies of scale, poor accessibility, limited infrastructure and institutional mechanisms, and a high degree of dependency on external forces (Britton, 1982; Connell, 1988; Pearce, 1995; Wilkinson, 1989). Considering such problems, it is hardly surprising that islands have long attracted the attention of social scientists such as anthropologists, economists, geographers and sociologists (Lockhart, 1993).

Over the last two decades or so, numerous tourism researchers have also trained their attention on islands. Their research has been prompted by the fact that in many such settings tourism has emerged as a dominant activity with significant economic, physical, and sociocultural ramifications. Small islands often have few realistic alternatives for generating economic growth other than the adoption of traditional mass tourism (Bastin, 1984; Wilkinson, 1989). The 'inevitability' of this development form commonly means that these insular regions have become true 'tourist economies' where travel-related receipts account for a major portion of the Gross Domestic Product (GDP). On many tropical or sub-tropical islands foreign tourists and tourist-related activities dominate the landscape, particularly of fragile coastal areas, often leading to a host of adverse environmental and social problems (Britton, 1978; Kousis, 1989). Pearce illustrates tourism's high profile in numerous insular settings arguing that because of their small population and area, the 'ratio of tourist arrivals to the host population, and particularly to the land area, is much greater than in North America and many parts of Europe' (1995: 118).

In addition to these characteristics, islands are also interesting to researchers because they are, quite simply, convenient to study. King aptly describes them as 'small-scale spatial laboratories where theories can be tested and processes observed in the setting of a semi-closed system' (1993: 14). Ironically, although their small territorial extent often serves as a handicap, it also makes islands attractive and suitable for the purposes of fieldwork. Island destinations (e.g., the island microstates of the Caribbean) commonly have a rich collection of reliable longitudinal tourist statistics relating to arrivals, receipts, and the supply of tourist accommodation and services. This phenomenon is perhaps unsurprising considering the relative importance that tourism plays in these destinations' economies compared to mainland areas. Also, because tourists can only access these islands through a few well-defined points of entry (e.g., airports or seaports) it means that it is relatively easy to track tourist flows compared to mainland areas. Our own experience has in the past shown that it is easier to obtain reliable chronological data relating to tourist arrivals on islands such as Mauritius or Jamaica than it is to track such flows to certain communities in the United States.

Much of the attention of tourist researchers has been focused on the islands of the Caribbean (Bryden, 1973; Erisman, 1983; Potter, 1983; Wilkinson, 1989). More recent studies have been carried out paying attention to tourism development in insular regions of the South Pacific and the Indian Oceans respectively (Hall and Page, 1996; Milne, 1992; Saleem, 1996). Nevertheless, Butler (1993) and Pearce (1995), among others, have criticized much of the existing research on island tourism for its descriptive, case study-oriented nature that offers little in terms of developing the generalizations necessary for the building of theoretical constructs. There are, of course, exceptions such as the political economy perspectives offered by R. Britton (1978) and S. Britton (1992). Moreover, in recent years, an increasing number of academics have produced a number of volumes that provide a comparative perspective of sustainability and tourism development in island destinations throughout the world (Apostolopoulos and Gayle, 2001; Briguglio *et al.*, 1996; Conlin and Baum, 1995; Wilkinson, 1997).

Considering all the attention that has been paid to tourism development in insular environments, it is perhaps somewhat surprising that there are no comprehensive English language publications offering a comparative perspective of tourism development in the Mediterranean insular region. This is despite the fact that these destinations 'may have a longer history of use as tourist places' than the Caribbean or the Pacific regions (Butler, 1993: 73). Most studies of tourism-related development in the insular Mediterranean have focused on individual islands such as Cyprus (Ioannides, 1992), Crete (Kousis, 1989) and Malta (Oglethorpe, 1984), or relatively concentrated island groupings such as the islands of Greece (Loukissas, 1982) and Croatia (Mikacic and Montana, 1994). There are obviously plausible explanations for this gap in the literature. With the exception of Cyprus and Malta, the region's only two microstates, and unlike most Caribbean islands that are independent states, the islands of the Mediterranean are territories controlled by neighbouring mainland countries (e.g., Corsica as part of France, Sardinia as part of Italy, and Djerba as part of Tunisia). This means that it is not always as easy to gather disaggregated information relating to various tourism-related characteristics in these destinations, especially if a specific island forms only a portion of a broader region (e.g., Mykonos within the Cyclades island grouping). Additionally, the fact that there is no umbrella organization for the entire insular region along the lines of the Caribbean Tourism Organization (CTO), which publishes information in a single language, means that it is hard to find accurate comparative travel-related statistics relating to the numerous islands of the Mediterranean.

On a broader note, the absence of comparative works relating to tourism development on the islands of the Mediterranean seems to reflect the general unwillingness of academics representing a variety of disciplines to adopt pan-Mediterranean approaches in their respective research areas. In *The Corrupting Sea*, Horden and Purcell explain that the possibility of a true integrative approach when studying the Mediterranean's history has essentially been thwarted by prevailing 'historical traditions' (2000: 15) that do not allow the development of an accurate definition of the region as a whole. Moreover, unlike the Caribbean insular region that can be easily conceptualized as a single entity, the Mediterranean Sea has a fragmented geography since it touches three continents and numerous countries.

Tourism Development in the Mediterranean Insular Region

In many respects, the smaller Mediterranean islands exemplify admirably the concept of the marginal ... They tend to instantiate especially well the variety of landscape — aspect, geology, relief, soil, altitude, hydrology — that creates a microregional topography.

(Horden and Purcell, 2000: 224)

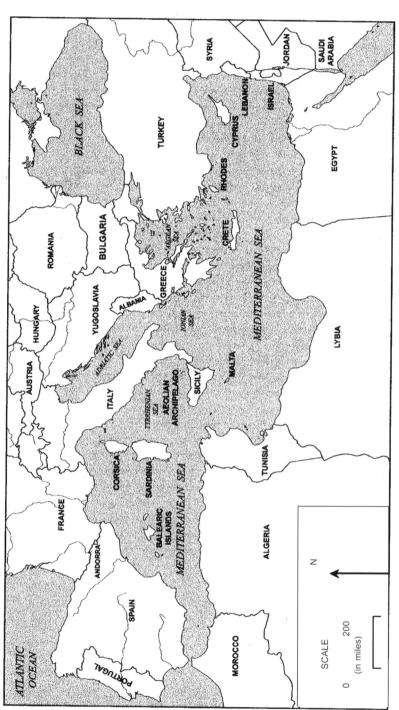

Figure 1.1 The Mediterranean islands

Historical antecedents

There are literally thousands of islands scattered throughout the Mediterranean (Figure 1.1). With the exception of Sicily, Sardinia, Cyprus, Corsica and Crete, all of which are relatively large in terms of area and population (each covers over 8,000 km^2 and with population exceeding 500,000), most islands are smaller than 500 km^2 and rarely have a population above 50,000. There are, of course, notable exceptions such as Majorca and Malta which despite their small territories have substantial populations (Ioannides, 2001). Many of the smaller islands are uninhabited since they have few or no resources. These include thousands of tiny islands that are little more than rocky outcrops. Only 337 of the roughly 2,500 islands in the Aegean and Ionian archipelagos show signs of human settlement (Leontidou, 1988).

Considering their relative proximity to the European mainland, it is perhaps surprising to note that tourism development did not occur on the Mediterranean islands until relatively recently. There are of course notable exceptions such as Capri, which was an established vacation spot for wealthy Romans more than 2,000 years ago (Conlin and Baum, 1995) and re-emerged as a popular venue of the aristocratic Grand Tour during the nineteenth century (Bonini, 1993). It was also during the nineteenth and early twentieth centuries that islands such as Corfu, Majorca and Rhodes began to attract the attention of a small number of wealthy and, often, famous visitors (Ioannides, forthcoming). For instance, in the 1830s George Sand brought her lover Chopin to Valdemosa on the island of Majorca to recover from an illness, while a few decades later D.H. Lawrence spent some time writing poetry in Taormina on the island of Sicily (Theroux, 1995). The introduction of regular steamboat services along the Adriatic coast during the 1800s led to the development of travel-oriented activities on the Croatian islands of Krk, Rab, Hvar and Korcula (Mikacic and Montana, 1994). Additionally, during the 1930s and 1940s certain resorts on the Troodos mountains in Cyprus became popular destinations for wealthy Middle Eastern visitors, including members of the Egyptian royal family who wished to escape the heat of the summer months in their native lands (Ioannides, 1994).

The real boom of insular tourism in the Mediterranean only began in earnest during the post-World War II period, especially the 1960s. Capitalizing on their relative proximity to northern European markets and the introduction of affordable package tours, places such as Corfu, Majorca, Malta, and Rhodes became increasingly popular for sun-seeking tourists. Realizing the potential of tourism as an economic development tool and, especially in the case of Spain and Greece, as a means of achieving political legitimacy of dictatorial regimes, national and regional governments also played a significant role in stimulating tourism development on many islands (Pearce, 1989; Valenzuela, 1988). For instance, both Cyprus and Malta saw tourism as an important post-independence development strategy given their limited options for economic growth (Ioannides, 1992; Oglethorpe, 1984). During the late 1960s and early 1970s the growth of Greece's tourist industry in coastal areas, including insular regions, was a result, among others, of the introduction of various incentives by the military junta to promote foreign-based investment in tourist activities (Leontidou, 1988).

The water in Majorca don't taste like what it 'oughta': Impacts of tourism development on Mediterranean islands

At first glance it is apparent that tourism development in the Mediterranean insular region has been highly uneven. While some destinations such as Corfu, southern Cyprus, Malta, and Majorca have grown very rapidly as tourist destinations, other islands (e.g., certain islands in the northern Aegean) remain quiet backwaters offering few formal visitor-based facilities. Moreover, although certain islands cater predominantly to northern European sunlust tourists, others attract domestic visitors from nearby mainland areas. Tinos, a popular destination for Greek Orthodox pilgrims, and the Aeolian islands of Italy fit the description of non-international tourism destinations in the Mediterranean (see, for example, Chapter 7 in this volume).

The observed differences in terms of type and level of tourism development that has taken place on the various islands has a lot to do with their location and, particularly their accessibility. It is not surprising, for instance, that the islands which have emerged as popular destinations for international package tourists are the ones offering direct airline connections to major European cities. Majorca, which attracts approximately 10 million tourists, now has one of the largest airports in southern Europe. By contrast, many of the islands that are unable to provide airport facilities due to their mountainous terrain (e.g., Symi) have generally seen fairly modest rates of international tourism development (Ioannides, 1994). According to Costa *et al.* (1996), Sardinia and Sicily draw a very small proportion of the international tourist arrivals registered in Italy because of the country's elongated shape, which means that southern areas including the islands are fairly isolated from European markets. Moreover, these peripheral destinations face stiff competition from other intervening coastal resorts in northern parts of the country (e.g., Rimini).

Historical contingencies including politics have also influenced the rate of tourism development on many islands. For instance, Corsica does not attract as many tourists as its size and diversity might lead one to expect largely because of its unstable political situation, especially the terrorist campaign waged by the Corsican national liberation front (F.L.N.C.) for the past 25 years or so. Tourism growth in northern Cyprus has been inhibited by the fact that this territory lacks international political recognition and cannot be accessed from the more popular southern part of the island. Charter airlines travelling from European countries to northern Cyprus have to make a stopover in Turkey, a stop that adds to the cost and duration of the flight (Ioannides and Apostolopoulos, 1999).

Despite such obvious variations in their level of tourism development, however, it is obvious that many Mediterranean islands have now emerged as leading destinations in their respective countries. Crete, for instance, accounts for 16.4 per cent of all official tourist accommodation establishments registered in Greece (Dagonaki and Kotios, 1998) and with Corfu, the Cyclades, and Rhodes comprises one of the leading destinations in terms of international tourist nights in Greece (Briassoulis, 1993). The Balearic islands are second only to Catalonia (a much larger region in area) in terms of lodging facilities (Albert-Pinole, 1993) and account for 37 per cent of all overnight stays by international tourists in Spain (Instituto Nacional de Estadística, 1998).

On many islands the growth rate of accommodation facilities has been truly astounding (Cyprus Tourism Organization, 1996; Greek Tourism Organization, 1996). Importantly, most of this development has been spatially polarized in a small number of coastal areas, which are often located close to existing urban settlements, airports or seaports. Pearce (1995) points out that on Majorca there are two principal clusters of tourism development, one around Palma and the other around Alcudia on the island's northeastern corner. On Rhodes, the most intensive tourism development has taken place on the northern and northeastern part of the island close to the capital city, while on Crete a major portion of the accommodation capacity is located in communities along the more developed northern coast. The coastal orientation of tourism development on many Mediterranean islands has reinforced their image as mass tourist destinations catering to sun-seeking package holidaymakers.

While it is true that tourism activities have often generated substantial economic growth on a number of islands resulting in improved living standards for their inhabitants, few people would argue that these destinations are presently sustainable. Examples of the adverse impacts resulting from rapid and to a large extent uncontrolled tourism growth abound and are similar to problems reported in other insular destinations throughout the world (Briguglio and Vella, 1995; Britton, 1978; Kousis, 1989). On a number of islands tourism-induced development has caused socio-economic concerns such as labour shortages, excessive hikes in property values, and rising costs of living overall (Vassiliou, 1995). Environmental problems include aesthetic pollution resulting from the ribbon-like over-development of unsightly hotels along large expanses of coastal land. Tourist-related growth has threatened natural resources such as indigenous fauna and flora as well as freshwater supplies and agricultural land. Loss of open space has continued at alarming rates. Inadequate infrastructure has often led to sewage spills in coastal waters around popular resorts (Loukissas and Triantafyllopoulos, 1997). Sociocultural problems, such as increasing incidents of crime and vandalism and the breakdown of cultural norms, have also been reported throughout the region (Boissevain, 1996; Ioannides, forthcoming; Stott, 1996).

The largely undifferentiated mass tourism product that has emerged on many of the islands of the Mediterranean has meant that in recent years their competitiveness as destinations has generally been reduced. The fact that these insular destinations are heavily dependent on exogenous actors, especially major tour operators based in northern European countries has compounded this problem. Because travel wholesalers tend to focus on product type (this being sun-based mass tourism in the case of the Mediterranean) rather than displaying loyalty to specific destinations, the 'could be anywhere' sun, sea and sand resorts of the Mediterranean island are highly substitutable. As Goodall and Bergsma (1990) argue, if these powerful tour operators lose interest in particular destinations for any reason, they can always substitute these with other destinations offering a similar product either in the Mediterranean or further afield (Ioannides, 1998). The vulnerability of the Mediterranean islands to competition from other insular regions in the Indian and Pacific Oceans and the Caribbean has become more obvious in recent years especially because an increasing number of northern Europeans are demanding less crowded and unpolluted destinations in more 'exotic' settings. Unfortunately, few such destinations remain in the Mediterranean region.

Policy-makers and others are gradually taking note of the many serious problems that have accompanied rapid tourism growth within the insular realm of the Mediterranean. A common theme found in many tourism-related policy documents is the call for enhancing the quality of the islands' product. The prevailing argument is that a more diversified and 'upmarket' oriented tourism product will attract higher spending individuals who can replace the larger numbers of budget-minded travellers. Theoretically, this would mean that the destinations' sustainability could be enhanced since fewer tourists would lead to reduced environmental impacts without reducing the economic benefits of the industry. Evidence in this volume, as well as from other sources, suggests that the results of this approach can be described, at best, as inconclusive. While certain destinations have had a certain degree of success in terms of moving towards more balanced development forms, others have found themselves unable to escape the vicious cycle of unsustainability. In the latter group it appears that the adoption by government officials and industry representatives of the labels 'sustainable development' and 'quality tourism' are nothing more than rhetoric.

This book explores the approaches taken in different insular settings throughout the Mediterranean Sea to achieve goals of balanced growth. Efforts have been made as far as possible to include case studies from all the major insular groupings plus the two island states in the Mediterranean. To represent the whole spectrum of perspectives, we have attracted contributions from a number of academics based in or with intimate experience of various parts of the Mediterranean, including Croatia, Greece, Italy, and Spain. Moreover, the approach in this book is truly interdisciplinary with the contributing authors representing fields such as anthropology, economics, geography, sociology, and urban planning.

Structure and Themes of the Book

This edited collection is divided into four parts. The Prologue includes a contribution by Tom Selwyn who sets the scene for the rest of the text. Selwyn argues that tourism cannot be studied in a vacuum without recognizing the sector's interrelationship with broader social, environmental and political issues. The chapter begins by providing a useful overview concerning tourism's role as an engine of socio-economic, cultural, and environmental transformation in insular areas of the Mediterranean. By referring to case studies from Majorca and Malta, Selwyn points out that in many instances the largely unregulated pattern of tourism development has accentuated regional imbalances between the islands' coastal and interior areas and has led to the decline of traditional activities such as agriculture. He expresses scepticism about the common assertion of many islanders that tourism has been inevitable for wealth creation in places such as Majorca, offering evidence that the quality of life, at least in some of these insular settings, had been satisfactory to its residents before the ascendancy of tourism. An important point that is highlighted throughout this chapter, and one that is reiterated by many of the contributors in the rest of the text, is that the fortunes of the islands' tourist developments are not solely determined by external forces, such as exogenous tour operators or major airlines. Rather, a multitude of local players, such as landowners, private developers, and returning immigrants, plus a host of characteristics such as land tenure patterns determine tourism's evolutionary dynamics. Thus, according to Selwyn, issues relating to sustainable development in the context of tourism should not be viewed solely as a power struggle between local players and transnational companies, but instead must be considered within the framework of democratic control. The chapter concludes appropriately with the thorny question as to whether tourism development has 'de-Mediterraneanized' the Mediterranean. On the basis of the evidence provided by Selwyn and many of the other contributors, it may be hard to deny such an argument.

Part 1 points to the key issues that need to be accounted for when examining tourism development on the Mediterranean islands. Some of the questions explored by the contributing authors are the following: What are some of the ways to plan for and manage further tourism development within the scope of sustainability? Who are the major players controlling the pattern of tourism development on many of the islands and what, if anything, can be done to ensure that local players can increase their say in the industry's fortunes? What are some of the key sociocultural implications emerging from the study of Mediterranean island tourism?

In Chapter 3, Vera Rebollo explores the problems of insularity and focuses on the uncertain future of Mediterranean island destinations in the face of their weakening competitiveness *vis-à-vis* other tourist hotspots around the world. He examines the dynamics of tourism development on Mediterranean islands and discusses many of the problems arising from unplanned developments in coastal areas. The chapter reinforces the point made by Selwyn that the highly polarized pattern of tourism development on most islands has caused serious regional imbalances. Referring to islands throughout the region, the chapter indicates that there is little variability between the tourism product of many of these destinations and, as a result, many of them tend to compete on the basis of price rather than product quality. Such characteristics place these destinations in a weak bargaining position when it comes to their negotiations with key travel industry representatives located in the principal origin countries of northern Europe. This point is reinforced in Chapter 4 by Francesc Sastre and Inmaculada Benito who explore the actions of tour operators as key gatekeepers in control of international tourist flows to mass tourist destinations in the Mediterranean. Sastre and Benito indicate that on the Balearics, just as on many other islands, the oversupply of tourist accommodation has resulted in a situation where tour operators have tightened their control over the destination as they can negotiate favourable rates with hoteliers who are desperate to fill their beds. This, in turn, means that many Mediterranean islands become further dependent on low-spending package tourists, a phenomenon that hardly bodes well for the future sustainability of such insular destinations.

Both Chapter 3 and Chapter 4 highlight the point mentioned previously that the growing problems associated with mass tourism development in the Mediterranean have led to calls for the introduction of 'quality' forms of tourism. The rationale behind these measures is that tourism development can become more sustainable if a large number of budget-minded tourists are replaced by a smaller number of more sophisticated and higher spending individuals. Vera Rebollo emphasizes that the best means to achieve this goal is for the islands of the Mediterranean to diversify their tourism products. By contrast, Sastre and Benito discuss the merits of enhancing the role of information technologies and distribution channels for island-based establishments as a means to bypass traditional travel intermediaries. Both these themes are revisited in later chapters by many of the contributing authors.

The final two chapters in Part 1 explore key social and cultural issues relating to tourism development on Mediterranean islands. Chapter 5 by Julie Scott laments the fact that gender issues have been largely absent from general discussions relating to sustainability. She also questions the traditional 'technical' solutions that are commonly used to implement sustainable solutions (e.g., techniques such as environmental analyses or carrying capacity studies) within sociocultural contexts since these tools generally do not account for various characteristics that influence human actions. The chapter offers a fresh perspective by examining gender's role and its effect on tourism development dynamics in the Mediterranean insular region. Scott asserts that depending on the sociocultural and economic context of each destination, women play an active role in tourism's development as participants but also beneficiaries of its impacts. She concludes by highlighting two major implications relating to the future of Mediterranean island tourism. The first is that policy-makers need to address the concerns of women when searching for sustainable development options. Second, she stresses that in addition to quantitative techniques, qualitative tools should be addressed when searching for sustainable solutions in tourism environments, particularly when dealing with the needs and priorities of various stakeholders including women.

In Chapter 6, Selänniemi reinforces the sociocultural perspective of sustainability issues in Mediterranean islands. His case study of Finnish tourists on Rhodes indicates that many northern European mass tourists visiting the Mediterranean's insular regions are often unaware of these destinations' cultural heritage. Selänniemi argues that since these tourists are satisfied by their sun, sea, and sand holiday experience they are commonly not interested in pursuing other interests. The chapter indicates that this lack of attention may not necessarily altogether be a bad thing as it means that the vast majority of tourists remain highly concentrated in a small number of coastal spots, thus reducing the negative impacts on many historical sites. Selänniemi takes the opportunity to dismiss as folly the increasingly common practice throughout the Mediterranean of pursuing 'quality' tourists (see earlier discussion) in an effort to enhance the sustainability of tourism. He argues, for instance, that one of the many negatives associated with cultural tourists is that these visitors are less likely to revisit a certain destination compared to conventional mass tourists. This and other critiques of cultural tourism are ones echoed by other authors in later chapters of this text (e.g., Ioannides and Holcomb in Chapter 12). Chapter 6 concludes on a cynical note by stressing that alternative tourism forms are rarely realistic options for places such as Rhodes that have already become mass tourist destinations. The real challenge, according to Selänniemi and an opinion that is echoed by many of the contributors, is for policy-makers to develop mass tourism in more sustainable ways.

In Part 2 the book's focus turns towards tourism practices in the various islands and insular groupings of the Mediterranean. The case studies examine the consequences of tourism development and attempts to enhance the sector's contribution to sustainable development in insular regions of Italy, Greece, Croatia, Spain, as well as the island states of Cyprus and Malta.

Chapter 7 by Giavelli argues that despite ample rhetoric concerning the merits of sustainable development, its implementation in many island destinations has been unsuccessful. A case study of some of the smallest insular settings in the Mediterranean, the Aeolian islands, reveals the negative impacts associated with unplanned and largely speculative tourism-related development. It is noted that this development has not been accompanied by the provision of adequate services and infrastructure that can benefit the local inhabitants. A particularly serious problem, common to many islands throughout the Mediterranean, is that of chronic water shortages, which have been accentuated by rapid tourism development. The Aeolian islands are especially disadvantaged, since they have no aquifers and rely exclusively on rainwater or, increasingly, supplies that have to be transported in from the mainland by tankers or pipelines. The chapter ends with a series of recommendations for ensuring that future tourism development dovetails with the environmental priorities of such destinations.

One of the major problems associated with the unqualified use of the term 'sustainable tourism' is that it often ignores tourism's interconnections with other sectors such as transport, housing, employment, or the environment. All too often 'tourism-centric' solutions focus primarily on the industry's immediate survival while the region's long-term prosperity is overlooked. In Chapter 8 Buhalis and Diamantis stress that sustainability has to be emphasized to guarantee the success of destinations not only in terms of their immediate profitability, but also to ensure that they remain competitive in the long run. Arguing that sustainable development and competitiveness are intertwined, they maintain that sustainability concerns are not, as some analysts believe, contradictory to the aims of tourism development. The chapter provides a detailed overview of the dynamics of tourism development in the insular regions of Greece and examines the role of small and medium tourism enterprises as important players who are in a position to determine the future sustainability of local resources. Buhalis and Diamantis end with a call for superior environmental auditing practices with the aim, among others, to increase the environmental awareness of islanders and tourists and to improve the islands' tourist destination profile.

In Chapter 9, Weber *et al.* provide yet another case study of tourism development and its impacts on small islands. The authors describe the dynamics of tourism evolution on Croatia's insular settings and examine how these destinations were affected by armed conflict during the early 1990s. The chapter recognizes that war and a number of other constraints such as limited accessibility have not allowed tourism to develop as rapidly on Croatia's islands as in certain other Mediterranean destinations. This situation may actually prove a blessing in disguise as it has meant that the severe environmental and societal impacts seen in many other Mediterranean destinations have not been as evident on the Croatian islands. In turn, this means that the islands of Croatia find themselves in a strong competitive position as long as they pursue future tourism development within an holistic planning framework that promotes sustainability.

One of the regions in the Mediterranean that has witnessed first-hand the extreme adverse impacts of uncontrolled tourism is the Balearic archipelago and particularly the island of Majorca. By the 1980s this region had lost its competitiveness and gained the reputation of a seedy destination for low-spending package tourists. This undesirable situation has prompted the government of the autonomous region to embrace a series of planning measures aimed at enhancing the sustainability of the islands. In Chapter 10, Bardolet provides a detailed account of the events that are leading to a change in the image of the Balearics. A turning point in terms of tourism-related policies occurred in 1983 when the islands gained their autonomy from the Central Government in Madrid. Bardolet maintains that the regional government was more aware of the dangers of unrestricted tourism development and, thus, better placed to create constructive policies for managing the sector in a more sustainable manner. The chapter provides a detailed description of all plans, laws, and regulatory instruments that have a bearing on the future pattern of tourism development in the Balearics. It is obvious that while there is a long way to go before the region achieves sustainability, it has already embarked on the right track by developing a comprehensive territorial planning model that focuses, among others, on strict capacity standards and growth management strategies. These measures are aimed at enhancing both the quality of the tourism product as well as that of the islands' overall environment. Importantly, it appears that the reaction of most stakeholders to these government-led efforts have been largely positive. It remains to be seen if the lessons learned from the Balearic experience can serve as an example for the other Mediterranean islands that are now struggling with the effects of uncoordinated tourism growth.

Approaches towards sustainable development are largely determined by territorial contingencies. This is a point made in Chapter 11 by Kousis who offers a comparative viewpoint of economic, environmental and social aspects as they relate to varying approaches towards sustainable development on four large islands of the Mediterranean, namely Sicily, Sardinia, Corsica and Crete. She reinforces the point that environmental and social concerns have historically been overlooked by the 'product-led' tourism of the region and stresses that these issues are only considered in cases where they may have a negative influence on tourism flows. The last part of the chapter examines the perceptions of host communities concerning the environmental impacts of tourism, noting that these rarely result in environmental protests against the industry. She attributes this lack of action to the communities' heavy economic dependence on tourism. A case study of environmental protest cases in Crete reveals that even though the number of mobilizers is fairly small, these stakeholders usually have a clearer vision of what sustainable development should entail than national or regional governments, which generally adopt a 'weak' or 'treadmill' approach to sustainability.

In the last chapter of Part 2 (Chapter 12), Ioannides and Holcomb reiterate the opinion put forth earlier by Selänniemi that policies focusing on upgrading the quality of tourism in order to lure luxury tourists are more often than not flawed. Through a case study of tourism evolution on the Mediterranean's only two island states, Malta and Cyprus, the chapter demonstrates that recommendations to improve the quality of these destinations in order to attract wealthy visitors have backfired. One of the problems is that policy-makers who call for quality tourism often confuse cultural tourists with high spenders even though this usually is not the case. Moreover, luxury facilities aimed at attracting high spenders commonly lead to high costs of energy and excessive use of valuable water resources. The fundamental trouble with quality-oriented proposals is that they reflect the governments' primary fixation with maximizing tourism's economic returns. According to Ioannides and Holcomb, if true sustainability is to be achieved in destination areas such as islands, surely a more appropriate approach would be for policy-makers to pursue tourism development in a manner that achieves overall balanced growth while also seeking to expand the opportunities for economic diversification. The chapter ends with a call for the creation of a supra-national organization of Mediterranean islands as a way to achieve broader environmental protection objectives.

The Epilogue presents two chapters focusing on new directions for planning and management issues as well as research relating to tourism development on Mediterranean islands. In Chapter 13, Apostolopoulos and Sonmez offer a novel approach to sustainability by arguing for the need to include socio- and geo-medical factors when implementing balanced development options in touristic environments. Because travel and tourism are activities with enormous implications for public health in origin as well as destination areas, the chapter contends that in order to achieve sustainable tourism development in the insular regions of the Mediterranean, maintenance programmes of disease prevention should be adopted. Such an approach will ensure that policy-makers expand their definition of risks to the environmental health of destinations to include actual threats to the medical well-being of visitors and host populations.

The final chapter by Butler and Stiakaki serves as a good synthesis of many of the points that have been highlighted in earlier chapters concerning tourism and sustainability in Mediterranean islands. The chapter points out that no island destination in the Mediterranean has achieved sustainability, although the Balearics have begun to take steps towards this goal, and current circumstances indicate that this is a situation that is likely to continue in the foreseeable future. The authors believe that a practical first step towards achieving more sustainable forms of tourism development would be for policy-makers on insular destinations to move away from the prevailing view that tourism growth should continue at all costs. Instead, the key decision-makers who affect the industry at these destinations should consider the adoption of quantity management strategies recognizing that tourism must operate within a region's capacity limits. While it is obviously impossible to set precise carrying capacity limits by determining 'how many [tourists] is too many?' (Bosselman *et al.*, 1999: 111), it would be folly for each destination to ignore the identification of capacity controls in the long run since the damage caused by over-development will inevitably result in lower numbers of arrivals and receipts. In contrast to the argument of some of the other contributors (e.g., Selänniemi), Butler and Stiakaki indicate that policy-makers should seriously consider encouraging less concentrated patterns of visitation in both spatial and temporal terms. They acknowledge, however, that this may be hard to achieve in most Mediterranean island destinations because of their geography and the type of tourism product they offer. They end by reiterating the underlining message of the book, namely that there is no hope of promoting sustainable development in the Mediterranean's insular regions without recognizing tourism's inter-links with these destinations' other sectors, activities, and resources. An important move towards sustainability in the region is to coordinate local, regional, national and supra-national planning objectives. Policy-makers who make decisions affecting the future of the Mediterranean's islands would do well to heed these calls.

References

Albert-Pinole, I. (1993) Tourism in Spain. In W. Pompl and P. Lavery (eds), *Tourism in Europe: Structures and Developments*. Wallingford: CAB International (242–61).

Apostolopoulos, Y. and Gayle, D.J. (eds) (2001) *Island Tourism and Sustainable Development: Experiences of Caribbean, Pacific, and Mediterranean Islands*. Westport: Praeger.

Bastin, R. (1984) Small island tourism: development of dependency. *Development Policy Review*, 2: 79–90.

Boissevain, J. (1996) 'But we live here!' Perspectives on cultural tourism in Malta. In L. Briguglio, R. Butler, D. Harrison and W.L. Filho (eds), *Sustainable Tourism in Islands and Small States: Case Studies*. London: Pinter (220–40).

Bonini, A. (1993) Tourism in Italy. In W. Pompl and P. Lavery (eds), *Tourism in Europe: Structures and Developments*. Wallingford: CAB International (302–23).

Bosselman, F.B., Peterson, C.B. and McCarthy, C. (1999) *Managing Tourism Growth: Issues and Applications*. Washington, DC: Island Press.

Briassoulis, H. (1993) Tourism in Greece. In W. Pompl and P. Lavery (eds), *Tourism in Europe: Structures and Developments*. Wallingford: CAB International (285–301).

Briguglio, L., Butler, R., Harrison, D. and Filho, W.L. (eds), (1996) *Sustainable Tourism in Islands and Small States: Case Studies*. London: Pinter.

Briguglio, L. and Vella, L. (1995) The competitiveness of the Maltese Islands in Mediterranean international tourism. In M.V. Conlin and T. Baum (eds), *Island Tourism: Management Principles and Practice*. Chichester: Wiley (133–47).

Britton, R.A. (1978) International tourism and indigenous development objectives: a study with special reference to the West Indies. Unpublished PhD thesis at the University of Minnesota.

Britton, S. (1982) The political economy of tourism in the Third World. *Annals of Tourism Research,* 9(3): 331–58.

Bryden, J. (1973) *Tourism and Development: A Case Study of the Commonwealth Caribbean.* London: Cambridge University Press.

Butler, R. (1993) Tourism development in small islands: past influences and future directions. In D. Lockhart, D. Drakakis-Smith, and J. Schembri (eds), *The Development Process in Small Islands.* London: Routledge (71–91).

Butler, R. (1999) Sustainable tourism: a state-of-the-art review. *Tourism Geographies,* 1(1): 7–25.

Campbell, S. (1996) Green cities, growing cities, just cities? Urban planning and the contradictions of sustainable development. *Journal of the American Planning Association,* 62(3): 296–312.

Conlin, M.V. and Baum, T. (eds) (1995) *Island Tourism: Management Principles and Practice.* Chichester: Wiley.

Connell, J. (1988) Contemporary issues in island micro-states. In M. Pacione (ed.), *The Geography of the Third World: Progress and Prospect.* New York: Routledge (427–62).

Costa, P., Gambuzza, M., Manente, M. and Minghetti, V. (1996) *Accessibility and Mobility Conditions and Tourist Development: The Case of Southern Italy.* Venice: International Centre of Studies on the Tourist Economy, University of Venice.

Cyprus Tourism Organization (1996) *Annual Report.* Nicosia: CTO.

Dagonaki, Z. and Kotios, A. (1998) Cultural tourism and regional development (in Greek). Paper written at the Department of Planning and Regional Development, University of Thessaly, Greece.

Erisman, H.M. (1983) Tourism and cultural dependency in the West Indies. *Annals of Tourism Research,* 10: 337–61.

Goodall, B. and Bergsma, J. (1990) Destinations – as marketed in tour operators' brochures. In G. Ashworth and B. Goodall (eds), *Marketing Tourism Places.* New York: Belhaven Press (170–92).

Greek Tourism Organization (1996) *Tourist Movement of the Dodecanese for 1996* (in Greek). Rhodes: GTO.

Hall, C. M. and Lew, A. (eds) (1998) *Sustainable Tourism: A Geographical Perspective.* Harlow: Longman.

Hall, C.M. and Page, S.J. (1996) *Tourism in the Pacific: Issues and Cases.* London: International Thomson Business Press.

Horden, P. and Purcell, N. (2000) *The Corrupting Sea: A Study of Mediterranean History.* Oxford: Blackwell.

Instituto Nacional de Estadística (1998) *Moviemento de Viajeros en Estableciementos Hoteleros* (MVEH). http://www.caib.es/kfgo/htm (accessed 19 June).

Ioannides, D. (1992) Tourism development agents: the Cypriot resort cycle. *Annals of Tourism Research,* 19: 711–31.

Ioannides, D. (1994) The state, transnationals, and the dynamics of tourism evolution in small island nations. PhD dissertation, Rutgers, State University of New Jersey.

Ioannides, D. (1998) Tour operators: the gatekeepers of tourism. In D. Ioannides and K. Debbage (eds), *The Economic Geography of the Tourist Industry: A Supply-side Analysis.* London: Routledge (139–58).

Ioannides, D. (2001) Tourism development in Mediterranean Islands: opportunities and constraints. In Y. Apostolopoulos and D.J. Gayle (eds), *Island Tourism and Sustainable Development: Experiences of Caribbean, Pacific, and Mediterranean Islands.* Westport: Praeger.

Ioannides, D. and Apostolopoulos, Y. (1999) Political instability, war, and tourism in

Cyprus: effects, management, and prospects for recovery. *Journal of Travel Research*, 38(1): 51–6.

King, R. (1993) The geographical fascination of islands. In D.G. Lockhart, D. Drakakis-Smith and J. Schembri (eds), *The Development Process in Small Island States*. London: Routledge (13–37).

Kousis, M. (1989) Tourism and the family in a rural Cretan community. *Annals of Tourism Research*, 16: 318–32.

Leontidou, L. (1988) Greece: prospects and contradictions of tourism in the 1980s. In A. Williams and G. Shaw (eds), *Tourism and Economic Development: Western European Experiences*. London: Belhaven Press (80–100).

Lockhart, D.G. (1993) Introduction. In D.G. Lockhart, D. Drakakis-Smith and J. Schembri (eds), *The Development Process in Small Island States*. London: Routledge (1–9).

Loukissas, P. (1982) Tourism's regional development impacts: a comparative analysis of the Greek Islands. *Annals of Tourism Research*, 9: 523–41.

Loukissas, P. and Triantafyllopoulos, N. (1997) Factores competitivos en los destinos turisticos traditionales: los casos de las Islas Rodas y Myconos (Grecia). *Papiers de Tourisme*. Valencia: TOURISME Generaliat Valenciana Agencia, Valenciana del Tourisme: 114.

McCool, S.F. (1995) Linking tourism, the environment, and concepts of sustainability: setting the stage. In S. McCool and A. Watson (eds), *Linking Tourism, the Environment, and Sustainability*. Ogden, UT: United States Department of Agriculture – Intermountain Research Station (3–7).

McCool, S.F. and Stankey, G.H. (1999) *Searching for Meaning and Purpose in the Quest for Sustainability*. Missoula, MT: School of Forestry.

Mikacic, V. and Montana, M. (1994) Island tourism in Croatia and the economics of small scale. *Insula: International Journal of Island Affairs*, 3(1): 37–40.

Milne, S. (1992) Tourism development in South Pacific microstates. *Annals of Tourism Research*, 19: 192–212.

Milne, S. and Gill, K. (1998) Distribution technologies and destination development: myths and realities. In D. Ioannides and K. Debbage (eds), *The Economic Geography of the Tourist Industry*. London: Routledge (123–38).

Mowforth, M. and Munt, I. (1998) *Tourism and Sustainability: New Tourism in the Third World*. London: Routledge.

Oglethorpe, M. (1984) Tourism in Malta: a crisis of dependence. *Leisure Studies*, 3: 147–61.

Pearce, D. (1989) *Tourist Development*. Harlow, Essex: Longman.

Pearce, D. (1995) *Tourism Today: A Geographical Analysis*. Harlow, Essex: Longman.

Pigram, J.J. and Wahab, S. (1997) The challenge of sustainable tourism growth. In S. Wahab and J.J. Pigram (eds), *Tourism Development and Growth: The Challenges of Sustainability*. London: Routledge (3–13).

Poon, A. (1993) *Tourism, Technology, and Competitive Strategies*. Wallingford: CAB International.

Potter, R.B. (1983) Tourism and development: the case of Barbados, West Indies. *Geography*, 68(1): 46–50.

Saleem, N. (1996) A strategy of sustainable tourism in Sri Lanka. In L. Briguglio, R. Butler, D. Harrison and W.L. Filho (eds), *Sustainable Tourism in Islands and Small States: Case Studies*. London: Pinter (50–62).

Stott, M. (1996) Tourism development and the need for community action in Mykonos, Greece. In L. Briguglio, R. Butler, D. Harrison and W.L. Filho (eds), *Sustainable Tourism in Islands and Small States: Case Studies*. London: Pinter (280–305).

Theroux, P. (1995) *The Pillars of Hercules: A Grand Tour of the Mediterranean*. New York: Fawcett Columbine.

Valenzuela, M. (1988) Spain: the phenomenon of mass tourism. In A. Williams and G. Shaw (eds), *Tourism and Economic Development: Western European Experiences.* London: Belhaven Press.

Vassiliou, G. (1995) Tourism and sustainable development: lessons from the Cyprus experience. In UNU World Institute for Development Economics Research. *Small Islands – Big Issues: Crucial Issues in the Sustainable Development of Small Developing Islands.* Helsinki: The United Nations University (38–62).

Wahab, S. and Pigram, J.J. (eds) (1997) *Tourism Development and Growth: The Challenges of Sustainability.* London: Routledge.

Wall, G. (1997) Sustainable development – unsustainable development. In S. Wahab and J.J. Pigram (eds), *Tourism Development and Growth: The Challenges of Sustainability.* London: Routledge (33–49).

Wilkinson, P.F. (1989) Strategies for tourism in island microstates. *Annals of Tourism Research,* 16: 153–77.

Wilkinson, P.F. (1997) *Tourism Policy and Planning: Case Studies from the Commonwealth Caribbean.* New York: Cognizant Communications Corporation.

Williams, A. and Montanari, A. (1999) Sustainability and self-regulation: critical perspectives. *Tourism Geographies,* 1(1): 26–40.

World Commission on Environment and Development (1987) *Our Common Future.* Oxford: Oxford University Press.

2

Tourism, Development, and Society in the Insular Mediterranean

Tom Selwyn

Introduction: Islands, Tourism, and Space

The purpose of this chapter is to use studies of Mediterranean island tourism to reflect on several broader regional issues. The exercise is a reminder that the study of tourism is not only an end in itself, but is also a prism within which to discuss questions of more mainstream regional social, environ-mental and political concern. The overall orientation of the chapter will be towards a concern with space. Specifically, it examines questions of control over space and those various types of spatial transformations within the region upon which tourism exercises a major, and sometimes determining, role.

The starting point will be the tourist-induced movement of the centres of gravity in Mediterranean islands from inland settlements to coasts. This will allow consideration of some of the issues arising from studies of coastal development, the forces shaping that development, and the extent to which the coastal mode of (tourism) production has spread into the rest of island political economies. The second part will consider some of the consequences of this shift for the culture and nature of the region.

Shifting Centres: *Balearization* and Beyond

I begin, then, by making some generalizations about the role of tourism in Mediterranean island development. All are familiar. First of all, tourism development was one of the main engines within the region leading to the transformation of semi-feudal to capitalist island economies. Second, this transformation was accompanied by the decline in influence of traditional landowners (both local and absentee) and the rise in influence of a combination of development companies, banks, and foreign tour operators. Third, there were at least two accompanying demographic consequences: the movement of indigenous populations from island centres to coasts, and incoming migration by hotel and other workers for the expanding tourist industry. Fourth, the ownership and control of space are presently, and often bitterly, contested. On the one hand, there are the forces of speculative development, favouring a *laissez-faire* approach to building. On the other hand, there are the forces associated with such public authorities as local municipalities, attempting to contain private speculation within a framework of public interest. Fifth, one of the main questions for Mediterranean island development in the decades to come will be concerned with the way in which this contest is played out.

The process of simultaneous marginalization and under-development of island interiors and economic development of coasts, often achieved through rapid and unplanned, building, with all its associated social, environmental and political consequences, came to be known, in relation to the Balearic islands, as *balearization*. This process has also become familiar in many other parts of the Mediterranean islands. Sivri (1997), for example, reports depopulation of some of the inland settlements of Thasos in the face of coastal development, and also draws attention to the better known cases of such development in islands such as Mykonos and Rhodes. She also points out, however, that some of the inland villages and towns in Thasos have retained a mixed economy, including both tourism and agriculture. Thus, for example, Panagia, the island's nineteenth-century capital, has retained a strong identity in terms of its social structure, economy and the quality of its architecture (Sivri, 1997: 50).

The ingredients of *balearization* and its associated consequences, then, included the radical disruption of local inland economies. The *polyculture*, mixed agriculture, characteristic of the historical Mediterranean has, to a large extent, been replaced by the mono-crop of coastal tourism. This has had, of course, environmental consequences such as the falling into disrepair of many inland agricultural terraces. At the same time, the populations of inland towns and villages have declined – a fact that is particularly noticeable in the case of young men and women. This process, in turn, has led to various types of changes in family organization.

At the local level, municipal and other planning authorities have found it consistently hard to assert or retain local control over tourist developments. It needs to be said, though, that while many of these developments may be wholly or partly controlled from the outside by outsiders – multinational tour operators and their associated financial institutions, for example – there are often significant local players on the inside. These include returning immigrants with capital, such as those described by Kenna (1993) for the

Greek island of Anafi. The issue is thus not so much one of insiders versus outsiders (a red herring of an argument much favoured by some sustainable tourism lobbies in northern Europe), but rather of the extent to which tourism development is subject to democratic control (cf. Boissevain, 1996). These processes may be illustrated by taking a small number of indicative examples from Majorca and Malta.

Coastal Development: The Case of Majorca

Rapid tourist development of the coast of Majorca in the 1960s was accompanied by the abandonment of much of the agricultural land in the island's centre. This has caused Picornel *et al.* (1997) to observe that space on the coast, which was once economically marginal to the island, has now become of central importance to its economy. At the same time, the once most economically significant space covering much of the interior has become economically marginal since it has not traditionally been included in the development plans of the tourist industry (see also Chapter 10 by Bardolet in this volume). Other research in Majorca (Selwyn, 1997; Waldren, 1996) has broadened the ethnographic base from which further generalizations about the nature of coastal development and the forces unleashed by this may be made.

I begin with the case of Calvia District located southwest of Palma, the district which now has one of densest stretches of tourism development in Europe and includes such well-known tourist resorts as Magaluf and Santa Ponsa. The district of Calvia underwent radical transformation from a semi-feudal agricultural economy to one based on tourism in the space of a very few years. The first boom in tourist building on the Calvian coast happened in the early 1960s. It took place as a result of the confluence of three local and global trends: the growth of mass tourism following post-war austerity in northern Europe; the *laissez-faire* economic policies of the Franco era; and the complete absence of local government and local planning policies. Together, these factors provided the context for a free-for-all building bonanza. The boom lasted for about 15 years and consisted in the main of hotel building. The Middle East War and subsequent oil crisis ended this period, and for about 10 years building was largely confined to the construction of apartments. A second boom of hotel building began in the mid-1980s and coincided with the simultaneous growth of effective local planning. At the same time a new regional level of government came into existence. More recently, in the last years of the 1990s, hotel building has slowed while apartment building has continued.

Much effort has been spent by local and regional authorities to check the growth of building development and to continue the long process of salvaging the coast from the effects of the speculative builders of the 1960s. In many respects this effort has met with considerable success. The effectiveness of Calvia Municipality itself as a planning authority has been recognized throughout the Mediterranean. Nevertheless, there are some observers who are far from complacent, noting that speculative building and the forces fuelling this have only temporarily retreated from the island. Furthermore, despite being one of the most powerful in Spain, Calvia Municipality has found it difficult to achieve the level of control which can assure that such building is contained within what it considers reasonable bounds. At any rate the coast of Calvia is one of many locations in the island Mediterranean where the struggle between speculative private development and publicly organized and controlled development, shaped by concern for the social and economic well-being of those who live and work in the district, will take place in the decades to come.

It is important to reflect at this stage about what existed *before* the building boom of the 1960s. Elderly residents speak of general poverty, lack of public facilities, persistent emigration (notably to France, Cuba, and elsewhere in Latin America) and seem to be in no doubt that mass tourism has brought previously unknown levels of wealth to Calvia. Nevertheless, it would not be accurate to paint an unremittingly gloomy picture of the life and times of the district before the coming of tourism. Photographic evidence from the municipal archives spanning the past 100 years (Amengual, 1990) shows clear evidence of enterprise, style, and good living. There are photographs of musical bands and dancers in Calvia village at the turn of the century, of family picnics and celebrations on the Santa Ponsa headland, of the festivities of St Jaime, of women enjoying the La Granja café – well known for its ice cream and tapas – in 1945, of the village football team in 1949, and so on. Furthermore Calvia's valleys are reminders that the district contained areas of considerable abundance. There is good, fertile, land there suitable for vegetable and fruit production, and there is plenty of evidence of former orchards and market gardens. Further up the valley slopes there are dry stone walls supporting terraces on which dry farming (carob, almond, fig, olive) was practised. These areas of agricultural production were, for the most part, managed as part of large estates, some of which were extremely wealthy.

It is even worth locating the history of, say, the past few hundred years, in a longer-term context. Describing the estate (*possessio* or *finca*) of Valldurgent, named possibly after the French *Val d'Argent* (i.e., valley of silver), Andreu remarks that it would be easy to imagine that before the conquest in 1229 by the Catalan King Jaume I of the then Muslim population of the island, the land produced all kinds of fruit and vegetables, with men and women coming and going, busily working or having fun, among the din and bustle characteristic of places of abundance (1987: 27).

The purpose of this small historical reflection is not to deny that the island is now a great deal wealthier than it was historically. That would, of course, be unrealistic. Equally unrealistic, however, would be claims about the benefits of contemporary tourist development, which rest upon assumptions of the island having been nothing but a poverty-stricken backwater or economic *tabula rasa*. As in many other parts of the island and mainland Mediterranean, coastal development in Majorca has been accomplished at the cost of substantial under-development of the agricultural interior.

In more recent times, Calvia's coastal development has caused substantial demographic changes. Not only was there the pronounced population drift to the coast from the centre of the island which has already been noted, but Calvia District has the highest population of mainland Spanish workers of any municipality on the island. This is the main factor that has ensured a consistent, if narrow, majority in the municipality ever since its inception in the early 1980s, for the Spanish socialist party (i.e., the *Partido Socialista Obrero Español*, or PSOE).

As far as the tourism offer is concerned, the present concern among municipal planners is that an appropriate balance between hotel and self-catering apartment accommodation might be disrupted in favour of a greater number of the latter. Such a shift would, they argue, reduce the demand for labour in the hotel industry, thus causing unemployment. Were that unemployment to translate into return emigration to the mainland of part of the hotel work force, then it is thought that that would affect the political make-up of the municipality, tipping the balance of power towards the Spanish Conservative Party, the *Partido Popular*, or PP.

The significance of the party differences is as follows. While, in Calvia, the PSOE has always stood for interventionist policies in matters of property development and administration, the PP favours a much more *laissez-faire* approach. In the present context this means that the PP would tend to take a much softer line in relation to landowners closing off their land to the public, be more reluctant to introduce more natural parks, and generally be less interested in legislative controls on property development. As indicated, the consistent PSOE majority in Calvia owes most to the hotel workers from the mainland. A possible future electoral weakness might derive from the increasing number of foreign residents, many from the UK, who, post-Maastricht, have rights to a vote in local municipal elections. Ironically this army of pensioners with largely Thatcherite tendencies is coming to hold the electoral balance of power and could tip it in favour of the PP almost at a stroke.

While the details of party affiliations, party policies, voting patterns, and so on, vary from island to island, the *general* significance of the Calvia case in this regard lies in the different policy and planning dispositions and capacities held and enacted at the local level by local authorities. As has already been said, this is a landscape where the forces of speculative building and controlled development are increasingly in fierce competition with one another. Since the mid-1980s development in Calvia itself has taken place within the framework of the municipality's *General Plan*, an extremely detailed document describing the environmental and urban consequences deriving from the municipality's economic dependence on tourism. It outlines the strategies and legal frameworks to be followed by developers. The central aim of the *Plan* is the rational organization of space, including tourist space. Furthermore, it is self-consciously informed by a *regional* perspective on Mediterranean tourism, being based on the forecast that an island such as Majorca will not be able to compete with such new destinations as Turkey for the cheap holiday market. The implication is that the island's hotels and other tourist structures need to be upgraded in order to attract higher spending tourists. The *Plan* itself is backed up by an impressive team of professional planners, architects, landscape designers, and others working in the municipality.

Calvia's *General Plan*, drawn up and implemented by a team of experts, is illustrative of a dominant principle of the council itself, namely its belief in strategic local intervention backed up at regional, national and European levels. This principle is found in many of the council policy initiatives. These include the declaration of a large area of the district as a Natural Park and an ongoing programme involving opening up its interior to tourists by re-opening ancient paths used in the past by peasant farmers, wood-cutters, charcoal burners, shepherds, and others. It is precisely these kinds of actions, as well as the principles which guide them, which have brought the council into conflict with a number of local landowners and developers who are pressing for controls on public access to land in favour of more exclusively private access.

In Calvia itself, therefore, the 1960s' era of unplanned and haphazard development gave way in the 1980s and early 1990s to a planned and regulated development in such a way as to make private development seem contained within a public planning framework. The question remains. For how much longer can private speculative building development be contained by public policies?[1] How might the balance between public and private tip towards the dominance of the latter? In order to answer this we may take the following indicative case.

Part of the business of a development company in Calvia District consists of the building of tourist-related residential developments that, increasingly, have consisted of estates of luxury apartments for sale to foreign residents. Along with the apartments themselves, there is the associated infrastructure to make such developments attractive to potential buyers, golf courses being a particularly popular offering. Closely linked to both of these is the other main part of the company's business, namely the building of public roads, which are not only for use by the general public but also part of the infrastructure of the company's own developments. When complete, the roads are sold to Calvia Municipality. This is where the weak link appears. Because in the early days of its existence the municipality borrowed large sums of money, it presently pays an extremely high fraction of its budget on interest payments, a fact that periodically makes it late in paying for its roads. This puts the municipality in something of a vulnerable condition, opening the way for arrangements to be made between it and the development company. These may take a number of forms. Granting permission to build golf courses might be one. It was recently argued in Calvia, for example, that there are substantial economic benefits to the municipality to be obtained from the hosting of international golf tournaments. Dilution of legislation governing natural parks (in which building development is forbidden) might be another. Allowing road building to serve further private developments, might be a third.

The Disputed Landscapes of Coasts and Interiors: Cases from Majorca and Malta

Before making some generalizations about the shape and character of tourist development in the island Mediterranean, I should consider the implications the general forces and processes taking place on the coast have for interior areas. This may effectively be done ethnographically using one example from Majorca and two from Malta.

Waldren (1996) points towards the ever-increasing power of the private construction sector on Majorca in general and, particularly in its interior, by showing how road building programmes adopted by the regional government of the Balearics have been pushed through at enormous expense. Such projects, as the hotly disputed widening of the coast road between Deia and Soller, for example, are frequently carried out in the face of local opposition and informed environmentalist criticism. According to estimates of the Majorcan Green Party and the island's well-respected *Grup Balear d'Ornitologia i Defensa de la Naturesa* (GOB), road development projects in the single year of 1997 destroyed 700 hectares of forest, agricultural terrain, and protected natural spaces. Waldren points out that these developments are at odds with the Majorcan Tourist Board's rhetoric about the desirability of forms of sustainable tourism based on existing traditional local agricultural economies. As she says, the very direction of these projects is in complete contradiction to the new types of tourism the tourism board wants to attract (1996: 127). At the heart of the matter, Waldren argues, is the fact that the development programmes of the island are generally driven by private interests articulated through municipalities and the island's parliament which take precedence over collective and/or environmental objectives.

Boissevain and Theuma (1998) sharpen the focus of this pattern of power relations in their analysis of the recent Hilton and Cottonera cases from Malta. In the first of these, permission was granted by Malta's planning authority for the development of a US$122 million project involving the construction of a new Hilton hotel, together with a development of 250 luxury apartments, yacht marina, and business centre. Apart from the general dislocation and inconvenience to local residents and businesses, the project involved the destruction of a unique part of the island's historical fortifications built in 1530 by the Knights of St John and the causing of pollution to nearby sea grass meadows and beaches. Environmental groupings vigorously opposed the project. Indeed, the project involved high profile legal and political engagement, since the public was very largely opposed to the development. In the second case, a US-led development corporation was on the point of receiving permission to take over the front of one of the famous three cities opposite Valletta across the Grand Harbour. This particular idea became the focus of a political trial of strength between the then ruling Labour party which, with its majority of one, was publicly selling the project on the grounds of it bringing inward investment and providing employment opportunities to a part of Malta marked by poverty and unemployment, and the opposition Nationalist Party who took the opportunity to oppose the plan. Following a rejection by the former Prime Minister Dom Mintoff of his party's whip on this issue, the government itself fell and in the ensuing election lost its majority to the Nationalists. Though yet to be seen whether they will revive the Cottonera project itself, Boissevain and Theuma conclude with the wry observation that the Nationalists certainly are committed to the implementation of many of the other ambitious upmarket tourist projects which the Labour Party had adopted. In their view the confrontations over Malta's landscape are set to continue.

This notion of the landscape being subject to confrontation and disputation is an accurate one that finds echoes throughout the Mediterranean islands. In Malta's own case, for example, the number of tourists visiting the island's ancient capital, Mdina (upwards of 750,000 annually) has for some time been thought by residents (who number 220) to be excessive (Boissevain, 1997). But, or so it seemed to them, there was little that they could actually do about controlling numbers. Malta lacked any system of local government and there appeared few other effective avenues to take appropriate action. Recently, however, a system of local municipalities has been introduced throughout the island. One of the first actions taken by the newly constituted municipality of Mdina was to limit visitor numbers. Clearly, however, it will be a while before the long-term effectiveness of Mdina council in asserting control over the spaces of its town in the face of the island's tourist industry can be assessed.

Summary

These ethnographic sketches allow us to make several working assumptions. The tourism-related development in Mediterranean islands in the second half of the twentieth century started with the relocation of the centres of economic activity from inland agricultural settlements to coastal tourist areas. In the process, a semi-feudal, remittance-aided, agricultural mode of production, which in some islands, such as Majorca, were dominated by large estates, gave way to a modern capitalist economy based on tourism. One important aspect of this transformation involved land on the coast, which formerly had little agricultural use value, rapidly acquiring development value. Some of the owners of coastal lands (typically younger sons or daughters of families whose elder siblings owned land in the interior) became rich. The majority, lacking capital to develop the lands themselves, sold them to developers. In the early days, coastal development in many islands was essentially opportunistic and unplanned. As the tourism industry grew, the centres of economic gravity expanded to include tour operators, many of them foreign. Thus, economic power is presently increasingly located in combinations of development companies/banks and (often foreign) tour operators — although the extent to which individual members of previously dominant families, and/or some whole families themselves, have retained power in the new economic climate must be a matter for ethno-financial investigation. The mode of tourism-related development on the coasts has had wide-reaching effects in inland areas. With few exceptions (where elements of traditional agricultural economies have managed to co-exist with tourism), inland areas have also been incorporated, even if only through their own under-development, in tourist-dominated island economies. In the process, development decisions are often taken in locations that are out of reach of those who live and work in the sites of actual tourism development. In general the forces of private speculative development are a good deal stronger that those of combinations of local municipalities, non-governmental organizations, and public movements. For example, it is clear that, from the point of view (and involvement) of those living or working near the sites, or those who simply care about them, the development of the Deia/Soller road and the Malta Hilton have passed out of any form of democratic control. However, there *are* times when alliances between environmental groups, local government authorities, and tour operators anxious about the sustainability of their product, can come together in opposition to the development companies. This is what happened briefly in Majorca in the mid to late 1990s. As far as the ownership and control of space is concerned, it is these unfolding structures of alliances, and the sites of struggle in which they operate which provide the most interesting set of questions for students of tourism and tourism development.

So far I have discussed aspects of the political economy of tourism development in Mediterranean islands. The next stage is to consider some of the social, cultural and environmental consequences.

Tourism, Culture, and Nature

The raw material of the tourism industry consists of the culture and nature of its destinations. We may take them in turn.

Cultural questions

The term culture itself is, of course, complex and catch-all. It covers just about everything in all areas of life and is thus to be found as much in the spheres of economic and political practice as it does in religious, artistic or culinary ones. Thus, when we speak of culture in the Mediterranean, as indeed anywhere else, we need to think in terms of such categories as family life and values, economic and productive practices, religious, artistic and architectural practices, and so on. The term refers to the way people live in a general and inclusive sense, together with the accompanying symbolic paraphernalia. But the particular interest of the present chapter is with the *cultural uses of space*. In what follows, therefore, there is a concern with the social spaces occupied by families, communities, and individuals and the physical spaces in which these are located. There are several social and cultural changes associated with the kinds of economic transformations that have been discussed. I begin by considering the changing structures of family and kinship.

The relationship between the generations, to take one aspect of family life, has clearly been affected by the movement away from the centrality of agriculture/pastoralism in inland areas to participation in coastal tourism-based economies. Thus, Black (1990) has written of the emancipatory effect of tourism in Malta for young women, many of whom have moved away from patriarchal and matriarchal structures by finding economic roles in the tourist-dominated economy of the island, making them less dependent on parents and the Catholic Church. Eber and Aziz (1997) have described how Bedouin children, particularly females, work the beaches of the Sinai selling friendship bracelets to tourists on the coasts, again re-defining their role *vis-à-vis* their parents, particularly their mothers. Evidence from Corfu suggests that there is a radical loosening of the authoritative proximity of generations following the leaving by young men of villages in the interior to pursue business opportunities on the coast. This generational dislocation has been one of the contributory causes behind the spread of AIDS as well as several well-publicized outbreaks of violence on the island.[2]

Examples such as these suggest a pattern not so much of family breakdown but of growing autonomy and individualism within kinship structures. At the same time there is less overlap between the spaces inhabited by the family and the spaces in which moral decisions are taken. Formerly, with a core of members of extended families inhabiting contiguous space, there was an overlap between kinship and spatial boundaries, providing a recognizable spatial arena in which moral sanctions were exercised. Increasingly, with the growing autonomy of family members in tourist-dominated economies, moral sanctions are becoming more of a matter for individual consideration.

Movements from island centres to coasts and the development of tourist economies, then, involve the dispersal of family members into heterogeneous spaces within and beyond the boundaries of the island. The same applies to larger communal structures, such as those working-class inhabitants of the quarters of historic cities. Schembri and Borg (1997), for example, describe the exodus of the working-class population of the Three Cities in Malta, a pattern repeated in some of the historic cities in Turkey, Greece and elsewhere (Orbasli, 1997). Typically what has accompanied this exodus has been the *inflow* of middle-class investors into second homes from the metropolis. Investors from Rome are the most visible in the case of the Three Cities, while wealthy Athenians are investing in the settlements and towns of Greek islands (Chelidoni, 1997; Sivri, 1997).

As this movement of population takes place and the basis of the economy of such towns and settlements is determined to an ever greater extent by the tourism and second home economy, the character of island towns undergoes a spatial transformation which may be introduced as follows.

One of the most remarkable features of the *historic* Mediterranean urban landscape has been a distinctive structure of spatial order and economy. This is based upon the capacity to construct spaces – public, semi-public, private – in which different individual persons, families, groups of families, and communities may live closely together, simultaneously maintaining senses of difference and coherence, separateness and commonality. This is typically achieved, as in the *Casbah* in Algiers or in the historic Old City of Jerusalem, through subtle combinations of the use of courtyards, which are more or less closed to the streets, openings to roof terraces, organization into communal *quarters*, and so on. In the case of Valletta and the Three Cities (as in some quarters in the Old City of Marrakesh or the Ottoman parts of Nicosia), it is partly achieved by the use of balconies jutting out into the street from the upper floors of houses. This gives residents (particularly women) opportunities to move at ease between the realm of the semi-public and the private. Such spatial economy and order at the level of the house find expression at the level of the whole town in such features as historic grid systems, as in Valletta and parts of the towns of the Canaries. It is also expressed in the tendency of historic Mediterranean cities, in general, to have mixed economic use linked to residential patterns. This has placed people of different economic and social standing in close proximity to one another. For example, there are Romas in the heart of Palma, while in several Mediterranean cities craftsmen and working-class families often live in the lower floors of buildings whose upper stories are inhabited by the wealthy (see Leontidou, 1990: 10–14; Amyuni, 1998). I would like to place these features within a single category that may appropriately be termed *socio-spatial counterpoint*.

Similar processes are at work in the Mediterranean countryside. The *polyculture* and mixed usages of historic Mediterranean agricultural land mirror the kind of processes noted above for urban settlements. For example, on the large canvas, the relationship between the desert and the coast (in the south of the region) or the mountains and the coast in the north and in most islands, provides us with another example of *socio-spatial counterpoint*. In the fourteenth century, Ibn Khaldun argued that the society and history of the Arab Mediterranean were structured by the relationship between the desert and the city. In the desert resided pastoralists, herdsmen, and shepherds. In the city there were labourers, craftsmen, moneylenders, scholars, priests, soldiers, and the court. Agriculturists were in between. But as the middle classes move in to town and country, as coasts become separated from interiors (by roads and tourist development), and as whole categories of occupation (from pastoralist to most types of craftsperson) disappear, and the overall basis of island economies changes, spaces become increasingly individuated, decorative and cut off from the field of relations in which they were embedded.

In sum, then, the historical landscape of the Mediterranean, both urban and agricultural, was one in which boundaries of space and family tended to coincide. It was also a landscape in which considerable value was placed both on public space and on the routine ability to enter the spaces of others. Indeed, elaborate codes of hospitality and politeness were available to guide strangers through the spaces of others (Selwyn, 2000a). Moreover, marginal categories of people – pastoralists, those involved in transhumant shepherding, Romas – found convenient and available spaces for themselves either inside or outside the city. Towns and villages could cope with the periodicity that was a feature of their lives.

It was also a social landscape marked by *patronage* of several kinds. There was the type of patronage of the rich and powerful by the poor made famous by the anthropological literature on Mediterranean society (Campbell, 1964; Gellner, 1969). There was patronage of the arts and sciences in the historical Mediterranean by cities, courts, and prominent families. There was the patronage of local churches and mosques by rich members of congregations, and the patronage by smaller towns and villages of festivals of patron saints and/or holy figures.

But as can be seen, many of these features and relationships are changing under the influence of economic shifts to contemporary tourist-dominated free market economies. The historic spatial economy, and what I have termed socio-spatial counterpoint, is breaking down. The landscape generally is in the process of being privatized and access to spaces in both town and country is increasingly restricted. At the same time, and partly as a result, pastoralism and transhumance are disappearing and some Bedouin, shepherds and Romas are being marginalized. Allied to such movements, systems of patronage are also breaking down (except perhaps in cases of competitive religious or nationalist competition and/or conflict where foreign patrons might support some kinds of buildings and activities to curry favour in scrambles for political influence).

The new cultural landscape of the Mediterranean is one shaped by the increasing emancipation of the individual from such overarching social structures as family, communal city quarter, estate, constituency of patron, and so on. One implication of this is that properties and spaces in both town and countryside are also shedding remaining links with larger communal spaces. The Archduke Salvador and a well-known Hollywood film star share the distinction of being the owners (the former in the nineteenth century, the latter in the twentieth) of the same Majorcan *possessio*. However, while the estate in the nineteenth century was accessible to Majorcan residents, including hunters, fishers, and collectors of wild fruits and other edible species of plant, the twentieth-century estate is surrounded by fences. As a result, it has become a significant political issue in Majorcan politics – not only of itself but for what it represents, namely the removal of public space. At the same time, in the centre of Palma city, now a heavily commercial area full of privately owned bars and restaurants for tourists, the presence of Romas using urban spaces previously able to accommodate them, has also become a political issue. There is mounting pressure by the bar and restaurant owners to remove such 'unsightly' citizens. The issue takes different forms but the question everywhere is the same: as space is being privatized, how are communal rights (including those held by different constituencies and categories of people working and living in them) to those spaces going to be exercised and maintained?

Tourism and Culture

Apart from the above processes, all of which are consequences of tourism-related development and the kind of politico-economic changes it brings in its wake, tourism also takes part more directly in cultural formations. Of the many possible examples, here are three. The first is the appropriation of cultural sites and practices by national and international authorities in the name of tourism and tourist-related conservation practices. The second consists of one of the ingredients of such appropriation, namely what has been called (Orbasli, 2000) facadism. The third has to do with a phenomenon that appears to be at odds with the spatial privatization identified above, but which is in fact closely tied to it, namely the nationalization of cultural spaces.

Cultural appropriation

Odermatt (1996) has described how the Sardinian bronze/iron age monuments, the *nuraghi*, are presently the focus of a dispute between the

Italian authorities, who claim that the site is of major importance to world heritage and needs protection (including fencing off) and local residents of the nearby village for whom the monuments are a popular meeting place in the evening. The latter argue that since the site is located in their village it is they who should take responsibility for its management and protection.

This case is just one illustration of a particular kind of cultural appropriation: in the name of protection and/or conservation historical sites are removed from everyday access. Nowhere better are the complexities of this process described (albeit in a different geographical context) than in Bender's (1998) *Stonehenge*.

The making of national or natural parks is another example of the appropriation by state authorities of sites that are often used for everyday purposes by nearby communities. Crain's (1996) work on the Andalusian Doñana National Park is an excellent case in point. This park, one of Europe's largest game reserves, was identified by the European Union and ecologically aware local and national planners, together with those predominantly wealthy locals who stood to gain out of increased ecotourism, as a good site for international protective status. Appropriate measures were taken, including the donation by the European Commission to the government of Spain to make the park into a European heritage site. Environmentally friendly tourism by bird- and animal-loving northern Europeans was encouraged. The only snag was that, for centuries, the area was a hunting ground for the predominantly working-class inhabitants of nearby villages.

The issue of hunting in Mediterranean islands raises several questions that are not as easy to answer as might at first be supposed. Who has the right to hunt? Who has the obligation to conserve? What processes of decision-making are there to resolve contradictory and conflicting demands on the land and its produce? Who owns the space on which hunting takes place? Who should own it? And so on.

These are precisely the issues in relation to historical monuments and even whole towns (such as Mdina) which have been taken over, to a greater or lesser extent, by tourists and tourist authorities. Once again the question concerns the control and organization of space, including sites of national and international scientific significance.

Facadism, Internet-ism, museumization, experience-ification

These are processes stimulated by the tourist industry, which Boissevain and Theuma (1998) describe in terms of a movement from utilitarian space to heritage. These take several forms.

There is, first of all, the urban facadism (i.e., the emphasis on conserving the facades of buildings) much debated by architects concerned with historic towns. This 'preservation at any price' approach to the historic cities on the tourist trail is one emphasizing external appearance above all else and is, suggests Orbasli (2000), a fear-laden response to spoiling a desired image (cf. also Selwyn, 1996). As she goes on to explain, such an approach is ultimately the enemy of urban conservation, since towns and cities need constantly to be renewing themselves to remain alive. However, it is legitimate to ask when considering the three UNESCO World Heritage Sites on Mediterranean islands, namely Valletta, Rhodes Old Town, and Paphos, how can such renewal be achieved? And who is going to achieve this renewal? One may also wonder about the extent to which the authorities (whether from the tourist sector or UNESCO itself) are, indeed, concerned with image more that the gritty day-to-day life of one these cities.

Then there are the various forms of what one might term Internet-ism: the offering on the Internet of properties and sites for sale which are described effusively in terms of their cultural, natural and historic value. Internet-ese builds on the kinds of language (of tourist/real estate brochures) described and analysed by Dann (1996) and others. In one of the Sardinia web sites, for example, the viewer is offered for rent:

> Villa Ebner ... sleeps 8 ... a holiday villa of 6000 Sq. meters of Mediterranean bush, pinewood and eucalyptus wood ... located close to Port Pino ... an area which boasts a wide range of typically Mediterranean natural habitats, most of which are very much unspoilt ... Inland there is a rich archeological heritage, which includes settlements of the first inhabitants of the island, the Nuraghe, the typical Sardinian houses dating back to the Bronze Age.

Nestling in a box on the bottom left-hand side of the web site, at once discreet and reassuring, is the additional information that 'Restaurants and Pizzerie are in Porto Pino, 2 km from the property. Supermarket, pharmacy, bank, Post Office are in Santa Anna Annesi village. There is a golf club at 50km.' Such language is, as noted, familiar from sales brochures of Mediterranean properties in other islands, such as the 1993 brochure offering a luxury apartment in Calvia: 'Los Pampanos offers reminiscences of the old Mediterranean wrapped in subtropical gardens, created from materials of the finest quality, bringing forth a dream of architectural excellence combined with comfort.' Once again there was a golf course as part of the package for the buyer of a Los Pampanos apartment, the whole complex being built and supplied by the development company whose other function was the building of roads over much of the island. Apart from these connections, the other point of significance is that Los Pampanos is framed by an appeal to a private domain in which the Majorcan landscape serves as a backdrop. These two cases suggest that we have arrived in a dreamlike world of sensual experiences of an essentially private kind.

The emphasis on *experience* follows seamlessly from the villas Ebner and Los Pampanos. In Valletta tourists are invited (by varieties of strategically placed advertisements, including those offered in the in-flight glossy magazine distributed by Air Malta) to visit the permanently running show called the Malta Experience. This is a multimedia presentation of the best-known pieces of Maltese history, its foundation by the Knights, the siege of the island by the Turks, the heroism of the island and its people in World War II, and so on. Mdina has an equivalent, Mdina Experience, which is advertised by a sign at the entrance to the old city. As Orbasli (2000) observes, tourists seeing the Mdina sign for the first time are liable to be confused for unless there is the knowledge of the associated multi-media and film show, does the unsuspecting visitor not assume that the walled town itself is the experience?. In other words, the tourist is taken a step away from experiencing the site itself in order to sample an off-site experience of the site. Furthermore, the Experience feels as if it were an *authoritative* experience, a super guidebook, the real McCoy.

Such experience-ification is not far removed from the sort of museumiza-tion described, amongst others, by Boissevain (1997). He estimated that Mdina could earn itself around $2 million annually by redefining itself as a museum – its citizens losing the right to be treated as objects in the process.

Nationalization of tourist space

Tourism is related to nationalism in several ways. One of these is the overlapping nature of promotional and nationalist rhetoric. Akay (1997), for example, has shown that northern Cyprus is promoted in nationalistic terms. Turkish Cypriot tourism authorities, he argues, are engaged in recasting the Cypriot historical and cultural mosaic in terms of a Turkishness which is counter-posed to the Greekness of the south. Sites with Greek associations are increasingly defined in terms of them being Byzantine or Roman. Villages with Greek names have been given Turkish names that now appear on tourist maps. At the same time, the south is presented by the Greek Cypriot tourist authorities as if the foundation of Cypriot history was co-terminous with the first traces of the Greek population in Cyprus. Akay effectively demonstrates that while the heritage of North Cyprus (as the territory typically appears in English language guidebooks) is presented as Turkish, this process cannot be disconnected from the comparable processes engaged in over the years by Greek Cypriots in Hellenizing the whole island of Cyprus (1997: 89). He further observes that because guidebooks subtract politics from culture (in the sense that gives the impression to the naïve tourist that the north is *culturally* Turkish and the south Greek), they take part in the process of nation-building in both territories. That is, they add legitimization to the political entities of the Turkish Republic of North Cyprus, on the one hand, and the state of Cyprus on the other.

The notion of an island's cultural mosaic being manipulated by rival nationalist movements is one that resonates elsewhere in the Mediterranean. Selwyn (1997), for example, has argued that Majorcan/Catalan nationalism has a very clear link with the Majorcan political economy of tourism and that there is a fairly close correlation between economic downturns and the rise of anti-Spanish and pro-Majorcan nationalist expressions. Such association is to be expected in a context in which many workers in the hotel industry on the island come from the mainland. Selwyn further argues that one of the reasons why Majorcan and Spanish nationalisms have not, unlike Greek and Turkish nationalisms in Cyprus, resulted until now in hot conflict in Majorca is that government (particularly local government) on that island is powerful enough to have regulated the provision of services (health, education, and so on) and employment to both indigenous Majorcan and immigrant Spanish workers in the tourist industry to safeguard the well-being of both communities. It achieved this in the early days of its existence, namely in the aftermath of the death of Franco and the setting up of municipalities in Spain in the early 1980s, by borrowing significant sums of money to build schools, homes for the elderly, sports centres, and other facilities. This is the reason why presently the municipality is still in debt (see above). Selwyn also speculates that were tourism development policies to be adopted that failed to meet the employment needs of the present population of the island, and if there were to be a sustained period of unemployment, then expressions of nationalist sentiments would be likely to increase. In the case of Majorca such unemployment could easily be imagined were the ratio of self-catering apartments to hotels (the former being much less labour-intensive than the latter) to increase.

It would be tempting, following these two examples, to link strong nationalist sentiments to weak civil institutions, and vice versa and there is probably something to be said for such a link. But there are clearly also other factors, not least those coming from forces outside the islands in question.

Tourism studies suggest three topics of interest within the general framework of discussions about the relation between tourism and nationalism. The first arises from the disjunction between the fact that the organization of tourism within the Mediterranean requires co-operation between potentially conflicting national communities. For instance, on the one hand, Majorcan tourism needs Spanish workers, Israeli and Palestinian tourism need each other, and so on. On the other hand, there is the promotion of nationalist agendas in the tourism context. The second topic of interest concerns the capacity of public authorities to contain rival nationalisms through economic regulation (so that all sides feel senses of well-being). The third, the political extension of the second, concerns the extent to which public authorities, including local municipalities, can so include and involve their populations, to use contemporary Third Way language, as to reduce the propensity for nationalist expressions.

Environmental Questions

Tourism and tourism-related developments are writing a script on the natural and built spaces of Mediterranean islands, the decoding of which involves looking three ways: backwards at features of the historic Mediterranean environment, sideways at how that environment is presently changing, and forwards at how it may become in the future.

The best way to introduce a discussion on the natural environment of Mediterranean islands is to refer back to the extensive and now very well-known description and analysis of the region's environment by Grenon and Batisse in 1989. In their *Futures for the Mediterranean Basin: The Blue Plan* these authors identified six primary features of the Mediterranean environment.

The first consists of the environmental *diversity* of the region. This may be seen in the interplay among mountains (acting as a physical boundary between the region and what lies beyond), pastures on the mountain slopes, the forests with their chestnut groves and variety of other trees, the villages with their associated terrace farming, the shrublands (home to birds and other fauna), meadows leading to cultivated crop lands, lagoons and marshes, and the pines on the edge of the sea. The diversity which is to be found in these different terrains and niches may also be seen in another feature of the region's agriculture, namely the practice of what is termed, in French, *polyculture* – the growing of many different kinds of agricultural products next door to one another. The second feature is the close *interrelationship* between nature, on the one hand, and agriculture and other productive or extractive practices, on the other: everywhere in the Mediterranean basin, human activity has always been one agent of environmental and geological change and development The third, which arises from the first two, consists of the *systematic nature* of the region's environment. Thus, for example, the ancient cycle of pastoral transhumance, whereby sheep, goats and other livestock would be shepherded down to the plains in the winter, where they would give birth in the spring before being taken back up to the mountain pastures in the summer, is illustrative of the fundamentally cyclical nature of the Mediterranean environment as a whole – spaces and times of agricultural use and activity followed by spaces and times of inactivity and renewal, the year itself being dominated by a water cycle fed and regulated by mountains which capture snow and rainfall which they feed to the slopes and valleys. The fourth follows from this: the *relatively scarce resources* of the region mean that the systematic interrelationship between the various parts of the natural environment and between it and the cultural environment depends to a large extent on the sparing use of those resources. Indeed, as the Plan itself makes clear, this is a fact which underlies not only much of the region's agriculture, but also much of its culture. As Grenon and Batisse say:

> There is a common stock of attitudes and behaviour with deep cultural and religious roots. These are related to the realities and features of the environment. For example, agricultural methods made sparing use of the land, soil, water and landscape. [For this reason] food consumption was always tinged with frugality. (1989: 12)

The fifth point is that it is precisely the *blend* of natural and cultural heritage that is the true wealth of the Mediterranean basin (ibid.: 4). The final point is that the very rapid *technological, economic, demographic, and social changes* in the region in the past half century – in which the growth of tourism and tourism-related development has played a substantial role – have placed the environment of the region under threat. (One French research report produced in the late 1980s, for example, estimated that 526 types of plant species were under threat of extinction, a fact which in turn had led to the radical reduction if not actual extinction of several animal species – the large forest mammals such as bears and lynxes, antelopes, and large birds of prey such as eagles and vultures all being examples.)

Mediterranean Tourism, Mediterranean Landscapes and Natural Environments

What contribution may we begin to make to the understanding of the features and structures of the Mediterranean landscapes and environments? We may start from observing that what we have called the coastal mode of (tourism) production has significantly changed the relationship between people and land. The radical decline of biodiversity, manifested as much in the decrease of the *polyculture* characteristic of the historical Mediterranean as in the (over-)use, abuse and neglect of the *garrigue*, is both cause and consequence of this changed relationship. Second, it is clear that the systematic interrelationship between nature and agriculture symbolically marked most potently by the seasonal transhumance of sheep and shepherds in the north, goats and Bedouin in the south of the region, has been replaced by a different sort of seasonality. This is driven not by the needs and lifecycles of livestock but by the dispositions and demands of northern European tourists coming and going from the region in the summer months. One of the several implications of this kind of seasonality is the enormous demand for food and other resources in the high season. Thus from being an area characteristically 'tinged with frugality' to use Grenon's and Batisse's nice phrase, it has become an area subject to regular bouts of over-demand and over-use of resources, particularly water.

The processes of social relocation and dislocation described here have had their affect on the landscape and environment. One (of many) ways into this discussion is provided by Hordern and Purcell (2000). Speaking of Mediterranean terraces and irrigation, and following the spirit of Grenon and Batisse, they observe that 'terracing and irrigation are represented within the microregion as strategies of improvement in miniature, part of that symbiosis between production and the environment which is so characteristic of the Mediterranean' (ibid.: 237). This idea of 'improvements in miniature' relates closely to the way Horden and Purcell describe one of the special agricultural and environmental characteristics of small Mediterranean islands (ibid.: 224–30). They refer to the 'tiny niches of high potential for intensification ... [being] ... long recognised as special features of the Mediterranean landscape'. But they qualify this generalization by also observing that while some historical periods have, indeed, provided contexts for flexible micro-agricultural responses by islanders to regional market opportunities, other periods have been marked by the incorporation of islands into regional market systems, dominated by mainland centres. In these latter contexts islands were often forced into monocrop production. No wonder, they say, that the population of early modern Corsica begged the authorities in Genoa to 'spare them economic growth or improvement' (ibid.: 229). The relevance of this to our present theme is clear. The monocrop of tourism has, in some senses, drawn islands into a kind of dependency on centres elsewhere. In the process the landscape itself, no longer shaped and constantly reshaped by small farmers and pastoralists, has become increasingly objectified and aestheticized in its transformation into a tourism product.

Conclusion

Tourism development in Mediterranean islands has been accompanied by a series of social and cultural changes. Spatial and kinship boundaries are becoming disassociated from one another. The working-class communities of the inner areas of historic island towns and cities are giving way to incoming second homeowners. As this happens, a social economy embedded within a system of spatial counterpoint is giving way to a system based on the occupancy by largely unrelated individuals of privatized space. This, in turn, gives rise, in both urban and rural settings, to a kind of aestheticization of the landscape that is increasingly unrelated to the uses to which it is put. The tourism industry itself (which, in this case, includes the various arms of the heritage and conservationist industries) thrives off such aestheticization, paying increasing attention (partly under the influence of tour operators anxious about their cultural products) to the façades and appearances of historic buildings and other sites of cultural interest. Just as tourism stimulates nostalgia for the communal spaces of the past, so it also can take part in efforts to nationalize space. As for the natural world, the diversity and polyculture of the historic agricultural Mediterranean is giving way to the homogeneity of the monocrop of tourism (one of the consequences being that terraces are being largely left to decay). Many of the historic interrelationships of agricultural practices and social relations are being broken up in the wake of the development of the coastal mode of tourist production. Resources, historically used frugally, are being used up. There is talk, for example, of replenishing water in north Cyprus with Turkish water transported to the island in balloons on their way to Israel.

We are left with a question: to what extent and in what ways are tourism and tourism development, some of the characteristics of which have been sketched out here, taking part in a process we might describe as the de-Mediterraneanization of the Mediterranean? It is an appropriate question on which to end.

Acknowledgements

A version of this chapter was published in Selwyn (2000b) by kind permission of the publisher of the present volume. I would like to thank the participants of the Atlas Conference in Savonlinna, Finland, in July 2000, and colleagues at the Joint Seminar of the Anthropology Department and DICE Seminar at the University of Kent as well as Dr Raoul Bianchi of the University of North London for comments on earlier drafts of this chapter. All errors, however, are my responsibility.

Notes

1. For comparative purposes, see the review in *Mediterranean Magazine* (June, 1991) of the conflict in the island of Minorca between private building speculation and public policy in the late 1980s.
2. I am indebted to students from the Tourism and Society course at the University of North London for this piece of information gained from their experiences as tour representatives on the island.

References

Akay, K. (1997) Tourism and nationalist discourse: the case of North Cyprus. In C. Fsadni and T. Selwyn (eds), *Sustainable Tourism in Mediterranean Islands and Small Cities*. Malta: MED-CAMPUS (91–4).

Amengual, J. (1990) *Cent Anys a Calvia*. Calvia: Ajuntament de Calvia.

Amyuni, M. (1998) *La Ville: Source d'inspiration*. Beirut: Franz Steiner.

Andreu, M. (1987) *The Landscape of Calvia*. Calvia: Ajuntament de Calvia.

Bender, B. (1998) *Stonehenge: Making Space*. Oxford: Berg.

Black, A. (1990) In the eyes of the beholder? The cultural effects of tourism in Malta. *Problems of Tourism*, 13: University of Warsaw, 112–43.

Boissevain, J. (1996) *Coping with Tourists: European Reactions to Mass Tourism*. Oxford: Berghahn.

Boissevain, J. (1997) Problems with cultural tourism in Malta. In C. Fsadni and T. Selwyn (eds), *Sustainable Tourism in Mediterranean Islands and Small Cities*. Malta: MED-CAMPUS (19–30).

Boissevain, J. and Theuma, N. (1998) Contested space: planners, tourists, developers and environmentalists in Malta. In S. Abram and J. Waldren (eds), *Anthropological Perspectives on Local Development*. London: Routledge (96–119).

Campbell, J. (1964) *Honour, Family and Patronage: A Study of Institutions and Moral Values in a Greek Mountain Community*. Oxford: Clarendon Press.

Chelidoni, K. (1997) Presentation of an interventionist policy: a case study of the island town of Kos. In C. Fsadni and T. Selwyn (eds), *Sustainable Tourism in Mediterranean Islands and Small Cities*. Malta: MED-CAMPUS (125–35).

Crain, M. (1996) The Danona National Park. In J. Boissevain (ed.), *Coping with Tourists: European Reactions to Mass Tourism*. Oxford: Berghahn (27–56).

Dann, G. (1996) *The Language of Tourism: A Sociolinguistic Perspective*. Wallingford: CAB International.

Eber, S. and Aziz, H. (1997) *Bedouin and Tourist Landscapes in Sinai*. Aix-en-Provence: Centre International de Recherches et d'Etudes Touristiques.

Gellner, E. (1969) *Saints of the Atlas*. London: Weidenfeld and Nicolson.

Grenon, M. and Batisse, M. (eds) (1989) *Futures for the Mediterranean Basin: The Blue Plan*. Oxford: Oxford University Press.

Horden, P. and Purcell, N. (2000) *The Corrupting Sea: A Study of Mediterranean History*. Oxford: Blackwell.

Kenna, M. (1993) Return migrants and tourist development: an example from the Cyclades. *Journal of Modern Greek Studies*, 11: 75–81.

Leontidou, L. (1990) *The Mediterranean City in Transition*. Cambridge: Cambridge University Press.

Mediterranean Magazine (1991) (25), June, 32–8.

Odermatt, P. (1996) The Sardinian Nuraghi. In J. Boissevain (ed.), *Coping with Tourists: European Reactions to Mass Tourism*. Oxford: Berghahn (84–112).

Orbasli, A. (1997) Historic towns and tourism in Turkey. In C. Fsadni and T. Selwyn (eds), *Sustainable Tourism in Mediterranean Islands and Small Cities*. Malta: MED-CAMPUS (36–46).

Orbasli, A. (2000) *Tourists in Historic Towns: Urban Conservation and Heritage Management*. London and New York: E. and F.N. Spon.

Picornel, C., Benitez, J. and Ginard, A. (1997) Tourism, territory and society in the Balearic islands. In C. Fsadni and T. Selwyn (eds), *Sustainable Tourism in Mediterranean Islands and Small Cities*. Malta: MED-CAMPUS (30–6).

Schembri, J. and Borg, M. (1997) Population changes in the walled cities of Malta. In C. Fsadni and T. Selwyn (eds), *Sustainable Tourism in Mediterranean Islands and Small Cities*. Malta: MED-CAMPUS (114–24).

Selwyn, T. (1996) *The Tourist Image: Myth and Myth Making in Tourism*. Chichester: Wiley.

Selwyn, T. (1997) Tourism, culture and cultural conflict. In C. Fsadni and T. Selwyn (eds), *Sustainable Tourism in Mediterranean Islands and Small Cities*. Malta: MED-CAMPUS (94–114).

Selwyn, T. (2000a) The anthropology of hospitality. In C. Lashley (ed.), *In Search of Hospitality: Theoretical Problems and Debates*. Oxford: Butterworth-Heinemann.

Selwyn, T. (2000b) The de-Mediterraneanisation of the Mediterranean. *Current Issues in Tourism*, 3, 3, 226–45.

Sivri, M. (1997) Tourism and development policies for traditional settlements: the case of Thasos and Dimitsana. In C. Fsadni and T. Selwyn (eds), *Sustainable Tourism in Mediterranean Islands and Small Cities*. Malta: MED-CAMPUS (46–60).

Waldren, J. (1996) *Insiders and Outsiders: Paradise and Reality in Mallorca*. Oxford: Berghahn.

Part 1
Key Issues Pertinent to Mediterranean Tourist Islands

3

Increasing the Value of Natural and Cultural Resources: Towards Sustainable Tourism Management

José Fernando Vera Rebollo

Introduction

When examining the factors affecting tourism development in Mediterranean islands at least two important issues should be considered. First, because of their insularity, these regions face a number of structural handicaps from the point of view of their territory, environment, society, culture and economy. The second issue is more global in nature and relates to the Mediterranean's future role as a tourist destination in view of strengthening competition from other places around the globe. Even though the Mediterranean basin attracts a major portion of the world's international visitors, a number of destinations in the region, including certain islands, face an uncertain future as their popularity wanes and as new, more exotic tourist areas emerge further afield.

Throughout history, the Mediterranean has witnessed the communication and exchange, both of cultural relations and civilization. In more recent times, tourism has emerged in the region as an extension of these processes. In the nineteenth century a number of Mediterranean destinations offered part of the romance of the Grand Tour. In the last few decades, however, the ascendancy of mass tourism with its many adverse economic, cultural, social and environmental dimensions has threatened the very resources that made these destinations attractive in the first place. Therefore, there is a need to redefine the region's tourist product and give it a new direction. Specifically, for the Mediterranean region to recapture its competitive position as a tourist destination it is important to replace a product geared towards the steady growth of arrivals with one emphasizing the region's natural and cultural qualities.

The primary aim of this contribution is to examine the potential role of natural and cultural resources in managing sustainable tourist development in the Mediterranean islands. The chapter begins with a definition of insularity and discusses its effects on the pattern of tourist development. Next, the focus switches to the rapid emergence of mass tourism and the problems associated with this growth. Attention is paid to possible new development scenarios resulting from changes in demand and from requirements for resource management in the context of sustainable development on the islands. This is followed by recommendations for planning and managing tourist activities. In order to adopt a sustainability approach focusing on natural and cultural resource management, the chapter attempts to system-atize local and regional experiences that have, thus far, only been treated in scattered studies.

Mediterranean Insularity as a Tourist Scenario

The prevailing image of the Mediterranean basin as a homogenous landmass facing similar climatic conditions and environmental problems throughout (e.g., soil erosion and lack of water resources) masks the region's diversity in terms of natural, historic, and cultural characteristics. Certain insular regions more than others face a number of problems, such as pressure on natural resources, fragility of ecosystems, and abandonment of traditional systems of land use and management while witnessing the polarization of population and economic activities towards coastal areas. Often these processes have been fuelled by increased tourist activity (see Chapter 2 in this book).

The development of mass tourism on many islands of the Mediterranean has created a stereotypical image based on the appeal of sun, coast and landscapes, inevitably leading to fairly standardized resort models and an undifferentiated supply of facilities. Nevertheless, there are also major differences relating to the size, shape and topography of the islands as well as their location, economic and political status.

The largest island, Sicily, covers 25,700 km^2 and has 5 million inhabitants. Sardinia, with 24,000 km^2 has a population of 1.6 million. The Balearics are a group of islands with an area totaling 5,000 km^2 and a population of 760,000. Both the Ionian and Aegean archipelagos include hundreds of small islands and islets with total populations of 191,000 and over 450,000, respectively. The island microstate of Malta with 372,000 inhabitants squeezed into an area of 315 km^2 has the highest population density of all the Mediterranean islands: almost 1,200 inhabitants per km^2. There are also variations between the tourism products of the islands of the western Mediterranean and those in the east. The few relatively large islands (the Balearics, Sicily, Sardinia, Corsica) in the western Mediterranean generally mirror the wide-scale mass tourist product witnessed on the coastal areas of neighbouring countries (e.g., Spain, Italy, and France, respectively). On the contrary, many of the islands of the eastern Mediterranean, some of which are tiny, have witnessed the development of fairly small tourism attraction poles.

Even though these islands are all part of the Mediterranean basin and share a number of common characteristics affecting their environment (e.g., climate), and fairly similar histories, they have all evolved quite distinctly. Certain islands have historically had agricultural-based economies; others have relied heavily on mining activities while a number of them have depended on a sea-based economy. In other words, unique geographical characteristics of each island as well as their territorial organization have played an important role in shaping the distinct fortunes of these insular regions.

In some cases, variations in the topography or geographical location have been responsible for the divergent historical evolution of socio-economic systems on each island. For instance, many littoral areas have historically been dedicated to fishing and sea trade. Inland areas have often been used for grazing of cattle, goats, and sheep. Forests cover other areas, such as many of the mountains. Mining activities and even manufacturing industries have evolved on some of the islands. There are a number of insular societies that have scorned the coastline, preferring instead to inhabit inland areas. By contrast, the smaller islands of the eastern Mediterranean have historically developed close trading and cultural ties with each other. Long-term maritime exchanges between these islands have led to the development of a number of sea-oriented urban cultures.

There are considerable variations in terms of economic development levels from island to island. The Balearic Islands have demonstrated an economic growth well above the Spanish average and their GDP per inhabitant is above the average for European Union countries (109 per cent of the EUR12 average). By contrast, the Greek islands where the GDP per inhabitant is just 53 per cent of the EUR12 average, Corsica (76.8 per cent), Sardinia (75.3 per cent) and Sicily (70 per cent) are clearly below that level. The non-European Union countries of Cyprus and Malta are also below that average. Unemployment rates on many of the islands tend to be above or even twice as high as the national average. There is also the widespread problem of a poorly qualified workforce on many islands, thus reducing their ability to foster development based on local initiatives as opposed to external forces.

Towards a New Model for Mass Tourism: Exploiting the Islands' Comparative Advantages

Since the 1960s, the tourism boom witnessed on many Mediterranean islands has depended on the widespread demand, especially in northern European countries, for a sun, sea, and sand product. Of course, a number of places such as Sicily and many of the Greek islands had drawn travellers since

Table 3.1 Tourist movement in selected Mediterranean countries, 1996

	Main Generating Markets							
	France		Germany		Italy		United Kingdom	
Main destinations	Percentage of the total of emitted tourism	Tourists (thousands)	Percentage of the total of emitted tourism	Tourists (thousands)	Percentage of the total of emitted tourism	Tourists (thousands)	Percentage of the total of emitted tourism	Tourists (thousands)
Spain	15.3	3,357	13.6	10,628	12.9	2,165	20.3	9,807
France	–	–	17.2	13,378	31.6	5,299	22.9	8,691
Italy	10.8	2,368	11.23	8,780	–	–	3.75	1,601
Greece	2.05	446	2.26	1,768	2.95	487	3.7	1,608
Croatia	(*)		0.57	448	2.79	467	(*)	
Cyprus	0.18	40	0.32	249	(*)		1.75	746
Malta	0.29	64	0.24	184	0.53	89	0.93	398

Note: *This country does not appear among the 50 main destinations of the corresponding generating market.

Source: World Tourism Organization (1997a)

the early nineteenth century when they became destinations for the aristocratic Grand Tour (Marchena and Vera Rebollo, 1995).

Over the past 40 years, the growing importance of package holidays organized and controlled by tour operators based in certain European countries (e.g., the United Kingdom, France, Germany, and Italy) (Table 3.1) has fuelled the rapid development of insular sun-based resorts. Taking advantage of technological improvements in transportation and because of their ability to generate significant economies of scale these operators were able to reduce the cost of travel, thus accounting for the growth of tourist peripheries in the southern and eastern Mediterranean. Tours organized by operators account for 60 per cent of international arrivals in Greece, while in Cyprus and Malta as many as 80 per cent of the tourists arrive on inclusive package tours. In Spain, organized travel amounts to 40 per cent of the total number of arrivals (see Chapter 4 in this book).

The growth of tourism has also been shaped, albeit to varying degrees, by the policies of the region's countries. For instance, the massive growth of tourism in Spain during the 1960s was actively promoted by the national government 'amongst other things to broaden the political acceptance of Franco's regime' (Pearce, 1989: 41). The devaluation of various currencies has also had a lot to do with the increase in the demand for certain destinations (Pearce, 1989). For instance, the growth of international coastal tourism in Greece between 1970 and 1990 took place, to a great extent, thanks to that country's competitive prices compared to those countries in the north-western Mediterranean. (See Table 3.2 on the ratio between the countries' tourist income and the number of arrivals.)

Table 3.2 Relationship of international tourist arrivals to tourism revenues, 1997

Countries	Arrivals (thousands)	Position in world rankings	Revenues (US$ million)	Position in world rankings
France	66,800	1	27,947	3
Spain	43,403	3	27,190	4
Italy	34,087	4	30,000	2
Greece (*)	8,987	18	3,660	29
Cyprus(*)	1,950	49	1,670	46
Malta (*)	1,053	–	618	–

Note: *1996
Source: World Tourism Organization (1997a)

The rapid growth of mass tourism, particularly in the coastal areas of so many Mediterranean destinations has resulted in a highly standardized product displaying many of the characteristics of what some authors term a 'Fordist' phase of tourism development (Ioannides and Debbage, 1997; Poon, 1993; Shaw and Williams, 1994). This means that major tour operators located in northern countries such as Germany and the United Kingdom commonly determine the fortunes of the tourist industry on the Mediterranean islands. Because these tour operators 'market holiday type rather than [specific] place[s]' (Ioannides, 1998: 143) and since they employ a multi-locational strategy, they will not hesitate to pull out of certain destinations if these no longer prove profitable. Thus, these players find themselves in the driver's seat when it comes to negotiating with local representatives of the travel industry, particularly hotel owners. Since there is relatively little variation in the tourist product of most Mediterranean islands, it is easy for these operators to substitute one destination with another, in response to changing consumer demands.

There is little doubt that tourism has become a major engine behind the economic and social transformations witnessed on so many islands. Before the tourism boom, most islands experienced severe depopulation brought upon by the lack of economic growth opportunities. The rapid growth of tourism offered a whole range of new economic opportunities leading to the reversal of migration patterns and, in many cases, population growth. For example, Mykonos saw an increase of its population from 2,872 in 1961 to over 8,500 in 1991 (Coccossis and Parpairis, 1995). Parallel to this, many islands have seen a spectacular growth in their seasonal population.

In 1965, the Mediterranean islands received 2 million tourists, whereas by 1993, 16 million arrivals were recorded. This rapid growth in visitor numbers coupled with the increase in population of many islands has become a major problem for resource management in a variety of insular settings. In Greece, half of the country's tourist accommodation is on the islands, with the Cyclades and the Dodecanese alone accounting for more than 25 per cent of this country's arrivals, while Corfu and the Ionian Sea islands receive another 8.5 per cent (Lanquar, 1995).

The Balearic Islands, the archetype of the mass sun and beach model catering to the markets of industrialized northern European countries, respectively account for approximately 28 per cent and 10 per cent of Spain's total capacity in hotels and other forms of lodging establishments. In terms of overnight stays in hotels, this region is the country's leader accounting for 21.3 per cent of the total. Foreigners, especially Britons and Germans, are responsible for over 80 per cent of overnight stays in the Balearics. In 1996, more than 8.5 million tourists visited these islands making them the leading island destination in the Mediterranean.

As opposed to the insular regions of Greece and Spain, the Italian islands (Sicily and Sardinia) and the French island of Corsica respectively account for a relatively small proportion of tourist arrivals in those two countries. For instance, the islands still draw only 6.5 per cent of tourists in Italy (4.9 per cent of international arrivals), in part because of the historic importance of that country's northern and central regions as tourist destinations (Banco Nazionale del Lavoro, 1997) (Tables 3.3 and 3.4).

In terms of the Mediterranean's two island states, Cyprus and Malta, the growth of tourist arrivals in the late 1970s and 1980s has been particularly impressive following a slow but steady increase during earlier years (1960s and early 1970s). For instance, while only 127,000 arrived on Cyprus in 1970 there were 1,950,000 in 1996. Similarly, Malta saw an increase from 171,000 to 1,053,000 arrivals between 1970 and 1996.

Problems and Conflicts Arising from Mass Tourism Development

In the 1980s, the rapid growth in terms of tourism supply and demand in a variety of insular settings resulted in many problems (Lanquar, 1995). Disorderly development has often caused the destruction of unique cultural and natural spaces. In many destinations, the lack of infrastructure and services has led to serious bottlenecks. The undiversified nature of the tourism product resulting from the oligopolistic control of demand by major international tour operators has caused the perpetuation of an unsustainable growth model based on cheap package tourism and has reduced the opportunities for product diversification. Moreover, the highly specialized tourism form that has emerged in these Mediterranean settings has often led to the dismantling of traditional land use systems and, importantly, caused significant regional and functional disparities. Thus, one thing that is obvious is that if tourism's development is to be more sustainable in the future, it is imperative to understand the rational limits of such spatial and functional reorganization processes.

What follows is a, by no means exhaustive, list of problems relating to rapid mass tourism development.

Table 3.3 Selected characteristics relating to Mediterranean islands

	Size (thousands km²)	Population (thousands)	Density (humans/km²)	Accommodation capacity	No. of tourist arrivals
Island states					
Cyprus	9.2	767 (1996)	78.7	35,000 rooms in hotels and similar establishments	2 million tourists in 1996
Malta	0.315	372 (1996)	1,177	37,308 beds (50,000 in 1993, according to Blue Plan)	1.053 million tourists in 1996
Insular regions/island regions					
Corsica	8.7	258 (1994)	28	N/A	1.5 million tourists/year
Sardinia	24.0	1660 (1996)	68	120,503 beds (50% in hotels)	Nearly 900,000 Italians and around 200,000 foreigners
Sicily	25.7	5094 (1996)	201	108,138 beds (64.6% in hotels)	1.7 million Italians and 971,000 foreigners
Balearics Majorca Minorca Ibiza Formentera	5.014	760 (1996)	153.2	393,850 beds 67.4% in Majorca island (hotels, hostelries, campsites, legal tourist apartments	8,537,700 tourists in 1996 (225,000 came for the sea). Majorca: 5,147,800 Minorca: 2,377,000 Ibiza/Formentera: 1,012,900
Ionian Islands	2.3	191 (1991)	83		
Kefalonia	0.9	32 (1991)	36		
Corfu/Kerkira	0.5	105 (1991)	164		
Kevkas	0.35	20 (1991)	59		
Zakynthos	0.4	32 (1991)	81		
Aegean Islands (Northern and Southern)	10.4	481 (1991)	50	North Aegean: 13,000 beds in 1990.	More than 259,000 tourists in Mykonos (Cyclades).
Cyclades	2.6	100 (1991)	39	South Aegean:	
Dodecanese	2.7	162 (1991)	60	22,000 beds in	
Rhodes	1.3	67 (1991)	51	Cyclades and 71,000	
Lesbos	2.2	103 (1991)	48	in Dodecanese (1990).	
Kos	0.9	52 (1991)	58	Only in Mykonos	
Samos	0.8	41 (1991)	54	(Cyclades) more than 16,000 beds.	
Crete	8.2	540 (1991)	64	77,678 beds in 1990	15% of the international tourist arrivals in Greece

Source: WTO, Calendario Atlante Agostini, Encyclopedia Britannica, Inc., Comisión Europea, Ministry of Aegean, ISTAT (Italy).

Table 3.4 Charter flight traffic to Italy's insular airports, 1986 and 1996

	1986	*1996*	*Growth rate 1986–96 (%)*
Cagliari	50,563	74,331	47.01
Olbia	33,562	74,016	120.54
Tortoli	–	7,841	–
Alguero	55,798	42,821	−23.26
Catania	226,611	371,299	63.85
Palermo	206,659	309,947	49.98
Trapani	9,792	–	–
Pantelleria	626	1,252	100.00

Source: Civilavia (Italy), Banco Nazionale, p. 201.

Imbalances related to the environment and resource management

Tourism-related activities in insular environments tend to develop in a small number of coastal areas, often in and around existing communities. For instance, according to Pearce, 'over half the accommodation on Mallorca in 1986 was located in the Bay of Palma' (1995: 118). Moreover, because of weak or non-existent land use regulations, this development has often spread out of these communities in a ribbon-like fashion along the coast. On the island of Cyprus, for instance, intensive development has taken place along fairly narrow stretches of land extending east of Limassol and Larnaca respectively (Ioannides, 1992). By contrast, in rarer instances, large-scale construction of tourism accommodation has taken place in 'one pole' entertainment complexes or enclaves that are physically separate of existing localities (Lozato-Giotart, 1990).

The increasing density of coastal settlements has created a host of problems including the seepage of raw sewage into the sea. Some islands do not even have sewage treatment plants and in those that do, many have insufficient capacity. In Sicily, for instance, only 15 per cent of the sewage treatment plants are operable. Yet another problem is the lack of suitable landfills for solid waste disposal.

Perhaps the most significant problem most coastal areas in the Mediterranean face has to do with the shortage of water resulting from chronic droughts and, in many cases, the lack of ground water supplies. Ironically, the warm and pleasant weather which are important factors determining the high intensity mass tourism product in the region have meant that these destinations face severe shortfall in terms of water resources. The problem of water shortages is particularly acute on the island destinations of the Mediterranean since unlike the mainland coast they do not receive water from rivers coming from mountainous regions (e.g., the Rhône and the Po). In the Balearics, for instance, the growth of tourism has caused the over-exploitation of aquiferous layers. Other islands, such as Cyprus, have occasionally had to resort to receiving water transported from other areas by tanker. Malta and Cyprus have also had to construct desalination plants to cope with extreme water shortages. Malta now has the world's largest desalination plant producing 200,000 cubic metres of water every day (Gil Olcina, 1997). Mykonos and Capri also use desalination plants for their water needs since they have no other source of water other than scarce rainfall. Islands such as Capri and Ischia consume enormous amounts of water relative to their area and populations (Maury, 1990). In quite a number of cases, it is the poor quality of infrastructure that makes it impossible to move or use water resources. Such problems indicate the need for suitable resource planning that should integrate the reuse of treated sewage water.

Imbalances related to the commercialization of a trivialized product

A content analysis of holiday brochures supplied by major international tour wholesalers and operators based in the major origin countries clearly demonstrates an emphasis on the following elements. The brochures tend to focus on holiday resorts and establishments located very close to large white sandy beaches. The calm blue sea commonly features as a background. Often, the brochures also concentrate on purpose-built sports facilities and refer to various water sports. In some instances, the brochures also offer information concerning entertainment opportunities or local festivals. Only the literature relating to the Greek islands pays attention to local culture and heritage although these attractions usually play second fiddle to the sun, sea, and sand product.

Essentially, there are two main types of package holidays in the Mediterranean, those involving organized itineraries in one particular destination and, perhaps, excursions to surrounding coastal areas or islands, and those focusing on circuit travel with stops on a number of islands and/or mainland destinations. Tourists participating on the first type of package stay mainly in one destination (e.g., a town in Rhodes or Corfu) from where they may take a number of excursions to other communities or even surrounding islands. The length of stay at each ancillary destination may vary from just a few hours to a whole day. For instance, tourists in Sorrento may take a whole day visiting Capri and Anacapri and the Grotta Azzura. On a larger island, such as Sicily, the package holiday may combine stays in several localities.

Circuit tourism usually takes place in the form of cruises (e.g., around the French and Italian Rivieras or through the Aegean). Certain organized cruises can combine visits to Egypt and Israel or Turkey (e.g., from Cyprus). In these cases, tourists have the option of disembarking for a few hours from the cruise ship and taking shore excursions (e.g., passengers on cruise ships visiting Santorini can take organized mule rides to Fira, a traditional village).

The prevailing standardized tourism landscape found in Mediterranean insular environments demonstrates that in most instances there have been few serious efforts to promote attractions catering to alternative travellers interested in more individualized travel based on resources other that sun, sea and sand (e.g., related to cultural resources). Likewise, instead of promoting product differentiation in order to become more competitive, most Mediterranean islands compete on price alone. Additionally, only limited efforts have been made to seek the development of alternative accommodation in rural inland areas of most islands compared to the widespread practice of constructing luxury-oriented, standardized hotels in coastal areas.

Qualitative Changes in the Requirements for Competitiveness and Sustainability in Destination Areas

It is important to point out that most Mediterranean destinations have witnessed reduced average growth rates in tourist arrivals and receipts during the last few years. In many instances, this decline reflects the fact that the destinations have reached saturation, although in places like the Balearics the shifts in arrival rates have to do with changes in these destinations' quality and product diversification. In Croatia tourist arrivals were actually estimated to have grown by 20 per cent per year between 1995 and 2000 (WTO, 1997b) after this country's recovery from war (see Chapter 9 in this book). Although armed conflict in nearby Bosnia and, more recently, Kosovo, have inevitably disrupted its recovery, Croatia has made major steps to attract investors and developers while simultaneously adopting strict standards to protect natural areas, especially in its insular region and along the coastline.

Obviously, the serious economic, sociocultural and environmental impacts caused by rapid development of mass tourism on Mediterranean islands have been a key reason behind the region's declining popularity. Generally, as Mediterranean island destinations have reached the stage of maturity in their respective destination life-cycles (Ioannides, 1992), a number of serious problems have emerged including the destruction of natural habitats and the loss of traditional ways of life. Many islands are presently seeking to rejuvenate their image as destinations by paying attention to international trends suggesting that travellers have become more sophisticated and environmentally aware, thus seeking 'authentic' experiences. Growing awareness about consumer preferences coupled with the emergence of rival destinations in locations such as the Caribbean, the Indian Ocean, or the Pacific, many of which offer less spoilt natural environments, have fuelled the desire in Mediterranean destinations to improve the quality of their tourism product.

Increasingly, following the stance of the World Tourism Organization, many national tourist organizations around the world have recognized the importance of studying tourism's negative impacts and implementing strategic long-term plans to mitigate some of the most important problems. In particular, in numerous destinations 'sustainability' has emerged as a key requirement for directing the future development of tourism as an economic activity.

There are a number of examples of environmental problems that have led to a change in government attitudes. For instance, severe coastal pollution in Cyprus during the mid-1980s inspired certain Swiss ecological organizations to declare a boycott against this country (Lanquar, 1995). This, in turn, caused a change of attitude on the part of Cypriot authorities. In Greece, the impressive growth of tourism and the associated problems this caused provoked an image problem at the beginning of the 1990s. Again, this forced governmental agencies to change their attitude towards this sector. Environmental problems arising from mass tourism in Malta during the same period led to calls for higher quality tourism (see Chapter 12 in this book). Curiously, despite this emphasis on quality, the number of arrivals has continued to grow on this island, a result perhaps of expanding the tourist season and having a more balanced distribution of visitors throughout the year.

The new global trends indicating a growing demand for more individualized travel forms seem to support the hypothesis that tourism, like many other economic sectors, has begun to adopt the 'post-Fordist' traits of enhanced flexibility through demand-led product differentiation and niche marketing. Nevertheless, despite these trends it should be emphasized that the 'Fordist' type of conventional mass tourism is still very much alive (Ioannides and Debbage, 1997). Although there have been quite a few developments of exclusive destinations and custom-made tourism products have become more commonplace around the world, the World Tourism Organization (WTO) also predicts good prospects for reduced-price destinations and organized tours (Frangialli, 1998).

The Mediterranean insular regions should take into account these global trends when deciding how to manage their tourism resources in the twenty-first century. Clearly, these destinations should explore ways to improve the quality of their existing mass tourism product, taking into account their environmental and social carrying capacities while simultaneously searching for means to develop alternative tourism forms. The challenge for these destinations is, of course, to enhance their competitive position by promoting products not exclusively based on the exploitation of traditional comparative advantages such as reduced prices, proximity to major markets, and beach-oriented attractions.

The Blue Plan for the Mediterranean (Lanquar, 1995) stresses the need to develop new coherent and responsible approaches that show awareness of the fragility of the Mediterranean environment. It is not hard to find examples marking the sharp contrast between conventional mass tourism forms and alternative tourism products. The latter, if planned properly, generally consume less territory and can be better integrated into the receiving society (Weaver, 1993). Of course, the attainment of sustainable development through alternative tourism forms in the Mediterranean insular environments may appear utopian especially if one considers the enormous bargaining power held by oligopolistic tour operators in the principal origin countries. Still, the emerging global trends suggesting the shift in demand towards more individualized forms of travel indicate that destinations such as the Balearics, the Greek islands, and Malta should expand their efforts in terms of targeting new markets while seeking ways to decrease seasonality and dependence on a narrow product.

It appears that gradually the changes in consumers' values and habits, plus the commitment on the part of local policy-makers and other players to better manage their resources is leading to a new, more qualitative, phase of tourism development which uses sustainability as its reference. As expressed by the European Tourism Forum (Crauser, 1998), the sustainable management of natural and cultural resources forms the basis for a competitive advantage supported by quality. Such trends have been particularly obvious in the case of the Balearic Islands where both the authorities and entrepreneurs have taken major steps to enhance the quality of the tourism product even though the principal focus remains on mass tourism.

Recommendations for Increasing the Value of Resources

Sustainable practice in tourism implies attaining a balance between the economic objectives of tour operators and receiving societies, the satisfaction of visitors, and responsible management of the host territory and its natural and cultural resources. In destinations such as many Mediterranean islands that have gone through a stage of rapid growth and especially those that have attained maturity, the purpose of sustainable development should be to reposition their image as attractive, quality-oriented destinations and seek to draw clients from diverse market segments. Particularly, these destinations should target visitors who will prove profitable from an economic as well as an environmental standpoint. Within this context, attention should be paid to the WTO's focus on tourism's growing relevance as a socio-economic element and the organization's increasing concern about the sector's impacts, matters that necessitate long-term strategic planning.

One key repositioning strategy towards sustainability for destinations that have already experienced the negative impacts of mass tourism should surely be based on product differentiation through the creation of a new image associated with more profitable products/markets (Monfort Mir, 1999). Price alone should no longer feature as a key component of the holiday. Instead, emphasis should be placed on cultural activities, opportunities for sport, conferences, health tourism, and so on. Strategies for tourism's future development should lead to less overcrowding compared to what has been witnessed in conventional mass tourism areas, although this does not mean that the sun and beach tourism product should be abandoned. Instead, efforts should also be made to promote balanced development in mass tourism resorts.

In order for this to be achieved, policy-makers must focus their attention on improving the global competitiveness of their destination through the promotion of quality, regulation of services, upgrading of infrastructure, staff training, and so on. Of course, the actions of policy-makers cannot be successful without the involvement of the business community. For instance, the various enterprises responsible for the tourist product of a destination should also be committed to improving its competitive position.

With this in mind, it is important to highlight the pivotal role played by major tour operators in terms of producing and distributing tourist products. The hegemonic position these powerful players have in relation to the tourism product of Mediterranean island destinations means that independent businesses at the destination, especially small-scale lodging establishments, find themselves in a weak bargaining position when it comes to negotiating commissions and tour cut-off dates. Perhaps more importantly, small-scale local tourist businesses have limited direct access to their markets, particularly when they do not feature on computer reservation systems (CRSs) and global distribution systems (GDS) (Milne and Gill, 1998; Monfort Mir, 1999). It should be emphasized that for sustainability practices to be successfully implemented on the islands, it is imperative that local independent operators and entrepreneurs gain more direct access to product distribution channels. From a positive standpoint, the growing demand for alternative tourism has led to the proliferation of speciality travel agents and tour operators who are more likely to support small-scale businesses at the destinations. Concurrently, improved technology (for instance, the Internet) has meant that independent-minded travellers can bypass intermediaries and directly interact with local players offering a tourism product, for example, through the World Wide Web.

The role of natural and cultural resources in product diversification and differentiation

The wealth and variety of resources associated with marine ecosystems support a number of tourism modes ranging from sunbathing, water sports, and circuit tourism in the form of cruises to more sustainable practices associated with a select few resorts such as hiking in Corsica or agrotourism in Cyprus. Whatever the type of tourism that ultimately evolves in the various destinations, the use of coastal environments in the Mediterranean necessitates the consideration of a number of conditions that justify the implementation of carrying capacity and area protection measures (Bosselman *et al.*, 1999).

One of the biggest problems in the region has been the impact of rapid coastal development on a number of endemic species of fauna and flora. In particular, the conditions essential for the development of the life-cycle of various animals and plants have gradually been eroded throughout the Mediterranean (Araujo, 1997). A vital factor to be considered when dealing with the preservation of coastal environments is the amount of time required for the water in this sea to be renewed. For example, it takes years for pollutants dumped into the Mediterranean to disappear. According to Araujo (1997), each year 350,000 metric tons of dumped oil remain in the Mediterranean. In Lesbos, sea pollution has affected the quality of beaches in the gulfs of Kalloni and Ghera. Moreover, there is a major problem concerning the treatment of solid waste and sewage, as there are not enough recycling or sewage treatment facilities (Nijkamp and Verdonkschot, 1995).

Because of rapid tourism growth, many insular destinations have begun to lose the very qualities that put them on the tourist map in the first place. This has certainly been the case on the Aegean island of Santorini, as Bosselman *et al.* describe:

> Twenty years ago [Santorini] was a jewel among the Cyclades, and tourists weathered long ferry rides to ride donkeys up the steep path from the dock to the town to enjoy the spectacular views and village ambiance. Now the narrow lanes are clogged with tourists, Americans serve as waiters in the 'authentic' tavernas, there is a constant clamor of motorscooters, disco music reverberates through most of the night, and guidebooks warn of congestion and inflated prices. (1999: 109)

Since the nineteenth century, the Mediterranean's warm and sunny weather has led to heliotropism and balneotropism. Nevertheless, the opportunity exists for differentiating the region's product, for example, by extending the tourism season into the winter months. For instance, some islands offer the opportunities for health tourism (a number of them have thermal spas). Others could use their hotels more often, for example during the off-peak season, for conventions or incentive trips. Much of the Mediterranean is also ideally suited for sailing and other water sports, activities for which there is increasing demand by international tourists. Such activities may offer one of the best promises for diversifying the traditional product of the islands.

Many islands offer great opportunities for nature-based tourism as long as appropriate planning and management techniques accompany the use of these resources. Some of these destinations have already suffered considerable deforestation associated with over-development, fires (many of them deliberate), or logging activities. Ironically, on some of the mountainous larger islands, the polarization of human activities in coastal areas, along with the abandonment of traditional agricultural or mining practices in the interior, has led to a situation where there are still fairly large, relatively unspoiled areas offering the opportunity to diversify the tourist product. Proposals for ecotourism, agrotourism, hiking holidays, and so on have become increasingly commonplace on many of the islands. In Cyprus, for instance, where one-seventh of the territory (most of it on the mountains) is still covered with pine, cedar, and cypress forests there is enormous potential for the development of hiking holidays. In the province of Nuoro on Sardinia, the promotion of *non solo mare* is geared towards utilizing the island's wealth of landscapes and cultural attractions in interior areas for alternative tourism. One attraction of great interest is Gennargentu Park. In sum, natural resources especially in interior areas offer a basic ingredient for the sustainable development of tourism on the islands though, again, this requires rational planning and management systems.

Throughout the Mediterranean basin, including the islands, there is a wealth of cultural/historic features, a result of the long succession of civilizations that have existed in the region. As empires have come and gone they have left behind an exceptional heritage including Neolithic settlements, Roman villas, Greek amphitheatres, and monuments. In addition to these archaeological treasures, millennia of human activity have transformed entire physical landscapes, while the region has also inherited rich traditions and folklore resulting from the intermingling of civilizations. Obviously, a sustainable tourist strategy should focus on this attribute as long as efforts are made to not trivialize local cultures through the commercialization of heritage. Such an approach is essential if the quality of life of the islands' local inhabitants is to be maintained.

Yet another potential tourism resource in the Mediterranean is its agricultural areas, which essentially are landscapes shaped by centuries of human influence on the natural environment. Unfortunately, however, traditional farming and other rural practices are fast becoming an extinct way of life in the region, resulting in severe rural depopulation and economic downturn in numerous areas. Rural tourism or agrotourism is one way to revitalize disadvantaged agricultural areas, many of which are in isolated inland areas. Such a strategy could lead to the functional integration of coastal areas with more disadvantaged inland regions, eventually resulting in a reduction of spatial imbalances. Sustainable tourism strategies geared towards the promotion of rural-based tourism or inland cultural tours would be most beneficial on some of the larger islands such as Corsica, Sicily, and Sardinia, where many inland areas face chronic economic problems.

For alternative tourism forms based on cultural and natural features to become more competitive in the Mediterranean insular region it is essential that, along with the basic focus on quality and sustainability more attention should be paid to developing 'value for money' attractions such as historic theme parks. One of the major criticisms of most archaeological sites in Greece, for example, is that they offer poor interpretive facilities (e.g., diaromas, and educational displays). It is frustrating for an individual traveller to arrive at a particular historical site and not really know much about it other than what is in the guidebooks. Thus, one way by which the quality of archaeological sites, museums, and other tourist attractions can be enhanced would be to use information technologies (e.g., computer graphics, and interactive displays) in order to enhance the educational experience at historical sites (Frangialli, 1998). Moreover, the managers of historical and other attractions should explore ways to improve the entertainment aspect of their facility. For instance, an archaeological site could include a section indicating scenes of how people lived in a past era. Such heritage parks have been developed throughout Western Europe and North America and, as long as they do not trivialize history and are developed tastefully so as not to offend local sensitivities, can be an important means of diversifying the tourist product of a destination.

In final analysis, then, for Mediterranean islands to be able to enhance their competitive edge *vis-à-vis* rival destinations there is a need to establish an appropriate combination of nature, sea, landscape, history, and myth. Such an approach would certainly boost, among others, the cruise industry, which until now has accounted for a very small portion of international arrivals in Mediterranean islands. Although Cagliari is one of Italy's cruise-receiving harbours, it accounts for only 1 per cent of cruise arrivals in that country. If the islands have more to offer than the beach and retailing facilities (see Chapter 14 in this volume) perhaps more cruise ships will visit for longer periods.

Towards the Management of Sustainability in Tourism

Working guidelines

Following a number of important international meetings in recent years the message of sustainability (Stabler, 1997) appears to at last have been heard by a large number of institutions (e.g., the Action Plan for the Mediterranean, Blue Plan) and administrations (programmes like ENVIREG and LIFE, which include plans for the regulation of tourist supply and advocate coordinated actions between the European Union and Mediterranean countries). The message has also been heeded by NGOs (for instance, Ecomediterranea), as well as other enterprise organizations and local societies. Nevertheless, the concept of balanced growth is hard to implement in most cases since it is based mainly on qualitative long-range principles that often appear antithetical to more immediate profit-oriented objectives (Ioannides, forth-coming). Thus, it is hardly surprising that measures aimed at managing and protecting a destination's resources often arrive too late and are insufficient since they reflect reactions to specific problems rather than a proactive approach (Lanquar, 1995).

Happily, certain island societies have been able to reach a consensus on growth-limiting measures (e.g., through moratoria on further construction of standardized accommodation facilities). Some islands have been able to promote a new course of tourism development (e.g., see the discussion on Local Agenda 21 in Chapter 10 of this book) that includes an emphasis on the educational or ecological features of their tourism product. In short, these destinations have managed to implement a development model that is in line with the host region's natural and human environments and perceives tourism as a factor that will increase the value of the local heritage.

Strictly speaking, it should be emphasized that in the case of Mediterranean islands there is not a single set of guidelines for achieving sustainability in tourism. Importantly, before implementing a sustainable approach for tourism development it is imperative that a high degree of social consensus should be sought. Without a host society's active participation in the planning process, sustainable development strategies cannot be effective (McCool and Stankey, 1999).

A number of authors have discussed environmental policy instruments used to achieve sustainable development in tourism (Nijkamp and Verdonkschot, 1995). It is evident from the literature that a serious problem hindering the successful implementation of sustainable tourism is the lack of coordination between environmental policies and the actions of national and regional tourist organizations. Thus, for sustainability to be achieved in tourism environments it is imperative to integrate the strategies of the various organizations at the national, regional, and local levels which, either directly or indirectly, deal with this sector. An example of this integration concept appears in the Integrated Operational Plan for the Development of the Aegean (IOPDA) that was put forth by the Ministry of the Aegean. The objectives of this plan are oriented towards regional integration, promotion of economic activities, financing and management, and infrastructure planning.

In particular, the principles applied to the integrated planning and management of coastline areas can serve as a working strategy for the Mediterranean islands. The ENVIREG programme began in 1990 (DG XVI) with the aim of preserving the environment and consolidating the foundations for balanced development. At the moment a programme for the integrated regulation of island coastal areas is being applied in the Cyclades (Programme for Integrated Coastal Area Management in the Cyclades). This programme is within the framework of the European LIFE programme and is aimed at boosting development among different islands through coordinating essential aspects such as water resources, residue management, and problems related to the environment and landscape.

Another very useful tool for diagnosing and correcting environmental problems in tourist destinations is the introduction of environmental audit systems. These are designed to award environmental quality seals and badges to destinations that meet the requirements of sustainable development. The ECOTUR programme in the Balearic Islands is an example that could be applied to other destinations (Vera Rebollo, 1997).

The Environmental Impact Assessment (EIA) technique should also be applied to tourist projects, and rules relating to this should be harmonized between all countries in the region. EIA is not currently included in the environmental regulations of most countries. In the same way, carrying capacity studies, which combine physical and ecological, sociocultural and economic parameters, should be applied to island destinations for managing their future tourism development (Coccossis and Parpairis, 1992). For instance, authorities in Mediterranean islands could look at growth limitation strategies such as the ones adopted in Bermuda or Sanibel Island, Florida (Bosselman *et al.*, 1999). Growth limitation mechanisms are particularly suited for areas with clearly defined (inflexible) boundaries and a small number of access points (such as islands) meaning that it is hard to expand their carrying capacity. According to Bosselman *et al.* (1999), among the strategies that have been included in the Bermuda Plan of 1991 is a 'Hotel Phasing Policy' to ensure that the supply of tourist accommodations is compatible with demand, policies restricting the numbers of charter flights and cruise ship arrivals, and rigid standards for obtaining approvals for hotel construction. Such measures for ensuring that tourism does not exceed its carrying capacity should be considered by local and regional governments in the Mediterranean insular regions.

Because of the pressures witnessed on such small and fragile territories as the Mediterranean islands, certain areas should be declared protected. For instance, marine reserves should be created to protect the Mediterranean's sea life. Such marine parks exist in various parts of the world including the Great Barrier Reef Marine Park in Australia and the Saguenay–St Lawrence Marine Park in Quebec, Canada (Bosselman *et al.*, 1999). These approaches agree with the principles of sustainability since they combine the ecological and educational approach to tourism with protection. Examples of reserves that have already been set up in the Mediterranean include the Medas Islands (40 hectares) in the Costa Brava, Tabarca (1,000 hectares) in the Valencian Autonomous Community, and the Cabrera archipelago (a sea and land nature reserve of 1,570 hectares) in the Balearics. Marine reserves have also been set up in Sardinia, while in Corsica the Scandola Reserve preserves sea and land heritage. In Zakynthos in the Ionian Sea, the first centre in the Mediterranean for the reproduction of sea turtles has been set up.

Coastal ecosystems such as wetlands, estuaries, sand dunes, and cliffs should also be protected. Already there are a number of such nature reserves including S'Albufera (wetland area of 1,700 hectares) in Majorca, and Biguglia (a biotope with extraordinary ecological richness) in Corsica. In Cyprus, efforts have been made to establish the Akamas Peninsula Nature Reserve and the Cape Greco Reserve. Protected areas should also be created in the interior of some of the islands, partly to remedy the decline of traditional agricultural/pastoral or mining practices. These areas could be used for sustainable tourist and recreational activities. Examples of existing protected areas include the 100,000 hectare Gennargentu Park in Sardinia, the only nature reserve in the Italian islands. Other areas are the Sierra de la Tramuntana in Majorca, Corsica's Regional Nature Reserve, Enos in the Ionian island of Cephalonia, and so on. Furthermore, the declaration of the whole island of Minorca (Balearics) as an UNESCO Biosphere Reserve demonstrates a model that could become extremely appropriate for the achievement of sustainable development on distinct islands or archipelagos.

The protection of coastline stretches should also be made a priority in order to halt ribbon urban development or other inappropriate uses. This has already occurred in Corsica where 26 per cent of the coastline land has been acquired by *Conservatoire de l'Espace Littoral et des Rivages Lacustres*. In countries such as Greece, where there are only 60 kms of protected coastline, one way to preserve coastal land is through the implementation of land use regulations and building moratoria. In recent years this approach has met with considerable success in the Balearics. By contrast, in Cyprus during the early 1990s lack of enforcement of the statutory land use policy and the fact that building restrictions did not apply to developments for which permits had already been issued meant that these measures had little effect overall.

The islands' historical and cultural heritage should also be protected and managed. These include sites and monuments, many of which are internationally renowned and part of the world's heritage, that have a potential to be developed as tourist attractions. One project that has already been developed along these lines is the *EGÉE Archipelagos* International Programme for Cultural Development, a proposal to the UNESCO made by the Greek Ministry of Culture. This includes a global plan for the whole archipelago to be protected as a Mediterranean Sea Cultural Reserve.

As previously mentioned, there is a need to strengthen the cooperation between different islands and other destinations in the region in order to develop ways to combat common problems related to tourism and in order to develop pilot sustainable management programmes for tourism and establish information networks. EURISLES (European Islands System of Links and Exchanges) is one pilot project that has already been developed. This integrates certain Mediterranean islands such as Corsica and the islands in the northern Aegean. It is a project that counts on the support of the European Commission, within the framework of the RECITE Programme.

Finally, to better manage tourism development in the Mediterranean there is also a requirement to provide technical support and identify method-ologies for local management practices oriented towards sustainability. This includes placing Agenda 21 into daily practice. Training sessions could be set up to improve the professional and technical qualifications of all stakeholders at a destination. Information should also be widely disseminated to local communities since one of the foundations of sustainability rests on active citizen participation. After all, the objectives of sustainable tourism cannot be realized without giving priority to the receiving societies' aspirations for improved living standards (de Kadt, 1990).

Conclusion

It has become increasingly clear that most island destinations in the Mediterranean are faced with the challenge of reduced competitiveness arising from their standardized, mass tourism-oriented product that attracts budget-minded visitors from a small number of northern European countries. Evidently, for these destinations to improve their competitive edge, policy-makers should seek to promote product differentiation that focuses on enhanced quality based on the sustainable management of cultural and natural resources. Simultaneously, efforts should be made to boost cooperation between the islands by exploring, for instance, their complementary aspects in order to promote circuit tourism.

These objectives can only succeed if they are backed by public policies and particularly the efficient coordination of the different actions aimed at environmental and cultural priorities. For instance, goals of integrated coastal area management should be reconciled with those aimed at the recovery of historical and cultural heritage. In order to develop such strategies, it is essential to acknowledge tourism's true role in regional development and particularly its capacity to restore territorial balance. It is also important to realize the value of tourism in terms of its contribution to the preservation and management of a territory and its resources. This applies both to economies characterized by a low development level and facing a threat to their traditional systems, and to those islands which constitute truly specialized tourist systems and find themselves in the mature phase of their tourist product.

Unfortunately, experience has shown that the general principles of sustainability, and even its translation by means of public actions oriented towards the responsible management of tourism, will not be very fruitful unless they count on the participation of professional organizations and associations (local and international operators). Moreover, they must be coordinated by public–private actions. At the same time, it is essential for the local populations to get involved since they occupy, from the outset, the centre-stage of the process. It is particularly necessary to make local agents understand the meaning of sustainable management in tourism.

A good premise for launching sustainable tourism as the principal activity on which the islands can base their successful future should be to remember the meaning of 'the Mediterranean character' as:

> an art of living, of a refined civilization that, in other times, has been able to combine leisure and business, economic efficiency, aesthetics and ethics. Thus,

the Mediterranean could again be a meeting point between human beings, between different civilizations, between North and South, East and West, becoming, at the same time, a source of wisdom and culture. (Pérez, 1997: 95)

References

Araujo, J. (1997) ¿El Mediterráneo, un mar cansado? In *El Mediterráneo desde la Otra Orilla*. Alicante: Caja de Ahorros del Mediterráneo (157–72).

Banco Nazionale del Lavoro (1997) *Settimo Rapporto sul Turismo Italiano*. Roma: BNL y Presidencia del Consiglio dei Ministri.

Bosselman, F.P., Peterson, C.A. and Mccarthy, C. (1999) *Managing Tourism Growth: Issues and Applications*. Washington, DC: Island Press.

Coccossis, H. and Parpairis, A. (1992) Tourism and the environment: some observations on the concept of carrying capacity. In H. Briassoulis and J. Van Der Straaten (eds), *Tourism and the Environment*. Dordrecht: Kluwer (23–32).

Coccossis, H. and Parpairis, A. (1995) Assessing the interaction between heritage, environment and tourism: Mykonos. In H. Coccossis and P. Nijkamp (eds), *Sustainable Tourism Development*. Hampshire: Avebury (107–25).

Comisión Europea (1995) *Estudios de desarrollo regional. Estudio prospectivo de las regiones del Mediterráneo oeste. Europa 2000*. Luxemburg: European Community.

Crauser, G. (1998) Gestión integrada de la calidad. *Revista Valenciana D'Estudis Autonòmics*, 25: 13–18.

De Kadt, E. (1990) *Making the Alternative Sustainable: Lessons from Development for Tourism*. Brighton: Institute of Development Studies.

Frangialli, F. (1998) Mirando la bola de cristal. *Revista Valenciana D'Estudis Autonòmics*, 25: 7–12.

Gil Olcina, A. (1997) El agua en las regiones del Mediterráneo. In *El Mediterráneo desde Esta Orilla*. Alicante: Caja de Ahorros del Mediterráneo (173–92).

Ioannides, D. (1992) Tourism development agents: the Cypriot resort cycle. *Annals of Tourism Research*, 19: 711–31.

Ioannides, D. (1998) Tour operators: the gatekeepers of tourism. In D. Ioannides and K. Debbage (eds), *The Economic Geography of the Tourist Industry: A Supply-side Analysis*. London: Routledge (139–58).

Ioannides, D. (forthcoming) Sustainable development and the shifting composite of tourism stakeholders: towards a dynamic framework. In S. McCool and N. Mosey (eds), *Sustaining Tourism and Communities in a World of Change: Analytical Frameworks and Case Studies*. Wallingford: CAB International.

Ioannides, D. and Debbage, K. (1997) Post-fordism and flexibility: the travel industry polyglot. *Tourism Management*, 18(4): 229–41.

Ioannides, D. and Debbage, K. (1998) Neo-fordism and flexible specialization in the travel industry. In D. Ioannides and K. Debbage (eds), *The Economic Geography of the Tourist Industry: A Supply-side Analysis*. London: Routledge (99–122).

Lanquar, R. (1995) *Tourisme et Environment en Méditerranée. Enjeux et Prospective*. Paris: Economica et Plan Bleu.

Lozato-Giotart, J.P. (1990) *Méditerranée et Tourisme*. Paris: Masson.

Marchena, M. and Vera Rebollo, J.F. (1995) Coastal areas: processes, typologies and prospects. In A. Montanari and A.M. Williams (eds), *European Tourism: Regions, Spaces and Restructuring*. Chichester: John Wiley and Sons (111–26).

Maury, R.G. (1990) *L'Eau dans les Pays Méditerranées de l'Europe Communautaire*. Poitiers: Centre Interuniversitaire d'Études Méditerranéens, fasc. 15, 258–63.

McCool, S.F. and Stankey, G.H. (1999) *Searching for Meaning and Purpose in the Quest for Sustainability*. Missoula, MT: School of Forestry.

Milne, S. and Gill, K. (1998) Distribution technologies and destination development: myths and realities. In D. Ioannides and K. Debbage (eds), *The Economic Geography of the Tourist Industry: A Supply-side Analysis*. London: Routledge (123–38).

Monfort Mir, V. (1999) *Competitividad y factores críticos de éxito en los destinos turísticos mediterráneos: Benidorm y Peñíscola*. Doctoral thesis, Departamento de Estructura Económica (Economía Aplicada II), University of Valencia.

Nijkamp, P. and Verdonkschot, S. (1995) Sustainable tourism development: a case study of Lesbos. In H. Coccossis and P. Nijkamp (eds), *Sustainable Tourism Development*. Hampshire: Avebury (127–40).

Pearce, D. (1989) *Tourist Development*. Harlow, Essex: Longman.

Pearce, D. (1995) *Tourism Today: A Geographical Analysis*. Harlow, Essex: Longman.

Pérez, J. (1997) El Mediterráneo en la Historia. In *El Mediterráneo desde Esta Orilla*. Alicante: Caja de Ahorros del Mediterráneo (89–110).

Poon, A. (1993) *Tourism, Technology, and Competitive Strategies*. Wallingford: CAB International.

Shaw, G. and Williams, A.M. (1994) *Critical Issues in Tourism: A Geographical Perspective*. Oxford: Blackwell.

Stabler, M.J. (ed.) (1997) *Tourism Sustainability: Principles to Practice*. Oxon: CAB International.

Vera Rebollo, J.F. (ed.) (1997) *Análisis Territorial del Turismo: Una Nueva Geografía del Turismo*. Barcelona: Ariel.

Weaver, D. (1993) Ecotourism in the small island Caribbean. *GeoJournal*, 31(4): 457–65.

WTO (1995a) *Previsiones del Turismo Mundial hasta el Año 2000 y Después. Vol. 1, El Mundo*. Madrid: World Tourism Organization.

WTO (1995b) *Previsiones del Turismo Mundial hasta el Año 2000 y Después. Vol. 2. Estudios Regionales Sobre Previsiones*. Madrid: World Tourism Organization.

WTO (1997a) *Tourism Market Trends. Europe* (edition, 1997). Madrid: World Tourism Organization.

WTO (1997b) *Turismo. Panorama 2020. Nuevas Previsiones. Avance*. Madrid: World Tourism Organization.

4

The Role of Transnational Tour Operators in the Development of Mediterranean Island Tourism

Francesc Sastre and Inmaculada Benito

Introduction

Travel and tourism has become the world's largest economic sector, generating more income than any other economic activity including international oil production and arms sales (WTTC, 1993). The growth of mass tourism, a product of the late 1960s and early 1970s, was fuelled by several factors. On the demand side, post-war affluence and increased leisure in developed countries, plus a marked decline in the relative cost of travel, led to the industry's ascendancy. On the supply side, the mutually beneficial confluence of airlines, tour operators, travel agents, and hotel chains in conjunction with receptive government policies, has produced a vast worldwide network of vacation opportunities.

On many Mediterranean islands, tourism has become the most important source of hard currency, even exceeding the contribution of agriculture or manufacturing. For example, in the Balearic Islands agricultural activities represent less than 2 per cent of Gross Domestic Product (GDP) while industrial activities account for approximately 7.6 per cent of total GDP. Similar statements can be made for other islands in the Mediterranean.

Among the various factors linked to tourism (e.g., sociocultural, economic, etc.) in the Mediterranean islands, the pursuit of environmental conservation has emerged as a matter of particular relevance. This line of thought is supported by a number of empirical and analytical studies in the Balearic Islands (Riera, 1998). As stated by Opaschowski (1991), there is a strong link between establishing a good ecological balance and meeting the objective of quality leisure and tourism. In this context, the attractiveness of a given area's landscape and the manner in which this has been transformed (Haider,

1992), play a relevant role in providing a sense of welcome to the visitor. Environmental quality is particularly important for destinations such as islands because it often is the main, if not the only, draw for visitors.

Unfortunately, mass tour operators have historically ignored the negative environmental and sociocultural impacts arising from their emphasis on sun–sea–sand tourism in the Mediterranean. By contrast, specialist tour companies have emerged in recent years heeding the increasing demand for individualized tourism products in environmentally pristine areas (Ioannides, 1998). Unlike their mass marketing counterparts, these tour specialists have sought to target a 'small in volume but high in profitability' market through the offer of alternative tour experiences. Ironically, major tour operators such as TUI who have been seeking to protect their shrinking market share have gradually also jumped on the alternative tourism bandwagon by producing new niche products known as 'soft tourism' or 'ecotourism' (*Travel Indonesia*, 1993).

The primary objective of this chapter is to examine the tour operators' influence on the development of tourism on Mediterranean islands. The activities of tour operators are considered in detail in order to verify the hypothesis that these actors have been one of the major influences determining the nature of tourism demand relating to the region. It is suggested that tour operators affect the levels of demand for these insular destinations and are also instrumental in determining market trends. This chapter reviews trends in the tour operating business. It also examines the literature on the sector of travel suppliers and intermediaries, including airlines, reports on field research and findings, and discusses the relationship and effect of technology upon the chain of production.

The Intermediary Sector

Tour operators and travel agents respectively assemble and retail holidays mainly for the mass market. The role of tour operators is to create holiday packages and to facilitate the link between various suppliers located both in origin and destination countries (e.g., transportation companies, accommodation establishments, facilities and services) and the tourist. These gatekeepers of the tourism business procure the various components of the travel product, usually by negotiating discounted prices, and retailing the assembled package through travel agents (indirect distribution) or directly to the customer (direct distribution). Generally, tour operations are conducted in a number of ways: as an independent firm specializing solely in holiday assembly and marketing; as a subsidiary of a conglomerate business with diverse interests; as a division of an airline; or as a company linked with a travel agency (Gartner and Bachri, 1994; Ioannides, 1998; United Nations Center for Transnational Corporations, 1982).

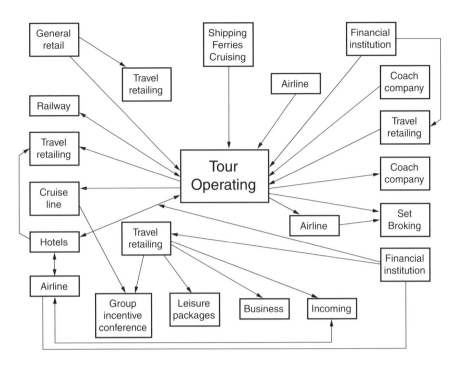

Figure 4.1 The tour operation system

The structure of the tour operating business

The demand for tourism is met by concentrating the marketing efforts of a wide variety of tourist services. Together, these services form the world's largest and fastest-growing industry. Some of these services are crucial to the generation and satisfaction of tourists' needs. Others play only peripheral or supportive roles. Figure 4.1 provides a framework for analysis based on those sectors commonly seen as forming the core of the industry. It also illustrates the chain of distribution in the travel and tourism business, representing the system by which a product or service is disseminated from its manufacturing source to the eventual consumers.

Apart from the relationship between principal and agent, the structure of the intermediary market – a significant issue in industrial economics – highlights certain interesting characteristics. One has been the increasing tendency towards industrial concentration (horizontal integration), with a handful of leading companies dominating the market place (Kingsley-Jones, 1998). The other characteristic has been a trend towards vertical integration, with tour operators controlling other tourism suppliers such as airlines, travel agents and, more rarely, hotels (Figure 4.1). According to Kingsley-Jones in an article for *Flight International*:

What already seems likely to emerge is a handful of powerful integrated groups, each with its own in-house airline. The next step in the battle also appears to be to expand beyond national borders – a challenge already laid down by the UK charter companies as they edge into Scandinavia and Germany. (1998: 64)

Already by the 1980s, the largest European tour operators had consolidated their position in the market through vertical and horizontal integration with other travel companies. Consequently, a number of major tour operators such as the UK-based Thomson's gained control over charter (holiday) airlines. By 1998 all the major charter airlines based in Britain had been vertically integrated with major tour operators while the independent charter companies (e.g., Air Europe and TEA-UK) had gone out of business (Kingsley-Jones, 1998). In general, tour operators have traditionally preferred to integrate with charter airlines rather than hotels. The industry avoids buying hotels because of the high risk associated with their non-transferability. Although tour operators could gain maximum control over every aspect of the holiday package by owning lodging establishments, there is always a danger that a destination may fall from favour, leaving the operator with hard-to-fill rooms. In contrast, there is less risk associated with tour operators' investment in charter flights since these can always be re-routed away from unpopular destinations to more fashionable areas.

As stated above, integration in the travel business has also been horizontal, with large tour operators buying up other tour operators to improve their market share and reduce competition. In theory, horizontal integration leads to economies of scale and, thus, to cost savings and, ultimately, price reductions for consumers. The cost savings may also enable a company to become more competitive, allowing it to develop a better range of products for its clients and to achieve superior quality control over its products. Through buy-outs a tour company may also reinforce its corporate image in the public mind.

Given the very competitive nature of the tour operating business and, in particular, the trend towards consolidation among some of the largest operators, it is not surprising that there has been a lot of turnover in the industry. For example, in the early 1990s a number of major British tour operators such as the International Leisure Group went out of business (Ioannides, 1998). Those small companies that attempted to stay afloat through low-cost packages were also driven out of business as they struggled to compete with their larger counterparts. Surprisingly, however, a sizeable group of smaller operators have managed to survive by specializing in market niches for which specific expertise is required. These companies may focus on parts of the world that are perceived as too remote to be worth the attention of larger companies. Moreover, these travel specialists are often able to build on a reputation for quality and exclusiveness and offer a more personal service than their larger counterparts.

The structure of the intermediary market in Europe and the USA is characterized by a relatively small number of large players in terms of ownership, control and market share. In the USA, there were approximately 1,500 operators in total in the early 1990s, 40 of whom (3 per cent) controlled almost a third of the market. In the UK, the top ten tour operators accounted for over 70 per cent of the 17 million seats of ATOL (Air Travel Organizers' Licence) licences granted in 1993–94. Just four companies, namely Thomson, Airtours, Owners Abroad (First Choice from 1994) and Cosmos, accounted for almost 60 per cent of the air holiday licences (Evans and Stabler, 1995).

Despite the high degree of market concentration in the tour operating industry, there has actually been a rise in the total number of firms. In the USA the number of companies increased from nearly 600 in the late 1970s to over 1,000 by 1985 (Sheldon, 1986). Likewise, in the UK while there were around 500 firms in 1985, by 1993–94 their number had nearly doubled (Evans and Stabler, 1995). Perhaps more significant, however, is the birth and death of tour operators, mostly of smaller firms. It has been estimated that in both the USA and Europe only a third of those in business in the late 1970s were still extant in the middle to late 1980s (Sheldon, 1994). In the UK, even though there was an increase in total number of firms, 24 firms ceased trading in the year 1992–93 and another 20 in 1993–94.

The performance of tour operators is extremely sensitive to market conditions, particularly variations in demand arising from such factors as changes in exchange rates, economic recession in origin countries and inflation, and real or perceived political instability in destinations. In the face of tourism development and the continuing emergence of new destinations, capacity has sometimes outrun demand. Furthermore, as in the hospitality industry, seasonality is a significant issue affecting the tour operating business. Large firms rely on a high volume of sales with low margins, a significant proportion of profit being generated by investing receipts from advanced bookings. A high rate of sales makes it possible to achieve substantial economies of scale and scope through operating efficiencies. Moreover, large companies have a wide knowledge of an extensive market and possess the market power to gain large discounts from carriers and hoteliers. Provided fixed investment is low, as in the case of smaller and more specialized tour operators, returns can be relatively high.

In the inclusive package market there is intensive competition to secure sales volume in order to generate cash flows. Consequently, discounting can be widespread at the launch of the upcoming season's package holidays to encourage early bookings. Discounting can also occur at the end of the season to fill excess capacity. The expectation of discounting by potential tourists, who delay making a firm booking earlier in the season, exacerbates tour operators' problems because not only do they have to dispose of holidays at little above cost but also their cash flow is adversely affected. In the early 1990s, late bookings in the UK accounted for almost 40 per cent of the summer sun package market. However, in August 1996 the leading tour operators withdrew holidays and raised prices in an attempt to deter such action by consumers since this had led to a considerable decrease in profits during the previous year. Discounting strategies are both a manifestation of the drive to maintain or increase market share and a reflection of the long lead times (often up to three years required for launching new holiday types) that enhance the likelihood of oversupply resulting from overestimated demand. Even large companies indulge in price wars with the market leaders often initiating these to safeguard their market position.

Factors such as ease of entry and exit, the number of tour operators, fierce price competition, low margins and often significant losses all point to contestable if not highly competitive market conditions in many countries. There is some empirical evidence, albeit very little, concerning the extent of economies and diseconomies of scale, economies of scope, capital indivisibilities, fixed capacity and fixed costs. Nevertheless, the larger operators in the top tier who have invested in charter airlines and some travel agents appear to enjoy economies of scale and scope. These large tour operators are able to overcome the problems of indivisibility and high fixed costs related to the concomitant fixed capacity by increasing average load factors on aircraft and occupancy rates overall.

Generally, a high degree of concentration of market share in the package holiday segment suggests an oligopolistic structure while a low incidence of market concentration indicates a highly competitive market. However, there is a problem in using relatively crude measures, such as the number of firms. It is conceivable for a few firms to be engaged in fierce competition with each other while many firms, because they are spatially separated or serving different segments of a market, might be relatively uncompetitive, representing the Chamberlinian notion of monopolistic competition. It is, therefore, necessary to take account of the relative size of firms, as well as price, cost, profit levels and market shares, to establish how competitive the market really is. Even factors like the extent of links between firms have a bearing on the degree of concentration.

Air Travel

The operation and regulation of air transport have been widely investigated in the context of both business and holiday travel (Button, 1991; Levine, 1987; Shaw, 1987). Useful reviews of the situation in the early 1990s are given in Ferguson and Ferguson (1994) and Lundberg *et al.* (1995) while Melville (1995) has provided a thorough overview and evaluation of economic studies of the sector, including econometric modelling approaches. Evidence of the conditions and the structure of the air transport sector illustrates a number of tourism and economic issues related to other transport markets, especially the economic environment created by regulation and deregulation and the resulting level of competition. An associated factor is the process of privatization of a number of airlines.

The cost structure of airlines is quite complex and operating costs and efficiency are related to technical factors depending on the distance travelled, the size and type of aircraft, the payload, as well as support services such as marketing and reservation systems. By contrast, capital costs are likely to be affected by whether the aircraft are owned outright or leased, or whether they are new or second-hand. Direct and indirect costs, such as airport charges and ground handling, are outside the control of the airline. *Prima facie*, airlines are high fixed cost enterprises with fixed capacity meaning that they need to attain high payloads to break even. Short-haul flights, involving fewer hours in the air and more take-offs and landings, are relatively more expensive than long-haul carriage. Furthermore, aircraft are designed to fly specific distances as efficiently as possible so, for example, employing a Boeing 747 on European routes under 2,500 km is uneconomic. In general, there are economies of scale, stemming from technical efficiencies in operating large aircraft depending, of course, on the route.

The market served influences the economics of airline operations in a number of ways. In order to maximize the payload and revenues for scheduled services demand has to be ascertained in advance to discover, for example, its composition with regard to the numbers of business and economy customers. The approach adopted by airlines is termed 'yield management' which in its most developed form is akin to perfectly discriminating monopoly pricing. Pricing policy also needs to take account of the route, destination and stage stopovers, the pressure of competition and longer-term level of demand. Chartered services reduce market uncertainty because it is possible to ascertain the payload well in advance. However, the distinction between these two main types of services (scheduled and charter) has become increasingly difficult to discern, as charter airlines have now moved into the scheduled market and vice versa. This has occurred because travel on what used to be holiday charter routes has become so regular warranting scheduled services. Conversely, certain under-utilized scheduled services (perhaps those operated as social services when airlines were state-owned), may be operated more irregularly by special charters.

The advent of deregulation and privatization has dramatically altered airline operations and has had some interesting economic consequences. The US experience, where deregulation occurred in 1978, holds implications for what might happen elsewhere, especially in the European Union where actions to relax controls have already been initiated. Competition has certainly intensified as new companies have moved into the market because of reduced entry barriers. Chartering, leasing or buying second-hand aircraft facilitate ease of entry. Barriers to entry are also reduced through the negotiation of reservations, ground-handling services and maintenance agreements with specialist contract firms or established major airlines. In the short run, increased competition has reduced fares and extended the market, also forcing airlines to be more sensitive to their customers' needs.

However, recent developments have thrown up the negative effects of deregulation with some formerly major airlines been forced out of business because of severe financial problems. For instance, the US-based Pan-Am is a well-known example of an airline that no longer operates. Also some major national airlines in Europe, such as Air France, Iberia, Sabena and SAS, have had problems in adapting to severe competition, especially on key routes. This is mainly because of inflexible structures, engendered by highly restrictive international fare policies and the state support they receive as national flag carriers. Moreover, the benefits to consumers may be short-lived as the number of airlines will almost certainly decrease in the long run through mergers and reciprocal agreements and the failure of smaller, newer entrants. This concentration and consolidation is likely to lead to higher fares eventually as the larger companies take control of key routes and gain the market power to dictate price levels and limit choice.

The development of the hub and spoke pattern of air travel where long-haul flights are concentrated on major airports provides opportunities for smaller feeder airlines to create a market niche, although the larger airlines usually determine the terms on which spoke routes will be served (Wheatcroft, 1998). Additional concerns arise where airlines cut costs in order to remain competitive since such actions may lower the quality of service or result in less attention being paid to maintenance and safety margins.

The pattern of air travel is still evolving given the differences in the rate of growth in sub-markets and the fact that deregulation has not yet had a full effect on the airline structure and market. However, as already mentioned, there are signs that market power will eventually be concentrated in the hands of a few international giants. A case in point was the proposed agreement between British Airways and American Airlines, two of the largest airlines in the world, which together control around 60 per cent of the UK–US routes. Market concentration in the European airline industry looks increasingly likely especially as state support for national airline companies declines under privatization programmes and agreements. The European Union already forbids subsidies for unprofitable airlines.

Evidence from this brief description of the airline sector suggests that although a domestic monopolistic or oligopolistic structure has historically been common because of state-supported airlines or a small number of competing airlines, deregulation has made certain markets competitive in the short run. In the international arena certain routes have become highly competitive, given the high number of carriers that serve these. Conversely, most of the other routes are served by only two carriers, indicating an oligopolistic market, while a handful of routes are served by a single carrier which may be tempted to exercise monopoly powers. This does not undermine the ability of the theory of the firm to explain the market structure. Instead, it signifies a need to divide the sector into sub-markets and to consider each one separately. The airline sector, in common with the tour operating industry, is in a fluid state, reflecting deregulation and the changing demand for foreign air travel.

Tour Operators as the Driving Force Behind Tourist Development in Mediterranean Islands

The development of tourism has been the major factor behind some of the changes witnessed on the majority of Mediterranean islands (see, for example, Chapter 2 in this book). The industry's growth in the region began in earnest during the early 1960s with the arrival of charter flights carrying large numbers of central and northern European tourists to purpose-built holiday resorts.

The rapid development of tourism has led to cultural, social, economic and environmental changes. In mature holiday destinations the sector's most common repercussions include the rapid destruction of natural resources and the degradation of the landscape in general, concentration of activities within the service sector and the creation of a tourist monoculture, and a growing dependence upon tour operators as travel intermediaries. From the very outset of mass tourism development in the region tour operators have featured as key manipulators of tourist flows from the principal origin countries and have held the upper hand in negotiating rates with the local owners of accommodation establishments (Aguiló and Payeras, 1997).

Shortage of natural resources

The geographic nature of an island means that its resources and ecosystems are both limited and fragile, to an extent that in many cases this type of region can be paralleled to a 'species in danger of extinction'. Natural resources are fundamental for human requirements, either directly because of their use value or indirectly as a component of the product offered to tourists. However, when these resources have been over-used, as has been the case in numerous Mediterranean island destinations, the consequence has been environmental deterioration. In turn, there are plenty of instances where northern European tourists have voted with their feet and chosen to shun overcrowded and environmentally degraded Mediterranean destinations in favour of remote coastal and insular areas in their early stages of tourism development (e.g., islands in the Caribbean or the Indian Ocean).

Tour operators are well aware that the declining environmental quality of many insular regions in the Mediterranean has resulted in growing consumer dissatisfaction with these destinations. Indeed, many companies appear to pay lip service to improving the environmental quality of the Mediterranean and some major players have gone as far as to set up environmental departments, maintaining that they are 'committed to protecting the environment' (Iwand, 1995). Moreover, a number of major tour operators have used their trade associations (such as the UK-based International Federation of Tour Operators) 'to adopt a tough stance against environmental and noise pollution in popular destinations' (Ioannides, 1998: 147). Nevertheless, one wonders how sincere these efforts by these powerful stakeholders will be in the long run particularly given their tendency to promote holiday type and not specific destinations. Because the destinations of the Mediterranean are highly substitutable, many tour operators may simply refocus their attention on new destinations that offer a superior quality product.

To better understand the level of influence tour operators exert on demand patterns relative to Mediterranean insular destinations we now turn our attention to a case study of Spain's Balearic region. This insular region has traditionally depended very heavily on mass tour operators based in northern European markets (e.g., the UK and Germany).

The Balearic Islands: A Case Study

The Balearic islands depend almost exclusively on tour operators. A total of 92 per cent of tourist arrivals on the Balearic islands are on package tours whereas the remaining 8 per cent are individual travellers (Conselleria de Turisme, 1999). It is interesting to note that this distribution in terms of arrivals has kept constant for years. The five largest tour operators account for 52 per cent of the package tour market while the remaining 48 per cent of the market is divided among a large number of small-scale operators. Mass tour operators target large numbers of visitors by offering packages at low prices. Their aim is to get the highest possible return from every operation. Tour operators based in the UK, Germany and Scandinavia account for a major share of the packages sold for this destination. Some of the major companies serving the Balearics include British-based Thomson, Airtours, and First Tours, the German companies TUI, NUR-Neckerman, and LTU, and the Scandinavian tour operators Spies and Vingressor (Sastre, 1999). By contrast, few package tourists come from Italy and France, a phenomenon that is not altogether surprising considering that these countries have their own sun, sea, and sand destinations on the Mediterranean.

Figure 4.2 indicates the increase in number of package tourists arriving on the Balearic islands by main countries of origin between 1992 and 1998. As can be seen, the number of package tourists from Germany alone increased from around 1.6 million in 1992 to approximately 2.8 million in 1998. Similarly, UK-based tour operators saw an increase in their sales from less than 1.5 million in 1992 to over 2 million in 1998. The largest German tour

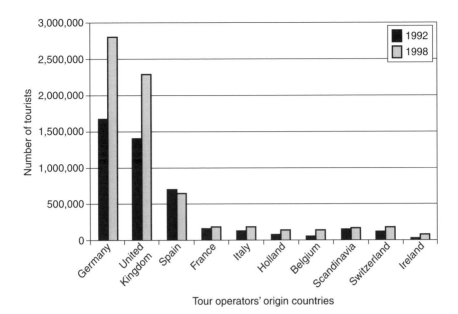

Figure 4.2 Number of package tour arrivals by country of origin, 1992–98

operator, TUI, witnessed an increase in its package tour sales to the islands from around 600,000 in 1992 to over 900,000 in 1998 (Sastre, 1999). The growth in the number of package tours is proportional to the increase in total number of tourist arrivals on the islands. It is important, however, to note that despite the overall increase in package tour arrivals, the number of operators responsible for these tours has declined as a result of accelerated market concentration in the industry. This means that the islands' economy is increasingly dependent on an ever-shrinking number of major tour operators. As a reflection of this dependence, it is perhaps not surprising that the German tour operator TUI boasts that it, alone, 'accounts for 10 per cent of the gross domestic product in the world's most successful holiday destination, the island of Majorca' (Iwand, 1995: 1).

Ironically, the large supply of tourist accommodation on the Balearics has historically been responsible for the tour operators' expanding control over this destination. Much of this accommodation was constructed, to a large extent in coastal locations, in the early 1960s with partial financial support provided by tour operators. Because of the large supply of bed spaces, the tour operators are in a strong bargaining position when it comes to negotiating terms with the operators of lodging establishments. In turn, this means that in order to fill these rooms and ensure healthy occupancy rates, the islands now have to depend on large numbers of tourists participating on low cost package holidays. Such a scenario does not appear to bode well for the future sustainability of these settings.

Fluctuations in demand

Over the years, tourism has increased its share as an economic sector in the Balearics due to the overall growth in demand in northern Europe for a 'sun, sea, and sand' product. Through their travel brochures and their ability to offer discounted holiday packages tour operators have been an important force behind the historically strong demand for this particular insular destination. However, despite these actors' strategic position as manipulators of tourist flows, there are a number of cyclical or sporadic circumstances outside their power that must also be taken into account. For instance, factors such as seasonality, the impacts of widespread economic crises, and the crises the sector itself faces at the destination all influence the behaviour of the tour operators and have a bearing on the fortunes of the tourist industry.

Seasonality

One of the main characteristics of tourism in Mediterranean islands, including the Balearics, is the highly seasonal nature of demand. After all, these destinations depend heavily on beach-oriented mass tourism. Seasonality in Majorca, for instance, means receiving 80 per cent of arrivals between May and October. This is possibly one of the greatest structural problems faced by a 'sun and sand' tourist destination such as this. Seasonality also has repercussions in terms of the product offered, since a large proportion of holiday accommodation remains closed and vacant during the low season. Because of this, occupancy rates are generally lower on islands than in other Mediterranean destinations.

Inevitably, tour operators have managed to exploit the issue of seasonality to their advantage because it is they and not the tourists who are the hotel and transport (air and transfer) companies' clients. Essentially, it is the tour operators who hire these companies' services and pay any money owed. Because of their dual role as client and distribution channel and because of the oversupply of tourist accommodation, particularly during the off-season, tour operators have been able to exercise a considerable amount of power over the accommodation/transport package. Alternatively, the hotel and transport companies in destinations such as the Balearics have a minimal, if any, influence on the tourist.

Traditionally, the tour operator would reserve a guaranteed share of hotel accommodation at pre-established prices that varied according to the season and depended on the general condition of the economy (Sheldon, 1986). Nowadays, however, due to market fluctuations and an increase in the type and number of accommodation establishments, reservations are often not guaranteed and one cannot even rely upon the maintenance of original prices. This is because it is common for tour operators to advertise last-minute special offers to boost the market. Moreover, 'to avoid any financial loss due to cancellations of bookings, the operators normally negotiate a [favourable] release date with their accommodation suppliers; otherwise they will most likely be subject to a cancellation penalty' (Ioannides, 1998: 145). These cut-off date strategies place the risk squarely on the shoulders of the owners of smaller, non-affiliated establishments since it may be impossible for them to fill their rooms at short notice following a cancellation.

At the same time, it appears that tour operators have also strengthened their position *vis-à-vis* that of airline companies. Charter contracts with airline companies are now made either for a series of flights or rotational flights. Previously, the whole plane was chartered, commonly through a block-purchase agreement that forced the tour operators to pay for the airline seats reserved even if these were not filled, an arrangement that clearly placed the risk on the operator. This practice has become less and less common due to fluctuations in demand and the excessive number of holiday packages on offer. At present, with a few exceptions, 80 per cent or 90 per cent of a plane's capacity is chartered under guarantee while the rest involves a pro rata agreement between the tour operator and the airline company. Prices vary according to the sub-season, day of the week and time.

New products and new proposals

In recent years, the Balearic and other Mediterranean islands have sought to escape their heavy dependence on tour operators by diversifying their product (see other chapters in this book). Economic strategists and policy-makers in general feel that the only way to enhance the sustainability of the tourist product in the long run is by moving away from the traditional emphasis on mass tourists from a small number of markets. Among the recommended strategies is an attempt to market the islands to areas other than the UK and Germany. Moreover, an effort has been made to target tourists who are seeking more than seaside products and who may wish to visit during the winter months (Bull, 1997). Unfortunately, however, it appears that these efforts do not go far enough as, in reality, they have not been geared towards altering the nature of the islands' product and market. In other words, these attempts are still targeted overwhelmingly towards large numbers of mass tourists. This situation is well demonstrated in the case of Cyprus, for instance (see Chapter 12 in this book), where strong lobbying by hoteliers has forced the government to allow an increase in cheap package tours to the island despite a commitment to improve the quality of the island's tourist product.

The inflexibility of the product/service

The traditional form of 'package travel' is characterized by a standard bundle of products or services, very much like a 'set menu', displaying little flexibility when it comes to choosing the starting date or the length of the holiday. The lack of flexibility of this type of product means that certain segments of the market, even those with a medium to high purchasing power, face certain difficulties in finding a product suiting their requirements.

At the other extreme, a number of flexible products are now being offered in response to the growing dissatisfaction of many consumers for all-inclusive, standardized holidays (Ioannides, 1998). These products can best be described as 'à la carte' holidays and are, of course, more expensive than the traditional mass travel packages. While they usually include air transportation and a direct hotel booking, the rest of the holiday packet is tailor-made to the tourist's specific needs. Interestingly, because of the lower volume of sales, tour operators often book scheduled airline seats for such individualized holidays rather than relying entirely on charter flights.

Technology and Distribution Channels

Information technology has the ability to give businesses a competitive edge. Indeed, because of new technologies the international business scene has significantly altered, as wealth creation is no longer confined to traditional physical spaces. In the context of this chapter, we should highlight the potential role of information technologies such as global distribution systems (GDS) and the Internet for making the Mediterranean islands' traditional sectors and tourism more competitive.

The introduction of technology is especially essential for mature destinations since it can enhance the efficiency of various businesses. It also facilitates new, more efficient methods of promotion and provides the potential for island tourism establishments to personalize their products and market directly to the consumers. This can be done, for instance, through the establishment of regional distributional systems (Buhalis, 1993) or, more commonly, the Internet (Milne and Gill, 1998). Many locally owned hotels around the Mediterranean have developed their own web pages and enable direct booking at least for more adventurous consumers who wish to create their own holiday experience. While such developments offer the opportunity to locally owned hotels and other tourist facilities in island regions of the Mediterranean to bypass intermediaries, it is still unclear what their overall impact has been on such companies as tour operators and travel agents (cf. Milne and Gill, 1998).

Regardless of the impact of new technologies on destination-based establishments, one thing is certain. Travel intermediaries such as tour operators have also perceived the need to replace old technologies with more efficient systems in order to protect their competitiveness. They have fast realized that if they do not adopt new technologies, they will eventually face shrinking demand as more and more consumers turn towards more innovative companies (e.g., those that market directly through the Internet). Interestingly, smaller tour operators are not as well represented as some other sectors of the travel industry on GDS systems. According to Ioannides, this is because the 'display protocol [of such systems] is fairly rigid, meaning that it is easier to represent fairly standardized tours' compared to 'the flexible products of specialized tour operators' (1998: 154). By contrast, these travel specialists have been quick to embrace other types of information technologies, especially the World Wide Web.

The tourism product in the majority of the Mediterranean islands is now in a mature stage of its life-cycle (Krugman, 1990). Because of the insular nature of these destinations, they can be thought of as perfect laboratories for experimenting with innovative ideas which may lead to a more harmonious relationship between human activities (such as tourism) and the natural environment. Technology itself can play a fundamental role in the islands' search for improved quality of life while preserving their natural resources. For instance, in order to attract new activities and professionals, these islands will have to offer a technological infrastructure comparable with that found in traditionally innovative regions (e.g., in Western Europe). Cyprus' relative success as an offshore banking centre (see Chapter 12 in this book) has been dependent on its excellent telecommunications network and the rapid diffusion of Internet services. In the case of tourism, technological innovation could include the following: (a) the development of information services via the installation of 'state-of-the-art' terminals both on the islands and abroad; (b) the introduction of new methods of communication between the suppliers of tourist services who are not connected to major booking offices; and (c) research into the diffusion of systems of technology for tourism management.

In the Mediterranean islands, where the tour operators have traditionally played an important role in product distribution, trading down and centralized travel arrangements have become common practice in order to reduce overall travel expenses and operating costs and improving general efficiency. The awareness at the enterprise level of the need for efficient travel services tends to increase the role of travel agents in the decision-making process. The intensification of pressure from clients urges these actors to improve the quantity and quality of information provided and to enhance their negotiating power with tourism suppliers. Information and telecommunication technologies are a key factor that would help streamline the whole process. According to an in-depth investigation of the sector carried out by researchers at the University of the Balearics, the adoption of automated management systems would allow enterprises to reduce travel and entertainment expenses by 20–30 per cent. The use of new technologies such as the Internet can facilitate the quick and convenient transfer of information to on-line customers. At the same time, these innovations offer tour operators and other travel intermediaries a huge opportunity to re-engineer their approach to customers, from low value added service providers to global travel consultants who offer integrated and high quality travel solutions. This would be a way for tour operators to compete against the new 'virtual' travel agents who sell their products directly through the Internet.

Conclusion

The ability of tour operators to package the individual components of the travel experience (e.g., transfers, accommodation and services) into clearly identifiable products has made it possible for millions of people to travel at extremely reasonable prices. Because the profit margins of mass tour operators are generally low, they have a permanent need to sell their products to high numbers of tourists in order to guarantee the profitability of their operations. This situation has fuelled the growth of mass tourism, a phenomenon that has, in turn, generated noticeable financial and social development in different destinations, including the Mediterranean's insular regions. Mass tourism has generally taken over from other more selective travel segments leading to a decrease in their market share over the last four decades.

In theory, because tour operators traditionally faced many risks (more than hotel or transport companies did), they were able to lower their prices and operate on razor-thin profit margins. Increasingly, however, the risk factor has shifted to other players in the industry, especially locally owned accommodation establishments at the destinations. This has occurred because of a slowdown in the growth rates of tourism demand for the Mediterranean region coupled with the enormous supply of bed spaces in most destinations that has arisen from years of speculative construction. Because local entrepreneurs want to protect their occupancy rates they are forced to offer their facilities to tour operators at extremely low prices. Moreover, these players are at the mercy of the travel intermediaries since, for instance, the latter are able to negotiate cut-off dates when bookings are low. Perhaps more importantly, the mass tourism product the islands have come to depend on does not offer sufficient flexibility to adapt to new trends in demand for travel. Thus, most locally owned establishments seldom reach optimum profit levels.

The example of the Balearics demonstrates a familiar situation in many islands of the Mediterranean, namely a destination with a heavy dependence on tourism from just two origins, Germany and the UK. Additionally, most of these tourists, many of whom are lower income individuals, arrive on the islands during the summer months and concentrate their activities mostly in a few seaside resorts. At the same time, the Balearics (just like many Mediterranean destinations) depend heavily on a small number of mass tour operators who have become larger in recent years through mergers and acquisitions.

It would appear, as some authors have strongly argued, that the rapid diffusion of new technologies, particularly the Internet and to a lesser degree regional distribution systems, open up new opportunities for locally owned establishments based on Mediterranean islands to escape their dependence on powerful travel intermediaries. For instance, an increasing number of lodging establishments throughout the Mediterranean have set up their own web pages and it is possible for 'on-line' travellers to make direct bookings for these facilities. By the same token, however, there are a number of circumstances indicating the need for caution concerning the comments made about the opportunities new technologies may present to local actors in insular regions. Even though there is no consensus concerning the impact of new information technologies on travel intermediaries, it seems that these players could, in the short run, actually strengthen their bargaining position *vis-à-vis* destination-based establishments if they use these technologies to re-engineer their approach towards their customers. Many of the larger tour operators, for instance, can use their access to new technologies to strengthen their control of distribution channels and are, therefore, well placed in terms of adapting to changes in demand.

References

Aguiló, E. and Payeras, M. (1997) El coste de la insularidad en las Islas Baleares. Paper presented to IMEDOC (Iles de la Méditerranée Occidentale group), Minorca, 23–26 April.

Buhalis, D. (1993) RICRMS as a strategic tool for small and medium tourism enterprises. *Tourism Management*, 14(5): 366–78.

Bull, P. (1997) Mass tourism in the Balearic Islands: an example of concentrated dependence. In D.G. Lockhart and D. Drakakis-Smith (eds), *Island Tourism, Trends and Prospects*. London: Pinter (137–51).

Button, K. (1991) *Airline Deregulation*. London: David Fulton.

Conselleria de Turisme (1999) *El Turisme a les Illes Balears: Estadistica*. Govern de les Illes Baleares.

Evans, N. and Stabler, M.J. (1995) A future for the package tour operator in the 21st century? *Tourism Economics*, 1(3): 245–63.

Ferguson, P.R. and Ferguson, G.J. (1994) *Industrial Economics: Issues and Perspectives* 2nd edition. London: Macmillan.

Gartner, W. and Bachri, T. (1994) Tour operator's role in the tourism distribution system: an Indonesian case study. In M. Uysal (ed.), *Global Tourist Behavior*. Binghampton, NY: The Haworth Press, Inc. (161–79).

Haider, M. (1992) *Umgestaltung für die Zukunft: Prinzipien und Überzeugende Strategien*. Munich: Quintessenz-Verlag.

Ioannides, D. (1998) Tour operators: the gatekeepers of tourism. In D. Ioannides and K. Debbage (eds), *The Economic Geography of the Tourist Industry: A Supply-side Analysis*. London: Routledge (139–58).

Iwand, W.M. (1995) Instruments, procedures and experiences of integrating the environment into tourism development by a major tour operator. Paper presented at the World Conference on Sustainable Tourism, Lanzarote, 24–29 April.

Kingsley-Jones, M. (1998) Sunshine jetset resets: a round of restructuring will see a new order of travel giants emerge. *Flight International*, 154: 64–5.

Krugman, P.R. (1990) *Rethinking International Trade*. Cambridge, MA: The MIT Press.

Levine, M.E. (1987) Airline competition in deregulated markets: theory, firm strategy and public policy. *Yale Journal on Regulation*, 4: 393–494.

Lundberg, D.E., Krishnamoorthy, M. and Stavenga, M.H. (1995) *Tourism Economics*. New York: John Wiley.

Melville, J.A. (1995) *Some Empirical Results for the Airline and Air Transport Markets of a Small Developing Country*. PhD thesis, University of Kent at Canterbury.

Milne, S. and Gill, K. (1998) Distribution technologies and destination development: myths and realities. In D. Ioannides and K.G. Debbage (eds), *The Economic Geography of the Tourist Industry: A Supply-side Analysis*. London: Routledge (123–38).

Opaschowski, H. (1991) *Okologie von Freizein und Tourismus*. Oplanden: Leske & Budrich.

Riera, A. (1998) *Cap a un nou model d'elecció discreta en les bases del mètode del cost del viatge: Aplicació als espais naturals protegits de l'illa de Mallorca*. PhD thesis, University of the Balearic Islands.

Sastre, A.A. (1999) Distance learning material: international tourism markets. Unpublished paper, University of the Balearic Islands.

Shaw, S. (1987) *Airline Marketing Management*. London: Pitman.

Sheldon, P.J. (1986) The tour operator industry: an analysis. *Annals of Tourism Research*, 13(3): 349–65.

Sheldon, P.J. (1994) Tour wholesaling. In S.F. Witt and L. Moutinho (eds), *Tourism Marketing and Management Handbook* 2nd edition. New York: Prentice Hall (469–72).

United Nations Center for Transnational Corporations (1982) *Transnational Corporations in International Tourism*. New York: United Nations.

Wheatcroft, S. (1998) The airline industry and tourism. In D. Ioannides and K.G. Debbage (eds), *The Economic Geography of the Tourist Industry: A Supply-Side Analysis*. London: Routledge (159–79).

World Travel and Tourism Council (1993) *Progress and Priorities*. Madrid: WTTC.

5

Gender and Sustainability in Mediterranean Island Tourism

Julie Scott

Introduction

Although 'community' has become a regular feature of the language of sustainability, the discussion remains, on the whole, remarkably gender-blind. The approach common in the literature, whereby 'community' is treated as a 'black-box' category whose contents are never unpacked, generally fails to recognize sociocultural heterogeneity embedded in differences of status, class, gender and ethnicity. It also reflects a more general problem with the way society is conceptualized, all too frequently subsumed into a category of the natural environment, susceptible to technical solutions which rely on the use of tools such as 'impact analysis', 'carrying capacity', and 'tourist density' borrowed from environmental management techniques. These are extremely blunt instruments for use in a sociocultural context because they take little account of questions of agency, subjectivity and choice that characterize human activity. Their currency reflects a still unresolved confusion about the concept of sustainability and its applicability to culture and society (Harrison, 1996).

I make these points because they are fundamental to any discussion of gender issues in the context of sustainability. Straddling 'nature' and 'culture', gender is perhaps *the* primordial cultural category, structuring not only social roles and relationships but also the symbolic dispositions of widely disparate societies.[1] Culturally constructed gender relations and ideologies of sexuality form the basis not only for the division of labour but also the ownership and transmission of property (via marriage and inheritance) which are crucial factors in tourism development. They also inform the ethos of liberation, hedonism and eroticism which underlie the 'sexualized' nature of travel and tourism (Richter, 1995), as well as the images of 'domesticated sexuality' and wholesome fun of the family holiday (Marshment, 1997). At the level of social symbolism, women often occupy a contradictory position encompassing both tradition and modernizing forces, plus continuity and potential disruption. This has the result that societies may be particularly sensitive, or even resistant to developments that bring changes in the roles, behaviour or controls on women and girls (Scott, 1995; Harrison, 1996). Gendered relations not only shape tourism, but are themselves constructed *within* tourism (Kinnaird and Hall, 1994; Swain, 1995; Sinclair, 1997). To introduce the topic of gender is, therefore, to acknowledge the sociocultural context in which gendered actors operate, and which influences outcomes, such as the ability of women to participate in and benefit from tourism development, and, indeed, how these outcomes are judged.

My aim in this chapter is not to catalogue the facts and figures on women's involvement in Mediterranean island tourism (statistical data disaggregated for gender and for islands are, in any case, hard to find). Rather, I aim to suggest a framework within which the gender dynamics of tourism in the region can be understood, and which can also be applied to the case study chapters that follow. Such a framework, in short, will permit women's tourism employment in, say, Samos, to be encompassed as part of the same discussion with handicraft businesses in Sardinia, expatriate residents in Malta, migrant labour in Cyprus, and discotheques in Majorca. The framework I propose rests on adopting a more sociological approach to the concepts of sustainability, culture and society than that current in much of the literature.

Sustainability, Culture and Society

The Brundtland Report proposed a definition of sustainability which encompasses social and distributional justice (de Kadt, 1990; Harrison, 1996), but this dimension of sustainability has arguably come a poor third to environmental and broad economic concerns (Craik, 1995). Even the corrective of a concept of 'cultural sustainability' is often marred by failure to engage seriously with the concept of 'culture'. Craik, for example, despite including an economic and public consultation element in her cultural indicators of tourism impacts, works with an implicit folk model of culture as embodied in the local traditions of bounded communities acted on by 'external elements' which introduce 'extrinsic tourist values' (1995: 90). Such approaches ignore the theoretical input of disciplines such as anthropology, which stresses the interpenetration of the global and the local, and the extent to which culture is internally and externally differentiated and embedded in social and economic relations (Eriksen, 1993; Goody, 1992). As a consequence, there has been a tendency for sociocultural sustainability to be conflated with issues of authenticity and the 'loss of culture', which, as de Kadt points out, remain on the whole '[issues] of importance only to the tourists, or to the hosts insofar as they want to please the tourists' (1990: 5–6).

Change may be welcome to some sections of the community, and unwelcome to others. Attempts to fend off change in the name of traditional values, especially where these changes challenge entrenched gender roles, may even be inimical to the goals of social and distributional justice (Harrison, 1996).

In the discussion that follows, I address primarily the social equity aspect of sustainability, and attempt to link this to the concept of the gendered stakeholder in Mediterranean islands. Although gender, of course, refers to both men and women, for the purposes of this chapter I interpret this as the need to gain some understanding of the characteristics of *female* involvement in tourism development, since the particularities of women's experience are too often subsumed within an all-encompassing male/neuter category. Any serious engagement with social justice and distributional issues must pay particular attention to the situation of women. Women as a group are often excluded from economic development and their position is frequently made much worse by the consequences of gender-insensitive state policies (Rogers, 1980). A number of studies indicate that women and men do not benefit equally from tourism development (Harvey *et al.*, 1995). Furthermore, it has been recognized that there are specific ways in which women's tourism activities can contribute to sustainability objectives. Women's tourism enterprises are typically small-scale, low capital-intensive activities, often sustaining local farming, and the money they earn is directed largely to the care and education of children (Hermans, 1983; Garcia-Ramon *et al.*, 1995; Hemmati *et al.*, 1999). But women in tourism also face particular obstacles, in the form of barriers to training, credit and public influence, and the limitations imposed by socially ascribed gender roles. In some cases, women's activities are viewed as a threat to sustainability. Levels of prostitution, for example, are used as a standard indicator of negative cultural impact (Craik, 1995). Later in the chapter, I consider these specific aspects of women's tourism involvement under three main heads: employment and entrepreneurship; migration; and leisure and consumption.

By focusing on the stakeholder concept, I want to get away from the 'impact analysis' approach to sustainability, and highlight women's roles as active participants in and beneficiaries of tourism development, within the opportunities and constraints of particular social, cultural and economic contexts. This brings us again to the problem of a workable definition of culture. The approach I adopt here is Goody's, who writes: 'the cultural is the social viewed from another perspective, not a distinct analytic entity' (1992: 30). What, then, does it mean to think about 'gender and tourism on Mediterranean islands'? In order to begin to answer that question, we need first to unpack the implicit models of culture and society wrapped up in the terms 'Mediterranean' and 'islands'.

'Mediterranean Culture'

The Mediterranean region is large and diverse, encompassing countries from three continents, with populations embracing Islam, Judaism, Roman Catholicism and Eastern Orthodox faiths and speaking a multiplicity of languages and dialects. The 162 inhabited islands of the Mediterranean present enormous variation in size, population, level of urbanization and degree of isolation from and proximity to other islands or mainland urban centres (Kolodny, 1966). The intra-regional complexities alone are considerable; what then of the added complexities of relations with the nation-states of which most of the islands form part, of supra-national entities such as the European Union, and global relationships into which islands are drawn in the process of tourism development? Tourism itself, which one might think of as a unifying factor in this, the busiest tourism region in the world, takes diverse forms, from the Balearics which have become a byword for mass tourism and its associated problems, to the nascent and struggling tourism of Corsica, Sicily and Northern Cyprus.

The tendency to identify 'culture' with specific bounded communities is widespread in the tourism literature, and is particularly marked in reference to islands (Scott, 1995). But for anthropologists working in the region, the concept of a unifying 'Mediterranean culture' has long been problematic (Davis, 1977; Herzfeld, 1984). Claims for the cultural unity of the Mediterranean were for many years based on the prevalence of a specific pattern of gender interaction and ideology referred to as the 'honour and shame complex', characterized by notions of social worth based on sexual reputation and the control of women (Giovannini, 1987), segregation of the sexes, and strong mother–son bonds (Gilmore, 1987). But as Goddard (1994) has pointed out, preoccupation with the cultural unity of the Mediterranean, and in particular with codes of honour and shame as the defining feature of that unity, has led to a theoretical dead end, since attempts to explain social conditions and change in terms of 'Mediterranean culture' cannot move beyond the descriptive elaboration of 'traditional values'. They also fail to take account of the complex political, religious, institutional and economic affiliations alluded to above, which produce internal variation within the region as well as commonalities with other places outside the region. Goddard argues that the particularities of the very real cultural constraints affecting women in the Mediterranean have to be evaluated in the context of these wider relationships.

This tension is implicit in the very phrase 'Mediterranean islands', juxtaposing as it does the idea of overarching and unifying culture with the fragmentation of apparently self-evidently bounded local units. Before moving on to consider what happens on Mediterranean islands, it is worth examining in more detail what they actually *are*.

What are Mediterranean Islands?

The 'island' has come to stand for what is unique and isolated, but the pervasiveness of the metaphor can obscure the extent to which island populations are actually enmeshed in wider global and regional systems and structures (Eriksen, 1993). This fact can also be (consciously) obscured by island people themselves, who at times choose to emphasize their insularity and uniqueness, and at others their interconnectedness to the wider world.[2] Despite a long history of incorporation into larger geopolitical entities – regional and global empires such as the Ottoman and British, the medieval kingdom of Aragon (comprising parts of Spain, Italy and North Africa as well as Sardinia, Sicily, Malta and the Balearics), and latterly, mainland-based nation–states – the islands have frequently continued to maintain distinct local customs and practices contrary to mainland laws. It is interesting to note, for example, that island customs with regard to women's rights to own and deal in property after marriage were often considerably more liberal than the laws to which women on the mainland were subject.[3]

As the dependent peripheries of distant centres of power and in the absence of effective local state mechanisms or active concepts of citizenship, islanders of the Mediterranean have long relied on patronage networks in order to influence events and obtain resources (Schneider *et al.*, 1972; Boissevain, 1976). The phenomenon of mass migration, a response to conditions of poverty and scarcity for much of the nineteenth and twentieth centuries, extended existing local informal networks to include family and 'neighbours' living in the world's major towns and cities (Lopreato, 1967; Cronin, 1970). Associations of islanders living abroad and maintaining active links with 'home' have often been important investors in island tourism and thus influential in guiding the course of tourism development on the islands.[4]

Substantive patron–client relationships are usually between men, even though the point of connection may be through women (for example, between a woman's male relatives and her husband), and are activated by appeals to local identity and kinship. But alongside these informal networks, the European Union has in recent years put in place a series of formal networks which appeal to – in fact, seek to create – a sense of a common European identity and citizenship (Shore and Black, 1994). The Committee of the Regions, with its remit to promote greater cohesiveness within the EU, directs resources to peripheral regions, and to women as the marginalized citizens of peripheral regions, through projects backed by the European Regional Development Fund and New Opportunities for Women. Such projects in Sardinia, for example, have included the establishment of local equal opportunities offices, assistance to women in business, and training and public awareness programmes (Directorate-General XVI, 1997).

Incorporation into EU structures marks the latest stage in a long history of fluctuating island boundaries, which challenges the stereotype of the

autonomous isolated community, and potentially has far-reaching consequences for the position of women. Insularity, then, for the purposes of the
current discussion, is a relative term. It requires us to set the specificities of
local conditions, society and culture, in the context of wider state,
institutional and informal relationships. Paradoxically, the difference between
islands and other peripheral regions on the mainland may be precisely that
islands are *more* integrated into global networks, since, as Braudel's (1973)
study of the history of the Mediterranean illustrates, it is mountains that
divide, while the sea unites. This effect is particularly marked in tourism
because of the powerful attraction of island destinations (Conlin and Baum,
1995). While not all Mediterranean islands are full members of the EU, it is
worth bearing in mind the following comment from the Balearic Islands
General Information publication:

> Because of their tourist 'export' ... the Balearic economy is so open to the
> exterior that before Spain's entry into the European Economic Community
> (1986) it was said that the Balearic Islands had already been in Europe for more
> than 30 years. (IBATUR 1996: 16)

Women's Involvement in Tourism: Employment, Entrepreneurship and the Gender Division of Labour

Throughout the Mediterranean region, island communities struggling to
make a living from farming and fishing have embraced the economic
opportunities offered by tourism. It is often women who are the first to seize
the initiative, finding that tourism is an activity where their traditional areas
of competence, and cultural norms of hospitality, can be used to generate
income. Zarkia (1996) gives a detailed account of the early stages of tourism
on the island of Skyros, describing how the tourists themselves initiated the
process of commercialization, insisting on paying for accommodation freely
given in the spirit of hospitality. Women quickly adapted to the implicit
demands for a 'service' and the standards and extra work that requires. The
'duty' of hospitality has been transformed into a business.

> Now they know that to receive a 'tourist' means work and money ... Hot
> water is needed and clean sheets and towels. But the benefits are important.
> With this money they can finish the dowry house for their daughters, or they
> can pay for the children to study. (Zarkia 1996: 164)

Two factors have favoured women's involvement in the early stages of
tourism. The Mediterranean pattern of bilateral partible inheritance, giving
women equal rights to inherited property with men, and the tradition
common in many parts of the Mediterranean of endowing women with a
house on their marriage, mean that women have frequently found themselves
in possession of an asset made valuable through tourism. In some cases, this

has been an unexpected windfall, a result of daughters being bequeathed land near the seashore or an old town or village house, while more fertile inland fields and fishing boats were passed on to the sons of the family.[5]

Ownership of an asset does not, however, necessarily confer control. It is usually households – like 'community', another black-box concept (Harris, 1984) – rather than individual women, who make decisions about the disposal of property, the control of business run in it and the distribution of resources generated by it. On the Greek Aegean island of Samos, the shift away from agricultural production to the use of dowry houses in tourism has transformed women's position within the household economy and strengthened female kinship networks (Galani-Moutafi, 1993). In Skyros, on the other hand, where dowry houses have also come to represent an important economic asset, sons and brothers have started to challenge women's traditional rights, at the same time as they, as future husbands, insist on a good dowry for their wife. Zarkia concludes that: 'For the women this effect of tourism has not been favourable. Though the value of their property has risen, it has not meant a similar increase in their power' (1996: 151).

In North Cyprus, men generally run bed and breakfast businesses with little participation from their wives, even when it is the women who nominally own the property. The pattern here is influenced by the range of work possibilities open to women and men, the low status locally of the small-scale accommodation sector, the availability of a cheap migrant labour supply from Turkey, and the lack of a female tradition of entrepreneurship. Business requiring, for example, the registration of documents, visits to public offices, or making and maintaining informal networks for information and influence, generally remains a male province (Scott, 1997).

While in the early stages it may be relatively easy for women to earn some income by letting rooms to tourists, businesses become subject to increasing regulation as tourism assumes greater importance in the economic life of the community as a whole. Standards of safety, hygiene, and service quality imposed by government ministries, local authorities and professional tourism associations, can involve households in substantial financial layout on their property, and increase the burden of work on women. They may also call for expertise beyond the informally acquired skills of women running accommodation businesses as a spin-off of their domestic routine. By 1993, in Skyros the informal standards of service that had recently evolved from traditional hospitality were no longer considered appropriate to the competitive image of the island in an international market place. Zarkia reports mounting criticism by local businessmen concerning the lack of professionalism evident in 'the dirtiness of the houses, the poor organisation of house rentals, contradictory behaviour to foreigners, and the selection of the customers by the women' (Zarkia, 1996: 157). Elsewhere, however, women's agrotourism cooperatives have been successful in enabling women to pool skills and resources, and to tap assistance from local municipalities. The Petra agrotourism cooperative on the island of Lesbos was established in 1983 with 50 members. Each member lets between one and four rooms. Of the original 50, 15 have since successfully expanded their accommodation and left the cooperative to run their own businesses independently (Teta Rally, 1998, personal communication).

The support which the Petra cooperative received from the local municipality is significant not only as an example of community support for women's contribution through tourism, but also as recognition of the value of the 'quality market' to which this kind of tourism product now appeals, as 'cultural' and 'village' tourism take their place alongside the conventional '4S' attractions of the Mediterranean beach holiday. Agrotourism businesses with female proprietors are included in the high quality brochures sent out, for example, by the Republic of Cyprus Tourism Organization, with e-mail now adding to the range of contacts and networks available to women entrepreneurs.

Involvement in mass tourism

Despite the developments in cultural and village tourism, mass tourism remains the dominant form in the Mediterranean, particularly in the Balearics, Malta, southern Cyprus, and many of the Greek islands. The 'professionalization' that accompanies the development of a mass market tourism product is often criticized for restricting women to a narrow range of jobs (notably cleaning, reception, and secretarial work) and excluding them from managerial positions, compared to the small-scale businesses where women are frequently owners and managers (Scott, 1997). The gender division of labour reflects locally held values and beliefs about the innate skills of men and women, which are closely allied to ideas about behaviour appropriate to each sex (Ecevit, 1991). These norms are not set in stone, and as Brandes (1987) has observed, communities will modify them according to changing material circumstances. There is, in any case, considerable variation in the way they are applied within societies, depending on age, social class, urban or rural location, and so on. 'Traditional' values can be mobilized to justify women's marginal position as a reserve labour force when employment opportunities for men are scarce.

Concern about male unemployment in Malta during the 1970s, for example, led to government policies promoting specifically male employment and, in 1974, legislation which 'made it mandatory to employ males rather than females wherever possible' (Boissevain and Inglott, 1979: 272). Some 25 per cent of female hotel employees had already lost their jobs during the temporary slump in tourist arrivals in 1972, compared to 15 per cent of male hotel employees. In North Cyprus, in contrast to the situation 20 years ago when tourism employment was not considered 'respectable' for women, work in tourist hotels is now regarded as a legitimate and prestigious source of female white-collar employment. This gradual shift in opinion reflects not only changes in the status of the tourism sector, but also raised expectations due to increased female access to education and qualifications and relative lack of other comparable employment opportunities (Scott, 1997). In fact, both the female labour force, and the labour requirements of tourism businesses, are highly diverse, with age, level of education, family situation and social class all important factors affecting both women's and employers' employment strategies.

Mass tourism opens up the range of opportunities available to women, not only as a result of direct employment in hotels but also through indirect and induced employment (from travel agencies to car hire offices and bureaux de change, from grocers to hairdressers, from bank clerks and estate agents to civil servants). This has occurred in, for example, a region such as Calvia in Majorca which, thanks to tourism, has become one of the richest municipalities in Europe and, at the time of writing, has one of the few female mayors in Spain (Selwyn, 1994; Council of European Municipalities and Regions, 1998). In the case of Sardinia – not yet a mass market destination – women's entrepreneurial activities have been given a boost by the tourism industry, both in the small-scale workshops producing the textile handicrafts for which Sardinia is famous, and in a 'higher-tech' business purifying and bottling drinking water. These business initiatives have also been backed by EU support (Directorate-General XVI, 1997).

The expansion of the service sector in general is associated with increased levels of female employment. In Corsica, service sector employment has doubled over the past 20 years, and in 1990 accounted for more than 70 per cent of jobs and 75 per cent of the island's GDP. Tourism, along with the public sector, has been a source of new jobs since the mid-1980s. Yet despite the fact that more women have entered the labour market as a result of these developments, female unemployment started to climb again in the late 1980s, and continues to lag behind female employment rates in mainland France (SCAD-plus, 1990). These trends have to be seen in the context of a stagnant island economy with 62 per cent of household incomes coming from government sources, and a relatively low level of local involvement in the tourist industry (Richez, 1996; Assemblée Nationale, 1998).

Migration

Tourism has reversed the flow of migration in the Mediterranean islands. Since the middle of the twentieth century, when it was still marked by heavy out-migration that threatened the sustainability of many island communities, the net flow of people is now into the region, for work, both seasonal and permanent, and for retirement and settlement. In addition, the draw of tourism employment in towns has stimulated rural–urban migration among the island populations themselves. Majorca has received a massive influx of labour from the mainland to meet the demand for workers, with the population of the municipality of Calvia increasing six-fold between 1950 and 1986. According to the 1991 census, of the 20,500 residents of Calvia, 9,000 were born in the Balearics; 9,000 were born in mainland Spain; and 2,500 were born elsewhere in Europe (Selwyn, 1994). As Selwyn points out, these categories conceal a huge gap in the situations of EU foreigners, who have three different votes to use if they want to, and the precarious position of unenfranchised non-EU migrants.[6] During the same period (1950–86) the population of the inland agricultural town of Petra fell by 50 per cent, indicating the high level of internal migration as well as migration from outside the island (Selwyn, 1994).

Women, like men, move in search of work and a better life, both independently and with their families. The types of work and social roles available to them are a function of both their gender and their outsider status. To these considerations must be added the gender-related values and ideas generated within tourism and which, with regard to women, are often heavily laced with moral judgements (Zinovieff, 1991; Scott, 1995).

Motivation and characteristics of female migrants

It is worth stressing again the diversity masked in the catch-all term 'female migrants'. It embraces British travel company reps and Filippina domestic servants in southern Cyprus; Romanian croupiers and second-generation Cypriot-Australians in Northern Cyprus; Spanish mainland chambermaids in the Balearics; expatriate settlers in Malta; former migrants returning from Athens to the Greek island of Anafi; and so on. Motivations for migration vary. Social and political conditions, lack of jobs or low wages at home are common push factors, but women may also be drawn by a desire to travel or experience a different lifestyle – or a combination of these. Romanian croupiers interviewed in Kyrenia, Northern Cyprus, for example, listed among their motives: a desire to see the world; to escape from social unrest; the opportunity to earn more money; or the wish to save for some particular expense, such as a house in Romania or, in one case, to pay for a younger sister's education (Scott, 1995). In some cases the economic motivation is less salient. Bianchi and Clarke (1998) identify an itinerant, predominantly young and hedonistic, transnational workforce from the countries of the post-industrial north, for whom casual employment with mostly expatriate-owned businesses provides a means to finance a travelling lifestyle. For former emigrants, or the daughters of former emigrants, tourism makes it economically viable to return to the island that they – or their parents – still regard as home.

Demand for female migrant labour

There are a number of reasons why a local labour force may not be able to meet the demand for labour generated by tourism development. There may simply not be enough local workers available, especially for large-scale mass tourism, or they may not have the requisite skills. Employers may not be willing to pay the wage levels demanded locally; or the local labour force may avoid certain types of jobs.

Work in the hospitality industry is strongly gender-typed, with women generally preferred both for 'unskilled' (because 'innate') domestic work, and for front-office jobs requiring frequent smiling and a caring demeanour (Urry, 1990). Beyond this, both skills and status are important determinants of how female migrant workers are inserted into the workforce. Language skills and familiarity with the culture of the tourist market are important assets, and in Magaluf, Majorca, young northern European women are sought-after employees for tour companies, car hire firms, bureaux de change, cafés and bars, etc., which are themselves often owned by expatriate residents on the island (Hazel Andrews, 1998, personal communication). Hotel and apartment cleaning jobs may attract both local and migrant women depending on the pay rates and the availability of other jobs. Waldren (1996) reports that younger Majorcan women, who have benefited from the economic development and increased educational opportunities stimulated by tourism, are reluctant to take jobs such as cleaning.[7] In contrast, when teenagers took up summer jobs on the Greek island of Anafi (in 1993 still in the early stages of tourism development), it was the local girls who cleaned and prepared rented rooms, while returned migrants from Athens waited on table (Kenna, 1993). The availability of women to do paid cleaning work follows a consistent social and economic hierarchy. In the past, conditions of harsh poverty often forced families to send their daughters into domestic service in the households of the rich (Esmeijer, 1984, for Malta; Argyrou, 1996, for Cyprus), despite a strong antipathy to allowing women of the family to do domestic work 'for another man' — reported for Sicily (Giovannini, 1987), Mykonos (Stott, 1995), Malta (Briguglio and Briguglio, 1996), and undoubtedly also current on other islands. In the more affluent conditions of today, the demand for domestic servants on islands such as Cyprus and Majorca is now met by women from the poorest areas of less developed regions of the world, such as south-east Asia and Africa (reports in *Cyprus Weekly* 1998; Selwyn, 1994).

The range of jobs considered not suitable or respectable for local women varies from 'chambermaiding' in Malta (Black, 1996), waitressing, bar work and tour guiding, which have not yet been totally accepted for Turkish Cypriot women (Scott, 1995, 1997), to jobs which comprise an overt sexual element such as entertainers, night club hostesses and prostitutes. Such jobs are not, of course, new, and have generally been associated with women who were in some way marginal or outside conventional local society. Friedl (1967), for example, comments that in Greece girls accompanying musicians and singing with them at village festivals were considered 'shameless'. The availability of a migrant workforce to take on these jobs provides a clear group of outsiders for this role. While all migrant workers, both men and women, are vulnerable to some extent − for example, in Majorca, where the trend towards self-catering accommodation threatens the livelihoods of the Spanish migrant workforce (Selwyn, 1994) − those most vulnerable are probably the single women without the benefits or protection of EU citizenship working as domestic servants or in the sex industry.[8]

'Leisured migrants'

Brief mention should be made of one final category of female migrants: that is, the migrants of leisure who are permanent or semi-permanent residents on the islands. Again, it would be misleading to think of this as an homogeneous category; conversely, they are characterized by some common features including a combination of relative privilege, outsider status and gender role. Two published studies of expatriate residents in Malta (Esmeijer, 1984) and the Majorcan village of Deia (Waldren, 1996) show women attempting to engage in the life of the island. Female settlers in post-independence Malta in the 1960s and 1970s were very active in the movement for the emancipation of (local) women, and also in 'reading circles': 'trying to improve Maltese teenagers' (often the children of their Maltese friends and neighbours) knowledge of English, by discussing books borrowed from the British Council library in Valletta' (Esmeijer, 1984: 84). Their style of involvement reveals their own background in the colonial service, living out their retirement in a former British colony.

It was to prove increasingly problematic in the context of a Maltese Labour government committed to disengagement from its colonial ties and to reducing British influence on the island. In contrast, the attempts of the (generally younger) British residents of Deia to integrate themselves into the life of the community, by joining in activities such as local folk-dancing lessons and forming friendships within the village, showed greater deference to Majorcan cultural concerns. But other issues have highlighted a sharp divide in the interests of settlers and locals. Plans for a road development to the village were opposed by settlers who wanted to maintain the village's exclusivity, and supported by locals in favour of improving transport links and economic opportunities. The resulting dispute revealed the existence of grievances and resentment on the part of locals, of which the settlers had previously been unaware (Waldren, 1996).

The influence of expatriate residents on island life is likely to increase in the future, as growing numbers buy up property, and EU citizens exercise their right to vote in local elections (Hearst, 1998). There is potential for the development of a powerful expatriate lobby in closely fought municipalities such as Calvia. Throughout the autumn of 1998 the expatriate newspaper *The Majorca Daily Bulletin* urged foreign residents to register to vote, with headlines proclaiming 'Foreign residents could "tip the balance" in local elections' (1998b: 13). The situation poses some interesting questions. What role will foreign female residents play in the life of the island? Waldren's observations of some similarities in the gender constraints on local and expatriate women in Deia suggest that their role may be limited. The British women 'are seen in the same social spaces that local women use and like local women have little time for café life. Women, both foreign and local, provide the support system that allows their men to enter into public activities' (Waldren, 1996: 194). By contrast, in the run-up to the municipal elections, at least one British woman was being tipped as a possible candidate (*Majorca Daily Bulletin*, 1998a). Will conflicts of interests between locals and foreign residents polarize the sustainability debate still further, pitting environmental concerns against local development goals in a contest of outsider versus insider – as happened in Deia? Are there gender and/or national differences in the way expatriates relate to their foreign home that will be reflected in voting behaviour? What other factors might influence the ways female foreign residents use their vote? These are all issues that require further research.

The Fruits of Tourism: Women's Leisure and Consumption

Fears about the pace of changes accompanying tourism development in many Mediterranean islands are often expressed as misgivings about the effects on the family, the young and sexual morality. Growing equality between the sexes is sometimes traced to a process of liberalization, introduced from the outside, which threatens the integrity of island culture and, by implication, island identity (Picornel *et al.*, 1997). Such concerns focus squarely on women as the boundary markers of identity, implying that they are particularly vulnerable to tourism's 'demonstration effect'.

As early as 1978, Stott argued from data gathered in Mykonos that such changes as had occurred in patterns of consumption and behaviour were explicable in terms of increased income, TV, and the diffusion of Greek mainland fashions, rather than the emulation of foreign tourists. Indeed, evidence tends to indicate that the behaviour of tourists, particularly in its more excessive forms, is rejected by local residents, and the places frequented by tourists avoided (Black, 1996). What is striking is, in fact, the persistence of underlying gender norms and values despite the changes in employment, income and social opportunities for women. The Church in Malta has long been influential in upholding conservative traditions regarding women. In one village at least the priest has both adapted to new conditions and maintained the Church's position as moral guardian, by acting as intermediary in the recruitment of village women for tourism employment (Black, 1996). Black also notes the continued importance for women's reputation of keeping to high standards of housework, and the consequent pressures on women of combining both work and the maintenance of a proper home.

'Traditional' priorities are maintained, too, in the uses to which women's income from tourism is put, although there are differences between the generations, and probably also according to the general level of economic development of the community. Women who started taking in tourists on the island of Skyros put the money they made towards the education of their children (Zarkia, 1996). Tourism income is also used to build bigger and better-appointed dowry houses, enabling daughters to make better marriages. In Mykonos, the daughters themselves put their earnings towards their own dowry house (Stott, 1996), but in Samos the burden still falls on parents, with daughters using their income for personal consumption (Galani-Moutafi, 1993).

The theme of the increased workload and other pressures on women is taken up by a number of writers. Kousis notes that, in Crete, women working in family tourism businesses find not only that they have more work and less leisure time than before, but that their work is more isolated, compared to agricultural work previously done in cooperation with kin outside the immediate nuclear family (Kousis, 1989). Long-standing social relationships are also disrupted when houses are sold for tourism businesses, breaking up neighbourhoods that are an important focus for women's sociability (Waldren, 1996). By contrast, women's experience in Samos, according to the account given by Galani-Moutafi (1993), was quite different. In that case, men owned the productive resources for agriculture, and male kin relationships structured the cooperative labour of households. Tourism activity, in contrast, utilized female-owned assets (the dowry house), and favoured cooperation among female kin living in neighbourhoods of households related through sisters.

'Differential right of access to space is a common cultural form for expressing superiority and inferiority in social position' (Friedl, 1967: 99). Women's avoidance of public spaces has been noted for many different Mediterranean islands, including Malta, Sicily, Majorca, and Cyprus (Cronin, 1970; Black, 1996; Waldren, 1996; Scott, 1997), and their appearance in those spaces might well be understood as indicating an improvement in status. Women involved in agrotourism cooperatives have commented on their increased mobility and access to public spaces as a valued by-product of their business success, a sign of their improved status and confidence (Castelberg-Koulma, 1991; Teta Rally, 1998, Petra co-op, personal communication). Similarly, the unchaperoned presence of young unmarried women in bars, cafés and other public places indicates a relaxation in the restrictions to which women have been traditionally subject.

As Giovannini (1987) observes of women in Sicily (not specifically in the context of tourism), women can enjoy more freedom of movement at the same time as people still cling to long-standing codes of female chastity. The controls on the behaviour of women become a matter of family negotiation rather than rigid norms enforced by the community in general. The litmus test for the behaviour of young women is still, on the whole, what the likely consequences will be for their marriage prospects (Argyrou, 1996). In the case of Greek Cypriot women of the elite social classes, it has been argued that since their contacts are generally limited to young men of equally high social standing, indiscretions are not likely to lead to unsuitable marriages, and so more licence can be permitted (Attalides, 1976; Argyrou, 1996). Black (1996) also notes that in Malta, girls of the non-elite tend to avoid tourists, whereas elites like to flout local rules. In Northern Cyprus, most female socializing is done in the home, or closely chaperoned at family occasions such as weddings, although it is becoming more common to see mixed groups of young Turkish Cypriots out together. In fact, there still remains a sharp gender divide in terms of mobility, with men of all ages enjoying considerable freedom to form friendships and liaisons with tourists, however temporary (Boissevain and Inglott, 1979; Zinovieff, 1991; Black, 1996; Zarkia, 1996).

Ethnographic data paint a picture infinitely more varied and complex than mechanistic social impact or demonstration effect models suggest. The very real concerns which some sections of communities express about the socially, morally and culturally corrosive effects of tourism are part of the picture, but not the whole picture. As Goddard observes, it is important 'to identify the specificities of local contexts. We can thus avert the risk of reifying into "tradition" what in fact may be issues of power, domination and inequality' (1994: 65).

Conclusion: Implications for Sustainable Policy and Practice

A recent report for the United Nations Commission on Sustainable Development highlights two important reasons why gender perspectives need to be integrated into sustainable tourism policy. The first reason is ethical. If tourism is to be truly sustainable, it has to be socially equitable as well as 'green', and the particular needs of women as stakeholders – employees, entrepreneurs and members of destination area communities – need to be addressed. The second reason is pragmatic. Women's input is vital to finding workable solutions to the problems sustainable policies seek to address.

> Without women participating equally in capacity building and education, at the workplace, in policy-formulation and decision-making, we will neither achieve a proper understanding of the problems, nor find the necessary solutions or be able to implement them. (Hemmati *et al.*, 1999: 2)

With these points in mind, I would like to draw out two main implications for sustainable policy and practice on Mediterranean islands.

The first concerns the role of women as social actors with a stake in sustainable development. Planners and policy-makers cannot afford to treat women as an undifferentiated group. What I hope emerges from the foregoing discussion is the diversity in women's situations – in terms of wealth and income, family status, generational differences, education, nationality, and so on – which all affect women's expectations and opportunities. At the same time, there are characteristic features of women's engagement with tourism that are shared. Women are 'actors seeking to achieve desirable ends through culturally structured methods' (Galani-Moutafi, 1993: 245). The gender constraints on women – governing, for example, division of labour, access to and control of property and resources (including skills and knowledge) and public visibility – are culturally mediated, but are also modified by the impact of state policies, institutional relationships, and the impact of wider social and economic conditions. The traditional institution of the dowry house produces different outcomes for the women of Samos, Skyros, Mykonos and Crete, in terms of the level of independence and conditions of work they enjoy, depending largely on the extent to which other economic opportunities and valuable assets are available to men. State and EU immigration policies, combined with local ideas about social status, sexuality, and the division of labour, together with the up-and-downturns of the tourism market, make migrant women workers particularly vulnerable. Changes in destination image can serve to marginalize women's small-scale room-letting activities, if resources are not made available so that they can make the transition to a professionalized tourism sector. Women's domestic responsibilities and lack of access to the public arena can prevent them from seeking office and participating in policy-making.

These features of women's tourism involvement call for an approach to policy and planning that is simultaneously integrated and disaggregated. Integrated, because it is important to understand how these different factors inter-relate. Disaggregated, because it is also important to recognize the specificities of each case, and to establish disaggregated indicators for identifying, implementing and monitoring policies.

This brings me to my second point, which concerns the conceptual tools for achieving these ends. Calling for the integration of gender perspectives into sustainable policy and planning amounts to calling for the integration of a proper sociological perspective, taking full account of the extent and implications of social and cultural relations which are complex, often contradictory, and extend beyond the boundaries of village, town and island. This requires that a qualitative approach be incorporated into field research, identifying a range of stakeholders which includes women and their specific interests, and being always alert to the gender implications of what people say and do.

Acknowledgements

My thanks to Teta Rally, secretary of the Petra women's agrotourism cooperative, and to Janet Bagg (University of Kent at Canterbury) and Hazel Andrews (doctoral candidate, University of North London) for their contributions made as a result of fieldwork. I should also like to thank colleagues David Harrison and Jonathan Karkut for their helpful comments.

Notes

1. There is a wealth of anthropological literature on gender, which provides ample demonstration of this point. Key publications on this topic include: Reiter (1975); Rosaldo and Lamphere (1974); Ortner and Whitehead (1981); and Moore (1988).

2. Of the villagers of Deia, Majorca, Waldren writes:

   The conceptual boundaries of the village expand and contract in different contexts. The boundaries can include family members who live in Palma and as far away as France, whilst some people who live in the mapped area of the village are not conceived of as 'of the village' at all. (1996: 55)

3. For example, Zarkia writes of the Greek island of Skyros:

   The custom that designates the dowry as property of the woman and her matriline was always respected and applied as an unwritten moral law. Until 1983, state law, as opposed to custom, considered the dowry as the property of the husband and transmittable as part of his patrimony. In Skyros, the custom, being stronger that the law, always identified the dowry goods with the matriline: it was scandal for a widower to claim the dowry of his late wife. (1996: 148)

   The women of Majorca were granted a special dispensation by King James I to dispose of their own property as they pleased after marriage (Waldren, 1996: 69). An exception to the general rule appears to have been Corsica, where tradition favoured the consolidation of the patrimony by passing on the inheritance to the sons of the family, or often to a single son who seemed most adept at managing it. 'A girl's dowry generally contained only moveable goods, and it entailed the girl's renunciation of any part in the inheritance, a practice forbidden by the Civil Code, but nonetheless perpetuated until the end of the 19th century' (Chiva, 1963: 112).

4. One such organization, the Anafiot Migrants Association Committee in Athens, financed the construction and equipping of a village bakery on the island of Anafi. As a result restaurateurs on the island no longer needed to buy their bread from the mainland (Kenna, 1993). Associations of migrant islanders often try to influence island tourism development away from mass tourism and in the direction of conservation; by contrast, as individual investors, expatriate islanders and returned migrants are often in the forefront of mass tourism development (Kenna, 1993; Zarkia, 1996).

5. Though not in the category of Mediterranean *islands*, this phenomenon has been reported by Hermans for the Spanish seaside town of Cambrils (1983), and I was also informed of similar cases in the Turkish resort of Bodrum. Similar cases on the island of Corsica have also caused local comment (Janet Bagg, personal communication).

6. There are about 2,000 residents of North African origin, mostly male, working in agriculture, tourism and construction. In addition, single female migrants from countries such as the Philippines and the Dominican Republic form part of a 'developing underclass of workers', employed in domestic service and prostitution (Selwyn, 1994: 28).

7. The Balearic islands are the third richest region of Spain after Madrid and Gerona, and per capita income in the islands is about 35 per cent higher than in Spain as a whole (Hughes, 1994).

8. Particularly given the rumoured Mafia involvement in the organized trafficking of women in the Mediterranean (Selwyn, 1994). On the vulnerability of Eastern European croupiers in Northern Cyprus see Scott (1995).

References

Argyrou, V. (1996) Tradition and modernity in the Mediterranean: the wedding as symbolic struggle. *Cambridge Studies in Social and Cultural Anthropology.* Cambridge: Cambridge University Press.

Assemblée Nationale (1998) *Rapport fait au nom de la commission d'enquête (1) sur l'utilisation des fonds publics et la gestion des services publics en Corse*, No. 1077. Paris: Assemblée Nationale.

Attalides, M. (1976) Changing configurations of Greek Cypriot kinship. In J.G. Peristiany (ed.), *Kinship and Modernization in Mediterranean Society*. Rome: The Centre for Mediterranean Studies (73–90).

Bianchi, R. and Clarke, A. (1998) Identifying the cultural configurations of tourism's transnational workforce: cosmopolitans, locals and neo-proletarians. Paper presented to the XIVth World Congress of Sociology, International Sociological Association, Montreal, 26 July–2 August.

Black, A. (1996) Negotiating the tourist gaze: the example of Malta. In J. Boissevain (ed.), *Coping with Tourists: European Reactions to Mass Tourism*. Oxford: Berghahn Books (112–42).

Boissevain, J. (1976) Uniformity and diversity in the Mediterranean: an essay in interpretation. In J.G. Peristiany (ed.), *Kinship and Modernization in Mediterranean Society*. Rome: The Centre for Mediterranean Studies (1–11).

Boissevain, J. and Inglott, P.S. (1979) Tourism in Malta. In E. de Kadt (ed.), *Tourism: Passport to Development?* Published for the World Bank/UNESCO. Oxford: Oxford University Press (265–84).

Brandes, S. (1987) Reflections on honor and shame in the Mediterranean. In D.D. Gilmore (ed.), *Honor and Shame and the Unity of the Mediterranean*. Washington, DC: American Anthropological Association (121–34).

Braudel, F. (1973) *The Mediterranean and the Mediterranean World in the Age of Philip II*. London: Collins.

Briguglio, L. and Briguglio, M. (1996) Sustainable tourism in the Maltese islands. In L. Briguglio (ed.), *Sustainable Tourism in Islands and Small States*. London: Pinter (162–79).

Castelberg-Koulma, M. (1991) Greek women and tourism: women's co-operatives as an alternative form of organisation. In N. Redclift and M.T. Sinclair (eds), *Working Women: International Perspectives on Labour and Gender Ideology*. London: Routledge (197–212).

Chiva, I. (1963) Social organisation, traditional economy, and customary law in Corsica: outline of a plan of analysis. In J. Pitt-Rivers (ed.), *Mediterranean Countrymen: Essays in the Social Anthropology of the Mediterranean*. Paris: Mouton (97–112).

Conlin, M.V. and Baum, T. (1995) Introduction. In M.V. Conlin and T. Baum (eds), *Island Tourism: Management Principles and Practice*. Chichester: Wiley (3–13).

Council of European Municipalities and Regions (1998) *Men and Women in European Municipalities: Assessment June 1998*. Brussels: European Commission/CEMR.

Craik, J. (1995) Are there cultural limits to tourism? *Journal of Sustainable Tourism*, 3: 87–98.

Cronin, C. (1970) *The Sting of Change*. Chicago: University of Chicago Press.

Davis, J. (1977) *People of the Mediterranean*. London: Routledge and Kegan Paul.

de Kadt, E. (1990) *Making the Alternative Sustainable: Lessons from Development for Tourism*. Institute of Development Studies Discussion Paper No. 272. Brighton: University of Sussex.

Directorate-General XVI (Regional Policy and Cohesion) (1997) Le donne Protagoniste dello Sviluppo Regionale. Proceedings of the seminar held in Chia Laguna, Sardinia, 26–28 October.

Ecevit, Y. (1991) Shop floor control: the ideological construction of Turkish women factory workers. In N. Redclift and M.T. Sinclair (eds), *Working Women: International Perspectives on Labour and Gender Ideology*. London: Routledge (56–78).

Eriksen, T.H. (1993) In which sense do cultural islands exist? *Social Anthropology*, 1(1B): 133–48.

Esmeijer, L. (1984) *Marginal Mediterraneans*. Papers on European and Mediterranean Societies. Amsterdam: Anthropologisch-Sociologisch Centrum, University of Amsterdam.

Friedl, E. (1967) The position of women: appearance and reality. *Anthropological Quarterly*, 40: 97–108.

Galani-Moutafi, V. (1993) From agriculture to tourism: property, labor, gender and kinship in a Greek island village (Part One). *Journal of Modern Greek Studies*, 2: 241–70.

Garcia-Ramon, M.D., Canoves, G. and Valdovinos, N. (1995) Farm tourism, gender and the environment in Spain. *Annals of Tourism Research*, 22: 267–82.

Gilmore, D.D. (1987) Introduction: the shame of dishonor. In D.D. Gilmore (ed.), *Honor and Shame and the Unity of the Mediterranean*. Washington, DC: American Anthropological Association (2–21).

Giovannini, M.J. (1987) Female chastity codes in the Circum-Mediterranean: comparative perspectives. In D.D. Gilmore (ed.), *Honor and Shame and the Unity of the Mediterranean*. Washington, DC: American Anthropological Association (61–74).

Goddard, V.A. (1994) From the Mediterranean to Europe: honour, kinship and gender. In V.A. Goddard, J.R. Llobera and C. Shore (eds), *The Anthropology of Europe: Identity and Boundaries in Conflict*. Oxford: Berg (57–92).

Goody, J. (1992) Culture and its boundaries: a European view. *Social Anthropology*, 1: 9–32.

Harris, O. (1984) Households as natural units. In K. Young, C. Wolkowitz and R. McCullagh (eds), *Of Marriage and the Market* 2nd edition. London: Routledge (136–55).

Harrison, D. (1996) Sustainability and tourism: reflections from a muddy pool. In L. Briguglio (ed.), *Sustainable Tourism in Islands and Small States*. London: Pinter (69–89).

Harvey, M.J., Hunt, J. and Harris, C.C. (1995) Gender and community tourism dependence level. *Annals of Tourism Research*, 22: 349–66.

Hearst, D. (1998) Majorcans fight losing battle as invading Germans put their mark on the island. *The Guardian*, 25 July: 16.

Hemmati, M., Sinclair, T. and Marsh, L. (1999) Part 1: Introduction. In *Gender and*

Tourism: Women's Employment and Participation in Tourism. Report for the United Nations Commission on Sustainable Development 7th Session, April 1999, UNED-UK, 1–7.

Hermans, D. (1983) Spanish women in business: the case of Cambrils. *Etnologia Europea*, XIII (1): 13–27.

Herzfeld, M. (1984) The horns of the Mediterraneanist dilemma. *American Ethnologist*, 11: 439–54.

Hughes, P. (1994) *Planning for Sustainable Tourism: The ECOMOST Project*. Lewes: International Federation of Tour Operators.

IBATUR (1996) *Balearic Islands General Information*. Majorca: Consellaria de Turisme Govern Balear.

Kenna, M.E. (1993) Return migrants and tourism development: an example from the Cyclades. *Journal of Modern Greek Studies*, 2: 75–95.

Kinnaird, V. and Hall, D. (1994) *Tourism: A Gender Analysis*. Chichester: Wiley.

Kolodny, Y. (1966) La population des îles en Méditerranée. *Méditerranée*, 7: 3–31.

Kousis, M. (1989) Tourism and the family in a rural Cretan community. *Annals of Tourism Research*, 16: 318–32.

Lopreato, J. (1967) *Peasants No More*. San Franciso: Chandler.

Majorca Daily Bulletin (1998a) The foreign vote looming! 4 September: 24.

Majorca Daily Bulletin (1998b) Foreign residents could 'tip the balance' in local elections. 24 November: 13.

Marshment, M. (1997) Gender takes a holiday: representation in holiday brochures. In M.T. Sinclair (ed.), *Gender, Work and Tourism*. London: Routledge (16–34).

Moore, H. (1988) *Feminism and Anthropology*. Cambridge: Polity Press.

Ortner, S.B. and Whitehead, H. (1981) *Sexual Meanings: The Cultural Construction of Gender and Sexuality*. Cambridge: Cambridge University Press.

Picornel, C., Benitez, J. and Ginard, A. (1997) Tourism, territory and society in the Balearic islands. In C. Fsadni and T. Selwyn (eds), *Sustainable Tourism in Mediterranean Islands and Small Cities*. Malta/London: Med-Campus (30–5).

Reiter, R.R. (1975) *Toward an Anthropology of Women*. New York: Monthly Review Press.

Richez, G. (1996) Sustaining local cultural identity: social unrest and tourism in Corsica. In J.A. Edwards, H. Coccossis and G.K. Priestly (eds), *Sustainable Tourism? European Experiences*. Oxford: CAB International (176–88).

Richter, L.K. (1995) Gender and race: neglected variables in tourism research. In R. Butler and D. Pearce (eds), *Change in Tourism People, Places, Processes*. London: Routledge (71–91).

Rogers, B. (1980) *The Domestication of Women: Discrimination in Developing Societies*. London: Tavistock.

Rosaldo, M.Z. and Lamphere, L. (1974) *Woman, Culture and Society*. Stanford, CA: Stanford University Press.

SCAD-plus. (1990) Employment and job opportunities in the region: France. From *SCADplus Database*. http://europa.eu.int/scadplus/gui/en/fr/018216.htm#CORSE.

Schneider, P., Schneider, J. and Hansen, E. (1972) Modernisation and development: the role of regional elites and non-corporate groups in the European Mediterranean. *Comparative Studies in Society and History*, 14: 328–50.

Scott, J. (1995) Sexual and national boundaries in tourism. *Annals of Tourism Research*, 22: 385–403.

Scott, J. (1997) Chances and choices: women and tourism in Northern Cyprus. In M.T. Sinclair (ed.), *Gender, Work and Tourism*. London: Routledge (60–90).

Selwyn, T. (1994) Tourism, culture and culture clash in the Mallorcan region of Calvia: towards a model of sustainable tourism policy. The *ECOMOST Report*. Brussels: European Community.

Shore, C. and Black, A. (1994) Citizens' Europe and the construction of European identity. In V.A. Goddard, J.R. Llobera and C. Shore (eds), *The Anthropology of Europe: Identity and Boundaries in Conflict.* Oxford: Berg (275–98).

Sinclair, M.T. (ed.) (1997) *Gender, Work and Tourism.* London: Routledge.

Stott, M.A. (1978) Tourism in Mykonos: social and cultural responses. *Mediterranean Studies,* 1: 72–90.

Stott, M.A. (1995) Property, labor and household economy: the transition to tourism in Mykonos, Greece. *Journal of Modern Greek Studies,* 3: 187–206.

Stott, M.A. (1996) Tourism development and the need for community action in Mykonos, Greece. In L. Briguglio (ed.), *Sustainable Tourism in Islands and Small States.* London: Pinter (281–306).

Swain, M. (ed.) (1995) *Gender in Tourism.* Special issue of *Annals of Tourism Research* 22(2).

Urry, J. (1990) *The Tourist Gaze: Leisure and Travel in Contemporary Societies.* London: Sage.

Waldren, J. (1996) *Insiders and Outsiders: Paradise and Reality in Mallorca.* Oxford: Berghahn Books.

Zarkia, C. (1996) *Philoxenia*: receiving tourists – but not guests – on a Greek island. In J. Boissevain (ed.), *Coping with Tourists: European Reactions to Mass Tourism.* Oxford: Berghahn Books (143–73).

Zinovieff, S. (1991) Hunters and hunted: Kamaki and the ambiguities of sexual predation in a Greek town. In P. Loizos and E. Papataxiarchis (eds), *Contested Identities: Gender and Kinship in Modern Greece.* Princeton, NJ: Princeton University Press (203–20).

6

Trapped by the Image: The Implications of Cultural Tourism in the Insular Mediterranean

Tom Selänniemi

Introduction

When Brian Wheeller showed the audience at the 'Sustainable Tourism: Eco-Loving or Marketing Plot' seminar at the University of Westminster on 8 December 1998, an overhead slide that said: 'Don't believe anything (positive) anyone tells you about sustainable tourism' the laughter of the crowd was slightly uneasy. Wheeller does have a point, though, in the way he questions the foundations of the concept of sustainable tourism (Wheeller, 1997). It really is a pity that one of the key concepts, a crucial one for the future of tourism, has been inflated to the point that almost anything can be labelled sustainable these days. What is perhaps even more alarming is the tendency of planners, policy-makers, and researchers to brush the real problems under the carpet by concentrating on 'alternative', 'eco', 'small-scale', or 'whatever prefix' tourism as if they were a true answer to the existing problems that mass tourism in its many forms produces. Instead, attention must be focused to a greater extent than currently on the problems in existing mass tourism destinations.

Generally speaking, sustainable future in tourism rests on three foundations, namely the economic, ecological, and sociocultural foundations. If one of these foundations falters, the whole structure falls. It is easy to realize that in regions currently depending on mass tourism, ecological and sociocultural sustainability is dependent on the economic foundation. This means that any attempts to quickly limit the arrival of tourists to such a degree that it would actually have a positive impact would require a miracle in terms of the amount of money the few visitors would be willing to spend on their holiday. This is true for many Mediterranean mass tourism destinations, including Rhodes, where the local economy is dependent on tourism (Coccossis and Mexa, 1995). In fact, it has become a sort of a monocrop and, thus, any investments in the environmental or sociocultural infrastructure are ultimately dependent on the income from tourism. Therefore the problem should be phrased in the following question: 'How are tourists going to be attracted to an existing mass tourism destination without causing unacceptable impacts on the indigenous nature and culture and, simultaneously, how are these tourists going to enjoy positive tourist experiences?'

In this chapter, I will examine the interesting and partly disturbing paradox between a Mediterranean island destination with rich cultural history and its pleasure-seeking tourists who are not interested in that heritage. This is a situation that is fairly common to most mature mass tourism destinations in the region. Even though the conclusions in this analysis are based on a case study of Rhodes, I argue that the findings can easily be generalized to apply to many Mediterranean tourist areas. Based on field work conducted with tourists – especially Finnish charter tourists – on Rhodes in 1993 and 1997, I will compare these individuals' experiences and the contexts of these experiences with the rich heritage of the island. The Old Town of Rhodes is a unique medieval milieu included on the UNESCO World Heritage List (Plate 6.1). The acropolis of Lindos together with the

Plate 6.1 The Old Town of Rhodes – a World Heritage site

charming village below the hill form one of the most enchanting sights in Greece. Moreover, the archaeological sites of Kamiros and Ialisos together with nearby beautiful villages, remains of fortresses, and a diversity of landscapes form a perfect setting for the experiences of cultural tourists. Nevertheless, cultural tourists are rarely seen on the island. What entices most of the charter tourists to the island are good beaches, waiters and shopkeepers speaking their language, easy relaxation, cheap beer and an ample nightlife. Most of the tourists I interviewed were unaware of the cultural side of their destination. This did not, however, disturb their holiday experience because they were fully satisfied with their stay and their expectations of the destination. A few were pleasantly surprised about the rich cultural heritage of the island, but most of the tourists were not at all interested. Similar situations have been noted elsewhere in the Mediterranean, especially on the Spanish Costa del Sol (Barke and France, 1996).

The image of Rhodes, like those of many other destinations in the Mediterranean, is as a tourist destination offering the four Ss (sun, sea, sand, and sex) and not as a cultural destination. Just as on other island destinations in the Mediterranean, the authorities on Rhodes would welcome more cultural tourists, mainly because there is a broad perception among policy-makers that cultural tourists, as opposed to sunlust tourists, are high spenders. However, while cultural tourists would most likely view a holiday in Athens or Rome as acceptable, a fortnight spent on Rhodes would not convey the same esteem. Therefore Rhodes continues to receive mostly charter tourists not interested in the culture of the island. There is, however, a possible benefit from this situation as the masses of tourists that have been frequenting the island for about 40 years have tended to concentrate in a relatively limited area. Without interest in the historical sites or remote villages, most of the island has remained relatively untouched up to this date. This is, however, changing with the development of the southern parts of the island for tourism activities. The situation on Rhodes gives rise to a difficult question: is it possible that in some cases mass tourism can help preserve some areas by concentrating its impacts – at least in the long run? Would Rhodes be different today if only a fraction (e.g., 15 per cent) of the tourists visiting the island during the past 40 years had been really interested in what the island has to offer in a cultural and environmental sense?

These questions and problems do not limit themselves to Rhodes only. This became clear from a recent project (1999) conducted, under my supervision, in Limassol, Cyprus by six students of the Finnish University Network for Tourism. Just as on Rhodes, Malta, Majorca, and many other Mediterranean islands, cultural heritage as well as political/nationalistic history is a cornerstone for identity-building on Cyprus. These insular destinations often boast a distinctive heritage that could function as their main attraction. However, more often than not it is other assets such as their beaches and climate that function as the islands' leading attraction for consumers based in northern European countries. Thus, in most cases the host population is often faced with mass tourists who do provide a certain income but do not share the islanders' values concerning their homeland. In the most developed mass tourism destinations the tourists are often ignorant of or behave indifferently towards the local culture. Indeed, the visitors tours of island villages may often be experienced by the locals as 'peep shows'. To illustrate these points, I will also use material from Malta and other Mediterranean destinations for comparative purposes.

The Touristic Rhodes

The island of Rhodes is located just 20 km off the Turkish coast (see Figure 1.1). Being 65 km long and 20 km wide it is the largest island in the Dodecanese archipelago. Rhodes is very rich in history and has a favourable climate, elements that have contributed to the development of one of the most popular tourist destinations in the Mediterranean region. The main historical attractions on the island are the acropolis of Lindos, the archaeological site of Kamiros, and, of course, the medieval Old Town of Rhodes which is included in the list of UNESCO World Heritage sites. Approximately 1 million tourists visit the island per annum, arriving mainly on charter flights. Just as in most Mediterranean island destinations, cultural history is, however, not what brings tourists to Rhodes. The attraction of the island and especially the town of Rhodes rests in its good beach facilities, ample tourist services, a vibrant nightlife, and, most important (at least for Finnish tourists), almost guaranteed sunshine during the six summer months. The influx of tourists has been so intense in the town of Rhodes that the northern tip of the town where most of the hotels, restaurants and bars are located, resembles more closely the tourists' home cultures than anything Greek or Rhodian. The medieval Old Town and the vast areas of inland Rhodes have, however, preserved much of their originality and distinctiveness. This has been partly a result of the spatial concentration of tourists in only certain limited areas around the island. Also, when these tourists travel around the island, they seldom step off the beaten track.

The town of Rhodes with about 45,000 inhabitants has two touristic areas. The first one, where approximately 4,500 locals also live, is the Old Town. The population of the Old Town has seen a constant decline over the last few decades while that of the town of Rhodes had been increasing (Coccossis and Mexa, 1995: 111). Parts of the Old Town have already been transformed purely into tourist areas, while others still function as the residential areas of an ageing population. The medieval Old Town, one of the best preserved medieval milieus, is inside the fortification walls of the Knights of St John. The Grand Master's palace which was restored by the Italians to be the summer palace of Mussolini and the street of the knights (Ippoton Street) lined with medieval buildings are the main attractions. Most tourists walk by taking an occasional snapshot of Ippoton Street, and continue their stroll to the main street of the Old Town: Socratous Street. Most souvenir vendors, fur merchants and liquor sellers have their shops on Socratous Street alongside numerous restaurants, bars, and cafés (although there is a far bigger concentration of such establishments in the touristic northern part of town). Socratous Street is almost always crowded, but one can walk the winding narrow alleys of the Old Town for hours meeting mainly local people and stray cats and only a few tourists. Almost the same applies for Ippoton Street, the archaeological museum, and the Grand Master's palace. Obviously, most tourists have not come to Rhodes for its history.

The northern tip of town is the tourist district where local people are clearly a minority during the tourist season. The area is full of hotels, shops, and English, Swedish, Danish and Finnish pubs, cafés, restaurants, discos, and so on. On some streets there is not a sign in Greek. Rather, all signs are in English, Swedish, or Finnish, and occasionally German. On a quick walk around the quarter in the touristic part of Rhodes, one can spot signs in Finnish that advertise, for instance, Finnish coffee-shops and bars, liquor stores and restaurants with Finnish menus.

In the town of Rhodes, tourists have no problems ordering their meal in Finnish from a menu written in Finnish. Shopping is easy, because many merchants know at least a couple of Finnish words and, surprisingly, many shops have Finnish women working there either as hired help or because they are married to the shop owner. On the beach the soft drink sellers shout as they walk around 'Fanta, kola, hyvä kalja, kylmä kalja! (Fanta, cola, good beer, cold beer!)' so the Finns, dehydrated by intensive suntanning, have no trouble finding out what the vendors are selling. In the hotels, you can exchange your markkas into drachmas and ask for your key at the reception in Finnish. If you need a snack or lunch while sunbathing, the snack-bars and restaurants near the beach will serve you in Finnish or at least have a photo-menu from which it is easy to pick your choice. After lunch it is always pleasant to drop into Demis' Finnish Café for a cup of Finnish coffee where you will be served by a staff consisting entirely of Finnish women. Following an afternoon nap, there is always time to buy some aperitifs from Vävypojan Viinakauppa (the Son-in-law's Booze Shop) to drink on the balcony while contemplating where to dine during the evening. On the way to the restaurant, you may stop at the fur shop to have an extra ouzo with the Finnish shop assistant and discuss the prices (or anything else) before going to a Greek restaurant where your Finnish is often understood or, why not, to some of the Scandinavian restaurants, where you are sure to get familiar food so you will not have to wonder what you are eating. After dinner there are many options open if you want to continue your evening in this manner. During the tourist season almost every night there is a chance to see Finnish popular music artists perform live, or at least to dance to Finnish dance music. These examples indicate the existence of what could be called 'little Finland', an extension of the tourists' home culture (Hanefors and Larsson, 1989, 1993). The touristic culture of Finns on Rhodes is familiar and in many details similar to the tourists' home culture, but it exists outside its proper context (i.e., place and time of Finnish culture).

The Finnish Tourists on Rhodes

The Greek island of Rhodes has been one of the most popular destinations for Finnish vacationers since the beginnings of mass tourism from that country at the end of the 1960s. According to the statistics of the Dodecanese branch of the National Tourist Organization of Greece, 86,883 Finns spent their holiday on Rhodes in 1989. Finns were the third largest group of tourists on Rhodes by nationality after British and German visitors. Since then the number of Finns travelling to Rhodes decreased to just above 30,000 visitors in 1993 due to the economic recession in Finland, but has risen to around 50,000 arrivals yearly at the time of writing (1999). Finns are no longer the third largest nationality of tourists on Rhodes, but still represent a 5 per cent share of total arrivals.

Data relating to Finnish tourists on Rhodes collected by questionnaires in 1993 and 1997 (339 replies) reveal that the typical Finn travelling to Rhodes is less than 45 years old (68 per cent), has an upper secondary education (56 per cent) and lives outside metropolitan areas (77 per cent) (Table 6.1). He or she has made less than 10 trips abroad (50 per cent) and travels once a year or less frequently (75 per cent). According to the returned questionnaires, the single most important factor influencing the decision to make a tourist trip was the need to get away from everyday life (48 per cent) and to relax. Rhodes was chosen as a destination for two almost equally important reasons: it is safe and familiar (23 per cent), and the flight and departure dates were suitable (27 per cent). Reasons directly connected with the distinctiveness of Rhodes compared to other holiday destinations were mentioned in only 2 per cent of the replies. The sun and climate, which are interchangeable with almost any of the tourist resorts in the 'south', were mentioned by 9 per cent of the respondents as the most important reason for choosing Rhodes.

Table 6.1 Traveller profiles: the typical Finnish tourists on Rhodes and in Athens

	Rhodes	*Athens*
Age	Less than 45	36–55
Education	Upper secondary	University
Place of residence	Outside metropolitan area	Metropolitan area
Travel experience	Less than 10 trips	Over 10 trips
Travel frequency	Less than once per year	More than twice per year
Reason for holiday	Break from everyday life	Break from everyday life
Destination choice	Suitable departure and safety	Culture and history

By comparison, replies to questionnaires distributed as part of my earlier field work to Finnish tourists in Athens (64 replies in 1991 and 63 replies in 1992) indicate a clear difference in the tourists' backgrounds and motives for travelling. At that time, the typical Finnish tourist travelling to Athens was 36–55 years old (55 per cent), had a university degree or equivalent (57 per cent) and lived in a metropolitan area (63 per cent). He or she had made more than 10 trips abroad (70 per cent) and travelled more than twice a year (51 per cent). The decision to take a holiday trip came from the need to relax and get away from everyday life (35 per cent), but in contrast to Rhodes, Athens was chosen as a destination because of its distinctiveness as a place. The majority of respondents (67 per cent) gave the culture and history of Athens as the main reason for destination choice.

I also conducted time-use interviews with 61 Finnish tourists on Rhodes asking them what they had done the day before. Results from these surveys indicate that the tourists sleep relatively late and have breakfast around 9 or 10 a.m. The beach lures them before noon. At 10 a.m. almost 40 per cent of the respondents were at the beach and at 1 p.m. over 50 per cent were sunbathing. After that, the number of sunbathers dropped slowly but steadily so that by 4 p.m. 35 per cent were still tanning themselves, but by 5 p.m. only 8 per cent were at the beach. Based on these interviews, the tourists seem go out to dinner between 8 and 10 p.m. and continue partying and bar-hopping until late at night. At 1 a.m. almost 70 per cent were still partying in the town, at 3 a.m. 40 per cent, and at 5 a.m. 7 per cent.

My own observations and the diaries that some tourists kept for me during their stay on Rhodes confirm that Finnish tourists enjoy unstructured time usage while on holiday. The tourists do not have to conform to any timetables and have the freedom to eat, sleep, drink, and do whatever, whenever they please. The climate, particularly the warm sun, is always mentioned in the diaries, often in an implicit comparison to the uncertain weather of Finland. The sun clearly features as the most important entity in these travellers' holiday experience. For instance, there are sections in the diaries where people write about rainy or cold days and their trouble in finding anything to do. In fact, those Finnish tourists who experienced bad weather in Rhodes write about their frustration relating to the lack of the one thing they came all the way here to enjoy: the sun. One must keep in mind that the long dark winters of the northern regions of Europe are probably the strongest push factor in the travel motivations of Finns, while the sunshine and warmth of the Mediterranean region and the Canary Islands are the strongest pull factor.

Observations on the Island

What strikes me as particularly surprising when walking down the narrow alleys of the Old Town of Rhodes or along the inland paths in non-touristic areas is the total absence of tourists. This sounds somewhat unbelievable on an island that has been frequented by tourists arriving in large numbers over the past four decades. While the main shopping street in the Old Town, Socratous Street, is packed with tourists during high season, the small picturesque alleys just a few metres away might be empty. Even the most famous historical street in town, Ippoton Street, can offer the opportunity for a pleasant quiet stroll without crowds! The further one ventures into the labyrinth of tiny alleys, the further one gets from the crowds and the more likely it becomes to receive a friendly nod from the locals you meet in the streets. When leaving the town of Rhodes and travelling along the roads with least traffic, a traveller may find himself or herself to be a lonely tourist, especially along inland footpaths or in inland villages.

When interviewing Finnish tourists in the new parts of the town of Rhodes where most hotels are located, I found out that many of them never went to the Old Town during their stay. Very often, tourists coming for a relaxing sunlust holiday do not leave what some guides call the 'Bermuda triangle' of the new town. The area is roughly bordered by Mandraki Harbour and Elli Beach on the east side, Windy Beach on the west side, and the walls of the Old Town in the south. As described earlier, this is the area where most tourist facilities are located. Outside the town, the main tourist areas are Ialissos on the west coast and Faliraki on the east coast. New developments on a large scale can be seen especially in Gennadio.

Many of the tourists I interviewed saw no reason for going to the Old Town or making trips to the archaeological sites, including Lindos. Some of these tourists had been to these places, at least the Old Town and Lindos, on a previous trip to Rhodes, while others simply were not interested. They did not express any wish to get to know the history of the island or the local people. Participating in the 'Greek village feast' organized by the tour operators in a nearby village, like Afantou, where you were met by 'papa Ouzo' and taken to a tavern for dinner with a dance show, was as far into local culture as these tourists were prepared to go. The very simple explanation for this lack of interest is that these tourists were not on a quest for authenticity in the MacCannellian (1989) sense, nor were their travels motivated by a quest for the 'Other'. That is, they were neither trying to find authenticity in other times (e.g., historical attractions) nor were they looking for authenticity in the lives of other people. Their travel was more pleasure-oriented and had elements of a quest for the authentic 'self' (Brown, 1996).

When considering Finnish or indeed any type of northern European mass tourism to the 'south' (i.e., the Mediterranean region and the Canary Islands), it seems to be more important *that you travel* than *where you travel*. The chosen destination is of marginal importance as long as it provides the tourist with good opportunities for beach life and partying and provided there are ample visitor-related services. In this type of tourism, people choose to travel to another 'state of being' rather than to a different place. In an analogy to the anthropological theories of transition rites (van Gennep, 1960; Turner, 1978), mass tourists can be understood as striving to free themselves for a limited time-span from everyday life both at work and at home.

In transition rites, of which initiations are a case in point, the ritual subjects go through phases that are called preliminal, liminal, and postliminal. The preliminal is the normal profane state of being, the liminal phase is sacred, anomalous, abnormal and dangerous, and the postliminal is the normal state of things to which the ritual subject re-enters after the transition. The liminal is a state and a process in the transition phase during which the ritual subjects pass a cultural area or zone that has minimal attributes of the states preceding or following the liminal. This 'betweenness' has been compared, for example, to death, bisexuality, and invisibility (Turner and Turner, 1978). Nelson Graburn (1989) has, by using Leach's (1982) refinements on van Gennep's and Turner's theories, shown how tourism can be understood as a journey to the sacred in an analogy with transition rites.

The stage in tourism that resembles the liminal stage or phase in rites of passage could be called the *liminoid* or *quasiliminal* in Turner's terms. The liminoid is related but not identical to the ritually liminal. The main difference is that the liminoid is *produced and consumed by individuals* while the liminal is believed by the members of society to be of divine origin and is anonymous in its nature. The liminoid is also fragmentary compared to the liminal. Often elements of the liminal have been separated from the whole to act individually in specialized fields like art (Turner and Turner, 1978: 253). In art, popular culture, entertainment, and tourism products are made for consumption by individuals and groups that promise to remove the consumer from the everyday experience. They promise a transition into a stage that resembles the liminal for a limited time-span. The attraction of mass tourism lies in the possibility of being transported and transformed for a moment into the liminoid where 'everything is possible' (Selänniemi, 1997).

When tourists enter the *liminoid* stage, some changes take place. Normal social time stops in the marginal state of liminality, and it seems to stop also in the liminoid 'south'. In this stage, people who are normally confined to everyday timetables and routines forget the lapse of time and sleep late, eat whenever it suits them, follow flexible time schedules, party until they drop, and so on. One of the freedoms of the 'south' is that you do not *have* to do anything (Selänniemi, 1996). Social antistructure or the so-called *communitas* – undifferentiated, democratic, direct, and spontaneous social bonds or contacts – is characteristic of liminality. *Communitas* relieves the individuals from following the common norms. This has to be a temporary state so that society can continue its organized existence (Turner and Turner, 1978: 249–50).

If the 'south' is understood to be a liminoid 'play-zone' for tourists, it becomes obvious that the cultural and geographical location of this pleasure periphery has only marginal importance. In fact, it seems that the more placeless the destination is, the easier it is for the tourist to break away from everyday life. In this liminoid 'south' people behave in ways they would not normally do at home. This could be interpreted as a result of the anti-structure of the 'south' that entices the latent 'Other' in the tourist's self to come forth. On holiday the anti-self that drinks, hooliganizes, forgets safe sex, and so on or an ideal self that is social, sensitive and creative may take over. These selves may also alternate in the same person (Selänniemi, 1996, 1997).

Thus, leaving home and going on a trip seems to be a prerequisite for some people to attain a desired state of relaxation (Selänniemi, 1996). Instead of engaging in the more middle-class 'gaze' type of tourism (Urry, 1990), these tourists are seen as being on a sacred journey (Graburn, 1989) to a liminoid state of mind (Turner and Turner, 1978) as described above, where they might cross the boundaries of the sensible body subsumed to rules in everyday life (Falk, 1994) and enjoy their multisensorial and bodily tourist experiences (Veijola and Jokinen, 1994; Selänniemi, 1996). This is, of course, culturally determined. Only in western societies has tourism become to such a degree a democratic and common activity that it is seen as a normal way of getting away from 'everyday' for a while. Tourism is positively sanctioned in our culture (Smith, 1989). Thus, people buy time for themselves, their spouses and families, as much as they buy a place to visit, when they walk into a travel agent's office to purchase a mass tourism trip to Rhodes or Playa del Ingles. They buy time that is more their own than the time lived in everyday life, where you have to conform to the clock and the rational rhythm of work that do not synchronize with the natural rhythms of the body. Consequently, this tension between the rhythms adds another element of stress to our lives (Adam, 1995). In many ways, the liminoid time of the 'south' is like the time of our childhood summers that were always sunny and warm and lasted forever (Selänniemi, 1997).

Is Cultural Tourism a Viable Option for Rhodes?

The image of Rhodes as a tourist destination is one offering the four Ss and not a cultural destination. The authorities on the island would welcome more cultural tourists, mainly because they are perceived as bigger spenders. Boissevain describes these visitors as 'quality tourists':

> These mythical visitors, whom planners think of as more affluent and cultured persons (characteristics which by no means need coincide), are being hotly pursued by National Tourist Organisations all over the globe. They are widely viewed as the key to liberating destination communities from enervating dependence on hordes of low-spending package tourists. (1996a: 3)

On islands like Mykonos and Lesbos, planners see cultural tourism as one of the ways towards more sustainable tourism (Coccossis and Parpairis, 1995; Nijkamp and Verdonkschot, 1995; Stott, 1996). Nevertheless, this view can be rightfully criticized, as I demonstrate later.

Within the peer group of cultural tourists a holiday in Athens or Rome is regarded as acceptable but a fortnight spent on Rhodes does not convey the same esteem. This is mainly the result of the type of tourism that has developed on the island over the past 30 years or so and the image it has generated. After decades of being one of the major sunlust destinations for northern Europeans, Rhodes faces major problems in attracting cultural tourists who do not want to be identified as belonging to the 'masses'. Therefore, Rhodes continues to receive mostly charter tourists not interested in the island's cultural attributes. One also has to bear in mind that tourists are generally not really interested in authenticity, instead preferring 'genuine fakes' as Brown (1996) puts it. This produces a new form of 'tourist tradition' or tourist authenticity that has little to do with the 'real' authentic local culture (Zarkia, 1996). However, this staging of the destination culture is not inherently bad or a mere falsification as it may also function as a protective fence for the everyday reality of the locals as well as a way of revitalizing dying traditions. At least some forms of these traditions will survive, albeit in a touristified form.

The research carried out by Jeremy Boissevain on Malta clearly illustrates the problems that a destination faces when, on the one hand, it is a sunlust destination and, on the other hand, it has an abundance of culture, heritage and history to offer tourists (e.g., as Rhodes does). Boissevain (1996a, 1996b, 1997) describes how the inhabitants of the walled city of Mdina have become increasingly stressed by being under the constant gaze of tourists. Their attitudes towards tourism on Malta and the tourists visiting the island is much more negative than those of the Maltese public at large, including those inhabitants who live in the midst of mass tourism. From his research, Boissevain concludes that there are at least six negative structural characteristics associated with cultural tourism. These characteristics which are largely absent in seaside tourism are the following:

1. Entrepreneurs and tourist authorities commodify and market the local culture without consulting the inhabitants.
2. There is loss of privacy for the locals as they become the attractions.
3. Excessive tourist attention destroys the very culture tourists come to gaze at and, thus, transforms living communities into museums and heritage parks.
4. The inhabitants become hostile when they realize they are being exploited.
5. The locals are exposed to the attention of tourists throughout the year as cultural tourism is not necessarily as seasonal as seaside tourism.
6. Tourists are doubly intrusive when they arrive in the winter, when local

communities are used to going about their normal way of life. (Boissevain 1996b: 234–6)

Thus, it is not in the least clear that restructuring tourism on Rhodes from its seasonal sunlust charter character to a year-round cultural product would be a blessing, at least for all sectors of the Rhodian community. It is not a surprise, then, that the foremost spokespersons for this restructuring are the entrepreneurs or government officials, not the people who would mainly function as 'local colour'.

There is one thing, though, that planners and entrepreneurs might have overlooked. Very often, the importance of repeat visitors is emphasized when talking about sustainable tourism development at a given destination. Boissevain (1996b) reports that of the more than 1 million mainly four Ss tourists that visited Malta in 1993, half had been there before. In my data from Rhodes, in 1997 49 per cent of the Finnish tourists were repeat visitors. In fact, 6 per cent had been to the island more than five times. However, the results from a similar questionnaire distributed to Finnish tourists in Athens in 1991 indicated that only 22 per cent were repeat visitors. If one considers repeat visits to Greece as a whole, only 25 per cent of the Finnish tourists on Rhodes in 1997 had never been to Greece before. Of the 75 per cent who had been to Greece on holiday previously, 36 per cent had been to Crete and 24 per cent to Kos. The reasons for repeat visits to Rhodes were mainly that it was familiar and safe (28 per cent) and that the previous experiences had been positive (22 per cent). When thinking about the cultural tourist, the 'culture vulture' who collects places and cultures and who once she or he has been to a place and has seen and 'done' it all, the reasons for repeat visits to Rhodes do not make any sense. Once you have seen the medieval Old Town of Rhodes, the Acropolis, the Duomo in Florence or whatever, you can redirect your interest to new destinations on a never-ending quest for sight-related tourist experiences. But for the sunlust tourist who is not mainly interested in gazing at the 'Other', be it in past (museums, archaeological sites) or present (the culture of local people), the destination is not consumed or worn out by a visit. Very often the opposite happens. A nice holiday on Rhodes entices the tourist to return, whether or not that tourist ever ventured into the Old Town or made a trip to Lindos. Therefore, I would add a seventh characteristic to the list of (negative) characteristics of cultural tourism: cultural tourists tend not to repeat their visits to the same destination as the value of a destination lies mainly in its novelty for the tourist.

Discussion

It is important to know the motives of those tourists who prefer the ready-built resorts of the Mediterranean region and the Canary Islands as their destinations, because one type of sustainable tourism could actually be mass charter tourism, as long as the environmental infrastructure of the resorts can be renovated to cope with such a product. Tourists who are content with packaged charter trips can bring money to a well-planned polarized tourist region with a relatively low environmental and cultural impact on the host country. Charter flights transport large numbers of tourists with relatively low environmental impacts compared to the same number of 'individual tourists' who fly to the jungles of Borneo. If the tourists are content, as seems to be the case of Finns going south, with the hotel and leisure areas that have little or no resemblance to the 'authentic' local environment and culture, the services of the tourist industry's employees, the 'traditional' performances by professionals, and with air-conditioned sightseeing buses, they will have minimal contact with local people and a relatively low cultural impact on the host culture (compared with 'cannibal tourists') (Selänniemi, forthcoming).

We can consider that sustainable development in tourism rests on economic, ecological, and sociocultural foundations. If any of these foundations is missing, the structure can topple. What, then, does this mean in a Rhodian perspective? Let us examine mass tourism on an island destination from a perspective of pros and cons (Table 6.2).

As we can see from comparing the pros and cons of mass tourism on Rhodes, the picture one can paint of tourism is never black and white with some things being entirely positive and some things exclusively negative. Mass tourism can actually concentrate environmental degradation and, thus, perhaps make the impact more severe in its destinations. However, the impacts may be more manageable precisely because of this polarization. Even though one might consider the inadequate economic filtration to the local inhabitants plus the unequal job opportunities to be in conflict with the idea of sustainable development, one also has to ask what the realistic alternatives are. While tourists on Rhodes show little interest in local culture and, thus, do not intrude in the daily lives of local people, instead preferring to stay in the tourist areas, one might also argue that these same tourists, due to their lack of interest, act in a culturally insensitive manner. Moreover, the idea that their lack of interest can play a significant part in an acculturative process does not seem far-fetched. In the town of Rhodes a whole generation of people who do not remember the time before mass tourism has already reached adulthood. What impacts on their self-esteem and identity have these millions of visitors who do not pay much attention to their heritage and culture had?

Seasonality is often mentioned as one of the major downsides of tourism. That is very much so, but in 'living attractions' like the medieval town of Rhodes or Mdina on Malta local residents and the small-scale entrepreneurs who work long hours seven days a week during the season may regard the off-season as a welcome break for rest, social contacts, and renewing their strength before a new season.

At least Finnish tourists seem to be very happy with their holidays on

Table 6.2 Mass tourism on Rhodes: advantages and disadvantages

Positive impacts	Negative impacts
Concentrated and, thus, more manageable environmental and sociocultural impact	Concentrated degradation of the environment
Development only in certain regions thus limiting impacts	Inadequate economic filtration to the local level
Tourists not interested in local culture, thus, not intruding into the life of the locals	Unequal job opportunities
	Problems related to land use, access and ownership
Seasonality brings a welcome break from the tourist influx (at least for entrepreneurs)	Tourists not interested in the local culture, culturally insensitive, and possibly leaving a negative impact on local self-esteem and identity
Tourists (at least Finnish) are satisfied with the destination and continue to make repeat visits	Seasonality is problematic for tourism employees
	Seasonal crowding
Tourism to the island brings income to the region and helps to finance the preservation of the rich heritage (at least indirectly)	Rhodes is 'trapped by its image' – although it has potential for cultural and historical tourism it continues to attract the sunlust tourists
	Tourists coming to Rhodes are not interested in heritage and, thus, do not pay entrance fees that would help finance preservation

Rhodes and they make a significant number of repeat visits even though they are not interested in the history, heritage, or culture of the island. Their tourism brings income to the region and indirectly helps finance the preservation of its rich cultural heritage, but naturally a more direct financial contribution by cultural tourists willing to pay entrance fees (e.g., to gain access to the Old Town) would be welcome.

When discussing viable development alternatives for Rhodes, or for any mass tourism destination in the Mediterranean (or globally) one is rather quick to admit that the philosophically tempting solutions offered by spokespersons of 'alternative', 'eco', 'small-scale', or 'whatever-prefix-tourism' are idealistic opinions, not realistic options. We live in a world where many regions are totally dependent on the income generated by mass tourism, in this case, northern European sunlust tourism. Attempting to develop alternative tourism products alongside mainstream mass tourism is perhaps a strategy that should be supported. Nevertheless, it does not provide us with a real alternative. As I see it, the way forward is to develop the existing format of mass tourism in a more sustainable direction by renovating the destinations to become environmentally more sustainable. This may be achieved by favouring local entrepreneurs in negotiations between tour operators and hoteliers, and by trying to create increased awareness in the main origin countries by educating tourists, travel agents, and tour operators.

References

Adam, B. (1995) *Timewatch: The Social Analysis of Time*. Cambridge: Polity Press.

Barke, M. and France, L.A. (1996) The Costa del Sol. In M. Barke, J. Towner and M.T. Newton (eds), *Tourism in Spain: Critical Issues*. Wallingford: CAB International (265–308).

Boissevain, J. (1996a) Introduction. In J. Boissevain (ed.), *Coping with Tourists: European Reactions to Mass Tourism*. Providence, RI: Berghahn Books (1–26).

Boissevain, J. (1996b) 'But we live here!' Perspectives on cultural tourism in Malta. In L. Briguglio *et al.* (eds), *Sustainable Tourism in Islands and Small States: Case Studies*. London: Pinter (220–40).

Boissevain, J. (1997) Problems with cultural tourism in Malta. In C. Fsadni and T. Selwyn (eds), *Sustainable Tourism in Mediterranean Islands and Small Cities*. London: MED-CAMPUS (19–29).

Brown, D. (1996) Genuine fakes. In T. Selwyn (ed.), *The Tourist Image: Myths and Myth Making in Tourism*. Chichester: John Wiley & Sons (33–48).

Coccossis, H. and Mexa, A. (1995) Tourism and the conservation of heritage: the medieval town of Rhodes. In H. Coccossis and P. Nijkamp (eds), *Planning for Our Cultural Heritage*. Aldershot: Avebury (107–21).

Coccossis, H. and Parpairis, A. (1995) Assessing the interaction between heritage, environment and tourism: Mykonos. In H. Coccossis and P. Nijkamp (eds), *Sustainable Tourism Development*. Aldershot: Avebury (116–42).

Falk, P. (1994) *The Consuming Body*. London: Sage.

Graburn, N.H.H. (1989) Tourism: the sacred journey. In V.L. Smith (ed.), *Hosts and Guests: The Anthropology of Tourism*, 2nd edn. Philadelphia: University of Pennsylvania Press (21–36).

Hanefors, M. and Larsson, L. (1989) *Fardledaren: Turismkunskap for frontpersonal* (The tour guide: tourism knowledge for frontstage personnel). Malmö: Liber.

Hanefors, M. and Larsson, L. (1993) Video strategies used by tour operators: what is really communicated? *Tourism Management*, 14(1): 27–33.

Leach, E.R. ([1961] 1982) *Rethinking Anthropology*. New York: The Athlone Press.

MacCannell, D. (1989) *The Tourist: A New Theory of the Leisured Class*. New York: Schocken Books.

Nijkamp, P. and Verdonkschot, S. (1995) Sustainable tourism development: a case study of Lesbos. In H. Coccossis and P. Nijkamp (eds), *Sustainable Tourism Development*. Aldershot: Avebury (127–40).

Selänniemi, T. (1996) *Matka ikuiseen kesaan: Kulttuuriantropologinen nakokulma suomalaisten etelanmatkailuun* (A journey to the eternal summer: the anthropology of Finnish sunlust tourism). Helsinki: SKS.

Selänniemi, T. (1997) The mind in the museum, the body on the beach: place and authenticity in mass tourism. In W. Nuryanti (ed.), *Tourism and Culture. Toward a Sustainable Future: Balancing Conservation and Development*. Yogyakarta: Gadjah Mada University Press (293–303).

Selänniemi, T. (forthcoming) Pale skin on Playa del Anywhere: Finnish tourists in the South. In V.L. Smith (ed.), *The Hosts and Guests Revisited*. New York: Cognizant Press.

Smith, V.L. (1989) Introduction. In V.L. Smith (ed.), *Hosts and Guests: The Anthropology of Tourism*, 2nd edn. Philadelphia: University of Pennsylvania Press (1–20).

Stott, M. (1996) Tourism development and the need for community action in Mykonos, Greece. In L. Briguglio *et al.* (eds), *Sustainable Tourism in Islands and Small States: Case Studies*. London: Pinter (281–305).

Turner, V. ([1974] 1978) *Dramas, Fields, and Metaphors*. London: Cornell University Press.

Turner, V. and Turner, E. (1978) *Image and Pilgrimage in Christian Culture*. New York: Columbia University Press.

Urry, J. (1990) *The Tourist Gaze: Leisure and Travel in Contemporary Societies*. London: Sage.

Van Gennep, A. ([1908] 1960) *The Rites of Passage*. Chicago: University of Chicago Press.

Veijola, S. and Jokinen, E. (1994) The body in tourism. *Theory, Culture and Society*, 11(1): 125–51.

Wheeller, B. (1997) Here we go, here we go, here we go eco. In M.J. Stabler (ed.), *Tourism and Sustainability: Principles to Practice*. Wallingford: CAB International (39–49).

Zarkia, C. (1996) *Philoxenia*: receiving tourists – but not guests – on a Greek island. In J. Boissevain (ed.), *Coping with Tourists: European Reactions to Mass Tourism*. Providence, RI: Berghahn Books (143–73).

Part 2

Tourism Practices in the Mediterranean Island Groups

7

Tourism Development and Sustainability in the Aeolian Islands

Giovanni Giavelli

Introduction

Sustainable development is generally referred to as the goal of any economic activity favouring human well-being without compromising or endangering the survival of natural communities and their relationships within the common environment (United Nations Conference in Rio de Janeiro, 1992). In other words, sustainable development implies the recruitment of natural resources for human needs in such a way as to protect the often fragile ecological homeostatic equilibria. If one accepts both the 'natural environment component' as a value and the relevance of resilience mechanisms that drive such a component for the long-lasting satisfaction of human needs, then preserving these mechanisms ought to condition any kind of development.

The idea of sustainability is really an evolving vision representing the confluence of a great variety of concerns, disciplines and political pressures. Given the multiplicity of origins, definitions of sustainability abound and often diverge, depending on the nature of problems being addressed and the interests of the parties generating the definition (Bookman, 1994). Most academics and policy-makers would agree that for development to be sustainable, it should follow certain prescribed guidelines. First, development should ensure that future generations inherit a technological, capital, and environmental wealth greater than the one inherited by the present generation. Second, development should not interfere with the natural functioning of life-support systems or natural ecological processes (including protection of biodiversity). Third, it should foster equitable distribution of all costs and benefits. Finally, development should facilitate the participation of local populations from all societal sectors in decision-making, and must be carried out in a manner consistent with a thorough respect for the cultural values of the affected communities.

When tourism is directly and fully involved in the development perspectives of a territory, the first question that arises concerns the sector's sustainable relationship with the environment. This is particularly the case when examining tourism development in small islands. Scholars, economists and policy-makers have spent at least two decades discussing and debating the unfettered growth of mass tourism and its consequences on the environment, while seeking to devise feasible low-impact alternatives. Under-estimated and under-valued in the past, tourism in recent years has become one of the world's largest industries according to many economic measures, and there is a widespread view that it will continue to grow strongly into the foreseeable future (ENIT-ISTAT, 1995). This is certainly the case on the small islands of the Mediterranean, where the common features of peripheral location, import dependence, and limited resources and investment bases create a development pattern where options are few, and where a significant amount of economic activities is inevitably generated by tourism (Wilkinson, 1989).

Nevertheless, in the so-called modern tourist industry, the need to reconcile development and environment is especially evident, since natural heritage and the satisfaction of tourists are strongly related. The environmental compatibility of tourism can be pursued through a three-level approach:

1. The ecological approach aimed at: (i) long-term development without the depletion of resources, since irreversible damage to natural assets reduces the tourist attraction level; (ii) a decision-making policy based on the concept of sustainability; and (iii) solidarity toward nature and toward people (an environmental ethics approach, see Canestrini, 1995), focusing on helping people rediscover the concept of acting gratuitously for the sake of future generations.

2. A sociocultural approach aimed at avoiding or mitigating: (i) impacts on the social structure inevitably produced by imbalances in terms of per capita income derived from exogenous investments (Bresso and Torchio, 1992); (ii) impoverishment of local identity, since mass tourism may lead to the infiltration of extraneous cultural elements (e.g., non-traditional building designs); and (iii) levelling-off in the behaviour of local inhabitants, and, instead, enhancing the value of unique traditions, history, and folklore for which competition is at a minimum.

3. An economic approach geared towards pursuing: (i) an harmonious approach on environmental issues where the often conflicting interests of local or external groups seek quick profit on short-term objectives; (ii) the implementation of rational criteria to safeguard and enhance the value of nature as a common resource; and (iii) needs satisfaction within the ethics

of sustainability, which does not mean development adhering to the status quo, but rather economic growth below the limits of territorial carrying capacity. (Levi, 1995)

However, it appears that efforts to approach tourism development in the aforementioned manner have, thus far, proven elusive. Indeed, as the experience of the Aeolian islands demonstrates, unsustainable methods of tourism development continue to be the norm in many island environments.

Geography of the Aeolian Islands

The Aeolian archipelago, also known as the Lipari Islands, lies within a fascinating region. A deep sea separates the archipelago from the mainland and has always given it an aura of mystery. These tiny islands are located in the lower Tyrrhenian Sea, northeast of Sicily. Seven, in total, islands form the region (i.e., Lipari, Vulcano, Panarea, Stromboli, Salina, Filicudi, and Alicudi, see Figure 7.1). The archipelago that forms a Y-shape extends over 200 km and covers an overall surface area of 116.3 km^2.[1]

Lipari covers a surface of 37.6 km^2. The island's base is about 1,000 m below sea level, and its highest peak is Mount Chirica (602 m). Salina, located just 4 km northwest of Lipari, has an area of 26.8 km^2 and is the island with the tallest peaks, the steep Felci and Porri mountains (reaching 962 m and 860 m, respectively). These two volcanic cones are separated by the saddle of Valdichiesa (290 m) yielding the characteristic shape that led to the ancient name of *Didyme* (double, or twin).

Vulcano has a surface of 22 km^2 and its highest peak is 500 m above sea level. In fact, the island's peak is just the top part of a largely underwater volcano that is now in a permanent solfataric stage.[2] This means that major environmental risks still exist and, thus, the island is constantly monitored for gases and seismic activity. Panarea, with a surface of only 3.3 km^2 and a coastline of 7.4 km, is the second smallest island, after Basiluzzo (0.3 km^2). Stromboli is the only truly active volcano (although eruptions occurred on Vulcano as recently as 1890) and is currently experiencing continuous though moderate explosive activity. Unmistakable because of its conical shape and clouds of black smoke ringing the peak, Stromboli covers a surface of 12.6 km^2 and has a 15.8 km coastline marked by rocky crags and cliffs. With the exception of its verdant northeast side that is under cultivation, most of the island is bare (Barberi, 1995).

Filicudi covers an area of 9.5 km^2 and rises 774 m (the Felci Trench). It is the top part of a much more extensive volcanic structure whose main axis extends to a depth of 1,000 m. Finally, Alicudi is the westernmost island with a surface of 5 km^2 and a coastline of 8.4 km. Its peak, Filo dell'Arpa (675 m), is the projecting part of a volcanic structure that extends to a depth of 1,500 m and gives the island a conical shape.

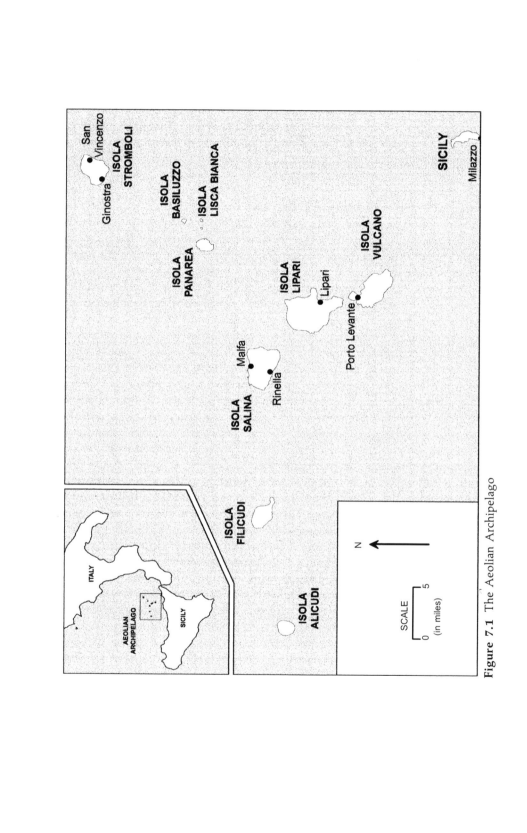

Figure 7.1 The Aeolian Archipelago

A typical feature of the archipelago is the uniqueness of each island. Because of different evolutionary paths, each island has its own specific environmental and socio-economic features, plus a unique morphology, fauna, flora and landscape (Genovese, 1995; Rossi *et al.*, 1996). However, in confronting the common problem of development constraints, the same general question arises for all islands. Specifically, how does each island reconcile economic growth with the preservation of its specific natural and cultural heritage?

The Aeolian Tourism Attitude

The beauty and uniqueness of small insular environments have always attracted visitors. The 'virgin' environment of these destinations, plus their charm based on archaic traditions, have become the major attractions for several tourist packages. People from highly urbanized and industrial northern European countries who commonly seek closer contact with nature, find a Garden of Eden on these land fragments (Francescato, 1991).

During the mid-1960s the Aeolian archipelago became part of a tourism circuit that attracted more and more people. In the late 1960s and 1970s throughout Italy, and on small islands in particular, the 'tourism boom' was a result of generalized well-being and an increase in leisure time in the principal markets (Figure 7.2). The need to expand their infrastructure caused Lipari and Vulcano to undergo a broad exploitation of their territories (Figure 7.3). Stromboli lost its traditional leading position as a destination because of connection and berthing problems while, conversely, in Panarea the availability of abandoned ancient houses led to the 'holiday house market' fed by tourists mainly from Northern Italy.

By 1966, Lipari and Vulcano accounted for the largest portion of the

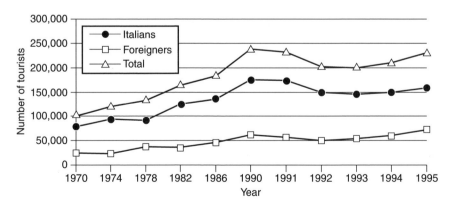

Figure 7.2 Tourism dynamics for hotels and guest-houses in the Archipelago, 1970–95

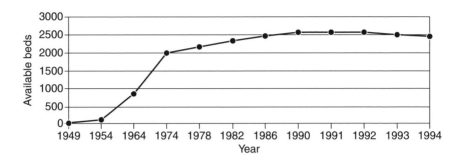

Figure 7.3 Available beds in hotels, Aeolian Archipelago, 1949–94

insular region's tourism accommodation capacity (44 per cent and 33 per cent, respectively). Unfortunately, this over-concentration of tourism facilities also caused the first signs of environmental damage on these two islands. Because of a total lack of urban planning, speculative building activities took place on a devastating scale. As a result, urban growth was haphazard and displayed no environmental awareness on the part of developers. Salina also began to experience tourism development through the purchase of old homes and speculative programmes, many of which were only partially completed. In this case, market saturation also led to a number of environmental hazards. For example, because of the large-scale construction of dwellings in Vulcano Porto particularly in the direction of the isthmus of Vulcanello, there has been a systematic degradation of uncontaminated scenic beauties. Today, Alicudi and Filicudi are the only islands left untouched by this phenomenon of rapid tourism expansion.

Interestingly, by the 1970s the number of foreign visitors on the islands had declined while that of Italians increased because of the expansion of the secondary residence market which had become a typical phenomenon throughout the archipelago (Cavallaro, 1987). Unfortunately, the proliferation of 'vacation homes' has historically made it difficult to determine the actual number of tourists. In fact, even today the number of arrivals is actually higher than what is indicated in official data.

By the 1980s, the available bedrooms on the islands had increased by 59 per cent from 913 to 1,455 while the number of hotel occupants grew from 46,009 to 105,327 (+60 per cent), and those staying in non-hotel businesses from 6,808 to 59,050 (+767 per cent). In 1986, after years of constant increase in the number of visitors, there were 354,381 recorded bed-nights, equally distributed among hotels and non-hotel structures or complementary businesses. However, only 26 per cent of the visitors on the islands were foreigners. These statistics, particularly the rapid increase in the number of day-trippers and tourists staying in non-hotel accommodation, indicate that over time the islands have become a destination for people with second homes and a growing number of budget-minded individuals.

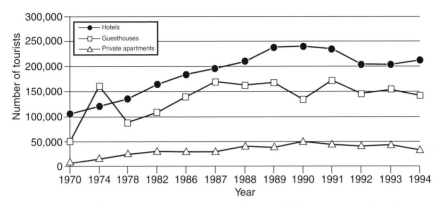

Figure 7.4 Trends in tourist occupancy (Italians and foreigners) in hotels, guest-houses and private apartments on the Aeolian islands, 1970–94

In 1994, the average daily amount spent for food, lodging, transportation, and souvenirs was estimated to be 420,000 lire per tourist in a four-star hotel, 360,300 lire in a three-star hotel, 260,000 lire in a two-star hotel and 198,000 lire in a one-star hotel (A.A.P.T., 1990–1995; ISTAT, 1992; see Figure 7.4). The tourist function index, a measure that compares the total number of bedrooms available with the resident population, has gone from 79 in 1986, to 84.5 in 1990, and 81 in 1994.[3] The value of this index shows that the islands have become a 'predominantly tourist commune' (Pearce, 1995: 84).

It has to be borne in mind that the seven islands have always had different degrees of tourist penetration and density of visitors and, therefore, environmental degradation. Indeed, each of the destinations in the Aeolian archipelago seems to match one of the three stages of development of an evolutionary model for small-island tourism (De Albuquerque and McElroy, 1992).

1. Emerging/pioneering: this refers to exploratory tourism, a stage when there is a low density of visitors. The only tourists are persons who, despite the inconvenience caused by the poor quality of infrastructure and services, choose the destination for its unspoiled natural features.
2. Transitional/expansionist: this involves a rapid growth in tourism flows matched by a large increase in the number of hotel facilities. During this stage environmental problems begin to arise.
3. Mature/saturation: during this stage there is a high density of tourists and, therefore, a high impact in terms of exploitation of resources and urban expansion. These impacts lead to landscape degradation. At this stage, replacement of natural attractions with human-built diversions and services usually takes place.

More or less, each Aeolian island seems to fit one of these stages. After an initial tourism explosion, Filicudi and Alicudi have experienced more than a

50 per cent decline in arrivals, thus returning to a stage where the services offered are adequate for the visitors. Thus, these islands are destinations for adventurous travellers seeking peaceful, non-crowded places. Stromboli and Panarea can be classified as transitional destinations, offering both natural and human-built environments. Moreover, they have adequate hotel and entertainment structures to satisfy the tourists. Salina is difficult to classify according to this model, since it has witnessed a major reduction in the number of arrivals. Lipari and Vulcano have reached the mature/saturation stage of tourism development. The damages inflicted on these territories because of tourism are profound and hard to reverse. On these two islands the type of infrastructure and the facilities available are geared towards mass tourism.

Tourists coming to the Aeolian islands are still fascinated by the charm of these destinations although there are wide-ranging inefficiencies in terms of the hotel accommodation and services on offer. These facilities certainly do not match up to the fame that these islands' unique natural wonders have endowed them with. To gain a better understanding about the tourists who visit the islands Tables 7.1 and 7.2 present some results from a questionnaire conducted in 1996 with 400 visitors (Zacchi, 1997).

Evidently, many tourists come to the islands for the seaside and nature in general. The resorts and attractions also draw a sizeable portion of the visitors. By contrast, activities such as visiting archaeological sites, scuba diving, or participating in cultural events do not feature as major reasons for visiting this region (Table 7.1). Table 7.2 summarizes various problems the tourists would not like to experience while on holiday on the islands. Not surprisingly, most tourists are unwilling to witness unclean places or a polluted sea during their stay. A majority also mentioned that expensive goods would be off-putting. By contrast, less than 30 per cent of the visitors stated that they would be affected by the lack of resort areas. Overcrowding also did not seem to be a major issue for many tourists.

Table 7.1 Features most sought by visitors on the Aeolian islands

I look for . . .	no.	%
Sea	320	42.0
Nature	209	27.6
Resort and attractions	128	17.0
Archaeology	31	4.1
History	25	3.3
Tranquility and quiet	18	2.5
Elite tourism	14	1.8
Cultural events	10	1.3
Scuba diving	2	0.3
Environmental mystique	1	0.1

Note: Based on survey of 392 tourists (758 suggestions were offered in total).

Table 7.2   Features which tourists are unwilling to put up with while on holiday in the Aeolian islands

Scores*	Dirty places		Dirty sea		Excessive traffic		Crowded places		Expensive goods		Lack of resort areas	
	n	*(%)*	*n*	*(%)*	*n*	*(%)*	*n*	*(%)*	*n*	*(%)*	*n*	*(%)*
1	51	15.5	70	21.7	81	26.6	73	23.3	25	7.1	111	36.5
2	44	13.4	30	9.3	37	12.1	44	14.1	37	10.4	50	16.4
3	52	15.8	37	11.5	49	16.1	67	21.4	73	20.6	52	17.1
4	28	8.5	32	9.9	25	8.2	28	8.1	47	13.3	21	6.9
5	152	46.3	153	47.5	113	37.0	101	32.3	172	48.6	70	23.0
% responding		82.2		80.7		76.4		78.4		88.7		76.2

Notes: Based on survey of 392 tourists.
* Scores were assigned according to the tourists' attitudes as follows: 1 = marginal importance, 2 = small importance, 3 = modest importance, 4 = important, 5 = very important

It is interesting to note that those visitors arriving during low season have pointed out that, between October and May the islands seem to be completely different places compared to the situation during the summer. Indeed, during the summer months the main destinations are crowded, noisy, and generally chaotic and, thus, not just environmentally but also humanly unsustainable.

Degradation of the Aeolian Territory

Tourism development in the archipelago has not been matched by the provision of adequate services and infrastructure essential for civilized living. These facilities are, in fact, already insufficient for the local population during winter. A local magazine *Nuovo Notiziario delle Isole Eolie* has repeatedly and clearly outlined these inefficiencies. They include a shortage of berths, insufficient water supply and health structures, plus poor waste and transportation management (Singh, 1996). The lack of a General Regulatory Plan and unemployment are some of the additional problems addressed in most of the *exposés*. Tourism has generally been regarded as the relief valve needed for the archipelago to escape its state of abandonment that occurred after World War II (Cavallaro, 1987). However, the islands' discovery and their subsequent exploitation by tourism occurred in too explosive a manner to allow for the harmonious development of this `naturally rich but ecologically fragile territory.

As in so many island environments around the Mediterranean, the heaviest damage has been caused by speculative building activities. Such deleterious activities pay little regard to public interest and operate on the margins of lawful practices. Many private houses and hotel structures have actually been built illegally. Speculative building also consumes large tracts of land, is difficult to control, and is hard to quantify. A good example of how building speculation has resulted in general deterioration is indicated by the lack of facilities for rainwater collection in new houses. Traditionally these facilities have been seen as necessary for survival and would be, even today, important for saving such a precious resource. Because the islands are not served by efficient sewer systems (in fact, sewage is currently disposed of in cesspools), higher anthropogenic pressure will mean more health-related risks. Other environmental problems relate to excessive traffic, waste disposal, uncontrolled wood fires, and so on.

Thus, because of mass tourism and related rapid development there have been major impacts on the quality of life for all living entities within the archipelago. For instance, summer wood fires combined with the abandonment of agriculture and other traditional activities have led to the loss of many endemic species of pelagic flora. Many bird populations who have historically come to the Aeolian islands during mating season have to compete for shrinking space and resources with seagulls that proliferate in the dumping areas. Leisure boats disturb nesting falcons near the rocky cliffs. Every summer the islanders resent being forced to suffer the 'emergence of tourism' and, thus, the archipelago loses part of its charm as it projects an image of disorganized and reluctant hospitality.

Socio-economic growth can be long-lasting not only when it is based on the exploitation of many different resources, but also and above all, when it respects the local natural and cultural environments (e.g., traditions and folklore). Luckily, the inhabitants of the Aeolian islands feel they are a unique population. Their pride is also fostered by the specific actions of the 'Lipari History and Problem Study and Research Centre', an NGO devoted to keep alive past and recent history and the unique aspects of the islands' everyday life. This organization promotes initiatives aimed at rediscovering old feelings concerning Lipari culture and strives to keep intact this increasingly threatened identity. The attraction of these islands lies essentially in their natural, scenic and cultural aspects: if these qualities are compromised, growth and development will have no future.

Endemic Environment Hardship: Water Supply and Transportation

The archipelago has never had natural springs and, thus, the inhabitants have been forced to come up with various interesting ideas for collecting rainwater. One traditional method is the installation of rainwater tanks on the roofs of Lipari-style houses. Currently, tanker ships from Naples and Augusta supply the islands and, during the summer, they even come from as far as La Spezia in northern Italy. Large amounts of water brought to the archipelago and distributed through pipes or by means of tanker trucks (especially for the more distant villages on Lipari and Vulcano) impose a heavy cost on the

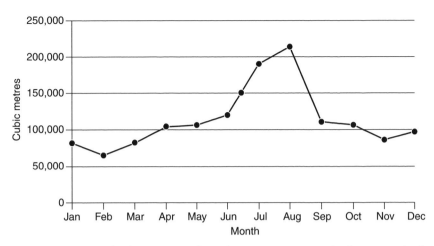

Figure 7.5 Lipari island: water supply (cubic metres per month) from outside the Archipelago, 1996

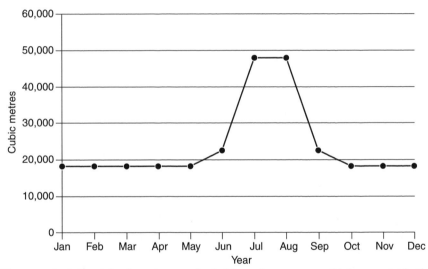

Figure 7.6 Salina island: water supply (cubic metres per month) from outside the Archipelago, 1996

islands. Thus, the distribution network must be managed efficiently to avoid waste. The supply of water increases significantly during summer to sustain the higher demand due to tourism (Figures 7.5 and 7.6). The residents of the island are well aware of tourism's impact on their precious water resources. Questionnaires filled in by a representative sample (Zacchi, 1997) have shown that the Aeolian islanders consider water supply as *good* for the entire year, although they rank it as no more than *fair* for the summer season.

The connection network between the islands and from the islands to the mainland is a major issue relating to Aeolian development, since it links the outside world to this naturally isolated microcosm (Di Geronimo, 1990; Moles, 1992). The main beneficiaries of a good transportation network are the various economic sectors. Nevertheless, other sectors, such as civil defence or healthcare, also require efficient services to carry out their duties. Transportation becomes vitally important to ensure the success of the tourist industry, especially when plans are made to deal with the seasonal nature of this sector. However, the only action taken so far has been to increase the prices of hydrofoil and ferry tickets for the June to September period.

Berthing facilities are permanently inadequate, not only because of the rise in popularity of leisure boating, but also because of regular maritime services. Indeed, during periods of bad weather, the latter are frequently cancelled since there are not adequate berths. In addition to structural technical deficiencies in all the islands that make it difficult to carry out embarkation and disembarkation operations, silting also occurs in the harbours of Panarea, Alicudi and Stromboli. The Lipari Administration has even submitted a complaint to report that 'serious delays in completing harbour works on the Aeolian islands have generated several inconveniences, in addition to economic damage' (*Nuovo Notiziario delle isole Eolie*, 1996). The 'Harbour Plan' aimed at rationalizing the management of ports and improving their functional capabilities, is still *in itinere.*

Towards 'Eco-compatible' Tourism

Tourism represents 5.5 per cent of the EU's gross domestic product (in some European States about or more than 10 per cent). As such, it is a strategic priority sector for economic development, one of the 17 sectors for which medium-term employment is expected to increase, making it an industry of real European interest. In the Green Paper *EU's Role in Tourism* (EU, 1995), tourism is explicitly mentioned as a sector of paramount importance for sustainable development in Europe. A number of key elements are seen as important for evolving toward such sustainability (Canova, 1995). Included in these are the internalization of environmental costs through tax plans, the transformation of environmental constraints into competitive factors, and the diversification of time (extension of tourist seasons), geography (tourist promotion in different environments) and typology as the best strategy to alleviate tourism's impact on the environment.

This context can help explain the Aeolian reality, which is common to that on many of the hundreds of inhabited Mediterranean small islands. A chief reason behind the archipelago's environmental degradation is the die-hard attitude towards mass tourism that has, either directly or indirectly, produced negative synergism (Schmidt di Friedberg, 1993). The progressive abandonment of traditional activities has not only led to a loss of the *modus vivendi* forming the roots of the local population's culture (Lipman, 1993). It has also enabled forms of social breakdown, since 70 per cent of the Aeolian families rely economically on 'single-culture tourism'. Indeed, most families carry out tourism-related activities without having any experience of the sector. Thus, they remain at the mercy of a tricky, fast-changing, and shameless market. The tourism resource cannot be governed unless solid alternative economic structures are first settled, based on the recovery of primary resources (Bodini and Giavelli, 1992).

High unemployment, the ups and downs of the tourism sector, recessions that threaten trade, recurring crises in traditional production activities are all convincing arguments for launching an alternative environment-aware 'tourism formula' with links to the unique characteristics of the archipelago, including its people and cultural heritage. Local administrations need to get involved and start taking action towards a recovery based on innovative methods and on upgrading the professional skills of operators (Calzoni, 1988). Agriculture and fishing, in particular, must not be allowed to fade away, but must be placed in a position where they can support tourism through the diffusion of D.O.C. (controlled origin of denomination) products, as is already occurring in the case of Malvasia wine in Salina.

In addition, complementary activities should be carried out, such as agrotourism and rural tourism. Agrotourism, ruled by national and regional laws, offers food and lodging in structures whose main activity is agriculture. Instead, rural tourism refers to the rental of restructured country homes to tourists. In Italy, there are no specific definitions nor any specific laws governing this sector (Lipman, 1993; Berni, *et al.*, 1995). The advantage of both agrotourism and rural tourism is that they allow conventional sea-based tourism to be integrated with cultural aspects. In addition, these alternative tourism forms can make it easier for locals to promote typical island products. Finally, the re-appropriation of arable land would put an end to the state of abandonment of farming areas, thus contributing to more efficient control of the territory. This will also prevent wood fires and intolerable forms of pollution caused by illegal waste dumping (Gandolla, 1992; Navarra, 1994).

Until recently, enthusiasm has been a sufficient stimulus for travellers to discover the natural wonders of the Aeolian Sea and islands. Any inconvenience in terms of services and accommodations was tolerated. Nowadays, however, there is an increasing demand for satisfactory quality/price ratios. Also, a more widespread ecological awareness among travellers implies the rejection of any form of degradation.

The seasonal nature of Aeolian tourism eventually has to come to an end, not only because the average occupancy of hotel accommodation is very low. Fortunately the presence of tourists in spring and fall is becoming increasingly more common. The absence of overcrowding, lack of traffic and noise pollution, and a clean appearance, mean that these off-season visitors can achieve a better quality/price ratio. However, this trend towards reducing seasonality must be enhanced by diversifying the product on offer and extending visitors' opportunities. One of the 'channels' readily applicable is the cultural one. For instance, in Lipari it is possible 'to read' the history of the Mediterranean civilizations and, by visiting the archaeological museum (Bernabò-Brea, 1995), review the fundamental milestones of western civilization. The importance of this cultural heritage can be emphasized through the development of a real archaeo-tourism that, when fully in operation, will be able to inject new life into the island economy.

Conclusion

In the short term, the economic rewards of traditional tourism can be a windfall for the Aeolian islands in need of external exchange to supplement their lagging economies. But the medium- and long-term effects of such a tourism product on the natural heritage can be more than the islands' socio-economic and ecological systems can sustain. The question arising is whether the wish to switch from mass tourism to more sustainable tourism forms masks more complex and less encouraging patterns for tourist destinations (Bookman, 1994). However, debating whether alternative tourism forms such as ecotourism are beneficial may be purely academic, since a variety of factors could eventually preclude economic alternatives for the islands.

At any rate, there is an urgent need to change existing trends, though alternatives are difficult to pursue. A rapid but balanced socio-economic development may involve a requalification of tourist activities on the Aeolian archipelago, since this is still considered by its inhabitants to be the best remunerative activity. But touristic development is subject to unpredictable fluctuations of demand in the international market and, thus, it needs to be integrated with and supplemented by other activities conceived and managed in up-to-date ways. There are at least three necessary changes to ensure that future tourism development takes place in a more harmonious manner with the natural environment.

1. Policy-making: landscape protection and tourism opportunities should persuade the public administrations to include environmental protection within the decision processes in a framework of sustainability. New forms of tourism (green, thermal, cultural, scientific, etc.) should be developed in order to eliminate the industry's seasonal nature. The reduction of arrival peaks during the summer as a consequence of an extended tourism season will allow the infrastructure and services to adequately support a higher number of visitors.
2. Marketing changes: each initiative designed to re-qualify tourism should include certified actions based on (recovered) environmental quality. New tourist packages should be advertised, not just in order to enhance tourism for its own sake, but also to initiate a truly environmentally

responsible product which can enter the market with a new image capable of handling foreign competition.

3. Technological changes: conditions such as exclusion and isolation, that notoriously have precluded these communities from developing 'natural' forms of economic growth, can be overcome by fostering initiatives for introducing innovations suited to the peculiarities of these ecosystems where strategic resources, like power and water, are chronically lacking. These innovations, however, should be positively related to human exploitation activities (agriculture, fishing, etc.) and always meet residents' needs and expectations. Without such a relationship, even a project highly favoured by the experts, will be refused by residents and could prove unfeasible.

Notes

1. The Aeolian archipelago is located between 38° 22′ and 38° 49′ north and between 1° 53′ and 2° 48′ east. The sea reaches a depth of 2,000 metres although off the shore of Lipari, the extended underwater geological structure, Secca del Capo, almost breaks the surface at a depth of only 7.5 metres. Administratively, the islands belong to the province of Messina and are unevenly divided into four municipalities: Malfa, Santa Marina Salina, Leni (on Salina island), and Lipari (the latter includes Lipari island and the remaining five islands).

2. The solfataric (named after the Italian volcano of Solfatara) stage refers to a late phase of volcanic activity that is characterized by sulphurous gases emitting from a vent. It is also known as a fumarolic stage.

3. The tourist function index is measured as $f(H) = HB/P * 100$ where HB = hotel bedrooms, P = local population, and $f(H)$ = tourism function index.

References

A.A.P.T. Lipari (1990–1995) *Dati di ricettivita turistica*. Messina: AAPT.

Barberi, F. (1995) I fuochi del mare. *Nuove Effemeridi*, 30: 92–6.

Bernabò-Brea, L. (1995) Archeoliana. *Nuove Effemeridi*, 30: 39–61.

Berni, M., Conti, F. and Canova, L. (1995) *L'eco-audit nelle strutture alberghiere*. Milan: Associazione Cultura Turismo Ambiente (ACTA).

Bodini, A. and Giavelli, G. (1992) Multicriteria analysis as a tool to investigate compatibility between conservation and development on Salina island, Aeolian archipelago, Italy. *Environmental Management*, 16: 633–52.

Bookman, S. (1994) Perspective on ecotourism in island development. *Insula*, 3(1): 19–21.

Bresso, M. and Torchio, M. (1992) Problemi di sviluppo e ambiente in microsistemi insulari: il caso delle isole Eolie. In *ISLAND 2000: The World of Islands: What Development on the Year 2000's Eve?* University of Messina (20–1).

Calzoni, G. (1988) *Principi di economia dell'ambiente e di gestione turistica del territorio*. Milan: Franco Angeli.

Canestrini, D. (1995) Ethnic tourism: the responsible way. *Insula*, 4(1): 20–3.

Canova, L. (1995) Principi per un turismo sostenibile. In *Per un turismo all'insegna della qualità*. Rimini: Movimento Consumatori (55–61).

Cavallaro, C. (1987) *Sistema territoriale Arcipelago Isole Eolie.* Genova: Sagep (19–43).

De Albuquerque, K. and McElroy, J. (1992) Caribbean small-island tourism styles and sustainable strategies. *Environmental Management,* 16: 619–32.

Di Geronimo, S. (1990) *Convenzione sulla Riserva Marina Isole Eolie.* Rome: Ministero della Marina Mercantile.

ENIT–ISTAT (1995) *Sesto rapporto sul turismo italiano.* Rome: ISTAT (439–72 and 533–76).

EU (1995) Tourism and the environment in Europe. Brussels: Official Publications of the European Community (3–22).

Francescato, G. (1991) C'è un tesoro nell'isola del futuro. *Airone Mare* (Supplement) 121. Milan: G. Mondadori (10–30).

Gandolla, M. (1992) Lo smaltimento dei rifiuti in isole e piccole comunità isolate. In *ISLAND 2000: The World of Islands: What Development on the Year 2000's Eve?* Messina: University of Messina (72–3).

Genovese, N. (1995) Arcipelago di celluloide. *Nuove Effemeridi* (Guida, Palermo) (135–8).

ISTAT (1992) *Popolazione e abitazioni 13th Censimento generale della popolazione e delle abitazioni (al 20. ottobre 1991).* Rome: ISTAT.

Levi, V. (1995) Notazioni psicologiche per la qualità del turismo. In *Per un turismo all'insegna della qualita.* Rimini: Movimento Consumatori (25–7).

Lipman, G. (1993) Più qualità ambientale per l'ecoturismo di massa. *L'impresa ambiente,* 2: 41–51.

Moles, A. (1992) On islands and isolation. In *ISLAND 2000: The World of Islands: What Development on the Year 2000's Eve?* Messina: University of Messina (127–8).

Navarra, E. (1994) *Il problema dei rifiuti solidi urbani nell'isola di Salina.* Salina, Messina: L.I.P.U.

Nuovo Notiziario delle isole Eolie (1996) Lipari, Messina.

Pearce, D. (1995) *Tourism Today: A Geographical Analysis.* New York. Longman.

Schmidt di Friedberg, P. (1993) Ambiente degradato turismo dimezzato. *L'impresa ambiente,* 2: 28–33.

Singh, N. (1996) Sustainable development and waste management in small island states. *Insula,* 5(1): 15–21.

Rossi, O., Vezzosi, M., Zurlini, G. and d'Ayala, A. (1996) Environmental profile of the Italian small islands. *Insula,* 5(1): 8–15.

Wilkinson, P.F. (1989) Integrating tourism into national development in island microstates. Proceedings of the Conference on Economics and Environment, Caribbean Conservation Association. Barbados, November.

Zacchi, G. (1997) Valorizzazione turistica e salvaguardia ambientale nell'arcipelago delle isole Eolie. Unpublished dissertation, University of Parma.

8

Tourism Development and Sustainability in the Greek Archipelagos

Dimitrios Buhalis and Dimitrios Diamantis

Introduction: Sustainability in Tourism

Over the last few years there have been ongoing discussions concerning the ability of tourist destinations, particularly islands, to adopt more sustainable-orientated practices. Increasingly, both the industry and planners realize that environmental sustainability is closely linked to profitability. This is especially the case in tourism where consumers appreciate natural resources and are willing to pay higher prices for superior environments. Sustainability in tourism has been widely discussed as people attempt to define the term and develop suitable tools that will enable them to maintain and perhaps enhance resources for future generations (Butler, 1996, 1997; Hall and Lew, 1998; Mowforth and Munt, 1998; Westlake and Diamantis, 1998).

Adopting sustainability in the context of tourism often creates 'tourism-centric' situations, where most of the approaches become partially divorced from the main principles of the sustainability concept (Hunter, 1995a, 1995b, 1997). In this case, decision-makers concentrate on tourism development as a short-term strategy, tending to neglect sustainability issues and the long-term prosperity of regions. This situation arises from the interpretation of sustainability. To some practitioners sustainability is expressed only with reference to products and/or segments, while to others it is a process of development, and to still others it is a principle which should be adopted by all tourism development and activities (Godfrey, 1996). The application of sustainability in tourism takes the form of either a tool used for the sector's long-term survival or for the maintenance of resources in order to generate more tourism demand (Fyall and Garrod, 1997). In both cases, it is recognized that sustainability is critical for the success of tourism destinations and enterprises, not only in terms of profitability but also to determine long-term competitiveness (Buhalis and Fletcher, 1995).

The challenge facing many islands and other destinations, which are heavily dependent on tourism (Colombo *et al.*, 1997), is to advance strategic planning and adopt new techniques embodied within sustainable development principles (Cooper, 1996, 1997; Butler, 1997; Buhalis, 1999b). This chapter concentrates on sustainable practices on insular Greece. Tourism development on the Greek islands is at a crossroads, as years of mass tourism development combined with inadequate and often irrational planning have resulted in unsuitable facilities and poor sustainability practices, jeopardizing the competitiveness of Greek tourism and the prosperity of the region in general. This chapter initially presents tourism practices in Greece and it provides an overview of the Aegean and Ionian archipelagos. The analysis aims to illustrate the policies of both the public and private sectors and their implications for the industry. The chapter also discusses environmental practices in Greece and illustrates their impact in the context of islands. It examines briefly the needs of small and medium-sized tourism enterprises (SMTEs) as they dominate the tourist industry and play an extremely important role in the sustainability of local resources. Finally, the chapter demonstrates the challenges facing the islands, and illustrates that sustainable tourism development should prevail in order to maximize the competitiveness of the destination and to ensure the conservation of its resources.

Tourism in Greece

Greece, including its island region, has a long tradition of tourism mainly due to its history and ancient civilization (Chiotis and Coccossis, 1992; EIU, 1995). Few regions globally can demonstrate a comparable concentration of heritage, cultural, natural and climatic resources. Warm Greek hospitality has been renowned over the centuries as *xenos* (foreign) was considered sacred and was protected by Zeus the father of the mythological Olympian Gods. Although the region is endowed with many resources, deficient public and private tourism-sector management and marketing constantly discount the benefits of tourist activities. This is reflected by the weak profitability of private enterprises and the negative impacts on destinations, all of which jeopardize the sustainability of local resources in the long term (Buhalis, 1998, 1999a).

Greece experienced a dramatic increase in tourist flows in the late 1970s and 1980s. This growth was facilitated by the maturity of competing destinations; the availability of natural, sociocultural and environmental resources; the existing airport infrastructure in major islands; and the lower cost of living in comparison with most of Europe (Buhalis, 1998; EIU, 1986, 1990; Leontidou, 1991). From a global perspective, in 1997 Greece was the 17th most popular destination worldwide with around 10.6 million tourism

Table 8.1 Greek tourism: international arrivals, bednights, capacity and exchange
earned

Year	Number of arrivals (m)	Number of bednights by foreigners (m)	Bed capacity (000)	Receipts exchange (m $)
1950	0.03	NA	NA	4.7
1960	0.4	3	57	49.2
1970	1.6	7.7	118.9	193.6
1980	5.3	27.2	278	1,733.5
1985	7.0	35.8	333.8	1428
1990	9.3	36.3	438.4	2575
1991	8.3	28.9	459.3	2,566.1
1992	9.8	36.3	475.8	3,268.4
1993	9.9	36.5	499.6	3,335.2
1994	11.2	40.7	908.4	3,904.9
1995	10.7	38.7	535.8	4106
1996	9.8	35.5	548.7	3660
1997	10.6	38.2	561.4	3800
1998*	10.9	NA	NA	6744
1999*	11.6	NA	NA	8309
2000*	12.2	NA	NA	9181
2001*	12.8	NA	NA	1,0115
2002*	13.3	NA	NA	1,1032
2003*	13.7	NA	NA	1,1939
2004*	14.1	NA	NA	1,2901
2005*	14.5	NA	NA	1,3919

Sources: GNTO (1998); HCG (1998); WTO (1998a)
Note: * Forecasts

arrivals, as illustrated in Table 8.1. Although there has been fairly consistent
annual growth, just like other European destinations, Greece has experienced
a decline in its market share to long-haul destinations.

Tourism remains a major export of the Greek economy and an important
contributor to the Gross Domestic Product (GDP) and balance of payments.
For instance, in 1993 it generated $3.3 billion, provided 4.4 per cent of the
GDP and covered 26 per cent of the country's merchandise trade deficit. In
1998, it was estimated that tourism generated around 18.7 per cent of the
total export of goods, an indication of its positive direct impact (HCG, 1998).
However, the true contribution of tourism to the Greek economy is
substantially greater, as the official figures ignore the 'para-economy' (black
or informal economy), estimated to be as high as 28–50 per cent of the
official GDP (Buhalis, 1998).

Tourism is also a major source of employment, accounting for somewhere
between 8 to 11 per cent of the total workforce (GNTO, 1998). Overall, the
importance of tourism to the Greek economy is expected to increase in the

following years, with estimates placing arrivals at 14.5 million and earnings at around $13.9 billion by the year 2005 (Table 8.1). This forecast inevitably affects the insular regions in Greece, as their economies are far more dependent upon this sector than the mainland due to their inability to attract successful industrial development. High transportation costs and a shortage of financial and human capital have prevented the growth of industrial sectors and forced the islanders to concentrate on agriculture and services. The seasonal nature of these activities enables them to combine and complement each other.

The Tourism Industry in the Greek Islands

Greece is blessed with about 15,000 mostly uninhabited islands (Figure 8.1). There are three main island regions: the Aegean and Ionian complexes as well as the island of Crete. The Aegean archipelago is the largest island complex in Europe, accommodating 4.5 per cent of the Greek population living on 95 of the 2,000 islands (Eurostat, 1993). The area is divided into two administrative peripheries: the North Aegean Periphery and the South Aegean Periphery. In the Ionian region, there are 15 inhabited islands, accommodating 1.8 per cent of the Greek population. The island of Crete, which is the largest island region of Greece, accommodates 5.3 per cent of the Greek population and is the fifth largest island in the Mediterranean. Due to their insularity, a great nautical industry and tradition were established hundreds of years ago on these islands. Apart from agriculture and an extensive fishing industry, the regional economy depends heavily on tourism. Insularity, poor infrastructure and the lack of qualified professionals have deprived the Greek islands of the ability to develop a competitive advantage in other economic activities (EIU, 1995; Papadopoulos and Kouzelis, 1998).

Naturally, the structure of local economies varies greatly from region to region, according to the resources and economic structure of each island. In most cases, the service sector (mainly tourism) generates over 50 per cent of their Gross Regional Product, although the multiplier effect magnifies the impact of tourism and stimulates the entire economy regionally and nationally. For instance, the South Aegean region has a surplus on its international trade and contributes to the reduction of the national balance of payments deficit (Finas, 1991). In terms of employment, the insular communities are mainly engaged in the tertiary sector, as demonstrated in Table 8.2. Nearly half the persons employed in the tertiary sector are employed in tourism, especially in the vast array of SMTEs.

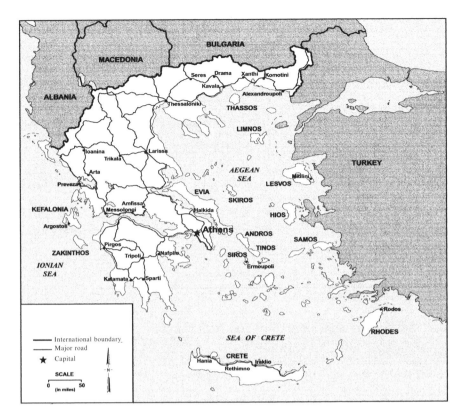

Figure 8.1 Greece
Note: Greek spellings of placenames have been used.

Table 8.2 Employment data in the Aegean and Ionian islands, 1991

Sectors	North Aegean	(%)	South Aegean	(%)	Ionian	(%)	Greece	(%)
Primary	13,926	25.3	11,315	12.7	19,778	28.6	698,738	19.6
Secondary	12,100	21.9	23,123	25.9	12,851	18.6	907,474	25.4
Tertiary	29,097	52.8	54,882	61.4	36,528	52.8	1,965,745	55.0
Total	55,123	100.0	89,320	100.0	69,157	100.0	3,571,957	100.0

Source: Papadopoulos and Kouzelis (1998)

Tourism demand

These regions attract more than a quarter of the national total of tourists, around 2.6 million visitors. A concentration in the summer months can be observed, as in the past ten years 37.5 per cent of the average arrivals were in

Table 8.3 Tourism arrivals on the South Aegean islands

Islands	1994	1995	1996	1997	1997 %
Rhodes	1,021,570	985,234	925,529	1,018,439	67.02
Kos	402,520	392,529	384,557	434,110	28.57
Kalimnos	15,734	15,735	11,806	11,411	0.75
Leros	3,382	3,301	3,426	2,656	0.17
Patmos	12,470	14,488	11,650	13,907	0.92
Karpathos	12,856	20,618	25,180	25,716	1.69
Kasos	175	174	20	185	0.01
Simi	2,715	4,954	5,859	6,301	0.41
Tilos	509	567	633	827	0.05
Nisiros	1,019	2,117	2,121	2,491	0.16
Megisti	583	533	577	533	0.04
Astipalea	421	1,299	1,147	1,128	0.07
Lipsi	NA	471	1,298	1,258	0.08
Halki	NA	NA	669	637	0.04
Total	1,473,954	1,442,020	1,374,652	1,519,599	100.00

Source: GNTO (1998); HCG (1996a, 1996b, 1997).

July and August, while the period May to September attracted 74.0 per cent of total arrivals. Although international tourists make 75 per cent of the bednights, domestic tourism is also a significant contributor as it enables the redistribution of wealth between metropolitan and peripheral regions. Unfortunately, there is a lack of reliable statistics for the entire archipelago region of Greece. Nevertheless, an example of tourist arrivals in the South Aegean Periphery is illustrated in Table 8.3.

The majority of tourists arrived on the two main islands, Rhodes and Kos, which accounted for almost 95 per cent of the total arrivals in this region. Similarly, most of the tourist arrivals in the Ionian region were concentrated in Corfu and Zakynthos (Zante), while in the North Aegean Lesbos and Samos received most arrivals (GNTO, 1998). The majority of foreign arrivals were Europeans, especially British, Germans, Swedish, Finnish, Dutch and Austrian. As a result, these nationalities are important markets providing more than three-quarters of the total demand for the region. Although the islands have unique heritage and environmental resources, their marketing and planning deficiencies mean they depend heavily upon mass tourism for their clientele. Demand is often undifferentiated and consumers frequently fail to appreciate the unique character of the destination. This is also a result of the practices of major mass tour operators who deliberately portray destinations as commodities, rather than regions of unique importance, in order to be able to shift demand to destinations that satisfy their commercial interests (Buhalis, 1999a, 2000). Similar practices are evident not only in the Mediterranean tourist industry but also in several destinations around the world (Britton, 1989; Roekaerts and Savat, 1989; Bote and Sinclair, 1991; Valenzuela, 1991; Sinclair *et al.*, 1992; Josephides 1993, 1994; Shaw and Williams, 1994; Sheldon, 1994).

Tourism supply

The Ionian and Aegean regions offer a great number of tourist facilities and resources. The EIU suggests that 'each island resort has a different market profile and there is a very wide variety from island to island in the type and geographical source of clientele' (1990: 61). Table 8.4 indicates the number of hotel units and their total capacity.

Table 8.4 Hotel capacity on the South Aegean and Ionian islands, 1997

Regions	Units	(%)	Beds	(%)
South Aegean	998	12.6	105,105	18.4
North Aegean	370	4.7	17,416	3.0
Ionian islands	641	8.1	55,613	9.7
Greece	7,916	100	571,656	100

Source: HCG (1998)

Furthermore, in 1997 total bednights spent on the Aegean and Ionian islands accounted for almost 40 per cent of the total bednights in Greece. The South Aegean Periphery dominated, accounting for 27.4 per cent of bednights, as illustrated in Table 8.5. Occupancy rates on the islands ranged between 54 per cent and 75 per cent, with the North Aegean demonstrating the lowest and the South Aegean indicating the highest rates (Table 8.6). This is due to better climatic conditions in the South, which have stimulated a higher degree of tourism development and demand.

Accessibility is one of the most critical factors in tourism development, especially for insular and peripheral destinations. The Aegean and Ionian islands have a fairly well developed transportation system linking them with the outside world. This incorporates at least one major port on each island and 21 airports across the islands, of which most are capable of receiving charter flights directly from Europe.

There are numerous flights both by private and public-owned airlines between the mainland of Greece and the islands, as well as between the islands themselves. The islands are also connected by ferry services, with the ports of Piraeus in Athens and Patras in the Peloponnese, as well as with smaller ports on the mainland (Cooper and Buhalis, 1992).

Both the demand and supply characteristics of tourism influence the planning and management functions of the industry and hence its ability to adopt sustainability practices. A number of other factors also determine

Table 8.5 Total bednights spent by foreign and domestic visitors (in millions)

Municipalities	1995	1996	1997	1997 (%)
Lesbos	544,272	586,946	588,575	1.10
Chios	172,569	177,775	178,290	0.33
Samos	921,485	885,556	977,906	1.83
North Aegean Periphery	1,638,326	1,650,277	1,744,771	3.27
Cyclades	1,306,503	1,330,767	1,470,332	2.76
Dodecanese	12,905,847	11,918,673	13,137,626	24.62
South Aegean Periphery	14,212,350	13,249,440	14,607,958	27.37
Corfu	3,535,969	2,943,619	3,250,964	6.09
Lefkada	268,436	129,175	223,163	0.42
Kefallonia	310,762	331,066	330,891	0.62
Zakynthos	595,221	542,129	754,519	1.41
Ionian Periphery	4,710,388	3,945,989	4,559,537	8.54
Greece	51,294,196	47,945,506	53,364,507	100.00

Source: GNTO (1998)

Table 8.6 Occupancy levels in accommodation establishments on the Aegean and Ionian islands (%)

Municipalities	1995	1996	1997
Lesbos	47.53	44.45	45.45
Chios	44.60	45.82	46.18
Samos	66.53	61.81	63.68
North Aegean Periphery	56.09	52.54	54.24
Cyclades	46.48	48.92	52.33
Dodecanese	74.96	70.76	79.00
South Aegean Periphery	70.97	67.73	75.15
Corfu	71.80	62.27	69.21
Lefkada	58.41	47.11	61.60
Kefallonia	57.22	49.46	45.49
Zakynthos	67.71	61.29	68.23
Ionian Periphery	69.20	60.20	66.15
Greece	56.62	54.37	58.37

Source: GNTO (1998)

sustainability practices, notably the policies and practices of the public and private sectors as well as environmental regulations and initiatives. In the following sections, an overview of these factors illustrates the sustainability of the tourist industry on the Aegean and Ionian islands. An analysis of the public and private sectors also illustrates their influence on sustainability issues.

Greek Tourism Policy and Development: Public Sector

The Greek National Tourism Organization (GNTO) and the Ministry of Development oversee most of the planning, development and promotion of tourism for the islands from their headquarters in Athens. The GNTO adopts the guidelines of the Ministry of Development and is the most important public body for tourism development in the Aegean and Ionian regions. It also operates several hotels, casinos, organized beaches, and the Athens festival. The GNTO is financed by the central government, and most of its budget is spent on marketing-related activities (WTO, 1995). Although there are three directorates of the GNTO on the islands, two on the Aegean and one on the Ionian, the central office is still responsible for nearly all decisions about tourism in the regions.

The primary aim of the National Tourism Policy is to upgrade the quality of the tourism product, in an attempt to enhance its competitiveness in the international tourism market. In this respect, Development Laws 1261/1982, 1892/90, 2234/94, 2601/98 were formulated to encourage tourism development in Greece. The first law concentrated on providing incentives for small hotel construction, resulting in the establishment of a vast number of enterprises. The second, third, and fourth laws aimed at improving the tourism infrastructure by encouraging development in the broader sense, not only of hotels but also of marinas, spas, ski resorts, as well as the restoration of traditional and historical buildings. However, none of these laws advocated environmental awareness or provided any strict legislation or substantial incentive for sustainable development. Instead they concentrated on developing facilities and infrastructure in order to enable the islands to attract more visitors.

Despite several attempts, there is still no comprehensive policy or a Master Plan for Greek tourism. Policies are often based on mid-term, unsubstantiated statements published by the GNTO, often as pre-general election pledges. Based on the assumption that tourism arrivals to Greece will increase indefinitely, tourism policy focuses invariably on several generic and unquantifiable tasks, as demonstrated in Figure 8.2.

Inconsistent political intervention has been the largest obstacle in developing a competitive and professional tourist industry in Greece. Unfortunately, tourism has extensively been utilized as a political vehicle, where each government uses it to gratify political needs and allies. In addition, research is often limited, and in cases where it does exist, it tends to be contradictory. Consequently, policy follows conventional wisdom and concentrates on attracting a larger volume of tourists, ignoring scientific methods for tourism development and management and failing to assess the economic, social and environmental impacts of each market segment (Buhalis, 1998). Therefore, a 'depoliticization of Greek tourism', towards a professionally managed public sector, guided through a strategic master

- Increase arrivals and foreign exchange income.
- Increase competitiveness of tourism products.
- Improvement of services in the industry.
- Reduction of seasonality and expansion of the tourism season.
- Attraction of high spenders and alternative types of tourism.
- Construction of facilities appealing to the upper-end of the market, such as luxury hotels, golf courses, congress centres, casinos and marinas.
- Development of tourism infrastructure, with emphasis on transportation.
- Support of social tourism for low-income domestic tourists.
- Geographical redistribution of tourism demand and supply to achieve an even spread.
- Training of tourism employees.

Figure 8.2 Generic policy objectives for Greek tourism
Source: Buhalis (1995)

plan is urgently required (Josephides, 1995: 11). Empowerment of the regional tourism offices and close interaction between all stakeholders could enable officials to assess resources and develop strategies with the local communities to maximize the sector's benefits.

Environmental Policies in Greece and the Peripheral Islands

As far as environmental policies in Greece and in the Aegean and Ionian islands are concerned, different ministries as well as different municipalities share planning and legislation responsibilities. Although the origins of environmental legislation can be traced back to 1912, it was not until the late 1980s that sound policies came to light. The overall objective of Greek environmental law is tailored to two sectors: agriculture and tourism. The law aims to battle against the decline in agriculture and to manage that sector's activities in coastal areas, where industry and urban habitation are concentrated. In addition, the law aims to minimize air pollution in large urban areas as well as to protect the 800 unique species of Greek vegetation and wildlife, the ecosystems and the marine environment (ECG, 1994).

As a member state of the European Union (EU), Greece has also adopted most of the legislative and environmental frameworks, such as the Treaty of Maastricht, the 5th Environmental Action Programme, and Directives for Environmental Impact Assessment (EIA). According to the EIA legislation, all major investments should be supported by a comprehensive evaluation of their environmental impacts before they are approved by planners and also before gaining financial support from the government. Nevertheless, there are practical inconsistencies, resting largely on delays in implementing EU directives. There have been numerous attempts to implement environmental-related policies at certain Aegean and Ionian destinations. Most of these

Programmes and Sub-programmes	Areas
Integrated Mediterranean Programmes	Related to the improvement of infrastructure
	Construction of biological waste plants
	Restoration of monuments
Regional Operational Programmes	Improvement of the quality of life
	Development of research and technology
	Establishment of data bank on tourism economic performance
ENVIREG	Protection of the environment
	Construction of biological waste plants
	Coastal area studies
LEADER I	Enhancement of cultural heritage
	Seminars on agrotourism
	Promotion of agrotourism
Integrated Programme for Tourism and Culture	Promotion of new forms of tourism
	Inter-regional cooperation between islands on tourism and cultural projects
	Enhancement of biotopes
	Studies on management of small islands

Figure 8.3 European Community programmes on the Aegean and Ionian islands
Source: Anagnostopoulou *et al.* (1996)

projects are supported mainly by the EU's Structural Funds and other leading bodies such as the United Nations Environmental Program (UNEP), UNESCO, and the World Bank. Some of the programmes, which were applied to the Aegean and Ionian islands, as illustrated in Figure 8.3, aimed to encourage sustainable economic development. Officials recognized that in order to achieve sustainable practices both micro and macro economic practices should ensure the prosperity of local communities, while European programmes should be adopted aimed at enhancing environmentally sound policies and providing implementable solutions for preserving scarce resources.

The islands rely heavily on these types of projects not only in order to achieve tourism development and growth, but also to sustain their resources (Chiotis and Coccossis, 1992; Nijkamp and Verdonkshot, 1995; Anagnostoloupou *et al.*, 1996). Significant changes are therefore required at both micro and macro levels in order to set appropriate targets and criteria for sustainable development. Policies and regulations should address a wide range of issues and problems, as illustrated in Figure 8.4.

Greece and the Aegean and Ionian islands have consistently failed to implement sound sustainable development policies. Encouragingly, however, over the last few years there has been an increasing awareness among Greek stakeholders and acknowledgement of these challenges. This has generated several projects and several realistic proposals have been put forward. As a

- Market failure of self-regulating and sustainable practices.
- Inefficiencies between national and peripheral administration and municipalities.
- Lack of funding for ecotourism and environmental assessment projects.
- Negligence with regards to the meaning of ecotourism and alternative forms of tourism.
- Lack of implementation of published environmental policies.
- Inadequate consultation of all the different tourism-related stakeholders.
- Lack of mechanisms to ensure that tourism-environmental conservation programmes are not threatened by tourism development.

Figure 8.4 Issues and problems that should be addressed by legislation

result, a number of actions have been taken at the local level, especially associated with Environmental Agenda 21.

However, it should be recognized that it is often the private sector and in particular SMTEs who dominate the industry and, in fact, are often responsible for the implementation of sustainable legislation and practices. This is more important in the context of the Greek islands, where the public sector is clearly unable to implement and control rational tourism development and, thus, often relies on the good will and intention of entrepreneurs to follow sustainable practices.

Tourism Planning and the Private Sector: Small and Medium-sized Tourism Enterprises

Family-run SMTEs dominate the private sector in the Aegean and Ionian regions. SMTEs account for over one third of the total 55,000 Aegean and Ionian firms. These enterprises facilitate the interaction between visitors and locals as well as increase the infusion of tourism earnings into the peripheral regions and local community. However, SMTEs suffer a wide range of strategic disadvantages, preventing them from developing a healthy industry. Furthermore, SMTEs are unable to increase their prices in line with inflation, mainly due to pressure from distribution channel partners and low occupancy levels (Buhalis, 1995, 2000). The over-supply of tourism services, both in Greece and worldwide, also contributes to fierce global competition for a less rapidly increasing demand (Josephides, 1993). In Greece, the average annual increase of the official hotel bed supply between 1983 and 1992 was 4.7 per cent, while the annual average increase in international tourist bednights was 2.7 per cent (Epilogi, 1994). Seasonality forces most of the resorts to operate between four and eight months, effectively reducing the period when SMTEs can be profitable (Cooper and Buhalis, 1992; Buhalis and Cooper, 1998).

The investment incentive Laws 1262/82 and 1982/90 boosted this over-supply as they promoted small, and unfeasible family-run accommodation units unable to offer a high quality of services, while they exaggerated the concentration of tourist units in under-supplied resorts. A large portion of the capacity growth during the past 20 years has been in the small unofficial and sometimes illegal accommodation establishments ('parahoteleria'), which provide low quality and low-priced accommodation and, therefore, appeal to the clientele of mass tour operators. This situation has not only increased unfair competition *vis-à-vis* the official hotels, but it has also reduced both tax revenues and employment at the macro level. As SMTEs are unable to undertake a comprehensive marketing approach, they are often over-dependent on European tour operators for their clientele. The competition experienced in main European markets forces SMTEs to reduce their prices to unrealistic levels. This is often at the expense of the quality of their products and the sustainability of local resources. Such practices not only reduce the profitability of SMTEs and reduce the economic benefits at both micro and macro levels, but they also jeopardize the long-term competitiveness of the destination (Buhalis, 1994, 1999a, 2000). In addition, inadequate profitability means that SMTEs are unable to reinvest for the refurbishment of their facilities and the regeneration of resources.

The combination of marketing and management weaknesses, with the pressure experienced by mass tour operators, has meant that newly established SMTEs have been unable to pay back their mortgages and bank loans. Therefore, these enterprises have experienced an increase in their interest rates from an expected 14–18 per cent, to penalty rates of up to 42 per cent. This situation has severe impacts on the ability of these accommodation establishments to survive and as a consequence, it is estimated that 1,250 newly established small and medium Greek hotels (almost 20 per cent) are already in receivership (HCG, 1996a, 1996b). The economic pressures experienced often force SMTEs to adopt unsustainable commercial practices and pursue short-term profit or minimization of costs. The pressure to develop mass tourism in order to take advantage of economies of scale is also fundamentally against sustainability practices. As a result, SMTEs are often pressured by commercial practices and needs to ignore legislation and effectively to 'cut corners' in order to be able to survive the competition both locally and internationally. For example, a small hotel that cannot operate economically due to high fixed and labour costs would possibly try to expand illegally by adding a few more rooms in order to reduce its costs and take advantage of economies of scale.

Nevertheless, it is evident that under the oligopsonistic situation in the marketplace, the private sector is almost unable to operate without subsidies from the public sector. Therefore, to a large extent, both the development of the Greek private sector and tourism demand are subsidised by the government, reducing the macro-economic benefits of tourism on the destination.

Tourism Impacts and Sustainability on the Aegean and Ionian Islands

As described in the previous paragraphs, the economic realities of the private sector as well as the strategic weaknesses of the public sector effectively jeopardize the sustainability of local resources, the competitiveness of the destination, and the tourist industry in general. Although environmental resources have become vital for the destinations' competitiveness, many regions continue to experience severe exploitation. As is the case in many islands around the world, because of a weak planning system, the Aegean and the Ionian regions have witnessed uncontrolled development of tourist facilities and their built environment in general. This rapid growth has resulted in deficient infrastructure as well as environmental impacts like water shortages and sewage problems (Table 8.7) (Diamantis and Westlake, 1997). The operational and strategic practices on the islands are highly dependent upon mass tourism, resulting in a myriad of negative economic, environmental and sociocultural impacts. Moreover, the insular regions seem to pursue tourism as a single regional development option, at the expense of

Table 8.7 Tourism impacts and improvement targets at the macro level for the Aegean and Ionian islands, 1994–99

Regions	Problems	Targets
North Aegean	Inadequate tourism infrastructure	Development of spa tourism, ecotourism and archaeological tourism Improvement of three ports Construction of road networks Construction of three marinas Development of three new airports
South Aegean	Uncontrolled tourism development Inadequate tourism services Negative environmental impacts	Development of cruise tourism Development of nautical tourism Development of new marinas The creation/improvement of tourist boat facilities
Ionian islands	Uncontrolled tourism development Negative environmental impacts Sewage problems Population problems Impacts on endemic species and turtle population	Development of quality tourism Development of alternative forms of tourism Development of conference centres Construction of marinas and boat facilities Increase in average length of stay Increase tourism employment

Source: Papadopoulos and Kouzelis (1998)

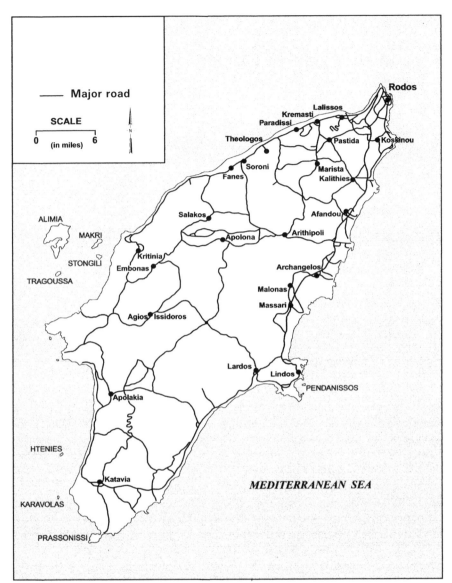

Figure 8.5 The island of Rhodes
Note: Greek placenames have been used.

other sectors such as manufacturing or agriculture (Chiotis and Coccossis, 1992; Nijkamp and Verdonkshot, 1995; HCG, 1997; PAP, 1997; Buhalis, 1998).

For example, the island of Rhodes (Figure 8.5), perhaps the most developed island in Greece, is highly dependent on the mass tourism market, while environmental resources are stretched to accommodate the industry's

- Lack of regional planning frameworks and integrated planning processes.
- Planning law is not enforced effectively.
- Land use planning centrally administered and poorly enforced.
- Resource management aim is the maximization of economic growth.
- Over-dependence of the economy on coastal tourism.
- Geographical concentration of tourism development along the northern and eastern coasts.
- High seasonality over-exploits resources during peak periods.
- Polarization of development along the north/south divide.
- Neglect of ecological and cultural resources.
- Weak enforcement of planning and environmental controls.
- Recurrent marine pollution in certain areas such as in Kolymbia (east coast).
- Over-exploitation of ground water on northern coast (e.g. Triada).
- Seawater intrusion in Rhodes city and in the south east (e.g. Kalathos).
- Litter and noise pollution in popular resorts (e.g. Faliraki).
- Hooliganism and conflicts between tourists and tourists and locals.
- Gradual deterioration of the beach quality (e.g. Rhodes town and Ixia).
- Transformation of villages into souvenir shops and exploitation of archaeological sites (e.g. Old Town and Lindos).

Figure 8.6   Problems and challenges for sustainable tourism development on Rhodes

needs. Several sustainability weaknesses (as illustrated in Figure 8.6) have significant implications for the economic structure and development of the island and its long-term prosperity. The lack of powerful regional planning frameworks and integrated planning processes often encourages a certain degree of anarchy at destinations like Rhodes where entrepreneurs take advantage of resources to improve their short-term profitability. To the degree that planning law is not enforced effectively and is guided by economic development criteria, it is inevitable that the industry is moving towards an over-supply of local products that consume more environmental resources. In fact, this process initiates a downward vicious spiral where over-supply intensifies the use of resources, reduces customer satisfaction and their willingness to pay and consequently decreases prices and quality of services. As a result, the economic benefits of tourism are reduced, while the ability to pay for restoring over-used resources is minimized, leading to the decay of facilities and resources. Thus, tourism development does not generate the benefits that destinations deserve and there are inadequate gains in terms of the resources utilized.

Several additional economic and sociocultural problems affect local people and jeopardize the well-being of Rhodes in the long term. Two resorts epitomize the problems and demonstrate that tourism development has failed

Plate 8.1 Lindos – a village transformed into a 'souvenir' flea market

to generate adequate benefits while jeopardizing the future prosperity of local people. Lindos village, for example, 50 km south of Rhodes Town, has been transformed into a vast souvenir shopping area with local enterprises covering every possible space and selling undifferentiated souvenirs, often made in mainland Greece or even in the Far East (Plate 8.1). Thousands of day-visitors visit the ancient Acropolis and spend a few hours in the village as part of packaged excursions, before heading back to their hotels in the north part of the island. Local men have been reduced to 'donkey-taxi' drivers (Plate 8.2), while local women spend most of their day selling handicrafts on the way to the Acropolis (Plate 8.3). Inadequate planning effectively means that Lindos has lost its character and a wide range of negative tourism impacts can be experienced such as heavy traffic, fumes from cars and coaches, and lack of public toilets. These impacts reduce the benefits of tourism for locals and also the satisfaction of visitors.

Closer to Rhodes Town, the holiday village of Faliraki is blessed with 6 km of sandy beach. However, the over-supply of low category and priced properties, particularly at the south end of the beach, has stimulated mass tourism well beyond the resort's carrying capacity. The northern part of the beach is occupied by four and five star hotels, which attract all-inclusive tourists from Germany and northern European countries. The southern part of the beach is dominated by smaller and often illegal properties, which attract a young, party-going clientele, primarily from Britain and Scandinavian countries. Alcohol consumption often starts at breakfast and continues all day long. In addition, several facilities have been introduced

Plate 8.2 'Donkey-taxi' drivers in Lindos

Plate 8.3 Lindos – local ladies sell handicrafts to tourists on the way to the Acropolis

such as two building cranes which are used for 'bungee jumping'. These facilities and the use of pleasure craft such as jet skis destroy the landscape of the resort. The town centre is packed with open bars playing extremely loud music, preventing both locals and visitors from sleeping in the early hours of the morning. Competition forces local bar owners to offer free drinks to tourists passing by, in order to induce them to visit their establishments. Effectively, tourists can and do drink as much as possible for free. As a result, after a certain time the resort is dominated by thousands of drunk people who misbehave, and generally act like hooligans.

Inevitably this situation results in friction among different groups of tourists as well as between locals and tourists. For instance, tourists of higher socio-economic classes who vacation in the northern part of the beach and in other resorts around the island are intimidated and seek alternative options for their holidays. These are the visitors who have a higher disposable income and are targeted by the Greek tourism policy seeking to attract quality tourists. Local residents are also threatened and forced to sell their properties and move to other parts of the island. Lack of serious legislation and enforcement policies have made the resort a dangerous and undesirable place. More importantly, they have destroyed the potential of tourism to generate adequate profits for the private sector and sufficient economic benefit for the destination. There are a few other resorts suffering from similar problems on both the Aegean and Ionian islands.

In order to overcome these problems, UNEP, under the Mediterranean Action Plan scheme, undertook a variety of projects in Rhodes, such as research on carrying capacity, the protection of historic settlements, and monitoring of pollution. Although the projects set up the framework for improving collaboration between different stakeholders, the overall results indicated that the existing legal and institutional frameworks were insufficient (PAP, 1997).

The disturbance of endangered species and their habitats is yet another problem experienced on several islands (Briassoulis, 1993; Van Den Bergh, 1993). For instance, on the island of Zakynthos (Zante) situated in the Ionian periphery, there have been many efforts over the years to conserve the marine turtle, known as *Caretta-Caretta*. Along the 3.5 km Lagana beach are the breeding grounds of the largest turtle population in the Mediterranean. Indeed, nests are found approximately every 1.75 metres. Environmental auditing of the area has indicated several problems, as illustrated in Figure 8.7. This location illustrates the traditional conflict between the push for greater tourism development and a higher number of visitors and efforts to preserve an endangered species. Tour operators driven by commercial motives attempt to bring charter flights during periods that are clearly in conflict with the activities of the turtles. Also, many tourists fail to follow sound environmental practices either because of ignorance or selfishness. Local authorities are threatened by private commercial interests and are

- Disturbance of turtle nests from motorized boats.
- Conflict between activities which use the area, such as scuba diving and turtle boats.
- The use of the beach during nesting periods.
- The large numbers of visitors and tourists in the area to observe the turtles breeding.
- Turtles being disturbed by the lights and noise from cars, hotels, and aircraft landing after hours.

Figure 8.7 Environmental problems at the Lagana beach in Zakynthos

reluctant to undertake action to protect the turtles as they feel that it will damage the economic benefits of tourism (Ottaway, 1992; Prunier *et al.*, 1993).

A number of projects have been undertaken on the Greek islands in order to protect certain endangered species. In particular, two programmes sponsored by the EU's Life Programme look at the conservation of turtles (*Monachus-Monachus*) on the Ionian islands and monk seals in the Aegean. The first project aims to minimize the conflict between tourism development and the protection of turtle nesting beaches by monitoring the movements of individual animals. The second project on the Sporades islands of the Aegean aims to establish a national marine park for the monk seal, as well as a rescue centre for the treatment and rehabilitation of injured seals. In both projects, campaigns were undertaken in the communities to enhance the awareness of the different stakeholders (EU, 1995).

Despite the need to protect economic priorities, environmental awareness is gradually emerging among the owners of tourism enterprises and the islanders. Often, initiatives geared towards safeguarding the natural environment have been pioneered by larger organizations in various destinations and tend to be imitated by their smaller counterparts. One such organization is Grecotel, the largest hotel company in Greece with 22 four and five star hotels. This company is partially owned by TUI, the German tour operator, and managed by the Daskaladonakis family. Most of the company's hotels are situated on the islands. In 1992, Grecotel became the first hotel group in the Mediterranean to form an environmental and cultural department that deals with a number of issues. As indicated in Figure 8.8, these issues not only affect the hotels but also the host communities.

However, several stakeholders have attempted to implement sustainable tourism policies on the Aegean and Ionian islands. Tour operators are under considerable pressure by consumers to provide environmentally friendly products. At the local level environmentalists also pressurize local authorities to improve the sustainability of resources by reinvesting in their preservation. Examples of initiatives include the development of a sewage treatment plant in Kos, the pedestrianization of the Old Town in Rhodes, and

- Creation of environmental policies (management).
- Encourage Greek suppliers to produce eco-friendly products (purchasing policy).
- Regular environmental audits monitoring and documentation (management).
- Creation of an environmental code of conduct (purchasing policy).
- Successful recycling and energy efficiency activities such as 78 per cent reduction of aluminium usage, 50 per cent reduction of glass consumption, and 30 per cent reduction of water consumption (technical).
- Recreation of local village areas in many hotels (built environment).
- Re-introduction of local plant species in hotel gardens (built environment).
- Inclusion of Grecotel environmental policy in personnel induction manual (communication).
- Co-operation with environmental organizations to protect endangered species and their habitats (natural environment).

Figure 8.8 Environmental and sustainable practices and initiatives by Grecotel

the redevelopment of several parts on islands such as Corfu and Kefalonia. Increasingly, entrepreneurs also realize the synergies between environmental practices and profitability and undertake suitable actions as illustrated in the Grecotel example. However, many of the current practices do not take into consideration the implications of equity issues in a generic geographical context. Most of the sustainable tourism practices are specific to certain islands and focus on local impacts. There is no community or government-led strategic co-ordination and enforcement for the entire region. As the regional economy is 'single-sector tourism motivated', development is extremely tourism-centric, rather than mutually targeted toward sustainability. Finally, there is a 'resources utilization' issue. The general concept of sustainability encourages the stewardship of all natural resources. However, sustainable development on the Greek islands typically protects only resources critical to further tourism exploitation and excludes resources that are not critical to tourism development or survival. Therefore, environmental management techniques (e.g., environmental auditing) should be used by providing incentives to destination authorities to overcome their 'tourism-centric' outlook (Diamantis, 1998, 1999).

Strategic Weaknesses and Challenges for Greek Tourism

Despite its popularity and growth over the past 40 years, the Greek tourist industry has reached a stage where both its potential and competitiveness have become questionable.

> The seemingly unstoppable growth of this market contributed to a degree of complacency that has led to Greece repeating some of the errors made in Spain. Rapid price increases mean the country is no longer perceived by mass

market clients as cheap in relation to comparable destinations in the Mediterranean, but much of the country's tourism infrastructure, hastily built in response to demand for cheap accommodation, does not meet the needs of a market less sensitive to price and more concerned with quality and value for money. (EIU, 1990: 45)

Unless both the public and private sectors address a number of critical issues immediately, their future can be seriously endangered, resulting in a potential disaster for both the Aegean and Ionian regional economies and the sustainability of their resources. The strategic weaknesses and threats for Greek tourism as well as the challenging factors can be summarized in Figure 8.9.

- Image of Greece as cheap, simple, unsophisticated, undifferentiated, sun and sea destination.
- Gradual deterioration of tourism product and lack of re-investment in improvements.
- Increase in tourism arrivals but decrease in tourism expenditure per capita.
- Inadequacy of the planning process and lack of efficient enforcement mechanism.
- Dependence upon major tour operators for promotion and distribution of the Greek tourism product.
- Plethora of anarchically developing and behaving SMTEs, aiming for short-term profitability.
- Inadequacy of infrastructure to serve the ever-expanding demand.
- Lack of coordination at the destination and disrespect for tourists' needs.
- Lack of professionalism and training in both state and private tourism establishments.
- Inadequate management and marketing abilities and failure to adopt IT.
- Individualistic behaviour by SMTEs and unwillingness to cooperate on a destination basis.
- Unsuccessful and inconsistent programmes of government intervention.
- Almost unregulated environment, with near complete lack of control.
- Development of tourism as a single regional development option.
- Failure of the private sector to invest in long-term projects.
- Deterioration of natural, social and cultural resources.
- SMTEs' inability to resist in global concentration in the tourism industry.
- Failure of both the private and public sectors to learn from internationally gained experience in tourism development and marketing.
- Lack of tourism research to identify the impacts of tourism.
- Negligence with regard to new tourism demand challenges.

Figure 8.9 Strategic weaknesses and challenges for tourism in Greece and the islands
Source: Adapted from Buhalis (1995, 1998)

As a result, Greece in general and the Aegean and Ionian islands in particular fail to attract the desired 'high-quality, high-expenditure' tourists, since they are increasingly unable to satisfy these individuals' requirements. The deterioration of the tourism product and image causes consumers to be less willing to pay, consequently leading to a further drop in quality, as the industry attempts to attract customers with lower prices. This is the vicious spiral which has been destroying the essence of developing tourism in several Mediterranean destinations. Hence, both the private and public sectors require radical measures in product formulation, promotional strategies and distribution channels in order to support the competitiveness of both destinations and SMTEs as well as their future profitability and prosperity. From the viewpoint of the public sector the development and implementation of a dynamic master plan need to safeguard the sustainability of resources and ensure that all stakeholders will gain benefits from tourist activities. Tourism policy should focus on optimizing impacts for the benefits of stakeholders, the satisfaction of consumers and the profitability of the industry. Failure to react by strengthening the competitiveness of the Aegean and Ionian SMTEs would have severe implications for the future of tourism activity in Greece, as the essence of its existence may be jeopardized, and its economic contribution become questionable.

Environmental awareness and sustainability of resources are critical for the quality of a tourism product and will increasingly determine the competitiveness of the industry. However, this relation can also be reversed. Unless the industry maintains its competitiveness and profitability there will be fewer resources available to be invested in environmental and sustainability projects. As a result, sustainability and competitiveness are interrelated and there are plenty of synergies evident. Perhaps both the private and public sectors should realize that sustainability concerns are not contrary to the aims of tourism development. By contrast, they should advocate a long-term tourism development which will enable the region to take advantage of its unique resources and maximize its long-term profitability and prosperity. To the degree that consumers increasingly appreciate high-quality environmental resources, they will be prepared to pay higher prices and increase their visitation to unspoiled regions.

International competition has also forced the industry and authorities to improve local resources and to reinvest in their regeneration. Long-haul destinations, which emerged in the last decade, have missed the mass tourism developments of the 1970s and have often undertaken superior preservation of their resources through legislation and careful planning. Closer to home, competing destinations such as Spain are undertaking serious steps to renovate their capacity and facilities as well as to regenerate their environmental and cultural resources. Initiatives in Calvia, Majorca as well as in Benidorm have improved the tourism product locally and have increased the profitability of local enterprises as well as reducing seasonality problems. In some cases, drastic interventions have taken place such as demolishing hotels to create open public spaces. Against this background, the Greek islands may find it increasingly more difficult to compete unless both the private and public sectors initiate and respect a regeneration programme for local resources and implement a strong framework for sustainable development.

Conclusion

The unique sociocultural, environmental and heritage resources of the Aegean and Ionian islands attract millions of visitors every year. Nevertheless, the destination fails to take advantage of tourism and ensure the sustainability of its resources for future generations. A combination of deficiencies relating to the public and private sectors are responsible for the inability to optimize tourism's impacts and to ensure the prosperity of local residents. The public sector has failed to develop a comprehensive master plan, which should guide policy and regulations as well as provide clear guidance for their enforcement. It has also failed to generate research on the area in order to support rational decision-making and long-term strategies. As a result, officials follow conventional wisdom and unsophisticated management and planning methods. Poor enforcement mechanisms are also responsible for a near anarchic development in several resorts. Conversely, the private sector is dominated by SMTEs, which have inadequate understanding of tourism management and marketing and fail to appreciate the long-term implications of their actions. Thus, they are dependent on international mass tour operators who force their mass/undifferentiated tourism strategy. Over-supply at the destination and globally in combination with lack of efficient marketing strategies also means that SMTEs are forced to accept extremely low prices from tour operators (Buhalis, 1999a, 2000). Therefore, environmental policies and sustainability are often considered luxuries by the private sector, which needs to concentrate on short-term profitability and often survival issues.

Greek tourism is heavily geared towards mass tourism, despite a number of policies promoting alternative tourism development. Current development in Greece and on the islands not only endangers the future of local resources, but also has direct implications for the short-term profitability of local SMTEs and the economic benefits at destination level. As a result, the benefits of tourism in Greece deteriorate and the product needs a drastic re-evaluation and repositioning in the marketplace, while tourism policies need to be refocused towards new realities and challenges. As far as environmental resources are concerned, thorough environmental auditing should be employed in order to monitor the actual and potential environmental impacts of tourism. In assessing the actual impacts, the current conditions of resources should be examined. Moreover, an evaluation of potential environmental impacts needs to take into account the implications of further development or change. Environmental auditing should aim, among other things, to improve the state of the aspects of the 'holistic' environment; to identify the types and magnitude of environmental impacts; to create an ongoing process to monitor environmental impacts; to enhance the profile of islands as tourist destinations; to increase the environmental awareness of islanders and tourists; and to minimize the potential risks associated with public health and visitor satisfaction.

Encouragingly, German and Scandinavian tour operators have begun adopting and enforcing environmental policies and, thus, may contribute to improvements locally. Larger organizations such as Grecotel, which partly belongs to TUI the German tour operator, have developed a comprehensive programme which not only assists environmental conservation but also contributes directly to its profitability. Local pioneers can motivate other players to imitate and adopt similar practices, improving the benefits of tourism. Nevertheless, the National Tourism Organization should develop a comprehensive framework to guide and enforce tourism development and management towards the sustainability of local resources and the development of regional prosperity. Failure to take such actions will eventually prove disastrous for local resources and long-term prosperity.

References

Anagnostopoulou, K., Arapis, T. and Micha, I. (1996) *Tourism and the Structural Funds: The Case for Environmental Integration*. Athens: Royal Society of Protection of Birds.

Bote, G. and Sinclair, T. (1991) Integration in the tourism industry: a case study approach. In T. Sinclair and M. Stabler (eds), *The Tourism Industry: An International Analysis*. Oxford: CAB International (67–91).

Briassoulis, H. (1993) Tourism in Greece. In W. Pompl and P. Lavery, (eds), *Tourism in Europe: Structures and Developments*. Oxford: CAB International (285–301).

Britton, S. (1989) Tourism, dependency and development: a mode of analysis. In T. Singh, H. Theuns and F. Go (eds), *Towards Appropriate Tourism: The Case of Developing Countries*. Frankfurt: Peter Land (93–116).

Buhalis, D. (1994) Information and telecommunications technologies as a strategic tool for small and medium tourism enterprises in the contemporary business environment. In A. Seaton *et al.* (eds), *Tourism: The State of the Art*. London: John Wiley and Sons (254–75).

Buhalis, D. (1995) The impact of information telecommunications technologies upon tourism distribution channels: strategic implications for small and medium sized tourism enterprises' management and marketing. PhD dissertation, Department of Management Studies, University of Surrey.

Buhalis, D. (1998) *Tourism in Greece: Strategic Analysis and Challenges for the New Millennium*. Monograph, Studies and Reports: (Series J) Planning and Development, Aix-en-Provence: International Centre for Research and Studies in Tourism.

Buhalis, D. (1999a) Tourism in the Greek islands: the issues of peripherality, competitiveness and development. Special issue: Tourism in the European periphery. *International Journal of Tourism Research*, 1(5): 341–59.

Buhalis, D. (1999b) Limits of tourism development in peripheral destinations: problems and challenges. *Tourism Management*, 20(2): 183–5.

Buhalis, D. (2000) Relationships in the distribution channel of tourism: conflicts between hoteliers and tour operators in the Mediterranean region. *Journal of International Hospitality, Leisure and Tourism Administration*, 1(1): 113–39.

Buhalis, D. and Cooper, C. (1998) Competition or co-operation: small and medium sized tourism enterprises at the destination. In E. Laws, B. Faulkner and G. Moscardo (eds), *Embracing and Managing Change in Tourism*. London: Routledge (324–46).

Buhalis, D. and Fletcher, J. (1995) Environmental impacts on tourism destinations: an economic analysis. In H. Coccossis and P. Nijkamp (eds), *Sustainable Tourism Development*. London: Avebury (3–24).

Butler, R.W. (1996) Problems and possibilities of sustainable tourism: the case of the Shetland islands. In L. Briguglio, R. Butler, D. Harrisson and W.L. Filho (eds), *Sustainable Tourism in Islands and Small States*. London: Pinter (11–31).

Butler, R.W. (1997) Modelling tourism development: evolution, growth and decline. In S. Wahab and J.J. Pigram (eds), *Tourism Development and Growth: The Challenge of Sustainability*. London: Routledge (109–25).

Chiotis, G. and Coccossis, H. (1992) Tourism development and environmental protection in Greece. In J. Van den Straaten and H. Briassoulis (eds), *Tourism and the Environment: Regional, Economic, and Policy Issues*. Dordrecht: Kluwer (133–43).

Colombo, R., Marin, C. and Ballesteros, P. (1997) *Integration of RES as a Vector for Sustainable Development in the Tourism Sector in Islands*. Ispa, Varese: European Union, Joint Research Centre.

Cooper, C. (1996) The environmental consequences of declining destinations. *Progress of Tourism and Hospitality Research*, 2(3–4): 337–45.

Cooper, C. (1997) The contribution of life cycle analysis and strategic planning to sustainable development. In S. Wahab and J.J. Pigram (eds), *Tourism Development and Growth: The Challenge of Sustainability*. London: Routledge (78–94).

Cooper, C. and Buhalis, D. (1992) Strategic management and marketing of small and medium sized tourism enterprises in the Greek Aegean islands. In R. Teare, D. Adams and S. Messenger (eds), *Managing Projects in Hospitality Organisations*, London: Cassell (101–25).

Diamantis, D. (1998) Environmental auditing: a tool in ecotourism development. *Eco-Management and Auditing Journal*, 5(1): 15–21.

Diamantis, D. (1999) The importance of environmental auditing and environmental indicators in islands. *Eco-Management and Auditing Journal*, 6(1): 18–25.

Diamantis, D. and Westlake, J. (1997) Environmental auditing: an approach towards monitoring the environmental impacts in tourism destinations, with reference to the case of Molyvos. *Progress of Tourism and Hospitality Research*, 3(1): 3–15.

ECG (1994) *EC Environmental Guide*. Brussels: EC Committee of the American Chamber of Commerce.

EIU (1986) Greece. *International Tourist Reports*, National Report, No. 3. London: Economist Intelligence Unit (45–60).

EIU (1990) Greece. *International Tourist Reports*, National Report, No. 4. London: Economist Intelligence Unit (45–62).

EIU (1995) *Greece Country Profile 1995–1996*. London: Economist Intelligence Unit.

Epilogi (1994) *Economic Review: The Greek Economy 1994*. Athens: Epilogi (in Greek).

EU (1995) *Projects Funded Under Life in the Field of Protection of Habitants and of Nature, 1991–1995*. Brussels: DG for the Environment, Nuclear Safety and Civil Protection, European Union.

Eurostat (1993) *Portrait of the Regions*, Vol. 3. Luxembourg: Office for Official Publications of the European Community.

Finas, K. (1991) *The Economy of Dodekanisos in the Period 1947–1989.* Rhodes: Economic Chamber of Dodekanisos (in Greek).

Fyall, A. and Garrod, B. (1997) Sustainable tourism: towards a methodology for implementing the concept. In M.J. Stabler (ed.), *Tourism and Sustainability: From Principles To Practice.* Oxford: CAB International (51–68).

GNTO (1998) Tourism statistics in Greece. http://www.gnto.gr.

Godfrey, K.B. (1996) Towards sustainability? Tourism in the Republic of Cyprus. In L.C. Harrison and W. Husbands (eds), *Practising Responsible Tourism: International Case Studies in Tourism Planning, Policy and Development.* Chichester: John Wiley & Sons (58–79).

Hall, M., and Lew, A. (1998) *Sustainable Tourism: A Geographical Perspective.* London: Longman.

HCG (1996a) *XENIA* monthly bulletin, No. 136, Hotel Chamber of Greece (in Greek).

HCG (1996b) *XENIA* monthly bulletin, No. 142, Hotel Chamber of Greece (in Greek).

HCG (1997) *XENIA* monthly bulletin, No. 155, Hotel Chamber of Greece (in Greek).

HCG (1998) *XENIA* monthly bulletin, No. 158, Hotel Chamber of Greece (in Greek).

Hunter, C. (1995a) Key concepts for tourism and the environment. In C. Hunter and H. Green (eds), *Tourism and the Environment: A Sustainable Relationship?,* London: Routledge (52–92).

Hunter, C. (1995b) On the need to re-conceptualise sustainable tourism development. *Journal of Sustainable Tourism,* 3(3): 155–65.

Hunter, C. (1997) Sustainable tourism as an adaptive paradigm. *Annals of Tourism Research,* 24(4): 850–67.

Josephides, N. (1993) Managing tourism in a recession. *Tourism Management,* 4(3): 162–6.

Josephides, N. (1994) Tour operators and the myth of self-regulation. *Tourism in Focus, Tourism Concern,* No. 14, Winter: 10–11.

Josephides, N. (1995) A sorry state for beautiful Greece. *Travel Weekly,* No. 1261, 5 April, 11.

Leontidou, L. (1991) Greece: prospects and contradictions of tourism in the 1980's. In A.M. Williams and G.J. Shaw (eds), *Tourism and Economic Development: Western European Experiences.* 2nd edn. London: Belhaven Press (94–106).

Mowforth, M. and Munt, I. (1998) *Tourism and Sustainability: New Tourism in the Third World.* London: Routledge.

Nijkamp, P. and Verdonkshot, S. (1995) Sustainable tourism development: a case study in Lesvos. In H. Coccossis and P. Nijkamp (eds), *Sustainable Tourism Development.* London: Avebury (127–40).

Ottaway, M. (1992) Turtle power. *The Sunday Times* (Travel and Style), 28 June, 3.

PAP (1997) *Guidelines for Carrying Capacity Assessment for Tourism in Mediterranean Coastal Areas.* Split, Croatia: Priority Actions Programme, Regional Activity Centre.

Papadopoulos, P. and Kouzelis, A. (1998) *Regional Development in Greece and Tourism.* Athens: Research Institute (in Greek).

Prunier, E., Sweeney, A. and Geen, A. (1993) Tourism and the environment: the case of Zakynthos. *Tourism Management,* 14(2): 137–9.

Roekaerts, M. and Savat, K. (1989) Mass tourism in South and Southeast Asia: a challenge to Christians and the churches. In T. Singh, H. Theuns and F. Go (eds), *Towards Appropriate Tourism: The Case of Developing Countries.* Frankfurt: Peter Land (35–69).

Shaw, G. and Williams, A.M. (1994) *Critical Issues in Tourism: A Geographic Perspective.* Oxford: Blackwell.

Sheldon, P. (1994) Tour operators. In S. Witt and L. Moutinho (eds), *Tourism Marketing and Management Handbook*. 2nd edn. London: Prentice Hall (399–403).

Sinclair, T., Alizadeh, P. and Onunga, E. (1992) The structure of international tourism and tourism development in Kenya. In D. Harrison (ed.), *Tourism and the Less Developed Countries*. London: Belhaven Press (47–63).

Valenzuela, M. (1991) Spain: the phenomenon of mass tourism. In A.M. Williams and G.J. Shaw (eds), *Tourism and Economic Development: Western European Experiences*. 2nd edn. London: Belhaven Press (40–60).

Van Den Bergh, J. (1993) Tourism development and natural environment: an economic–ecological model for the Sporades islands. In H. Briassoulis and J. Van Der Straaten (eds), *Tourism and Environment: Regional Economic and Policy Issues*. Dordrecht: Kluwer Academic Publishers (67–83).

Westlake, J. and Diamantis, D. (1998) The application of environmental auditing to the management of sustainability within tourism. *Tourism Recreation Research*, 23(2): 69–71.

WTO (1995) *Budgets and National Tourism Administrations*. Madrid: World Tourism Organization.

WTO (1998a) *Tourism Highlights 1997*. Madrid: World Tourism Organization.

WTO (1998b) *Tourism Economic Report*. Madrid: World Tourism Organization.

9

Tourism Development in the Croatian Adriatic Islands

Sanda Weber, Sinisa Horak and Vesna Mikacic

Introduction

Although Croatia's islands, thanks to their outstanding beauty and natural and cultural heritage, are among the country's greatest assets, their full potential has not yet been tapped. For almost a century little had been invested in these areas and, hence, year by year, they had witnessed economic and demographic decline. The development of tourism on the islands, which to a large extent resulted from the construction of road infrastructure on the mainland in the 1960s and the islands in the 1970s, slowed the decline and significantly altered the economic position of these environments. Significantly, by the late 1970s service activities had replaced traditional farming, fishing, shipping, and stockbreeding as the principal economic sector on the islands. Moreover, emigration from some of the larger islands halted, mainly for economic reasons, although the process of depopulation continued on the smaller insular environments. Unfortunately, the hostilities against Croatia during 1990–95 significantly hindered the growth of Croatia's economy, including its tourist industry. The consequences for island tourism were particularly hard. While Croatia's economy has gradually begun to revive in the last few years, the recovery of the islands has been slow, and problems have become increasingly serious. This situation calls for a major change in the state's policy towards the islands, because otherwise these degenerative processes will be irreversible.

Unlike many insular regions in the Mediterranean, the Croatian islands currently do not face serious ecological problems. Nevertheless, by paying heed to earlier lessons concerning the experiences and mistakes of other regions, the Croatian government has officially chosen sustainable development as the only acceptable scenario for the islands' future development. In this chapter, our purpose is to describe the evolution of tourism on the Croatian islands and indicate the sector's potential for future development. In addition, we discuss the problems these environments face, and the possible policy and development strategies which should be applied in the near future in order to enhance the value of existing resources while ensuring the long-term development prospects of the islands' population.

Sustainable Tourism Development on the Islands

Since the end of World War II, growing demand for travel has led to rapid and often uncontrolled tourism development in a variety of destinations. Because many tourist areas have been saturated with visitors, they have witnessed a number of negative environmental, economic and social impacts. These problems have often resulted in the reduced popularity of these destinations. Such processes were especially evident during the 1970s in areas where development was based to a large extent upon mass tourism. Therefore, in recent years, experts have begun searching for new means of development which will not lead to the rapid decay or exhaustion of resources and will not endanger the progress of future generations (De Kadt, 1990; Dragicevic, 1991; Misra, 1993). This premise is the basis for the concept of sustainable development as an alternative to uncontrolled mass tourist development (Leslie, 1993; Jafari and Wall, 1994; Hunter, 1997; WTO, 1998). A case study of various Mediterranean countries has enabled the international expert group of UNEP's Priority Action Plan Regional Activity Centre (PAP/RAC 1997), based in Split (Croatia), to elaborate on the methodology of the sustainable development approach (Klaric, 1989; Dragicevic, 1990; Travis, 1994; Muller, 1994). Such a concept has turned out to be particularly acceptable for the development of small island communities, particularly those susceptible to hasty and large-scale socio-economic changes (Taylor, 1996; Grant, 1997; Hall, 1998; Sofield, 1998).

Compared to western European Mediterranean countries (e.g., Spain and Italy), Croatia has only recently been able to attract significant numbers of international tourists. Initially, lack of investment funds for tourist infrastructure, as well as poor traffic connections, slowed down tourism development, especially on the islands. Interestingly, this slow development has actually meant that many of the negative effects associated with rapid and uncontrolled tourism development have been avoided. For instance, the natural environment has remained preserved, while the valuable cultural and historical heritage as well as the authentic social identity of the population has witnessed little change. Therefore, the question that arises is how to promote further tourism development on the islands in a sustainable fashion that will not exceed the carrying capacity of the ecosystem (European Island Agenda, 1997). If the Croatian tourism product is going to target international travellers who favour ecologically preserved destinations, it is necessary to include the following factors in the planning process for further development in order to ensure sustainability:

- protection of the environment and management of local resources;
- preservation of local identity and protection of cultural wealth;
- growth of tourism supply in accordance with the potential of the region;
- development of activities that are complementary to tourism;
- raise public awareness and participation of local people in decision-making.

Such an approach implies the overall economic development of the islands must take into account the potential of the region and particularly the specific needs of the communities on the smaller islands. In this context, a small-scale economy is better suited to the spatial and demographic resources of the islands, since it is oriented primarily towards the service sector generated by tourism (catering, transport, retailing, other services) and the traditional primary sector (agriculture and fishing). On the larger islands light manufacturing, which is more easily adaptable to technological changes and flexible to market shifts, also has potential.

The Attractions of the Croatian Islands

Basic facts

The insular region of Croatia includes almost all the islands in the eastern part of the Adriatic. This archipelago, the second largest island group in the Mediterranean, is commonly divided into three groups according to geographical position: the northern Kvarner islands, the central islands, and the southern islands (Figure 9.1). The entire Croatian archipelago consists of 718 islands, 389 rock formations, and 78 reefs in the territorial waters. The islands make up around 5.8 per cent of Croatia's land area, totaling approximately 3,300 km^2. The largest island is Krk, with 410 km^2 while a total of 20 islands are larger than 20 km^2. Due to their considerable indentation, the islands account for around 70 per cent of the total length of Croatia's entire coastline (4,057 km out of a total of 5,835 km). Some of the limestone outcrops of the largest islands reach up to 500 m above sea level, the highest being Vidova Gora on the island of Brac (778 m).

The island population makes up 2.7 per cent of the Croatian total (4.7 million) with some 130,000 people living in 287 settlements. According to the most recent census in 1991, there were 67 permanently inhabited islands while another 15 were inhabited on a seasonal basis (usually by shepherds).

Figure 9.1 The Croatian Adriatic – the biggest islands, national parks and airports
Note: NP = national park

The islands' attractions

The islands' potential for future tourism development can be based on many assets, all of which can help accelerate the region's recovery following the political turmoil of the early 1990s. Foremost are a favourable geographical position and pleasant climate, the beauty of the archipelago with many unique features such as a rich natural and cultural heritage and the exceptional suitability for nautical tourism. An additional quality is the islands' low population density, making them attractive to many individual travellers.

The geographical position of the archipelago, particularly the location of the northern Adriatic islands, is extremely favourable since these destinations are close to Croatia's main tourist-generating countries (i.e., Austria, Germany, Italy, and Slovenia). New high-quality roads currently under construction are due to be completed by 2001. These thoroughfares will make the Croatian coast even more accessible to the country's main tourist markets encouraging short visits such as day trips.

Both the Croatian mainland coastline and the islands have a climate that can be described as Mediterranean. Summers are hot and dry, while winters are mild and damp. Moreover, Croatia's islands are among the sunniest places in Europe. The annual average amount of sunshine ranges from 2,200 to 2,650 hours. The Adriatic is a warm sea since the surface temperature does not fall below 10°C in winter and rises above 25°C in summer. This climate favours the survival of numerous plant and animal species, many of them endemic. Mediterranean evergreen vegetation dominates the islands, while red soil is abundant. Not surprisingly, the list of officially protected natural heritage sites is exceptionally lengthy. Of Croatia's seven national parks, three are located on islands (see Figure 9.1) (Brijuni, Mljet, and Kornati), while the Telascica nature park lies on Dugi otok island. Furthermore, the Croatian islands have six ornithological reserves, seven forest parks, ten protected countryside areas, and other protected natural sites (Table 9.1).

The undersea environment around the islands is particularly attractive because it is, on the whole, unpolluted. There are numerous shipwrecks and

Table 9.1 Protected natural and cultural sites on the Croatian islands

Sites	Number
Natural	
National parks	3
Nature parks	1
Special reserves	10
Forest parks	7
Protected countryside areas	10
Natural monuments	13
Architectural monument parks	5
Total	49
Cultural/historical	
Memorial areas	3
Historical urban and rural entities	65
Historical complexes	16
Memorial monuments	52
Civilian buildings	164
Military buildings	27
Commercial buildings	13
Ecclesiastical buildings	262
Cemetery buildings and entities	5
Public sculptures and urban installations	3
Dry-land archaeological localities	34
Undersea archaeological localities	24
Total	668

Source: Ministarstvo kulture (1997)

examples of the undersea natural world. The clear, warm sea is ideal for scuba diving and other types of water sports.

The islands' cultural heritage is also an exceptionally valuable tourism resource. All the major historical periods (Palaeolithic, Neolithic, Illyrian, Greek, Roman, and Croat) have left their mark on Croatia's islands, resulting in 668 permanent monuments meriting protection as national heritage sites (Table 9.1).

Especially noteworthy is the architectural heritage of most of the urban and rural communities on the islands. Surrounded by abundant greenery, these picturesque places are built mostly of stone in a typical Mediterranean style and traversed by narrow streets. Most coastal communities have small but busy harbours, many of which are exceptionally scenic. All these factors combine to create a pleasant environment for tourists in search of a quiet vacation spot.

The islands' low population density (38 persons per km^2) also contributes to these destinations' attraction. Unlike the situation in many other Mediterranean islands, large expanses of coastal land are devoid of development while access to the sea is not hindered by large-scale ribbon development. Similarly, the interior of the Croatian islands has experienced only sparse development. Thanks to a low degree of urbanization and only modest business activity, this part of the Mediterranean is still relatively clean and swimming conditions almost everywhere along the islands' coastlines are ideal. Due to the high indentation of the coastlines (in this case the indentation coefficient, which can be calculated as the ratio of the actual coastline divided by the air-distance between the most extreme points, is equal to 11.09), this region is extremely favourable for nautical tourism. In fact, in the entire coastal and island region of Croatia there are 330 small harbours in various settlements. There is a total of 65 km of wharves where locals and visiting sailors can moor their boats. Croatia has a total of 42 nautical centres, half of which are located on the islands.

The long experience of many islanders with tourism is yet another exceptionally valuable and noteworthy resource for the sector's future development. After all, the islands' tradition as tourist destinations spans more than 100 years. This tradition places the Croatian islands in a strong position in terms of their ability to quickly revitalize their tourist industry once the conditions are favourable. Moreover, despite numerous obvious weaknesses, the existing infrastructure that includes 1,500 km of roads, 3 airports, 44 seaports, plus approximately 130,000 bed spaces, constitutes a firm foundation for redeveloping the islands' tourist industry whose development was forcibly interrupted by political upheaval during the early 1990s.

Brief History and Contemporary Tourism Development

Until the advent of the tourist industry the Croatian islands, like so many peripheral regions in the Mediterranean realm, had only limited opportunities for economic development. For centuries, this insular region depended on extensive farming, fishing, shipping, and shipbuilding, and traditionally lagged behind the development of other parts of the country. Over time, the region witnessed significant depopulation (Mikacic and Pepeonik, 1997). Tourism development first began in Croatia during the first half of the nineteenth century with the introduction in 1837 of a steamship route between Trieste and Kotor, and later a regular ferry route between Rijeka and Dubrovnik. This ferry service called at all the major islands. Thanks to their attractions and despite their relative inaccessibility, on the eve of World War II in 1939 the islands accounted for almost a quarter (23 per cent) of the 2.2 million bednights recorded in Croatia. Significantly, 61 per cent of tourist arrivals recorded on the islands during that year were from abroad.

The development of tourism in Croatia accelerated in the mid-1960s when fiscal policy measures encouraged greater financial investment in tourism facilities, while improvements in the domestic standard of living and liberalization of international travel contributed to increasing numbers of domestic and foreign tourists. During its initial phase, the tourism boom benefited mainland coastal towns and villages with better connections to international transport routes, while tourism on the islands started to develop rapidly one decade later. It is only in the past 25 years that the Adriatic archipelago has become interesting to a growing number of tourists thanks to the introduction of numerous ferry links and improvements to the island infrastructure (such as roads, water supplies and telecommunications). The opportunity to make a living other than through traditional island activities attracted many local people to seek jobs in tourism and catering. This phenomenon resulted in a slow-down of emigration and reversed the chronic decline of the islands' population.

Over the past 25 years the island tourist industry has accounted for between a fifth and a third of Croatia's tourist facilities. Most facilities offered on the islands are supplementary (e.g., campsites, rented rooms and apartments as well as company resorts) (Figure 9.2). Before 1990 when social tourism (Haulot, 1981) was the predominant form, company-owned and children's holiday resorts made up the largest proportion of tourist facilities (45 per cent), whereas today a large part of the available tourism capacity consists of private accommodation (50 per cent) and campsites (26 per cent). The share of hotels and tourist villages (20 per cent) as a proportion of all accommodation is 10 per cent lower than that witnessed on the mainland coast (30 per cent). Most hotels that were built to meet the needs of mass tourists in the 1970s belong to the three-star category.

A significant addition to Croatia's tourism product during the 1980s and

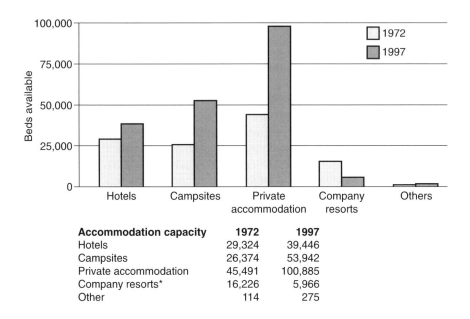

Accommodation capacity	1972	1997
Hotels	29,324	39,446
Campsites	26,374	53,942
Private accommodation	45,491	100,885
Company resorts*	16,226	5,966
Other	114	275

Figure 9.2 Breakdown of accommodation capacity on islands, 1972 and 1997
Source: DZS (1997a)
Note: *Company resorts include company-owned and youth accommodation capacity.

1990s were a number of yacht marinas. Because the insular region is particularly suitable for the development of this type of tourism, just over half (37,395) of all berths (72,128) are located on the islands. Significantly, these facilities attract visitors who have high purchasing power (DZS, 1997a).

In addition to the above mentioned commercial tourism facilities, private holiday houses and flats constitute a specific non-commercial holiday venue, since the owners do not have to pay for housing and related services. According to the latest housing and population census (1991), there were around 39,000 such holiday properties registered in Croatia's island region, roughly corresponding to 43 per cent of the entire housing stock of the islands. This type of holiday facility accounts for a significant number of visitors in those destinations that do not have additional tourist infrastructure.

The increase of tourist facilities on the islands since the 1960s has been matched by the growth trend of tourist arrivals. Over the period 1966 to 1997, the proportion of tourist overnight stays in commercial establishments on the islands ranged from a fifth to a third of the total recorded for the entire country (Figure 9.3).

When considering the regions separately, it is interesting to note that the tourist arrival growth trends on various islands have followed different patterns. In general, the fastest growth rate has occurred on the largest

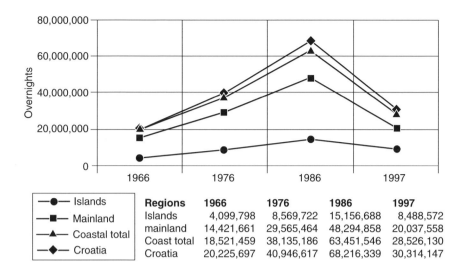

Regions	1966	1976	1986	1997
Islands	4,099,798	8,569,722	15,156,688	8,488,572
mainland	14,421,661	29,565,464	48,294,858	20,037,558
Coast total	18,521,459	38,135,186	63,451,546	28,526,130
Croatia	20,225,697	40,946,617	68,216,339	30,314,147

Figure 9.3 Tourist bednights on islands, mainland coast, and Croatia, 1966–97
Source: DZS (1997a)

islands, especially those closest to the mainland. Conversely, the more distant and scattered small island groups of Zadar County (central Adriatic) have developed quite slowly. This is partly because their population is older and less able to become actively involved in tourism. In the initial phase of island tourism development, up to the mid-1970s, the northern and southern island regions developed at a similar pace. Much of the accommodation capacity and related tourism services were similar in both regions.

The existing transport links made the islands of the Kvarner region and southern Dalmatia more accessible than the others (Horak and Weber, 1986). At that time these two island groups accounted for similar numbers of tourist bednights, representing 85 per cent of the total tourist flows to the entire insular region (Figure 9.4). However, significant changes began to occur in the early 1980s with the construction of a bridge to the largest island, Krk, the construction of an airport on the same island, and the introduction of fast ferry links. These improvements generated rapid development on the northern Kvarner islands (Horak, 1986, 1991). In fact, in 1986 when tourist arrivals in Croatia reached their peak, about half of all tourist bednights in the insular region were recorded on the Kvarner islands.

The drastic decline of tourist arrivals in Croatia including its island region can be attributed to a number of factors. First, one reason for this decline was the economic downturn that became increasingly pronounced in the former socialist Yugoslavia during the 1980s and the related overall deterioration of tourist facilities compared to those found in competing Mediterranean countries. Second and more importantly, a drastic decline in tourist arrivals

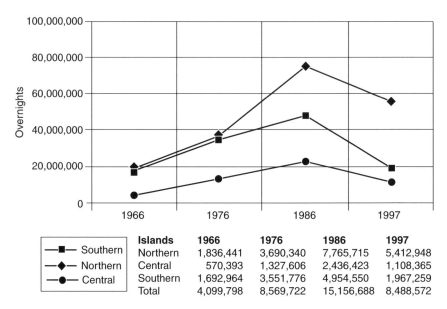

Islands	1966	1976	1986	1997
Northern	1,836,441	3,690,340	7,765,715	5,412,948
Central	570,393	1,327,606	2,436,423	1,108,365
Southern	1,692,964	3,551,776	4,954,550	1,967,259
Total	4,099,798	8,569,722	15,156,688	8,488,572

Figure 9.4 Tourist bednights on islands by region, 1966–97
Source: DZS (1997b)

occurred in the early 1990s because of the hostilities in Croatia. Based on projections derived from pre-war tourist flows, it is estimated that in the eight years during and following the war, from 1990 to 1997, 76 million potential bednights on the islands were lost.

This 65 per cent reduction in tourist arrivals has represented an enormous loss for the island region since it relies primarily on tourism. The repercussions of this decline will, unfortunately, continue over the next few years until tourist arrivals in Croatia return to their pre-war levels. Although in the past tourism development has contributed to the region's revitalization, the war-induced misfortune has highlighted the dangers of over-dependence on a single economic sector. This is especially the case for small islands since the disruption of tourist flows appears to have had a much greater effect on these environments than on neighbouring mainland areas (Mikacic and Montana, 1994).

Because of the quality of their natural resources, and the existing commercial and non-commercial tourist facilities, plus the small size of their population, the Croatian islands have traditionally been a region with tourism development indicators several times greater than the national average (Table 9.2). For instance, during a peaceful business year like 1989, the islands' tourist population, accounting for 4.5 million bednights, represented almost one-third (33 per cent) of the resident population's bednights (47 million bednights). At the same time, the number of tourist bednights on the Croatian mainland amounted to less than one-fifth (18 per cent) of the resident population's bednights. Perhaps more important is the fact that on the islands during peak season there were twice as many tourists (including persons visiting friends and relatives and those staying in their own houses or apartments) as residents (Radnic and Mikacic, 1994). Most likely, when the numbers of tourist arrivals increase to their pre-war peaks, the same situation will emerge. Historically, the average duration of tourist stays on the islands has also been longer than in Croatia as a whole accounting, on average, for nine days. By contrast, the occupancy rate on the islands has consistently been lower than the Croatian average due to the greater proportion of complementary capacities, and a more pronounced seasonality (Table 9.2). This situation, which is similar to that encountered in other insular regions around the world, indicates that it is imperative for Croatia to adopt a sustainable approach when considering further tourist and economic development for the islands, bearing in mind that these environments have limited space and extremely fragile ecosystems.

Table 9.2 Tourism development indicators – islands and Croatia, 1989 and 1997

Indicators	1989 Islands	1997	1989 Croatia	1997
Population*	120,900	129,300	4,747,740	4,893,980
Total tourist bednights	14,506,593	8,488,572	61,848,887	30,314,147
● domestic**	4,442,534	1,490,527	22,521,055	5,617,221
● foreign	10,064,059	6,998,045	39,327,832	24,686,926
Tourist population as % of total population	32.9	18.0	3.6	1.7
● domestic**	10.1	3.2	1.3	0.3
● foreign	22.8	14.8	2.3	1.4
Average duration of stay – in days	9.0	7.2	6.4	5.8
● domestic tourists**	8.6	6.7	5.6	4.1
● foreign tourists	9.1	7.3	7.0	6.4
Total commercial accommodation capacity	224,480	200,514	882,199	683,334
● occupancy rate in %	17.7	11.5	19.2	12.1

Source: DZS (1997b)

Notes: * Estimated population

** In 1989 domestic tourists include tourists from all republics of the Former Yugoslavia.

Main Characteristics of Croatian Tourism Demand

The development of the Croatian tourism product reached a peak in the early 1980s. At this time there were no significant differences between the type of products offered on the islands and those on the mainland. The tourist facilities were aimed primarily at mass tourism, largely of the 'sun and beach' variety. The loss of popularity of this type of product was already reflected in the declining numbers of tourists arriving in Croatia in the late 1980s and by the time the hostilities began in 1990 the flow of tourists, especially foreign visitors, had almost dried up completely. At a time when there should have been investment and market repositioning through renovation of accommodation facilities, introduction of additional services, and creation of new tourist products, holiday establishments were used to house refugees and displaced persons. This situation led to further deterioration of these facilities, many of which were already in a poor condition. Tourism is only now slowly returning to Croatia although eight years after the outbreak of hostilities only 60 per cent of the pre-war number of tourist bednights had been achieved.

Statistical data on recorded tourist flows and overnight stays by country of origin, backed up by survey results, confirm there are no major differences between the origin of tourists visiting the mainland and those arriving on the islands. According to data from 1997, the islands were visited mostly by Slovenian tourists (the only country to show a difference between visits to the islands and mainland regions), followed by domestic visitors and guests from the traditional generating country, Germany. It should be stressed that after the war the breakdown of tourists according to their national origin has changed significantly in Croatia; this, of course, is also the situation on the islands. More distant markets such as Britain have been lost while the numbers of arrivals from neighbouring countries such as Austria, Germany, Italy, and Slovenia have increased (Table 9.3). This is most likely since the population of these countries, because of traditional sociocultural ties, is better informed about events in Croatia.

The Institute for Tourism in Zagreb has been conducting a longitudinal market study since 1987 (in total, four surveys have been carried out) entitled 'Attitudes and Expenditures of Tourists in Croatia' – known by its trademark abbreviation TOMAS. This methodology has been developed based on the Swiss TOMAS (Touristisches Marktforschungssystem Schweiz 1983) and the Austrian 'Gastebefragung Österreich' (1984) studies. According to the latest survey, TOMAS '97 (1997), the social and demographic profile of visitors on the islands is not significantly different from that of the arrivals in Croatia's other regions (Institut za turizam, 1997). Nevertheless, small differences can be seen in other characteristics relating to the tourists visiting the islands.

A breakdown of the age groups (Table 9.4) shows that the largest number of tourists were in the 36 to 49 year-old category (30 per cent), followed by a

Table 9.3 Tourist bednights by country of origin, 1997

Country of origin	Croatia	Islands
Austria	9.4	9.8
Czech Republic	13.7	13.7
Croatia	18.5	17.6
Italy	11.0	12.1
Hungary	2.5	2.3
Netherlands	2.0	0.5
Germany	17.8	17.1
Slovenia	12.3	18.9
Britain	1.0	0.3
Other	11.8	7.7
Total (%)	100.0	100.0
Number of bednights	30,314,147	8,488,572

Source: DZS (1997b)

Table 9.4 Socio-demographic data of tourists

Socio-demographic data	Croatia	Islands
Age groups		
Up to 25	15.8	13.9
26 to 35	26.8	28.8
36 to 45	29.2	30.0
46 to 55	16.7	15.6
56 and over	11.5	11.7
Total	100.0	100.0
Level of education		
Primary school	7.5	6.2
Secondary school	46.0	46.4
Tertiary	22.2	22.5
Faculty and higher degree	23.7	24.6
Other	0.6	0.3
Total	100.0	100.0

Source: TOMAS '97, Institut za turizam, Zagreb, 1997

slightly younger group, 26 to 35 years (29 per cent). As is the case for Croatia as a whole, most of these tourists have completed secondary school (46 per cent), with nearly equal numbers (22 per cent and 24 per cent) having finished tertiary or higher education.

Tourists, usually accompanied by family members, visit the islands primarily to spend their main annual vacations. By contrast, the proportions of other types of trips (e.g., short breaks or business trips) are smaller than those witnessed in other parts of Croatia (Table 9.5). These results support

Table 9.5 Traveller characteristics

Characteristics	Croatia	Islands
Type of trip		
Main annual vacation	77.6	80.0
Short break	16.9	15.7
Travel for health reasons	2.4	1.8
Business trip	1.0	0.6
Attending a congress or a seminar	0.3	0.0
Tour	1.8	1.7
Total	100.0	100.0
Travel party		
Alone	4.6	4.1
With my partner	37.2	35.8
With other members of family	47.8	50.0
With friends	9.4	9.3
With organized tourist group	1.0	0.8
Total	100.0	100.0

Source: TOMAS '97, Institut za turizam, Zagreb, 1997

the conclusion that the island tourism product is aimed primarily at the main holiday season (July and August). Moreover, the facilities and infrastructure do not allow product differentiation (in terms of seasons or activities) that one might generally expect considering the differences in climate and quality and variety of resources compared to the mainland. Survey results show that the majority of tourists visit the islands primarily for rest and relaxation by the sea and to discover natural beauty. Only a small number of respondents identified other motives such as sport, recreation, fitness, or cultural interest.

Tourists generally come to the islands independently, without booking through a travel agent. Many are probably well acquainted with Croatia's tourism facilities, since around two-thirds have already visited Croatia several times. Data on tourists' activities during their visits show that on both the mainland and the islands the primary activities are the same, swimming and bathing, country walks, visiting restaurants, resting, and organizing independent excursions. Scuba diving is one activity that appears more popular on the islands than on the mainland resorts.

The overall picture painted by this brief summary of the survey results shows that the islands are still not making sufficient use of the potential of their resources in order to formulate a recognizable Croatian tourism product. In this context, it should be mentioned that those islands with marinas have nevertheless managed to position Croatia as a rather successful destination for sailing. According to a pilot study (Horak, 1995), yachtsmen come mainly from Austria and Germany, and most of them sail on to Croatia's competitor countries: Italy, Greece, and Turkey. In comparison with other countries that they have previously visited, these individuals identify Croatia's advantages as its natural beauty, the cleanliness and beauty of the sea, and the hospitality of the local people. By contrast, they view the high prices and the poor quality of service and level of equipment in the marinas as Croatia's major disadvantage.

Most Significant Limitations for Croatian Tourism Development

The most significant limitations for tourism development, which apply to a greater or lesser extent to every island in the Croatian archipelago, are as follows:

- social limitations: depopulation and the remaining working population;
- economic limitations: the state of the economy (ownership transformation of tourism companies) and the consequences of war;
- physical limitations: transport accessibility, water supply, and sewage systems.

Social limitations

A key factor limiting tourism development is the declining number of individuals of working age on the islands. In 1991 the recorded proportion of people of working age (15 to 60) was 58 per cent of the total island population, although because of certain methodological problems in the census this proportion was overestimated. Even so, this estimate is lower than the average for the whole country (64 per cent). The population age pyramid of the island is inverted and the proportion of aged people who are dependent on the younger population is twice that of the country as a whole. This means there are approximately equal numbers of active working people and aged dependents on the islands, while the average for Croatia as a whole is more favourable with twice as many workers compared to elderly dependants. The natural population growth on the islands is too low to maintain the present proportions, never mind overcome the serious structural imbalances. The situation is even more serious for the smaller islands.

Economic limitations

Under the previous economic system, tourism provided a relatively good living on most islands. Thanks to patchy income tax collection and inadequate controls over public companies, a sizable amount of wealth created by tourism found its way into private pockets. Most people working in tourism were employed throughout the year, even though businesses were closed for six months or more. In the summer, when tourism demand reached its peak, most people employed in the sector gained considerable additional earnings in their own households by offering accommodation and catering services to tourists. Although it came over a short period, this mainly untaxed tourism income in addition to regular earnings throughout the year provided a handsome living for a part of the island population. Therefore, the need to gain additional income from considerably harder work in agriculture and fishing gradually decreased. During this period many vineyards, olive groves, and farmland in general on the islands were abandoned.

With the introduction of a market economy and a much more rigorous taxation system the situation in tourism, already badly hit by the war and the drastic reduction in tourist arrivals, deteriorated sharply. In the 1990s, the island population gradually returned to traditional, more secure methods of making a living, since people have found it increasingly difficult to make a living from tourism. Inappropriate ownership transformation and out-standing debts to the banks (most of them dating from before or during the war), which are a burden on almost all tourism companies on the islands, and the lack of foreign investment hinder the necessary post-war recovery. In such circumstances any progress in tourism requires state support, and as a result the National Island Development Programme (Ministarstvo, 1997) was recently drawn up and ratified by the Croatian Parliament. This document defines and stimulates primarily long-term measures to revive the economy of Croatia's islands with the aim of maintaining and, if possible, restoring the island population and providing new development prospects.

Although the transition process has led to a transformation of ownership patterns in tourism businesses on the islands, the process of privatization is still largely unfinished. Most tourist companies are still under majority ownership of the state or the banks. There has been no legal restriction on the entry of foreign capital. However, the companies on the islands were assessed by various institutions according to criteria established by the Croatian government at considerably more than their market value, so there was no real interest from foreign investors. Unable to repay their mounting debts due to the war and the sharp drop in numbers of tourists and income, tourist companies passed into majority or partial ownership of individual commercial banks. Moreover, they have gone into further debt with no possibility of repaying the loans. The banks have no further interest in transforming those receivables into shareholdings because such companies cannot be sold on the market for even a third of their value, so the only way out of this position is through state assistance. Neither the banks nor the state have found an effective way of managing these tourism portfolios, so the privatization problem looms as a priority in resolving the entire log-jam of problems. However, the owners of tourist companies are, in fact, unwilling to sell their properties before they achieve a recovery and market repositioning, when they would be able to realize their true value and at least partially recover their investment. Greater involvement is expected from the state which, exhausted by the war, reconstruction, and the inherited inefficient economy, does not have the economic strength to resolve all these problems. Any solutions are merely palliative.

The restructuring and recovery of the tourism economy, following the resolution of the difficulties inherited from the previous economic system and those caused by the war in Croatia, will start a new development cycle in island tourism. This, according to several assessments by domestic and foreign experts, is potentially the most promising part for Croatian tourism. On a positive note this process, despite numerous difficulties, has already begun on some of the most developed islands.

Physical limitations

One of the most significant problems affecting the economic, and hence tourism development of the islands is their accessibility. The accessibility of the islands can be considered in three separate segments: (1) accessibility from the mainland; (2) accessibility between islands; and (3) accessibility between the towns and villages on each island. On the issue of access to the islands from the mainland, it should be pointed out that over 90 per cent of coastal ferry traffic is carried by the national ferry company Jadrolinija, which operates 38 ferries and 7 passenger ships on 30 permanent routes. Although trip frequency on the major routes increases considerably during the tourism season, long queues at the landing stages are commonplace. The acquisition and maintenance of additional vessels, however, would be completely unprofitable since usage of the existing fleet is only around 30 per cent. Therefore, Jadrolinija receives significant state subsidies to maintain its services.

Access to individual settlements on islands is provided by substituting unprofitable shipping lines with ferry transport and by building road networks, a programme that has been in progress since the 1970s. Since in most cases the ferries run from the mainland to the islands via the shortest route, and to only one point, it is important to build adequate road networks on the bigger islands, where these have yet to be completed. Links between islands are almost non-existent. There are only a few lines, which operate at unsuitable times for tourist visits. These companies only provide tourist charter services, if and when there is sufficient interest. Only five islands are linked to the mainland by bridges (Krk, Pag, Vir, Murter and Ciovo), and one of them has an airport for primary traffic (Krk). Another two islands (Brac and Losinj) have airports for secondary traffic. None of these three airports provide regular scheduled services. Since transport accessibility is essentially the basis of any development, these unsolved issues present an obstacle to the tourism development of individual islands.

Water management is a particularly important factor affecting the development of any island destination, since providing sufficient quantities of drinking-quality water for the population and business activities while concurrently protecting the marine environment by using adequate sewage disposal installations are strategic priorities. Therefore, the state of the water supply and sewage disposal is the next limiting factor for tourism development on the Croatian islands.

There are no natural watercourses on the islands (except on the island of Cres, where there is a natural lake that supplies the islands of Cres and Losinj). Thus, water is extracted from wells, piped from the mainland or transported by tanker. The state of water management on the islands is well illustrated by the Water Supply Development Programme (part of the National Island Development Programme (Ministarstvo, 1997)) which aims to bring water supplies to 85 per cent of the island population. This will require improvements in water supplies to various built-up locations on the 27 largest islands.

Unfortunately, the coastal waters around the islands receive sewage from all the coastal towns and villages. Similar to many islands around the Mediterranean, most of the permanent settlements have no sewer mains and sewage from most of the tourism facilities is discharged into the sea without treatment. On the plus side, the sea around the southern islands is quite deep and, thus, the polluting effects of such discharge are small. The same applies to some of the islands in the central and northern Adriatic (Brac, Solta, Krk, Hvar, Rab and Cres). By contrast, however, most of the remaining islands are not surrounded by deep water and do not witness strong enough currents so here the negative effects of such discharges are greater.

National Strategy Relating to Tourism Development on the Islands

As mentioned earlier, the National Island Development Programme was ratified by the Croatian Parliament in 1997 as a set of development tasks to be carried out by the state to ensure the islands' growth is sustainable and coordinated with Croatia's overall development. The basic goals of this programme are as follows: (1) sustainable development; (2) a socially satisfactory population density; and (3) the continued retention of the present population and the return of emigrants, primarily those who are young and actively working.

A sectoral study of the national programme entitled 'Conception of Further Development of Island Tourism' (Kunst, 1996) provides more detailed clarification of the aims of developing island tourism in the future, and the measures and actions necessary for this concept's realization. The following are the key aims for developing island tourism: restructuring and modernization of the existing products in order to adapt to market demand; more complete valuation and permanent protection of non-renewable resources of the islands; and building up a new identity and market repositioning of the islands as a leading micro-destination in Europe.

Toward the end of the 1980s before the outbreak of war in Croatia, a stagnation of actual tourist flows, accompanied by increasing discrepancies between the budgeted and actual accommodation prices (up to 40 per cent), was observed. Obsolescence of the tourism product had led to a loss of market position. Therefore, the existing accommodation facilities on the islands should be reduced (but above all modernized), while being supplemented with new, high quality facilities, taking advantage of the characteristics of the islands' natural resources, construction and horticulture.

In the context of tourism, sustainable development is the only acceptable scenario for the future development of the islands. In this way, development of the islands is based on improving the quality of life for their population while simultaneously increasing visitors' satisfaction. Although mass tourism development has been accompanied by numerous negative effects, the sector developed more slowly on the islands than on the mainland due to space limitations and poor transport links. Thus, the islands have succeeded to a large extent in preserving the environment, their valuable cultural and historical resources, and their original social identity. Today, they represent the strategic potential of Croatian tourism.

For the islands, market repositioning and establishing a new identity have become an exceptionally important priority. An analysis of tourism demand for the islands shows that this does not differ greatly from that for the mainland. This indicates an unsatisfactory use of the islands' resources. Therefore, in creating their image, the islands should emphasize their own ecological, cultural and social values in order to achieve the desired market image. The natural resource base of the islands is competitive in the Mediterranean and should, therefore, become the basis for repositioning. Island architecture, lifestyle, folklore, cuisine, and landscape can become the differentiating factors of the island tourism product.

For this situation to be realized it is essential to define priority tasks, actions, and measures and to appoint people responsible for the completion of such tasks. If island development is to be directed and systematically planned on the basis of sustainable development, it is necessary to draw up a tourism plan for the Croatian islands and then make detailed plans for the tourism development of each individual island (Kunst, 1996). This demands state incentives for the development of island tourism, primarily through direct assistance in building major infrastructure (transport, water supply, etc.), and non-repayable investment in restoring the monumental heritage of the island's culture and traditions. Other measures that could be included in the system of state incentives are: a special lower rate of value added tax; investment loans on more favourable terms than those available on the market; attracting foreign capital by reducing the nominal value of tourism assets to their realistic market value; reduced prices for electricity, water, and gas supplied to accommodation facilities; and exemption from profit tax during the initial years of operation for new investment projects in the tourism sector. Such direct concessions and incentives would have to be more generous in the initial stages of development and then reduced gradually according to the progress of development.

Conclusion

There is little doubt that the islands represent an extremely valuable natural resource that could contribute to the rapid recovery of Croatian tourism and the country's establishment as a high-quality destination on the Mediterranean. At the same time, the islands represent an extremely sensitive social, economic and ecological system, meaning that sustainable development is the most desirable development option. Sustainable tourism development makes use of the natural and cultural heritage with the aim of increasing the numbers of tourists and profit, but in a manner that does not damage and exhaust these resources but rather preserves them for future generations.

Until the advent of tourism, due to their natural characteristics and relatively meagre traditional economic resources, the islands had quite modest development prospects (such as agriculture, fishing, shipbuilding and marine transport). The rather rudimentary development of tourism brought short-term prosperity to the islands but eventually would have caused long-term damage. Obviously, the sector's growth in these environments was retarded by the obsolescence of the tourism product in the 1980s and then cut off by the war in the early 1990s. Therefore, the new opportunity for future sustainable development of tourism on the islands must not be missed.

The feature which sets the Croatian Adriatic islands most clearly apart from competing island destinations is their low level of tourism saturation. Given this, the Croatian islands must use their natural characteristics and cultural heritage to create a recognizable and unique tourism brand. The state's role should be to introduce appropriate measures and instruments to promote such development of the islands in a manner that considers the quality of life and well-being of the island population.

References

De Kadt, E. (1990) *Making the Alternative Sustainable: Lessons from Development for Tourism.* Discussion Paper No. 272. Brighton: University of Sussex.

Dragicevic, M. (1990) *Methodological Framework for Assessing Tourism Carrying Capacity in Mediterranean Coastal Zones.* Split, Croatia: UNEP/MAP/PAP.

Dragicevic, M. (1991) Towards sustainable development. *AIEST Reports*, 33: 29–62.

DZS Drzavni zavod za statistiku (Central Bureau of Statistics) (1991). *Popis Stanova I stnovnistva* (Housing and Population Census). Zagreb: DZS.

DZS Drzavni zavod za statistiku (Central Bureau of Statistics). (1997a). *Promet Turista u Primorskim Mjestima Hrvatske, 1966–1997* (Tourist flows in coastal resorts in Croatia). Zagreb: DZS.

DZS Drzavni zavod za statistiku (Central Bureau of Statistics) (1997b) *Promet Turista u Primorskim Mjestima Hrvatske 1989–1997* (Tourist flows in coastal resorts in Croatia). Zagreb: DZS.

DZS Drzavni zavod za statistiku (Central Bureau of Statistics) (1997c) *Statisticki ljetopis* (Statistical Yearbook). Zagreb: DZS.

European Island Agenda (1997) Commitments. Final Report. 1st European Conference on Sustainable Development, Minorca, April.

Grant, D.L. (1997) Sustainable tourism in islands and small states: case studies. *Tourism Management*, 18(5): 335–7.

Hall, D.R. (1998) Tourism development and sustainability issues in Central and South-eastern Europe. *Tourism Management*, 19(5): 423–31.

Haulot, A. (1981) Social tourism: current dimensions and future developments. *Tourism Management*, 2(3): 207–12.

Horak, S. (1986) Utjecaj prometne povezanosti na turisticki razvoj otoka Krka i Cres-Losinja. *Ceste i mostovi*, 8: 287–91.

Horak, S. (1991) Znacaj izgradnje Krckog mosta za razvoj turizma u opcini Krk. *Turizam*, 37(11–12): 273–7.

Horak, S. (1995) Tko je i kakv gost nauticar u Hrvatskoj. *Hrvatski turisticki magazin UT*, 10: 18–20.

Horak, S. and Weber, S. (1986) *Znacaj i uloga obalne plovidbe za razvoj turizma na Jadranu*. Zagreb: Institut za turizam.

Hunter, C. (1997) Sustainable tourism as an adaptive paradigm. *Annals of Tourism Research*, 24(4): 850–67.

Institut za turizam (1997) *Stavovi i potrosnja turista u Hrvatskoj – TOMAS '97* (Attitudes and Expenditures of Tourists in Croatia). Zagreb: Institut za turizam.

Jafari, J. and Wall, G. (1994) Sustainable tourism. *Annals of Tourism Research*, 21(3): 667–9.

Klaric, Z. (1989) Situation of tourist development in relation to environment in the Mediterranean setting. Seminar on tourism and environment in the European Mediterranean of the nineties. Diagnosis 89: Tourism and its effect on our environment. Valencia: Institut turistic, June.

Kunst, I. (1996) Koncepcija razvitka turizma na hrvatskim otocima. (Conception of further development of island tourism), *Turizam*, 44(9–10): 207–27.

Leslie, D. (1993) Developing sustainable tourism. *Tourism Management*, 14(6), 485–8.

Mazanec, J. and Schmidhauser, H.P. (1985) Monitoring behavioral changes through national guest surveys: Swiss and Austrian experiences. St Gallen: Edition AIEST, 26.

Mikacic, V. and Montana, M. (1994) Island tourism and the concept of small-scale economy. *Insula*, 3(1): 37–40.

Mikacic, V. and Pepeonik, Z. (1997) The importance of island tourism to the foreign tourist turnover of Croatia. *Conditions of the Foreign Tourism Development in Central and Eastern Europe*, 4(9): 143–54.

Ministarstvo Kulture (1997) *Program prostornog uredjenja Republike Hrvatske* (Spatial planning programme for Republic of Croatia). Zagreb: Ministarstvo Kulture.

Ministarstvo razvitka i obnove (1997) *Nacionalni program razvitka otoka* (National Island Development Programme). Zagreb: Ministarstvo razvitka i obnove.

Misra, S.K. (1993) Preservation in sustainable tourism development. WTO, 10th General Assembly, Bali, 30 September–9 October: Round Table on Planning for Sustainable Tourism Development.

Muller, H. (1994) The thorny path to sustainable tourism development. International scientific round table: Towards Sustainable Tourism Development in Croatia (Proceedings), December, Zagreb.

PAP/RAC-Mediterranean Action Plan (1997) *Guidelines for Carrying Capacity*

Assessment for Tourism in Mediterranean Coastal Areas. Split, Croatia: Regional Activity Centre.

Radnic, A. and Mikacic, V. (1994) Turizam i odrzivi razvoj hrvatskih otoka. (Tourism and sustainable development of Croatian islands). *Zbornik radova simpozija Strategija odrzivog razvitka hrvatskih otoka,* Hvar (332–47).

Sofield, T. (1998) Sustainable tourism in islands and small states. *Annals of Tourism Research,* 25(1): 250–3.

Taylor, G. (1996) Tourism and sustainable community development. *Tourism Management,* 17(4): 309–10.

Travis, A. (1994) Sustainable tourism concept and innovations in coastal areas and coastal city tourism. International scientific round table: Towards sustainable tourism development in Croatia. Proceedings, December, Zagreb.

World Tourism Organization (1998) *Guide for Local Authorities on Developing Sustainable Tourism.* Madrid: WTO.

10

The Path Towards Sustainability in the Balearic Islands

Esteban Bardolet

Mallorca, sometimes called the heart of the Mediterranean, for embodying all its virtues, is known in Britain as a package holiday destination, and so is a synonym for cheapness ... just pronouncing it, deliberately twanging it, calling it 'Majorca', and sounding the 'j', has the same effect as cracking a joke.

(Theroux, 1995: 50)

Introduction: Tourism in the Balearic Islands

In this chapter I deal with the unprecedented success of the Balearic archipelago as a European mass tourism destination. In particular, I focus on the efforts of the region's citizens to limit further tourism development now that they have reached living standards above the averages for Spain and the European Union as a whole.

Unfortunately, tourism sustainability has been endangered by the very success brought on by the sector. In this chapter sustainable tourism development is approached from planning and marketing viewpoints. In particular, sustainable development is examined from the point of tourists' satisfaction levels as well as from the residents' acceptance of territorial planning. In 1998, following a popular and political consensus, the Autonomous Government of the Balearics implemented two moratoria to stop the growth of tourist accommodation and the increase of residential dwellings outside existing urbanized areas. The following year, the Parliament of the Balearics passed a new tourism law and new territorial ordinance plans, thus ending the two moratoria and reinforcing its strategy to achieve sustainable development. To successfully achieve this goal, a major approach has been to push for sustainable tourism since this is the main economic activity on the islands.

I begin the chapter by describing the islands' transition from pioneers in mass tourism into leaders in sustainable tourism development. A major force behind this transition was the autonomy gained by the Balearics in 1983 from Spain. Initially the autonomous government did not have a long-term plan regarding tourist activities and paid little attention to the industry's environmental and sociocultural impacts. Everything, except for basic infrastructural works, was left to the private sector. Only since 1995 and especially after 1998 has the public sector taken a proactive role in tourism planning. The case of the Balearic islands deserves close attention. This is because it is one of the first places in the European free market system where policy-makers have tried to limit further growth in an economic sector such as tourism in order to safeguard scarce natural resources and a limited area.

Tourism Evolution Since 1950

Overall, the Balearic islands are an archipelago of 5,014 square kilometres situated in the western Mediterranean (Figure 10.1) The largest island, Majorca, has an area of 3,640 square kilometres. The Balearics (Baleares) is one of Spain's 17 autonomous regions with a total of 760,000 inhabitants. The region's capital is Palma. There are three international airports, one on each island except the smallest island, Formentera (Bardolet, 1996).

The Balearic islands are a Mediterranean holiday destination whose success has had no parallel in the history of modern mass tourism. By 1950, following the Spanish Civil War and World War II, the number of tourist arrivals in the Balearics had reached 100,000 (90 per cent of whom were recorded in Majorca). In 1998 the Balearic islands' commitment to tourism resulted in some 10.1 million arrivals, 12 per cent of whom were Spanish and the rest from European countries. Nowadays Majorca accounts for 75 per cent of all arrivals in the Balearics, while the Pitiusas isles (Ibiza and Formentera) and Minorca attract 15 and 10 per cent, respectively (Bardolet, 1999).

The evolution of tourism in the Balearics reflects the history of various transportation innovations. The first tourists arrived by sea (steam ships) while by the 1960s most visitors came by air (nowadays 97 per cent of the total). Moreover, tourism grew significantly especially after the 1960s because of the successful co-operation between private promoters and foreign tour operators. Nowadays, the latter are responsible for 87 per cent of the total number of arrivals. Since the early years of tourism development the local population has welcomed visitors and worked hard to achieve prosperity through tourism. By 1998, tourism expenditure contributed US$5.7 billion to the economy of the Balearics (Aguiló *et al.*, 1998). Nevertheless, it should be borne in mind that this amounted to just 72 per cent of the total cost paid by holidaymakers for their vacation. The remaining 28 per cent of the cost was mainly absorbed by foreign-owned tour operators and airlines.

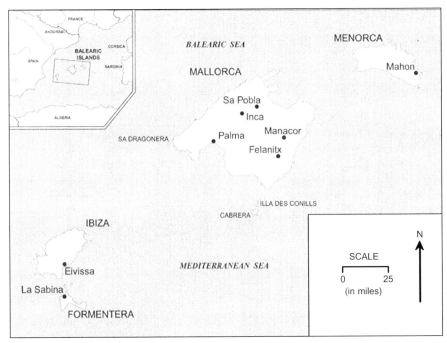

Figure 10.1 The Balearics
Note: Spanish placenames have been used.

The first island to develop its tourist industry as early as the 1950s was Majorca, followed by Ibiza (in the 1970s), Minorca (in the 1980s), and Formentera (in the 1990s). Since 1950, tourism growth has generally been steady although the industry has witnessed a number of downturns especially during the global energy crisis of 1973–76 and the Gulf War (1989–92). At approximately US$19,000 per capita, the island's gross regional product (GRP) has increased faster than that of Spain as a whole (130 per cent) and has been greater than the average growth for the European Union (110 per cent). The economy is highly dependent on tourism. This sector and related activities generate around 60 per cent of the Balearics' GRP. By contrast, manufacturing contributes little to the regional economy. The few existing manufacturing activities are fairly labour-intensive and include the production of shoes, custom jewellery, wooden furniture, artificial pearls, and construction materials. Agriculture is non-profitable due to the small scale of units and the chronic shortage of rain. This sector generates just 2 per cent of the islands' GRP although it is the most beneficial branch of the economy in terms of preserving the beauty of the hinterland. Nowadays, the market value of rural land is more dependent on its potential for residential or tourism development, rather than the profits generated from farming.

In 1998 the tourist accommodation capacity in both licensed and non-registered establishments reached 450,000 beds. The average length of stay was 10.5 days while the number of bednights amounted to 106 million. On average, less than 30 per cent of this capacity is in use during the winter season (November to April). Indeed, between November and April, the number of tourist arrivals is only 18 per cent of the annual total. Because of seasonality, despite the record number of tourists, the annual average occupancy rate is less than 55 per cent (Bardolet, 1999).

Until the 1960s, Spanish nationals accounted for the majority of arrivals on the islands followed by the French. By the 1970s, however, the British had become the leading nationality. In the 1980s, the British reached a record high (2.9 million in 1987) followed by the Germans (1.9 million in 1990). By 1995, however, the German market emerged as the leading source of tourists for the Balearics. In 1998 the number of arrivals from Germany reached a record high of almost 3.7 million, followed by the 3.3 million British and 1.1 million Spanish arrivals per year. In 1997, the Balearic islands accounted for an estimated 20 per cent market share of the total number of foreign tourist arrivals in Spain, and 10 per cent market share of European holidaymakers in the Mediterranean Sea.

Interestingly, the Balearics in the 1980s began an active campaign to develop winter products in order to reduce the effects of seasonality. The types of activities which have been promoted range from open air sports (16 golf courses, 60 marinas with 18,000 moorings, paths for almost 80,000 cycling tourists per year, etc.) to cultural events (visits to monuments, natural parks, and traditional celebrations) (Aguiló *et al.*, 1996). This strategy was reinforced during the 1990s following the development of two Tourism Marketing plans (1991–93 and 1996–98) by the Ministry of Tourism of the Balearic Islands.

Main Tourism Features

The most important characteristics of the tourist industry are mentioned in a white paper on Balearic tourism (Aguiló *et al.*, 1987). These include the following:

- The continuing importance and growth of summer tourism, despite major efforts to diversify the products for the winter months. The quality of the product (i.e., climate, clean beaches, safety, and hotel service) explains this continued growth.
- High seasonality, with only 18 per cent of annual arrivals recorded between November and April (less than 5 per cent of arrivals on the smaller islands of Pitiusas and Minorca).
- A heavy dependence on air transport (97 per cent of arrivals) and on tour operators (87 per cent of arrivals). Sea cruises bring half a million visitors

to the islands although these are not counted as tourists since they do not stay overnight. The same tour operators who are responsible for air package tours organize some of these cruises.

- An overwhelming reliance on the German and British tourist market since these two groups account for more than 70 per cent of all arrivals on the islands.
- The popularity of second homes purchases, predominantly by the British and more recently the Germans.
- A high level of satisfaction (86 per cent) partially indicated by the number of return visits (70 per cent) of tourists, despite the unpleasant side-effects of mass tourism during the summer months.
- The diversity in terms of supply of tourist facilities, landscapes, islands, and activities that a tourist can enjoy at any time because of relatively mild winters.
- Local ownership and management of most of the accommodation units, and tourism-related businesses. The major Spanish hotel chains, some of which are among the largest in the world, have their headquarters in the Balearics.
- A high level of tourism 'know-how' acquired after almost 50 years' experience in the industry. This 'know-how' is not just an asset for the islands but, nowadays, it is also exported to the Caribbean and other tourist destinations.

Tourism Policy in the Balearics: Before and After Autonomy

Since 1983, the Balearics have had full autonomy to set their own tourism policy, independent from the Central Government in Madrid. This date constitutes a major landmark for tourism evolution on the islands, particularly because the regional government had historically been far more aware than the national authorities of the dangers of excessive tourism growth. During the period of General Franco's dictatorship the tourist sector was the only hard currency earner; in the Balearic isles it featured as the main 'milk cow'. With the arrival of democracy in 1976, tourism was treated in Spain as a major job generator although the sector's environmental repercussions were widely ignored.

More recently, the main tourism regulations in the Balearics have adopted a common theme of 'sustainability'. Thus, it can be said that the Balearics are moving from a period of 'unsustainable success' into one of sustainable tourism (Bardolet, 1993). The various strategies geared towards achieving tourism sustainability are discussed below.

Environmental protection

The first obvious concern with protecting the landscape and environment was reflected in regional legislation passed in 1984 with a law protecting natural areas of special interest known as 'ANEIS'. During 1987 the law on territorial planning was also introduced. However, this law was only partially implemented after 1991 following the appearance of three types of regulations. These were the 1991 'Law on Conservation of Natural Areas and Landscape' (LEN), the 'Partial Territorial Plans' (for example, the one passed in 1997 for 'Es Pla de Mallorca', a geographical area of Majorca), and the 'Sectoral Activities Plans' (e.g., the 1995 'Regulatory Tourism Supply Plan' better known as POOT). It is important to mention, however, that because of the lack of political will, the 1987 'Law on Territorial Planning' was only fully approved by the Balearics Parliament in May 1999, more than a decade after it had originally been introduced.

It is also worth mentioning the 1988 nationwide 'Coastal Law' which constitutes one of the few attempts by the Spanish government to introduce land-use policy at the national level. This law established a green belt of 100 metres between the sea rescue zone and the non-urbanized hinterland (this figure was reduced to only 20 metres if the hinterland is already urbanized). Before 1988 when this law took effect some hotels and private villas had been built right upon the beach dunes.

The regional legislation of 1984 and 1991 (ANEIS and LEN, respectively) protects 39 per cent of the territory on the Balearics. This percentage is high due to the inclusion of the islands' mountain ranges. Nevertheless, the Balearics now boast among the highest proportion of protected land witnessed in Spanish and European resorts. Almost 54 per cent of the islands' remaining territory is rural and 7 per cent is classified as urban (already built-up or approved for development). The strategy of the recently approved Territorial Ordinance Plans (DOT), put forth by the Ministry of the Environment (Government of the Balearic Islands, 1997a), is to create a rational and long-term planning system for all activities on the islands. This would serve to limit the expansion of those mass tourism-related activities that consume large amounts of territory while concurrently fostering businesses and facilities aimed at higher quality tourists. Policy-makers assume that such an approach will reduce human pressure on the islands' natural resources.

This DOT strategy goes hand in hand with the 1997 ECOTUR Decree (Government of the Balearic Islands, 1997b), developed by the Ministry of Environment and partly financed by the EU. This programme is geared to conform to the overall sustainable territorial and tourism model for the Balearic islands, based on the 5th Environmental Action Programme of the EU for 1993–2000. This non-statutory programme applies to four areas: installations, resorts, tourism education, and applications. Specifically it assigns eco-labels and eco-audits for tourism-related units. According to this programme, the centres of tourism-related activity (broadly speaking lodging, catering and sports centres), which comply with management ISO 9000, environment ISO 14000, and eco-audits, are awarded 'environmental friendly' or 'environmental quality' labels. The amount assigned for this programme during 1998–99 was US$0.7 million. In 1998, a number of lodging establishments totalling 60,000 beds, plus a golf course and four marinas were awarded these labels.

The first designated 'natural' park of Majorca, Albufera Park, was created in 1988 while five others followed in the 1990s. These were Mondragó (a beach in Majorca), Albufera del Grau in Minorca, the island of Dragonera, and the archipelago of Cabrera which was labelled a 'national park'. UNESCO declared Minorca a 'biosphere reserve' in 1993, while Ibiza and Formentera have had their *salinas* (i.e., salt-lakes) declared a natural reserve. Formentera has recently adopted a unique programme in the Mediterranean aimed at protecting its environment through various policies and restrictions, including a plan to gradually introduce electric cars to replace conventional petrol-powered vehicles.

In July 1997 the 'Law of Rural Land' was introduced, limiting the construction of non-agricultural villas and cottages in rural areas, to minimize the negative impacts of such facilities on rural landscapes. While previous regulations required a minimum plot size of 7,000 square metres in these areas, the new law doubled the requirement to 14,000 square metres. By 1999, however, two years after the implementation of the law, there was evidence that the residential pressure on rural areas had not yet slowed down. This would not have been the case if the municipalities had strictly enforced the law and been less generous in granting permissions for 'refurbishing' small rural huts (e.g., former shelters for agromachinery). Increasingly, the owners of such buildings convert these into small weekend homes, which obviously no longer serve any agricultural purposes.

In 1998 the environmental pollution tax, originally drafted in 1992, finally saw the green light. This pollution tax was imposed by the Government of the Balearics upon companies such as public utilities (e.g., electricity, gas, and telephone) for environmentally damaging activities. The tax has been contested in the highest court of justice of Spain, although it has finally been confirmed. It has not yet been enforced, however, pending new court hearings. The tax rate is set at an annual 1 per cent upon the capitalization of a 40 per cent gross income average from the production assets of such companies located in the Balearics. This tax is the first of its kind to be instituted in Spain, following the advice of the European Union (Government of the Balearic Islands, 1991).

Furthermore, by 1999 a debate had started concerning the fairness and convenience of setting up a new 'ecotax' to be paid by tourists except during the winter season. This ecotax is meant to generate funds for the care of the environment and landscape that are severely damaged by mass tourism during the summer. The tax is also aimed at helping owners of large mountain area farms cover the increasing costs of keeping these establishments open for tourist visits.

Limiting tourism's growth

The first policy aimed at restraining the growth of tourist accommodation in the Balearic islands was included in the I Cladera Decree of 1984. This required 30 square metres of land for each planned tourist bed. The II Cladera Decree, introduced in 1987, increased the amount of required land to 60 square metres because the first decree had little effect. Nevertheless, the rush to have construction plans approved before the 1987 decree was passed led to an over-supply of lodging facilities, a situation made even more serious due to the decrease in tourism demand during the Gulf War of 1989–91. Eventually, however, the regulation proved to be one the best ways of limiting the growth of low category hotels in a free market economy. This legislation, still in effect today, indirectly led to the creation of luxury hotels since these were the only tourist establishments able to absorb the skyrocketing land costs.

In 1994 the ECOMOST (European Community Model of Sustainable Tourism) project was published pioneering research on the limits of tourism accommodation levels in Majorca and Rhodes. The POOT (Regulatory Tourism Supply Plan) of 1995, mentioned earlier, that aimed at controlling the supply of accommodation, resulted in the ECOMOST strategy being implemented in coastal areas of Majorca, by adhering to certain carrying-capacity parameters. Moreover, the 1992 Spanish Futures Plan and the 1995 Calvia Municipality Agenda 21 followed the same guidelines. These topics are discussed in more detail later on.

Since the 1950s the Balearics have been forced by tour operators based in the main markets to adopt the image of a 'subtropical' destination even though they did not really have the attributes of such destinations (e.g., warm winters for swimming). The high density of tourists during the peak summer months, most of whom are concentrated on the coast and beaches, has led to a major increase in lodging supply even though this is used only a few months of the year. This growth has worsened the environmental quality of the destination and reduced the stock of natural resources (mainly underground water), even though it has concurrently proved successful in terms of the high number of summer overnight stays.

During the 1980s the ratio of arrivals between the winter and summer seasons had worsened from a 25–75 per cent to a 13–87 per cent distribution. Thanks to the so-called 'D' Plan (1997), an off-peak season strategy aimed at balancing the distribution of winter *vis-à-vis* summer arrivals, the ratio has marginally improved to 18–82 per cent. The 'D' Plan was among the measures taken by IBATUR (the private Tourism Promotion Institute of the Balearics) to promote winter tourism through sports, cultural events and shopping incentives, with the co-operation of local Chambers of Commerce and the islands' private tourism boards.

The economic and social pressures arising from over-building in 1997 led the Balearic Government to pass two moratoria the following year. These related to new tourism lodging capacity and all types of new residential buildings outside urban areas. These moratoria were eclipsed by the middle of 1999 with the implementation of the new Law on Tourism and the new DOT (Territorial Ordinance Plans) (Government of the Balearic Islands, 1999). Through this legislation definitive limits on the capacity of tourism lodging and the islands' population will be set, although many problems remain to be solved.

Improving tourism products and infrastructure

After the Balearics gained their autonomy there were a total of six major tourism programmes. This section examines each one in turn. First, in 1989 a 'Global Sanitation Plan' was implemented aimed at constructing sewage treatment plants, to keep the sea clean. These projects were completed in 1997, at a cost exceeding US$200 million. As a result, beaches have generally been cleaned up and, indeed, the Balearics have been assigned 50 European Union 'Blue Flags'. Nevertheless, in some areas there is now a potential danger of contamination of underground water levels because of the uncontrolled disposal of improperly recycled water.

Second, in 1990 a plan aimed at embellishing tourism resorts was put into action. A second phase of this particular plan was instituted in 1994 (Government of the Balearic Islands, 1990a). The money invested for this programme exceeded US$100 million. The results have been extremely positive for the image of the islands, especially following work to improve or create sea promenades along the coast (lighting, pavement, green zones, urban elements, etc.). There is a downside, however, namely the fact that such projects have urbanized the seaside.

A third programme was passed by the Parliament of the Balearic Islands in 1990, the 'Hotel Accommodation Modernization Plan', aimed at all accommodation units built before 1984. These buildings had to pass a technical inspection to establish the need for renovations (Government of the Balearic Islands, 1990b). This modernization increased the quality of some 1,200 units and 200,000 beds. Those hotels that chose not to comply with the programme within three years could be forced to close down. However, since by 1997 around 30 per cent of these establishments had not yet finished their renovation work, a new deadline was supposed to be set. The amount for renovations spent by the hoteliers has already been approximately US$800 million. This modernization plan has been comple- mented by the 'Law on Modernization of Complementary Tourism Facilities' of 1996, that deals in a similar fashion with the catering sector (restaurants, cafeterias, etc.) (Government of the Balearic Islands, 1996).

The fourth tourism programme was implemented in 1995. This was aimed at fostering tourism education. For this purpose a new building was constructed on the campus of the University of the Balearic Islands for the School of Tourism (originally established in 1987) and for the brand new School of Hotel Administration. In 1998 the School of Tourism was integrated into the University of the Balearic Islands as part of the Faculty of Economics. The money invested by the Government of the Balearics in this building and equipment exceeded US$10 million.

Yet another programme was the 'Q Plan' (Tourism Supply Quality Plan) of 1995 (reviewed in 1998) that embraces the already mentioned improvements in modernization and education. Some of the most important forthcoming projects are ParcBIT (a Technological Innovation Park, close to the University campus) and the CITE (Centre for Research of Tourism Technologies, to be established inside the ParcBIT). These projects are partly financed by the EU.

The final tourism programme was the 1997 'Pla Mirall' (Mirror Plan) aimed at restoring the architectural identity of hinterland towns (Government of the Balearic Islands, 1997c). This was similar in purpose to the 'Embellishment Plan for Coastal Resorts'. Over two years, beginning in 1998, a total of US$280 million was to be invested in this plan. Funded partly by the EU, this programme is expected to conserve the traditional appearance of the towns and cities of the Balearics, especially by restoring monuments and historic façades.

Before the establishment of regional autonomy in the Balearics, there had been few attempts to regulate the excessive construction of tourist facilities at the national level. These included the national 'Decree for Minimum Structural Requirements for Tourism Accommodation' of 1970, but they generally had no practical effect in the Balearics due to the lack of municipal administrative controls. In 1974 the national 'Declaration for Territories with Preferential Tourism Use' focused on tourism-geared municipalities including coastal destinations such as the Balearics. This declaration was eventually over-ruled in the Balearics in 1989 when the autonomous government instituted a new stricter licensing system for tourism lodgings. However, the situation where municipalities actually have to obtain building licences from the Balearics Government before building tourism establishments was only achieved with the 1995 plan for regulating supply (POOT).

Compensating for the handicaps of insularity

The 1995 law concerning the Balearics' special economic and taxation status passed by the Parliament of the Balearics was finally confirmed by the Spanish Parliament in May 1998. The main measures of this legislation apply to sea and air transport discounts (33 per cent) for residents of the islands, cheaper (by 40–45 per cent) harbour fees for goods, vehicles, and raw materials to be imported, manufactured and exported, and for used items to be recycled outside the islands. The 1978 Spanish Constitution had already recognized the special situation arising from the insularity of the Canary Islands and Balearics, but only the former benefited from early programmes. The reason for that original discrimination was the higher per capita incomes that the Balearics enjoy. Paradoxically, the 1997 EU Amsterdam Summit recognized the importance of structural handicaps caused by insularity on European islands, even the ones not considered part of the 'ultra-periphery'. Since the islands' per capita income levels were disregarded, the Balearics were included in this group. The new EU approach to a large extent 'forced' the Spanish Parliament in 1998 to apply the original programmes of the 1978 Spanish Constitution to the Balearics.

In 1989 the so-called 'cost of insularity' of the Balearics in terms of extra transportation costs compared to those incurred in mainland areas was estimated to be 1.0 per cent of its GDP (Bardolet, 1989). A 1993 revision put this percentage up to 1.3 per cent of GDP. Still, the main problems caused by insularity are ones that cannot be quantified, as, for example, the qualitative handicaps arising from the absence of non-tourism sector investments because potential investors fear, among others, transportation costs. Investment in tourism may also be negatively influenced because of insularity as illustrated in the hypothetical case of choosing a location for a large theme park. Most investors are likely to choose a continental location over an island (even one as successful as Majorca) for such an attraction because the former is more likely to be closer to a major transportation node.

The Challenges of Tourism Quality and Tourism Sustainability in the Balearics

The ECOMOST project for Majorca

In 1990 the IFTO (International Federation of Tour Operators) promoted a scientific study termed the 'European Community Model of Sustainable Tourism' (ECOMOST). The study received funding from the DGXXIII in Brussels, Turespana (Ministry of Tourism) in Madrid, and IBATUR (Ministry of Tourism) in Palma. Work was carried out by a team of professors of the universities of Munich and the Balearics, led by Alfred Koch (DWIF) in Munich, and encouraged by the President of IFTO, Martin Brackenbury, in London. The resorts chosen for the study were two islands: Majorca and Rhodes, because of their fragile environments and their commercial success. The work began in 1992 and was presented in June 1994, after the end of the Gulf War (IFTO, 1994).

The model resulting from this study is based on four main requirements for maintaining a successful tourism destination in the long term in order to achieve sustainability. These are, in turn, the following:

1. The population should remain prosperous and maintain its cultural traits.

2. The destination should remain attractive to tourists.
3. Nothing should be done to damage the ecology.
4. An effective political framework should be implemented.

The key to the model is the analysis of the resorts' 'carrying capacity', based on such factors as the amount of natural resources, style of management, number of tourists and their behaviour, endurance of infrastructure, and attitude of residents. The model goes beyond the traditional ecological approach as it includes economic and sociocultural analysis. It sets up a list of critical values of indicators relating to the main topics. According to the situation, a set of measures is proposed to improve the carrying capacity, and some proposals are put forth relating to legal frameworks and territorial planning.

The four requirements covered by ECOMOST are then analysed according to their main components (e.g., for population these include preserving prosperity, economic efficiency, and cultural identity), and each of them monitored according to indicators (e.g., to preserve cultural identity it is necessary to examine the number of overnight stays per local inhabitant, the number of second residences per household, the number of seasonal employees, or the incidence of crime, and foreign infiltration). Thus, critical values are set up for each indicator (e.g., at the local level it is estimated that there should be a maximum of 20,000 recorded stays yearly per 100 inhabitants, or the ratio of residents to tourist beds must be less than 3:1).

The objective of ECOMOST was to provide tools for sustainable development since the tour operators and public institutions involved believed there was a lack of real understanding in this area. It is noticeable that many of the principal tour operators in Europe changed their strategy at the time ECOMOST was promoted in 1990. The same could be said for the main hoteliers and politicians in the Balearics, since these individuals were promoting limits to the growth of tourism to protect their own investments, thus becoming unlikely 'bed partners' with the ecologists.

The Futures Plan and 'Calvia Agenda 21'

The Spanish Futures Plan of 1992, also known as the 'Basic Plan for improving the competitiveness of Spanish Tourism', is now entering its second phase (1996–99). The total amount spent for this plan up to now has been $US380 million. The Futures Plan followed the recommendations of the 1990 Spanish 'White Paper on Tourism' (Spanish Ministry of Tourism, 1990).

Overall, the Futures Plan has the following aims: to promote the coordination primarily of public bodies, to modernize mainly in terms of quality and human resources, to develop new products to diversify away from the 'sun and beach' image, to improve promotion through the use of marketing techniques, and to support excellence by upgrading tourism-related activities in the eyes of the residents and improving information for tourists (Spanish Ministry of Tourism, 1994).

The second phase of the Futures Plan concentrates on three topics: new products and services, the internationalization of Spanish tourism companies, and technical innovation applied to tourism activities. The first phase was funded with US$350 million while up to now the second has spent US$30 million. Promotion is the one area that receives the greatest share of funding (US$215 million). The Futures Plan provides subsidies for private companies and public bodies that comply with the requirements of the Plan. Municipalities are among the major beneficiaries of the target objective to achieve excellence (US$30 million) and to promote new products (US$11 million).

By 1992, the Calvia Municipality in Majorca was the first beneficiary of the 'excellence' objective although it was not the largest beneficiary among Spanish Municipalities (e.g., compared to the Canaries). Other Balearic municipalities funded by the Futures Plan were Alcudia (Majorca), Sant Antonio (Ibiza), and Minorca. The Calvia Municipality in Majorca is a good case study of the history of Spanish and Balearic tourism.

The municipality covers an area of 143 square kilometres. This small town with only 41,000 inhabitants has almost 113,000 tourism beds (59,000 in hotels and similar establishments, and 54,000 in non-registered tourism lodgings including second homes) mainly spread along a coastline of 56 km. In 1997 the number of tourists was estimated to be 1.4 million, around 15 per cent of the total tourist arrivals in the Balearics. Calvia has 15 per cent of the registered tourism accommodation capacity of the Balearics, and 25 per cent of the total capacity (registered and non-registered). It is, in fact, ranked first amongst all Spanish Municipalities in terms of tourist arrivals and accommodation capacity. Despite this heavy concentration of tourism, Calvia has more than 80 per cent of its land classified as agricultural (i.e., not able to be urbanized).

One characteristic that singles Calvia out as a pioneer is its long-term effort to stop the downgrading of its territory. This strategy already began in the 1980s, although it was originally handicapped by lack of funds. Despite the success arising from large-scale tourism development, the municipality was hampered by heavy debts, amassed by the enormous investment on public infrastructure and the reduced amount of direct taxation to finance such projects. This shortage of funding was, and still remains today, a major problem for the fast-growing tourism municipalities in Spain which depend heavily on the red tape of Central and Autonomous Administrations in order to get a fair share of public finances.

Calvia adopted a two-fold policy: on the one hand, it made an exceptional effort to reduce the debt carried over from earlier years, and on the other it implemented an urban plan designed to support only new tourism developments aimed at modernizing and diversifying tourism activities. Some positive results were achieved although pressure from the private sector led to further overcrowding in certain beach resorts and further loss of quality. Nevertheless, in the 1990s certain events boosted Calvia's pioneering challenge. The Gulf Crisis served to cool down the rate of speculative development. Additionally, the regional government set up new measures to limit the growth of tourism (as seen earlier), and the Spanish Ministry of Tourism launched its Futures Plan. From 1992 to 1997 the Central Government, the Balearics Autonomous Government and the Municipality invested approximately US$8 million in Calvia in equal shares. The main feature of this investment was the demolition of five old shoreline hotels. The land occupied by these was converted into green areas.

Despite these improvements there was an ineffective dispersion of decision-making and, therefore, in 1995 the Municipality decided to unify the tasks by introducing 'Calvia Local Agenda 21'. This was based on Agenda 21 for the travel and tourism sector produced by the World Tourism Organization (WTO), the World Travel and Tourism Council (WTTC), and the EU, as a result of Programme 21 of the Rio Summit of 1992. The guiding principle of this agenda is sustainability geared to protect the environment, limit future building growth, modernize tourism facilities, extend off-season tourism, diversify the economy, and better the quality of life for all residents. The 'Calvia Local Agenda 21' has achieved its objectives, although with difficulties as some of the measures do not coincide with those passed by the Central and the Balearic Regional Governments.

The POOT (Tourism Supply Regulatory Plan) for Majorca

The POOT (Tourism Supply Regulatory Plan) is guided by sustainability principles. It was conceived in 1989 when the Balearic Parliament passed the 'General Criteria' for the 'Ordinance Territorial Plans' that should have implemented the 1987 law on territorial planning. That law gave tourism the highest economic priority but at the same time expressed concerns about the sector's unlimited growth. The POOT was, in fact, only implemented in 1995 as a sectoral plan within the framework of the non-enforced 1987 law following a decree of the Government of the Balearics (Government of the Balearic Islands, 1995). The delay in implementing the POOT is partially explained by the fact that municipalities were very concerned about losing their power of discretional authorization for tourism construction and building. These concerns led the Autonomous Government to develop the POOT through the uncommon procedure of sectoral planning.

The POOT was first designed for the 37 coastal zones of Majorca. In 1997 it was approved for the Pitiusas isles, while approval is still pending for the island of Minorca. The POOT requires that, prior to being issued a definitive building licence by the Municipalities, these areas must obtain permission from the Autonomous Government for the construction of any type of lodging. Resistance to the POOT requirements has remained strong. By 1999 only six of the 53 Municipalities of Majorca had adapted their local planning to the legislation's guidance on 'limits'.

The parameters fixed by the POOT in order to limit the growth of tourism are the following:

- A minimum of 7.5 square metres of beach per tourist in every zone. This requirement also takes swimming pools into account.
- In 13 zones preference is given for substituting obsolete beach-front tourism accommodation with new buildings on given plots of land situated 500 metres behind the urbanized resort. The formula for establishing the exchange of new for old tourism beds is as follows: 2 new beds for 1 old one up to a maximum of 100 new beds, 1.75 for 1 up to a maximum of 200 new beds, and a 1 to 1 ratio for more than 300 new beds. The grounds of the demolished obsolete buildings will be converted into green areas.
- There will be buffers of 1,000 metres perpendicular to the sea front, and as wide as the non-urban land separating neighbouring zones, in order to avoid ribbon development along the coastline.
- The population carrying capacity is calculated according to the drinking water supply, set at 200 litres per person per day.
- Implement a maximum limit of 60 persons per hectare (100 square metres) or 600 persons per square kilometre. The population density of Majorca currently averages 150 inhabitants per square kilometre but in some coastal zones it reaches 1,000.
- Only hotels or tourist apartments of 3, 4 and 5 stars may be built. The buildings will have a maximum height of a ground floor plus three storeys, and provide compulsory parking spaces and other facilities.

Other problems that have stood in the way of the POOT are related to financing. Specifically, there is a fear that millions of dollars may have to be provided in compensation, at market prices, to those developers who may already have obtained provisional building licences from the Municipalities, before the plan was approved. Fortunately, up to now, the Court of Justice has accepted only a few of these claims.

The cost of the POOT legislation has been estimated at US$250 million. This is to be shared by the Government of Majorca (65 per cent) and the Municipalities (35 per cent). There is a lack of agreement concerning these levels of funding and the tendency, especially on behalf of the Municipalities, has been to delay the POOT's introduction in public budgets. Thus, the POOT can be considered a virtual and not yet a real pioneering model of tourism sustainability. Nevertheless, other tourism destinations have been inspired by the POOT strategy to enforce regulations limiting undesirable tourism expansion (e.g., the case of the Canary Islands).

The New Marketing Plans and Approaches of the Balearic Islands

Since the 1950s one of the weakest points concerning the structure of tourism in the Balearics has been the scarcity of information relating to the demand-side of the business, specifically that part which is dominated by tour operators. The influence of the marketing and promotional strategies and the techniques of tour operators for the Balearics have generally overshadowed the role of host country organizations, particularly public tourism bodies. Nevertheless, while since 1980 there have been detailed data concerning the profiles of tourists by nationality, mode of transport, season of visit, and holiday expenses (Aguiló *et al.*, 1998), information relating to tourism-generating markets has been lacking. In 1990 the Ministry of Tourism set up for the first time a team (THR private consulting and the University of the Balearic Islands) to prepare 'Tourism Marketing Plan I' for 1991–93. Both this and 'Plan II' for 1996–98 (Aguiló *et al.*, 1996) reached similar conclusions. Specifically, they concluded that tourism sustainability might only be achieved by enhancing the competitiveness of tourism businesses and by off-peak tourism, as well as by keeping up environmental protection standards and protecting the social welfare of residents. Above all, the plans stressed that customer/tourist satisfaction is a key issue for understanding sustainability.

Middleton argues that:

> A marketing perspective is essentially an overall management orientation reflecting corporate attitudes that, in the case of travel and tourism, must balance the interests of shareholders/owners with the long-run environmental interests of a destination, and at the same time meet the demands and expectations of customers. (Middleton and Hawkins, 1998: 1)

He maintains that in an increasingly competitive environment it becomes imperative to understand what guides the choices of consumers. According to Middleton, this is the function 'primarily of marketing management' (ibid.: 9).

This argument has led to an examination of the motivations and satisfaction levels of tourists before and after their holidays in the Balearics. According to Aguiló *et al.* (1998), the summer holidaymakers are influenced by the following factors when choosing a 'sun and beach' resort such as the Balearics: climate, beaches, value for money, environmental quality, quality of accommodation. During the off-season, the mostly 'third age' tourists are influenced by air transport accessibility and the general tranquility of the destination. Although environmental quality and tranquility are most influential for tourists visiting between November and April, the analysis of tourist satisfaction levels indicates that these factors are also becoming increasingly important during the summer season.

An examination of tourists' complaints during the summer of 1998 noted, for the first time, dissatisfaction relating to the excessive level of tourism-related activities. Other complaints were made about the 'absence of country character' (e.g., architectural heritage, folklore, and gastronomy). Complaints also related to excessive noise and street untidiness. Despite these complaints, only 16.1 per cent of the tourists actually indicated any form of dissatisfaction about their holiday experience while only 1.6 per cent qualified their holiday as 'bad'. For the off-peak season the overall satisfaction levels were marginally higher than those relating to the summer months.

From a demand-side perspective, a 10-year analysis of the combination of motivations and complaints relating to pre- and post-holiday experiences respectively reveals that the Balearics must limit their tourism capacity. They must also strive to keep their original nature and character as far as possible to maintain the destination's sustainability in the future. Thus, it is important to use the information from marketing studies to support the territorial and tourism activity planning efforts described earlier. In some ways, the 1999 tourism regulation and especially the implementation of the so-called 'D' Plan (off-peak season strategy, since 1997) may be considered a form of marketing policy.

Conclusion: Moving Towards Sustainability

Tourism is not a 'smokeless industry', but a coordinated economic activity of the tertiary (services) sector. Moreover, tourism possesses important characteristics that cannot be managed by the private sector alone, namely the landscape and environment. Therefore, 'sustainable tourism' depends on the mix of products, services, and the environment under both private and public management.

To achieve tourism quality, better marketing and management practices are the main tools. Sustainability is a guiding principle to secure the tourism business. In order to achieve sustainability it is necessary to achieve product and environmental quality. Improved quality, in turn, enhances competitiveness. Sustainability is also a subjective concept, not just for individuals but also for collectives. Therefore, tourism sustainability may be defined as the 'continuous satisfaction of the tourist when visiting a resort resulting from the fulfilment of the expectations and the judgement of its value for money, while also maintaining specific levels of product quality, nature protection, and welfare of the host population'.

Such an operational and conceptual framework embraces not only the supply side of tourism but also the demand side. Customer satisfaction ensures competitiveness that leads to economic sustainability and, eventually to environmental sustainability. Without economic prosperity there can hardly be environmental protection, although an excess of success, as in the case of the Balearics, may lead to the abuse of nature. In the Balearics key issues that need to be addressed include the proper management of a limited territory, and the preservation of landscape and cultural identities, as well as the necessity to increase the quality of tourism products and services.

After the unique success that began in the 1950s following the introduction of popular mass tourism, sustainability was finally taken into account in 1983, when the insular region obtained its autonomous status. The path towards sustainability has been slow and without the aid of a definite long-term plan. Because of this, errors have occurred, such as the shortage of water supply in the capital Palma and surrounding areas (this was temporarily solved by costly water transshipments from the mainland and definitively solved by a new sea water desalinization plant), the inefficiency of waste disposal (recently solved by a new central disposal plant for the island of Majorca), and inadequate roads and public transportation facilities for islanders (within the islands and between islands). The latter issue is now being discussed. On Majorca certain abandoned railways are being restored and put into use again. However, the problem of excessive numbers of private cars combined with the overall scarcity of public transportation will not be solved in the near future, especially in Palma, unless drastic measures are adopted in the near future. This problem is aggravated by the fact that because of high living standards, the use of second homes in rural areas, and the fact that more than 60,000 cars are available for rent to tourists during the summer months, the Balearics have one of the highest car/population ratios in Europe. Moreover, sustainability in the Balearics is constantly held hostage by the fast growth of tourism demand that, unfortunately, exceeds natural resources and the size of the territory.

A major question that arises is the following. Can tourism growth be reduced or stopped in a free market economy? The solution chosen in the Balearics is for territorial planning and higher levels of quality requirements, thus setting capacity limits and standards for lodging units which have to be complied with. To set other tourism market limitations would be either politically and commercially unpopular or illegal, both in Spain and in the EU.

In practical terms, the question is how to limit summer tourism accommodation for an increasing number of visitors in the Balearics. That has been the main topic under discussion for a number of years, while the new Tourism Law and the new DOT (Territorial Ordinance Plans) were just approved in April and May of 1999 respectively by the Parliament of the Balearic Islands. The main resistance to these laws has come from municipalities, and the 'Consells' or island governments (one for each of the four main islands) since these want a share of discretional power to decide on their territorial issues within the regulation framework of the Government of the Balearic Islands. Because of this resistance, early in 1998 the Government of the Balearics passed exceptional regulations, by means of two 'moratoria' suspending any increase in tourism accommodation capacity or in residential non-urban capacity until definitive regulations were passed by the Parliament in 1999.

Laws presently protect almost 40 per cent of the Balearics' territory. The remaining 60 per cent of the territory consists of rural land (53 per cent) (already limited to building in plots less than 14,000 square metres) and 7 per cent of urbanized land. A total of 78 per cent of the urbanized land has already been built upon while the remaining 22 per cent is land that has been designated 'suitable for urbanization' and was the target of the aforementioned 'moratoria'. The DOT law of 1999 aims to close the 'loophole' for further licences authorized by Municipalities since this could lead to a potential increase of more than 1.5 million dwellers on the Balearics in the next 10 years, resulting in a population of a staggering 2.5 million inhabitants instead of the present 750,000. Instead the planned increase put forth by the DOT will be for around 300,000 residents, thus bringing the population to 1.2 million. A growth of only 10 per cent of the existing developed land is planned in the next 10 years. By contrast the new Tourism Law will try to save the 1995 POOT and will create a 'bank of obsolete tourism beds' to be sold to investors of new hotels or tourism apartments. A big remaining problem is how to prevent the obsolete tourism dwellings, once they lose their licence, from being transformed into other dwelling uses that will hinder the greening of coastal areas with high population densities.

The tourism stakeholders' reaction to this new strategy is by and large positive. In particular, established hoteliers, European tour operators (especially German), local ecological associations, and ordinary citizens have welcomed the strategy. Only the developers have been reluctant to accept the idea of limiting growth in new construction. Nevertheless, even they are now convinced that they have an opportunity for work in the long term due to the modernization, embellishment and restoration plans that are either in force or planned for the next decade. On the downside, the prices of real estate, urban land and city flats in the Balearics have risen dramatically since 1998 because of speculation concerning future scarcity.

The Balearics are now committed to follow the path towards tourism sustainability through quality and territorial planning. Fortunately, there is a supporting social and political consensus although the path will be slow and costly. This is because of the administrative work needed and the potential compensation to be paid to investors holding provisional building or tourism licences for projects that will not be developed, since the laws of 1999 have been approved.

Note

Parts of this chapter have already been published by CISET (International Centre of Studies on the Tourism Economy), University of Cà Foscari di Venezia (Italy), Volume II, 18. 2/98. This paper which was titled 'The ECOMOST Project and the case of Mallorca: path towards tourism sustainability', was presented at the international conference 'Competing in tourism through quality', held in Venice, in December 1997. No copyright on that paper has been yielded to CISET by the author.

References

Aguiló, E., Bardolet, E., et al. (1987) *Libre Blanc del Turisme a les Baleares*. (White Paper on Balearics tourism). Palma: University of the Balearic Islands.

Aguiló, E., Bardolet, E., et al. (1996) *II Plan de Marketing Turistico de Baleares 1996–98*. (Tourism marketing plan II for the Balearics). Palma: IBATUR Conselleria de Turisme (Balearics Ministry of Tourism).

Aguiló, E., Sastre, A. and Bardolet, E. (1998) *El Gasto Turistico en Baleares 1998*. (Tourist expenditure in the Balearics). Palma: Balearics Ministries of Tourism, Agriculture, Commerce, and Industry.

Bardolet, E. (1989) *El Coste de la Insularidad* (Cost of insularity). Palma: Camara de Comercio de Mallorca y Pitiusas (Chamber of Commerce).

Bardolet, E. (1993) The Balearic Isles: from unsustainable success to sustainable tourism within an archipelago. Unpublished paper presented at the 1993 Conference on Sustainable Tourism (Foundation of International Studies) Malta, 18–20 November.

Bardolet, E. (1996) *Baleares: General Information*. Palma: IBATUR Conselleria de Turisme (Press kit with tourism main features).

Bardolet, E. (1999) Evolución del turismo en Baleares 1997 Chapter IV AECIT (Asociación Española de Expertos Científicos en Turismo), *La actividad turística española en 1997*. Unpublished paper, Madrid (267–83).

Government of the Balearic Islands (1990a) *Plan de Embellecimiento de Zonas Turísticas*. (Tourism Coastal Resorts Embellishment Plan –1st phase 1990-93, 2nd phase 1994–97). Palma: Balearics Ministry of Tourism.

Government of the Balearic Islands (1990b) *Plan de Modernización de Alojamientos Turísticos*. (Modernization plan for tourism accommodation units, Law 3/90). Palma: Parliament of the Balearic Islands.

Government of the Balearic Islands (1991) *Normativa Fiscal sobre los Activos con Efectos Negativos sobre el Medioambiente*. (Special taxation procedures for activities with negative environmental effects, Law 12/91). Palma: Parliament of the Balearic Islands.

Government of the Balearic Islands (1995) *Plan de Ordenación de la Oferta Turística 'POOT'*. (Regulatory Plan on Tourism Supply, Decree 54/95 – extended by Decree 42/97 to Ibiza and Formentera). Palma: Parliament of the Balearic Islands.

Government of the Balearic Islands (1996) *Plan de Modernización de la Oferta Turística Complementaria* (Plan for Modernization of Complementary Tourism Supply, Law 6/96). Palma: Parliament of the Balearic Islands.

Government of the Balearic Islands (1997a) *Avance, análisis y diagnóstico de las Directrices de Ordenación Territorial (DOT)* (Draft on Territorial Ordinance). Palma: Conselleria de Ordenación del Territorio (Ministry of Territorial Ordinance).

Government of the Balearic Islands (1997b) *ECOTUR – Programa de ecoauditoras del sector turístico* (Programme for ecomanagement and ecoaudit of tourism centres, Decree 81/97). Palma: Conselleria de Ordenación del Territorio (Ministry of Territorial Ordinance).

Government of the Balearic Islands (1997c) *Pla MIRALL*. (Mirror Plan: a global plan of embellishment of hinterland municipalities). Palma: Conselleria de Ordenación del Territorio (Ministry of Territorial Ordinance).

Government of the Balearic Islands (1999) *Ley de Directrices de Ordenación Territorial 'DOT' y Ley General de Turismo*. (Territorial Ordinances Law and Tourism Law). Palma: Parliament of the Balearic Islands.

IFTO (International Federation of Tour Operators) (1994) *The ECOMOST Project*. London: IFTO.

Middleton, V.T.C. and Hawkins, R. (1998) *Sustainable Tourism: A Marketing Perspective*. London: Butterworth-Heinemann.

Spanish Ministry of Tourism (1990) *Libro Blanco del Turismo Español* (White Paper on Spanish tourism). Madrid: THR Consultants.

Spanish Ministry of Tourism (1994) *Futures-Plan: Marco de Competitividad del Turismo Español* (Spanish tourism competitiveness plan). Madrid: Secretaría de Estado de Turismo.

11

Tourism and the Environment in Corsica, Sardinia, Sicily, and Crete

Maria Kousis

Introduction

Before the 1980s, few social scientists had dealt with the tourism–environment nexus (e.g., Cohen, 1978). Since then, however, several researchers have studied the environmental and economic impacts of tourism (e.g., Farrell and Runyan, 1991; Zanetto and Soriani, 1996). Studies on the social dimensions of environmental issues focus either partially or exclusively on the host communities' attitudes and perceptions of tourism's environmental impacts on their surroundings (e.g., Liu et al., 1987, Urry, 1992). The more critical public health and/or socio-political impacts of ecosystem-intervening tourism-related activities are the focus of fewer and more recent works (Kocasoy, 1989; Richez, 1996; Stonich, 1998; Kousis, 2000).

The shift of the 'environment and development' literature towards research on sustainability has inevitably also pushed relevant tourism research in that direction. Focusing specifically on island-hosting communities, valuable recent works point to economic, environmental, or social sustainability issues (Briguglio and Briguglio, 1996; Butler et al., 1996; Burac, 1996; Boissevain, 1996; MCSD, 1998). Since sustainable development is a contested concept, Baker et al. (1997) propose that it is best visualized in terms of four alternative approaches: the *treadmill*, the *weak*, the *strong*, and the *ideal* sustainable development models. In the treadmill approach, ecosystems are viewed in terms of their utility to producers and production-related agencies. The more conservative wings of environmental social movement organizations (ESMOs) usually adopt the weak sustainable development approach. States and supra-national bodies are also more likely to embrace this approach, given their sector-driven orientations and the need for only minimal amendments to institutions. Strong sustainable development is characterized by changes in patterns of production and consumption and is more appealing to eco-centric ESMOs and grassroots groups, as well as to political ecology ESMOs. Finally, the ideal type aims towards more profound changes at socio-economic, ideological, and political levels. Only the more radical grassroots groups and ESMOs are likely to adopt this approach, as it would require a drastic restructuring of political, legal, social, and economic institutions.

The difficulties in pointing out exactly what determines sustainable tourism cannot, of course, be over-emphasized, especially in 'mass-tourism' hosting island communities. Butler *et al.* (1996) correctly point out the complicated and largely unresearched dynamics between 'bottom up' and 'top down' forces as well as the need to comprehend conflicting views about tourism's role at the community level, and to control the market tendencies imposed on the local ecosystem.[1]

This chapter focuses on aspects of tourism's inter-related economic, environmental, and social sustainability in the four large Mediterranean islands of Corsica, Sardinia, Sicily and Crete. Data from secondary sources describe the economic and environmental sustainability across the four islands, illustrating specific air polluting emission levels at the level of each prefecture. Social sustainability is examined through environmental protest cases related to tourism in Crete, using archival data. The analysis discusses two types of environmental protest claims, relating to the environmentally damaging sources, as well as to the negative ecosystem offences and the wide array of ecosystem and socio-economic and health impacts they produce. A discussion follows on the types of sustainable tourism development approaches promoted by various actors in the most developed tourist zone of the island of Crete. Finally, the findings relating to the economic, environmental, and social sustainability of tourism in the four islands are discussed in light of the Baker *et al.*'s (1997) approaches to sustainable development.

Economic Sustainability

Tourism has become a principal economic sector in most Mediterranean countries, since this region is the leading destination in the world. According to different Blue Plan[2] scenarios, it is estimated that the 135 million tourists visiting just the coastal regions of the Mediterranean in 1990 could increase by 235 to 350 million by 2025 (MCSD, 1998). For the Mediterranean's island regions, tourism is commonly viewed as the only activity that is capable of reviving local economies (MCSD, 1998; Eurostat, 1994). Thus, during the past three decades, the economic impacts of tourism for the Mediterranean islands have been well noted (Islands Commission [Eurisles], 1999) by national, supra-national as well as regional bodies.

Various analysts have argued that economic interests will drive the need for 'sustainable development' projects at the local level (Pridham and Konstadakopoulos, 1997; The European Coordination, 1998). Recent evidence addressing how tourism-entrepreneurs confront the environmental impacts of their activities is inconclusive. On the one hand, studies have pointed out that there is still a lot of reluctance in terms of seriously addressing the sector's environmental impacts by introducing ameliorating measures or showing concern (e.g., Stott, 1996; Stylianopoulou, 1998). On the other hand, an increasing number of local communities are taking steps towards the protection of local natural resources (e.g., Technical Chamber of Greece – Eastern, Crete Chapter *et al.*, 1995). In addition, participation in environmentally sensitive programmes, such as the one relating to the 'Blue Flags', is increasing (The European Coordination, 1998). The European Blue Flag Campaign, funded by the European Commission and operated by the Foundation for Environmental Education in Europe (FEEE), gives awards to beaches and marinas of environmental quality in 19 countries. These awards are based on specific criteria – environmental education and information, environmental management, water quality, as well as safety and services.[3]

Tourism indicators for the four islands are presented in Table 11.1. As shown by the percentage of jobs in the tertiary sector, tourism plays a critical role in the economy of all four islands.[4] Tourism density is highest in Corsica, followed by Crete, Sardinia and Sicily. Thus, tourism-related social impacts are expected to be of higher significance for the smaller islands of Corsica and Crete. The types of tourist accommodation vary across the four islands. Crete holds the lead in terms of the total number of hotel beds (Table 11.1). Other than hotel beds however, there are 263,000 beds in more than 50,000 second residences in Corsica (INSEE, 1997; INSEE, 1999), and many more in the 415,305 holiday homes in Sicily (Randazzo and Scrofani, 1996). The related figures presented in Table 11.1 may be higher when considering illegal tourist accommodation, which is persistent in Southern European countries (EC, 1997).

According to Table 11.1, the number of tourists is highest in Sicily, followed by Corsica, Crete and Sardinia. Other sources provide different estimates on the number of tourists (see, for example, Region of Crete, 1995, or Rizzo, 1997), probably due to different ways of measurement. Various estimates must be taken into consideration in view of the important implications they have for tourism's economic, environmental and social sustainability in a given area. As far as the importance of other indicators, such as the 'Blue Flags' programme, is concerned, one preliminary observation is that they do not appear to touch upon tourist density. Whether the quality of all beaches is positively correlated with the number of flags awarded remains an unresearched issue.

The intensity of tourism development in this region is depicted in Figure 11.1. According to 'Blue Plan' data, tourist inflows and the development of

Table 11.1 Tourism characteristics: Corsica, Crete, Sardinia, and Sicily

Indicator	Corsica	Crete	Sardinia	Sicily
Percentage of jobs in tertiary sector (1995)	75%	50%	62%	65%
Number of hotel beds**	12,027	115,491	Not available	74,567***
Number of campsite emplacements**	182	1580	3,120	950
Number of tourists (1994/95)	1,700,000	1,377,213	1,323,569	2,750,164
Number of tourists per 1000 inhabitants	6811	2,550	803	554
International airport passengers (1986)*	1,437,000	1,210,000	2,222,000	2,825,000
Number of air passengers (1994/95)	1,991,662	4,452,433	3,030,409	4,103,217
Blue Flags**** (1998)	5	32	13	4

Sources: Eurisles, the Islands Commission – web site
* Brigand (1991: 25) (Biggi and Spilanis)
** Eurostat (1994: 112)
*** Regione Siciliana – Assessorato Turismo, La constistenza ricettiva in Sicilia nel 1998
**** The European Coordination (1998)

tourism vary both across the four islands and within each one. Looking across the four islands the highest tourist frequencies occur in Sardinia's Sassari province, and Sicily's Messina and Syracuse provinces. The provinces with the lowest tourist frequencies are Oristano and Nuoro in Sardinia, and Enna in Sicily. The Italian islands are larger in size and more diverse in their total activities than Corsica and Crete. The latter are more similar in terms of tourist frequency both within and across these islands.

The smallest and peripheral French province, Corsica, is a mountainous island that experienced a fourfold increase in the number of tourists during the past two decades. Almost half of the tourist expenditures lead to production outside the island. Non-resident workers in the tourist industry amount to approximately all seasonal workers. Thus, even though it generates 15 per cent of market GDP, tourism is a highly seasonal activity (i.e., July and August). Tourism activities concentrate on the coastline and the major towns of Bastia, Ajaccio, Calvi, I'lle-Rousse and Bonifacio. Although unemployment is still a problem, during the last two decades, there has been a large increase (66 per cent) in employment which is partly attributed to the growth of the service sector as well as to tourism's impact on the island's economy. Employment in the tertiary sector doubled during this period. In the early 1990s, jobs in the distributive trades, the hotel trade and market services experienced the sharpest increase. Since there are no heavy industries or intensive agriculture, the environmental deterioration that is

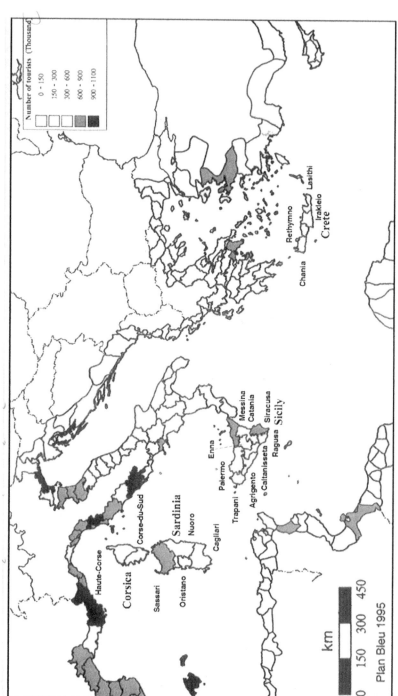

Figure 11.1 Estimated number of tourists during the peak season in Mediterranean regions
Source: Plan Bleu and UNEP (1998)

concentrated on the coastal areas is mainly due to urbanization and tourism development (Eurostat, 1994: 86–9).

The second largest island in the Mediterranean, Sardinia, is characterized by both developed (Sassari and Cagliari) and non-developed areas (Oristano and Nuoro). Tourism activities are concentrated in the more urban and industrialized Sassari and Cagliari provinces respectively. Industrial activities in these two provinces basically involve the generation of electricity, metalworking, processing of chemical and petroleum products, and mineral extraction. Although agricultural activities are widespread throughout most of the island, they are mainly a characteristic of the Oristano and Nuoro provinces where tourism activities remain low. The tourist industry constitutes a major part of the services sector but is not integrated with the more traditional farming and manufacturing sectors (Eurostat, 1994: 140–5).

Sicily, the largest and most populated island in the Mediterranean, is the most diverse in terms of society and economy. Heavy tourist flows are experienced especially in its coastal urban areas of Palermo, Catania, Messina, Syracuse and Agrigento for different reasons. Palermo is a political, economic and cultural centre, Catania is a commercial centre, Messina's geographical location makes it the gate to the island, while Syracuse and Agrigento are attractive for their archaeological and cultural resources (Rizzo, 1997). From the mid-1980s to the mid-1990s growth has been noted in the number of beds, although the number of tourist accommodation establishments has not increased as rapidly. This indicates the trend towards establishing bigger facilities catering to larger numbers of tourists (Loukissas *et al.*, 1997). The tourist season is mostly limited to July and August. Although there has been an increase in the number of hotel rooms, the capacity of the region is not yet adequate to satisfy the growing demand (Eurostat, 1994). The great majority of hotels, as in all of Italy and Greece (but unlike Spain), are small, family-owned businesses constituting a fragmented industry which is consistently confronted with competition and the problem of economic survival. Most official tourism-related data for Sardinia and Sicily, as in the case of Crete, do not reflect the 'underground' (unregistered or informal) tourism sector which many times is as large as the formal one (European Commission, 1997).

Crete has developed into a major tourist destination in Greece. Whereas in 1971 only about 4,000 people were directly employed in tourism, in 1988 the number was almost 190,000 (EOT-KEPE, vol. 1, 1994). During the 1990s, about 40 per cent of Crete's active population was directly or indirectly employed in tourism (Region of Crete, 1995). Crete contributed 58 per cent of Greece's monetary exchange from tourism, while it accounted for 27 per cent of the national total of luxury and 'A-class' hotel beds. In the last few years Crete has become the major tourist destination in the country, with the longest tourist season (7.5 months) (Region of Crete, 1995). The prefecture of Heraklion, especially its northern zone, has been the major destination of tourists on the island in the past decades, given its archaeological sites and its transportation infrastructure.

The significance of agriculture varies widely across the islands. It is vital in the case of Sicily whereas marginal in the case of Corsica (Eurisles, 1999). In the case of the Italian and Greek islands, agriculture plays a critical role in the life of the inhabitants. An examination of these regions' industrial profile shows once again that the two larger islands, Sicily and Sardinia, host more diversified and intensive activities. Petrochemicals, chemicals and various manufacturing activities appear there, but not in Corsica and Crete (Eurostat, 1994). Thus, not only is there a difference in the amount of activities but in the type and intensity of activities and the repercussions of these for the islands' ecosystems.

Environmental Sustainability

Southern European tourism is 'product-led' meaning that environmental issues come second to the need to come up with new tourism products while maintaining existing ones (Hunter, 1997). Under this type of tourism, powerful interest groups of the tourist industry aim exclusively for the economic growth of the sector, regardless of whether the area is over-developed, or not. Thus, these interest groups consider sustainability only in economic terms. Environmental and social concerns are important only if they negatively affect the tourist industry to the point that profits decrease (Saleem, 1996; Burac, 1996; Hunter, 1997). In the past four decades, Southern European coastal areas, especially the islands, have experienced drastic changes due to the development of tourism (Lozato-Giotart, 1990; Konsolas and Zacharatos, 1992). Tourism has become an important source of negative environmental impacts (MCSD, 1998).

Most islands tend to be small in size, with unique and fragile ecosystems, as well as lengthy coastlines. Their uniqueness arising from insularity makes the islands important contributors to biodiversity, while their fragility is due to low levels of resistance to outside influences (Briguglio and Briguglio, 1996). Therefore, it is particularly in the closed island ecosystems which entail delicate balances, that the growth of the tourist industry has led to negative environmental impacts (Konsolas and Zacharatos, 1992; Burac, 1996; Briguglio and Briguglio, 1996; Saleem, 1996; Stott, 1996; Mavris, 1998). The quantity and quality of local fresh water resources in such destinations have consistently decreased. Conversely, waste and sewage-related soil and water pollution have increased significantly. Wildlife and local natural resources are threatened (Chiotis and Coccossis, 1992; Konsolas and Zacharatos, 1992), while noise pollution has often caused problems (Sotiriadis, 1994; Mavris, 1998). All of these problems are evident in the islands under study.

Both formal and informal tourism (Briassoulis, forthcoming) are usually associated with a variety of ecosystem-offensive or polluting activities and sources. It is very difficult to estimate all the impacts created by the tourist industry. The more global impacts relating to the transport of tourists are hard to estimate, and studies have only very recently attempted to address them (e.g., Robbins, 1996). These include air or water traffic sources (e.g., airliners, cruise ships) leading to air pollution and water pollution. More global impacts also include various manufacturing activities related to products used in various stages of tourism-related activities. These vary widely from consumption-oriented ones (such as food, drink, clothes) to more accommodation-related ones (such as furniture, electrical products, infrastructure and construction material).

The more localized impacts relate to traffic (mostly in the form of local land traffic, but may also involve short-distance water transport). They also relate to the construction, extension, and operation of: (1) tourist-catering or hosting facilities, such as hotels, camping grounds, resort projects, holiday homes, etc.; (2) associated recreational facilities, for example, night life, entertainment clubs, golf grounds, aquatic parks, yacht clubs, ski areas, rally grounds, other sports areas; and, (3) infrastructural projects such as airports, roads, parking areas, and marine harbours. Other sources of such ecosystem intervention include water or sand extracting activities, traffic and congestion, waste and sewage problems, and lack or non-implementation of environmental protection policies. These tourism-related sources and activities create ecosystem offences such as water shortage, fresh-water, marine, coastal and soil pollution, noise pollution, damage to flora and fauna, and sometimes general destruction of local ecosystems. In turn, these offences lead to a wide range of impacts including negative aesthetic, recreational, cultural/historical, economic, ecosystem, psychological and public health impacts. The above constitute parts of the process of ecological marginalization (Kousis, 1998).

One example of how tourism development has affected water resources and led to health problems is eloquently described by Stonich (1998), for the Bay Islands, Honduras. The findings on three communities show that growth-oriented tourism development damages marine resources, imposing serious environmental risks on the islands' impoverished Latino immigrants and poor Afro-Antillean residents. With regards to local land traffic in Malta (e.g., Robbins, 1996), mass car use by tourists leads to traffic congestion, air emissions, and noise pollution, causing a wide array of negative impacts − including economic, environmental and health ones. Waste disposal and treatment facilities related to tourist accommodations have also at times created problems for host communities. Lack of proper infrastructure or problematic operation leads to the production of pollutants that negatively affect the immediate ecosystem, with subsequent harmful impacts for the community and the environment.

In Corsica, most pollution derives from domestic uses and usually affects the coastal zones where tourism activities tend to concentrate, especially in the summer time (Eurostat, 1994). In Sardinia, damage has been caused by industrial as well as by intense tourist activities, driving local authorities to pay more attention to natural resources. Hence, before expanding either the infrastructure network or existing tourist facilities, authorities must first examine environmental impacts, particularly in the already developed/ concentrated zones (ibid.). In Sicily, the tourism sector faces problems related to the environmental degradation of coastal areas from a variety of sources and activities, especially recent greenhouse/intensive cultivation, the petrochemical industries, as well as seaside tourism accommodations and holiday homes. The lack of tourism planning has led to uncontrolled and often illegal development of various forms of tourism accommodation on coastal areas without adequate infrastructure for sewage and solid waste (Randazzo and Scrofani, 1996). Negative impacts because of tourism have been noted on Sicily's archaeological sites as well as on its small islands in the Aeolian archipelago (Giavelli *et al.*, 1992). Tourism activities in Crete have also produced negative environmental impacts. These are mainly related to the lack of regional planning and the illegal construction of tourist accommodation/service facilities leading to their uneven geographical distribution and their concentration mainly in the northern urbanized coastal areas (Sotiriadis, 1994; Kousis, forthcoming).

It is already clear that although tourism intensity varies within as well as between the four islands, Corsica, Sardinia, Sicily, and Crete have undoubtedly played a significant role as Mediterranean tourism hosting areas (Figure 11.1). Figure 11.2 illustrates selected atmospheric environmental offences for the four islands at the provincial level. Carbon dioxide (CO_2) emissions, which usually stem from traffic and combustion processes, appear positively related to tourism-active provinces, as depicted in Figure 11.1. Figure 11.2 also presents nitrogen dioxide (NO_2) emissions, normally traced in all combustion processes such as those relating to vehicles and industrial activities. In addition to tourism-active provinces, high emission levels also appear in parts of the islands with industrial and other related activities. Sulphur dioxide (SO_2) emissions are also positively related to tourism intensity. Power plants, industrial processes, and traffic frequently produce these emissions. Finally, Figure 11.2 depicts non-methane volatile organic compounds (NMVOC) emissions. One major source of such emissions is traffic, leading to a positive correlation, when comparing tourism-intensive provinces to VOC polluted ones.

In conclusion, air pollution levels appear highest in Sardinia and Sicily, the two islands which host industrial as well as tourism activities. Nonetheless, Corsica and Crete also experience lower atmospheric quality in their active tourism provinces, albeit to a smaller extent. It cannot be doubted, however, that the mix of industrial, intensive agriculture, and tourism activities tends to impose more heavily on local ecosystems.

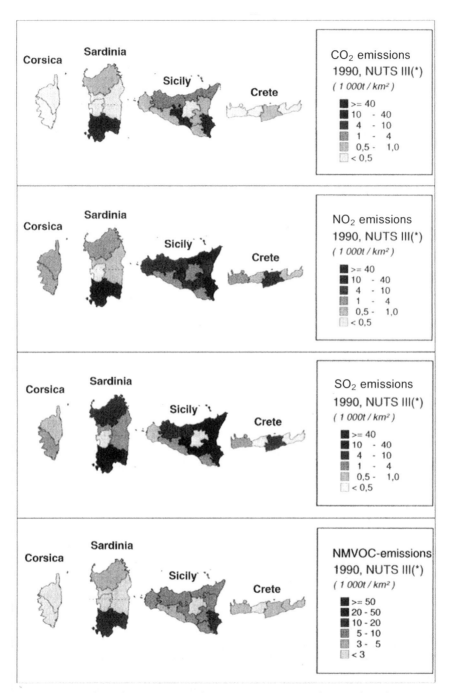

Figure 11.2 Selected air emissions for Corsica, Crete, Sardinia and Sicily
Source: Eurostat (1997)

Social Sustainability

Social sustainability usually refers to the host community's 'acceptance' or silent approval of tourism development and, thus, to the smooth transition of social life under tourism. Local social dynamics especially at the grassroots level, therefore, reflect the social sustainability of tourism in a critical manner. Endangering the local environment in a given social setting, however, does not always lead to social unrest or reaction. Host communities' social perceptions regarding the environmental impacts of tourism may not necessarily turn into action aimed at ameliorating these problems. Health impacts, for instance, have not always led to environmental protest against tourism activities (Stonich, 1998). This may be due to locals' economic dependence on these polluting activities as environmental protest has been found to be negatively associated with economic dependence (Gould *et al.*, 1996).

Nevertheless, intense protest is evident in Corsica, the least populated but highest in terms of tourist-density island. This island has a French, top-down imposed tourism sector. According to a recent study (Richez, 1996), local resistance to this outside-controlled development of tourism surfaced and climaxed with violent protest actions. Locals demanded the right to participate in the decision-making affecting their lives. The environmentalist supporters of regional autonomy who, as early as the late 1960s, warned the islanders of the dangers arising from the loss of local control of the island's fate had wide local support. From the early 1970s to the mid-1980s intense protest activities of various forms took place, including terrorist attacks on second homes, bars, restaurants, dance halls, hotels and holiday camps as well as other forms of violence. In addition to the disruption of daily activities at the local level, such protests succeeded in affecting tourist flows (Richez, 1996). However, these actions may have contributed positively to the protection of local natural resources, such as the creation of protected zones.

Although the exploitation of the Sicilian environment during the 1960s and 1970s through enforced industrialization, the adoption of intensive agriculture, and the construction of tourist accommodation establishments led to general environmental degradation and to considerable risks for public health, social protest has not been clearly visible (Randazzo and Scrofani, 1996). Generally, local resistance does not appear to be high in the region. Only in recent years has a small increase been noted in environmental awareness, as seen through the protests against land abuse around historical and natural sites, especially in Sicily's coastal zones.[5] In addition, the degradation of the environment in southeastern Sicily appears to have progressively reduced the awareness of local communities concerning the environment and the symbolic values essential for self-identity (Ruggiero and Scrofani, 1996). Hence, in this case economic dependence on tourism appears to hinder strong support for pro-environmental actions, especially before signs of negative economic effects become apparent.

In Crete, Sardinia and Sicily, social sustainability is intimately tied to economic sustainability, and environmental perceptions and actions are more likely to appear only when the former are in danger. Small family businesses, which may operate informally and struggle constantly to survive economically, control a considerable portion of the tourist accommodation establishments on these islands. In view of the related costs, large tourist industry entrepreneurs also resist taking ameliorative steps towards environmental protection. At the same time, other local groups from the host community, whose incomes may directly or indirectly also depend on the tourist industry, are not expected to show great signs of contention.

Evidence from Crete

Research on environmental protest or movements related to tourism has just surfaced (Kousis, 2000; Ruzza, forthcoming). Recent studies of local environmental activism indicate a bipolar treatment of tourism. Some localities consider tourism an environmentally offensive activity whose impacts should be curbed (Kousis, forthcoming). Other areas mobilize against polluting non-tourism activities (e.g., industrial activities) with the aim of protecting the local environment and supporting the development of existing, or expected tourism (e.g., Aguilar-Fernandez *et al.*, 1995; Kousis, 1997). Such environmental initiatives are defensive, lack the assistance of professional organizations, and usually challenge the state and private entrepreneurs by holding them responsible for the caused damages. The more interesting side of local protest, however, is its bipolar treatment of tourism in the same destination, such as on the island of Crete.

In Crete, tourism activities are concentrated on the north coast, and especially in the province of Heraklion, which accounts for almost half of the island's tourist bed capacity. The lack of, or improper, regional and urban planning and the uneven geographical distribution of tourist accommodation are considered the main reasons for the over-exploitation of natural resources and the subsequent negative environmental impacts (Briassoulis and Sofoulis, 1995; Sotiriadis, 1994). The degree of these impacts' severity is a debatable issue, since some people consider them very serious (Sotiriadis, 1994) while others view them as correctable (Rodalakis, 1995). In the 1990s, environmental questions have become more significant than before. One example of this is the evident increase in the participation of communities and tourism entrepreneurs in the 'Blue Flags' programme. Whereas in 1991 only five such flags were awarded in the province, by 1998 the number had increased to 17 (Hellenic Society for the Protection of Nature, 1998).

The data analysed for the study of local protest in Crete are the product of protest-case analysis, a specific form of manifest content analysis.[6] These data originated mostly in the form of procedural complaints to authorities by at least two persons, and were found in documents, newspaper articles, and other written material. This material was assembled from the archives of local, provincial, and municipal agencies in Heraklion, the province's capital, and covered the period 1983–94. Almost half of these claims were filed in the Prefecture's Health Department, followed by a smaller number of complaints to the police and local representatives of the Ministry of Planning, Public Works and the Environment. All documents were collated into 54 environmental protest cases and coded in terms of the specific environmental source or activity responsible for environmental degradation, the offences and impacts produced, the resolutions proposed and other involved groups.

Each case involves locals from different tourist-hosting communities in the Heraklion province who made environment-related claims. In 26 of the 54 cases locals claimed that tourism-related activities affected the local environment negatively, while in the remaining 28 cases it was claimed that non-tourism-related activities caused negative impacts on the environment. It is assumed that in cases where non-tourism activities have a negative environmental impact, there is also a negative effect on tourism. Both types of protest cases are more prevalent (65.4 per cent and 50.0 per cent respectively) in high-intensity tourism areas, while about one third occur in medium-intensity areas. The majority of cases occurred between 1989 and 1994. They only refer to already existing and operating, not planned, sources and activities. Residents are the leading group of protesters in both types of cases, followed by local government representatives and private entrepreneurs – who are more frequent in the pro-environment and pro-tourism cases. These groups are usually small in size (2–25 persons), especially for the cases against tourism activities, which do not have as wide social support as the other cases. In both types of cases, actions taken to publicize the claims of locals mostly appear in the form of procedural complaints to authorities. More intense actions (such as litigation, blockades, etc.), although limited, occur only in cases against non-tourism activities and pro-tourism development.

The different environment-offensive activities associated with the two types of cases appear in Table 11.2. For both types of cases, waste disposal, problematic sewage systems, construction and infrastructural projects, as well as lack of, or failure to implement, environmental laws are seen as significant polluting activities. Anti-tourism mobilizers often complain about hotel waste, while those who are against non-tourism activities complain about open landfills. Industrial activities and, to a smaller extent, animal husbandry are also targets of those cases favouring tourism. The majority of anti-tourism mobilizers claim that hotel owners/entrepreneurs are responsible for ecosystem disturbances, while in pro-tourism cases other producers are challenged in addition to the state and local governments. The majority of mobilizers propose the implementation of existing laws in order to

Table 11.2 Ecosystem-damaging activities by type of local protest case in the Prefecture of Heraklion, 1983–94*

| | Type of local protest case | | | |
| Ecosystem-damaging activities | Against tourism-induced environmental offences | | Against non-tourism-induced environmental offences (Pro-tourism activities) | |
	Frequency	(%)	Frequency	(%)
Animal husbandry	1	(3.8)	5	(17.9)
Various industrial			4	(14.3)
Land transport, Storage and communications	4	(15.3)	2	(7.2)
Construction/infrastructure	6	(23.1)	5	(17.9)
Hydroelectric power stations			1	(3.6)
Non-toxic waste disposal	1	(3.8)	6	(21.4)
Hotel waste	5	(19.2)		
Open landfill	3	(11.5)	10	(35.7)
Nonexistent/problematic sewage system	7	(26.9)	7	(25.0)
Biological treatment/sanitary landfill	1	(3.8)	1	(3.6)
Lack of environmental laws	2	(7.7)		
Failure/non-implementation of envir. laws	7	(26.9)	6	(21.4)
Miscellaneous	2	(7.6)	5	(17.8)

Note: * Each category has been coded as a dichotomous (yes/no) variable, thus percentages do not add up to 100 per cent.

ameliorate the present situation. Nevertheless, in cases of non-tourism polluting activities a considerable minority propose, alternatively, proper regional and urban planning as well as the closing or relocation of the polluting source.

According to the mobilizers the activities presented in Table 11.2 lead to a wide range of ecosystem offences. The subsequent environmental and social impacts are shown in Table 11.3. The two types of cases offer differing views of offences and impacts. For the anti-tourism mobilizers the two most frequent offences are noise and atmospheric pollution, while for the pro-tourism mobilizers air and coastal zone/marine pollution are seen as major problems. Different experiences are also evident concerning the impacts. Whereas the great majority of the pro-tourism mobilizers stress the negative impacts for the tourism sector as well as for the community's health, only half of the anti-tourism campaigners refer to the negative economic, and health impacts, as well as psychological impacts.

Table 11.3 Environmental offences and impacts by type of local protest case in the Prefecture of Heraklion, 1983–94*

Offences/impacts created by the environmentally-damaging activities	Against tourism-induced environmental offences		Against non-tourism-induced environmental offences (pro-tourism activities)	
	Frequency	(%)	Frequency	(%)
Offences				
Noise pollution	13	(50.0)	6	(21.4)
Atmospheric pollution	8	(30.8)	17	(60.7)
Fresh water pollution	2	(7.7)	5	(17.9)
Sea/coastal pollution	5	(19.2)	13	(46.4)
Local ecosystem destruction	6	(23.1)	1	(3.6)
Impacts				
Negative aesthetic/recreational	7	(11.5)	16	(57.2)
Negative economic	14	(53.9)	28	(100.0)
Wetland/land/fresh water	2	(7.7)	7	(25.1)
Coastal zones/marine ecosystems	5	(19.2)	11	(39.2)
Airsheds	8	(30.8)	17	(60.7)
Local ecosystem	4	(15.4)	13	(46.4)
Negative psychological	13	(50.0)	6	(21.4)
Realized health incidents	1	(3.8)	1	(3.6)
Expected/suspected health incidents	12	(46.2)	20	(71.4)
Life threatened/seriously endangered	2	(7.7)		

Note: *Each category has been coded as a dichotomous (yes/no) variable, thus percentages do not add up to 100 per cent.

In both types of cases, mobilizers approach local and state governing agencies demanding ecosystem protection, while they challenge private entrepreneurs responsible for the negative impacts they produce. However, the existence of only 26 anti-tourism environmental protest cases in a high-intensity tourist zone during a decade implies the silent non-resistance on the part of the local population regarding a variety of negative ecosystem and social impacts. Although small in size, on the basis of its demands, this group appears to hold a stronger sustainable development view than the state. This is especially the case since the general secretary of the Hellenic Tourism Organization replaced a 1983 pro-environment decree with one that permitted the continuation of construction activities in an already saturated area. At the same time, individuals in host communities who may be economically affected by non-tourism-related environmental damages are also adhering to a similar sustainable development perspective. The concerns of both types of protest cases could contribute to the environmental quality of the local ecosystem for hosts and guests.

Conclusion

Examining tourism and the environment in four Mediterranean islands has provided the opportunity to raise a number of issues regarding sustainable development and aspects of the relevant dynamics between top-down and bottom-up forces.

The variation of tourism development experiences across these islands shows strong as well as weak associations amongst them. While Corsicans have resisted French-imposed tourism planning which negatively affects their economic, environmental, and social sustainability, in the Italian islands and Crete, state-imposed plans were followed by local pro-tourism initiatives. Crete, Sardinia and Sicily which are more populous and economically diverse island communities than Corsica, did not reject tourism – an economically profitable activity which would solve unemployment problems. Based on these experiences, top-down development has decreased the quality of the physical environment in the islands where resistance was low or non-existent, and led to a treadmill sustainable development approach.

The diversification of economic activities at the island level may not necessarily imply its economic, environmental or social sustainability, as studies pointing to tourism dependency may suggest. This is clearly visible when looking at air quality in the more diversified economies of Sardinia and Sicily. Compared to tourism-oriented Corsica and Crete, the Italian islands experience heavier loads of air pollutants with more negative economic, environmental and social impacts, and the subsequent implications these may carry for tourism's future. Thus, tourism may be still seen as a less-intruding-on-the-environment activity, especially *vis-à-vis* heavy industrial sectors, particularly when it comes to certain types of environmental offences. Therefore, economic diversification, aimed at reducing an island's economic dependence, should be carefully assessed and critically evaluated in terms of its environmental impacts.

Although local environmental protest is difficult to trace, it does make explicit reference to the negative as well as the positive role played by tourism activities in environmental protection in all four islands. In Sardinia, Sicily and Crete, the low in number and intensity environmental protest cases may imply the prevalence of economic sustainability, since tourism-producing activities in Greece and Italy, involve small family-owned businesses struggling to survive economically. Nonetheless, when these environmental demands are voiced, they reflect the variety of tourism-related local problems, and a strong sustainable development view. Hence, small economic-scale producers should be assisted in their struggle to improve the local environment and raise the quality of life for themselves and the tourists.

Economic dependence appears to hinder environmental mobilizations and state agencies, pressurized by producers, proceed to solve environmental problems at low political cost for the state and low economic cost for the producers. Treadmill or weak sustainable development views characterize these actors, since economic sustainability is more important to them than environmental sustainability. It is expected, therefore, that solutions will follow these trends and that the rate at which economic interests will drive the need for sustainable development projects at the local level will be slow.

Finally, further research is warranted to assist policy-making in the transition towards sustainability. Such research should aim at revealing both those tourism entrepreneurs and related agencies adopting a weak, and those adopting a strong, sustainable development perspective.

Acknowledgement

Thanks to D. Ioannides and Y. Apostolopoulos for their help, as well as to all agencies and persons who provided access to various data and reports – especially Elizabeth Coudert at Plan Bleu. Data used in this work derive in part from project no. EV5V-CT94-0393, funded by EC DGXII.

Notes

1. Bottom-up forces relate to small entrepreneurs and residents and other local groups in host communities, with little or no control over policy decisions affecting their daily lives. Top-down forces include policy-makers, usually at the central state or supra-state level, and powerful interest groups who are key decision-makers in tourism development at the international, national, and local levels.

2. Located in France, the 'Blue Plan' is the regional activity centre of the Mediterranean Action Plan launched by all the Mediterranean countries and the European Commission (EC) under the auspices of UNEP. In 1996, following the 1992 UN conference on Environment and Development, the Mediterranean Commission on Sustainable Development (MSCD) was established in partnership with the 'Blue Plan'. All of the above constitute forces aimed towards sustainable development in the Mediterranean.

   The 'Blue Plan' has prepared scenarios to define futures of the Mediterranean basin, operated coastal management programmes and, with EC support, it has established a Mediterranean Environmental and Development Observatory (MEDO) (Plan Bleu and UNEP, 1998).

3. In 1998, 2,499 Blue Flags were awarded in 19 European countries. This was the highest number of awards in the programme's 12 years of operation. National member organizations (19) of FEEE call on national juries and prepare the presentation of applicants for the Blue Flag. The juries usually include Ministries of the Environment, Ministries of Tourism, environmental organizations, the Association of Local Authorities, the National Lifesaving Federation, educational experts, and marina experts (The European Coordination, 1998).

4. The least populated of the large Mediterranean islands is Corsica, which, although similar in size to Crete, has a population of only 250,000. The most populated island is Sicily with about 5 million inhabitants whereas Sardinia has about 1.5 million. Although the four islands vary in size, the length of their coastlines is

quite similar (ranging from 1,047 to 1,636 km) (Eurisles, 1999). Thus, coastline development is of equal importance in terms of the environmental implications for the islands' ecosystems.

5. Personal communication with Luigi Scrofani, Sezione di Geografia, Facoltà di Economia, Università di Catania.

6. For a more detailed presentation of the methodology see Kousis (2000).

References

Aguilar-Fernandez, S., Fidelis-Nogueira, T. and Kousis, M. (1995) Encounters between social movements and the state: examples from waste facility siting in Greece, Portugal, and Spain. Alternative Futures and Popular Protest, Conference Papers, Vol. II, Manchester: Faculty of Humanities and Social Sciences, The Manchester Metropolitan University, 4–6 April.

Baker, S., Kousis, M., Richardson, D. and Young, S. (eds) (1997) *The Politics of Sustainable Development: Theory, Policy, and Practice within the EU*. London: Routledge.

Boissevain, J. (ed.) (1996) *Coping with Tourists*. London: Berghahn Books.

Briassoulis, H. (forthcoming) Sustainable development: the legal or illegal way? In K. Eder and M. Kousis (eds), *Environmental Movements, Discourses and Policies in Southern Europe*. Dordrecht: Kluwer.

Briassoulis, H. and Sofoulis, K. (1995) Regional policies and environmental quality in Greece, 1970–1992. In M.S. Skourtos and K.M. Sofoulis (eds), *Environmental Politics in Greece*. Athens: Tipothito, Dardanos.

Brigant, L. *et al.* (1995). *Les Îles en Méditerranée: enjeux et perspectives*. Les Fascicules du Plan Bleu 5, Plan d'Action pour la Méditerranée. Paris: Programme des Nations Unies pour l'environnement.

Briguglio, L. and Briguglio, M. (1996) Sustainable tourism in the Maltese Islands. In L. Briguglio, R. Butler, D. Harrison and W. Leal Filho (eds), *Sustainable Tourism in Islands and Small States: Case Studies*. London: Pinter (162–79).

Burac, M. (1996) Tourism and environment in Guadeloupe and Martinique. In L. Briguglio, R. Butler, D. Harrison, and W. Leal Filho (eds), *Sustainable Tourism in Islands and Small States: Case Studies*. London: Pinter (63–74).

Butler, R., Harrison, D. and Leal Filho W. (1996) Introduction. In L. Briguglio, R. Butler, D. Harrison and W. Leal Filho (eds), *Sustainable Tourism in Islands and Small States: Case Studies*. London: Pinter (1–10).

Chiotis, G. and Coccossis, H. (1992) Tourist development and environmental protection in Greece. In H. Briassoulis and J. van der Straaten (eds), *Tourism and the Environment*. Dordrecht: Kluwer Academic Publishers.

Cohen, E. (1978) Impacts of tourism on the physical environment. *Annals of Tourism Research*, 5(2): 215–37.

EOT-KEPE (Hellenic Tourism Organization – Centre of Planning and Economic Research) (1994) *Preliminary National Economic and Spatial Plan for Tourism, Phase, Volume 1. Basic Tourism Data*. Athens (in Greek).

Eurisles (1999) European Islands System of Links and Exchanges: The Islands Commission http://www.eurisles.com

European Commission, Directorate-General XXIII, for Tourism (1995) *Tourism in Europe*. Luxembourg: Office for Official Publications of the European Communities.

European Commission, Directorate-General XXIII, for Tourism (1997) *Yield Management in Small and Medium-sized Enterprises in the Tourist Industry*. General Report. Luxembourg: Office for Official Publications of the European Communities.

The European Coordination. The Danish Outdoor Council (1998) *The Blue Flag Awards of 1998*. Copenhagen.

Eurostat (1994) European Commission, Directorate-General for Regional Policy *Portrait of the Islands*. Luxembourg: Office for Official Publications of the European Communities.

Eurostat (1997) *Environment Statistics, 1996 8A*. Luxembourg: Office of Official Publications of the European Communities.

Farrell, B. and Runyan, D. (1991) Ecology and tourism. *Annals of Tourism Research*, 18: 26–40.

Giavelli, G., Rossi, O. and Sartore, F. (1992) Socio-environmental enquiry in Salina Island (Aeolian Archipelago, Italy). *International Journal of Environmental Studies*, 40: 281–98.

Gould, K.A., Schnaiberg, A. and Weinberg, S. (1996) *Local Environmental Struggles: Citizen Activism in the Treadmill of Production*. Cambridge: Cambridge University Press.

Hellenic Society for the Protection of Nature (1998) *Blue Flags Program*, Athens.

Hunter, C. (1997) Sustainable tourism as an adaptive paradigm. *Annals of Tourism Research*, 24(4): 850–67.

Institut National de la Statistique et des Etudes Economiques (INSEE) (1999) *Tableaux de l'économie Corse*. Ajaccio: INSEE Corse.

Institut National de la Statistique et des Etudes Economiques (INSEE) (1997) *Economie Corse: Le tourisme en Corse*, no. 83, December.

Kocasoy, G. (1989) The relationship between coastal tourism, sea pollution and public health: a case study from Turkey. *The Environmentalist*, 9(4): 241–51.

Konsolas, N. and Zacharatos, G. (1992) Regionalization of tourism activity in Greece: problems and policies. In H. Briassoulis and J. van der Straaten (eds), *Tourism and the Environment*. Dordrecht: Kluwer Academic Publishers.

Kousis, M. (1997) Unraveling environmental claim-making at the roots: Evidence from a Southern European county. *Humanity and Society*, 21(3): 257–83.

Kousis, M. (1998) Ecological marginalization in rural areas: actors, impacts, responses. *Sociologia Ruralis*, 38(1): 86–108.

Kousis, M. (2000) Tourism and the environment: a social movements perspective. *Annals of Tourism Research*, 27(2): 468–89.

Kousis, M. (forthcoming) Tourism and the environment: local social claims in Crete. In P. Tsartas (ed.), *Tourism Development: Scientific Approaches*. Athens: Exantas (in Greek).

Liu, J., Sheldon, P.J. and Var, T. (1987) Resident perception of the environmental impacts of tourism. *Annals of Tourism Research*, 14(1): 17–37.

Loukissas, P. (coordinator) *et al.* (1997) Strategic management actions relating to tourism (Summary Report by University of Thessaly), Università di Catania, and Fundación Cavanilles de Altos Estudios Turísticos. Vol. 1, Brussels: European Commission, DGXXIII.

Lozato-Giotart, J-P. (1990) *Méditerranée et tourisme*. Paris: Masson.

Mavris, C. (1998) Sustainable cultural tourism in the island state of Cyprus. *Insula – International Journal of Island Affairs*, Year 7, no. 1: 51–60.

Mediterranean Commission for Sustainable Development (MCSD), Plan Bleu, UNEP (1998) Synthesis report of the working group: tourism and sustainable development in the Mediterranean Region. *Mediterranean Action Plan*, Monaco, 20–22 October.

Plan Bleu and UNEP (1998) *A Blue Plan for the Mediterranean Peoples: From Ideas to Action*. Sophia Antipolis: Blue Plan Regional Activity Centre.

Pridham, G. and Konstadakopoulos, D. (1997) Sustainable development in Mediterranean Europe? Interactions between European, national and sub-national levels. In S. Baker, M. Kousis, D. Richardson and S. Young (eds), *The Polit.,* *Sustainable Development: Theory, Policy, and Practice Within the EU.* Londo. Routledge.

Randazzo, G. and Scrofani, L. (1996) Economic development and coastal environment in Sicily (Italy) in an integrated coastal management policy. In E. Ozhan (ed.), *Proceedings of the International Workshop on MED and Black Sea ICZM,* 2–5 November, Sarigerme, Turkey.

Region of Crete, Secretary General (1995) *Summary of Regional Tourism Development in Crete.* Heraklion: Region of Crete.

Richez, G. (1996) Sustaining local cultural identity: social unrest and tourism in Corsica. In G.K. Priestley, A.G. Edwards and H. Coccossis (eds), *Sustainable Tourism: European Experiences.* Wallingford: CAB International.

Rizzo, C. (1997) Distretti Turistici Siciliani: Alcune Considerazioni. *Bolletino della Società Geografica Italiana.* Serie XII, vol. III: 275–90.

Robbins, D. (1996) A sustainable transport policy for tourism on small islands: a case study of Malta. In L. Briguglio, R. Butler, D. Harrison and W. Leal Filho (eds), *Sustainable Tourism in Islands and Small States: Case Studies.* London: Pinter (180–98).

Rodolakis, N. (1995) Environmental protection and tourism development in Mediterranean island areas. In Technical Chamber of Crete, Eastern Crete Chapter, Western Crete Chapter, Technical Chamber of Dodekanissos, and ETE of Cyprus, *Tourism and the Environment in the Island Regions, Symposium Proceedings.* Heraklion, 17–19 March (in Greek).

Ruggiero, V. and Scrofani, L. (1996) Il paesaggio culturale della Sicilia sud-orientale: tra processi di degradazione e di omologazione e tentativi di valorizzazione. *Riv. Geogr. Ital.* 103: 373–403.

Ruzza, C. (forthcoming) Environmental sustainability and tourism in European policy making. In K. Eder and M. Kousis (eds), *Environmental Movements, Discourses and Policies in Southern Europe.* Dordrecht: Kluwer.

Saleem, N. (1996) A strategy for sustainable tourism in Sri Lanka. In L. Briguglio, R. Butler, D. Harrison and W. Leal Filho (eds), *Sustainable Tourism in Islands and Small States: Case Studies.* London: Pinter (50–62).

Sotiriadis, M. (1994) *Tourism Policy.* Heraklion: Department of Tourism Enterprises, TEI (in Greek).

Stonich, S. (1998) The political ecology of tourism. *Annals of Tourism Research,* 25(1): 25–54.

Stott, M. (1996) Tourism development and the need for community action. In L. Briguglio, R. Butler, D. Harrison and W. Leal Filho (eds), *Sustainable Tourism in Islands and Small States: Case Studies.* London: Pinter (281–305).

Stylianopoulou, E. (1998) The formulation of an environmental strategy in the hotel sector: the introduction of environmental management systems to hotels in Cyprus. Paper presented at the 1st International Scientific Congress 'Tourism and Culture for Sustainable Development', Department of Geography and Regional Planning, National Technical University of Athens, Athens, Greece, 19–21 May.

Technical Chamber of Greece – Eastern Crete Chapter *et al.* (1995) *Tourism and the Environment in the Island Regions, Symposium Proceedings.* Heraklion, 17–19 March.

Tsartas, P. (1992) Socioeconomic impacts of tourism on two Greek isles. *Annals of Tourism Research,* 19: 516–33.

Urry, J. (1992) The tourist gaze and the environment. *Theory, Culture and Society,* 9: 1–26.

Zanetto, G. and Soriani, S. (1996) Tourism and environmental degradation: the Northern Adriatic Sea. In G.K. Priestley, J.A. Edwards and H. Coccossis (eds), *Sustainable Tourism: European Experiences.* Wallingford: CAB International.

12

Raising the Stakes: Implications of Upmarket Tourism Policies in Cyprus and Malta

Dimitri Ioannides and Briavel Holcomb

Once more, well met at Cyprus.

(Shakespeare, *Othello* (Act 2, Sc. 2)

Mr. Rutter immediately conducted us to an inn, which had now the appearance of a palace. We had an excellent supper, and good Burgundy; and as this is the king's birthday, we have almost got tipsy to his health.

(Brydone, 1792)

The palace, now occupied, by the Admiral commanding the station, was fitted up by Sir Alexander Ball, for the accommodation of strangers of distinction:- now, we have three good inns, where a prince may be accommodated; and 5 or 6 most excellent lodging houses ...

(MacGill, 1839)

Introduction

Cyprus and Malta are the only independent island microstates in the Mediterranean. Despite many obvious differences, the two islands share some important traits. Since their independence from Britain in the 1960s, one common characteristic has been both islands' excessive reliance on tourism as a strategy for economic growth. Moreover, in recent years, the Republic of Cyprus and Malta have adopted governmental policies targeting upmarket visitors as a means of increasing the economic 'yield' per visitor while hoping to minimize the adverse impacts associated with mass tourism. Obviously, an empirical evaluation of these upmarket tourist strategies would be premature given both the recentness of the policy shifts, the time lag required to overcome various obstacles and change market mix, and the paucity of data with which to measure the impacts. Thus, this chapter discusses some of the environmental, economic and social implications of the islands' quests for affluent tourists, concluding that the strategy is flawed.

Cyprus, with an area of over 9,000 km^2 (including both the Republic of Cyprus and the Turkish-controlled northern part of the island, the Turkish Republic of Cyprus) and an estimated population of approximately 770,000 is much larger than Malta which covers only 246 km^2 (Figure 12.1). Nevertheless, Malta's population (400,000 in 2000) means that this island's density (1,459 inhabitants per square kilometre) is among the highest for any country. Malta, located in the central Mediterranean about 144 kilometres south of Sicily, and Cyprus, in the far Eastern section of the Mediterranean close to Turkey, Syria and Lebanon, both have rich histories which include invasions and at least temporary settlement by (*inter alia*) Phoenicians, Greeks, Turks, and the British. Cyprus gained independence from Britain in 1960, as did Malta in 1963, but both maintained strong ties with their former colonial ruler, which still is among their major sources of tourists more than 35 years later. Both islands' economies have developed from agriculture and fishing to industry and services and both have been seeking entry to the European Union. Cyprus' application is probably closer to acceptance (European Union, 1998a), while Malta originally applied for membership in 1990 but suspended the application after a change of government in 1996. The application was reactivated in late 1998 and is currently pending (European Union, 1998b).

Although essentially stable politically, both countries have experienced perturbations (Cyprus' *de facto* division, Malta's swings from socialist to nationalist governments and its connections to pariah-state Libya) which have affected tourist arrivals to varying extents. The two islands have similar 'human development' indices – a measure of life quality based on life expectancy and educational attainment. While Canada, Norway and the USA rank 1st, 2nd, and 3rd respectively on the index, Cyprus is 26th and Malta 32nd (out of nearly 180 countries ranked) (UNDP, 1999).

Tourism is an important component of the economy of both islands, but one that faces challenges in each. Cyprus has in recent years lost competitiveness in the traditional tourism sector and has made efforts to reduce its overall economic dependence on the industry (European Union, 1998a). Malta too has faced strong competition in its traditional package tourist market and demonstrates characteristics placing it in the 'stagnation' phase of the resort cycle model (Butler, 1980). In the effort to rejuvenate an industry critical to the islands' economies, both have turned to a strategy of trying to lure upmarket visitors who, it is assumed, will generate higher per capita revenues for the industry, thus requiring fewer visitors for the same (or higher) returns. There is also the assumption among policy-makers,

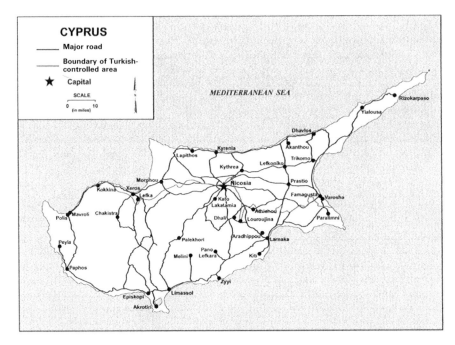

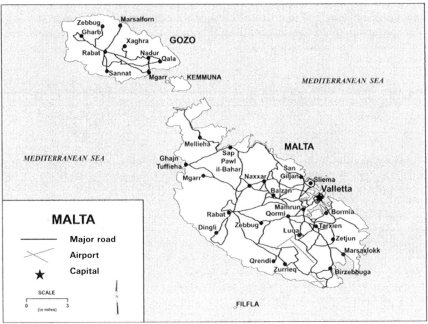

Figure 12.1 Cyprus and Malta

sometimes overtly expressed, that upmarket visitors offer other advantages. These tourists are, it is argued, more respectful of local culture and society and less disruptive than the 'lager louts' of Benidorm. These tourists supposedly appreciate high quality architecture, conserved nature, and preserved heritage. They are believed to generate more positive economic externalities and fewer negative social impacts than their downmarket, mass tourist brethren.

The search for more affluent, 'cultural' tourists while maintaining (or even decreasing) the number of mass sun/sea/sand seekers is a strategy congruent with much recent literature on 'sustainable tourism' including the recommendations of a UNESCO (1996a and b) report on sustainable tourism development in small island states. That particular report weighed economic, social and environmental aspects of tourism development in small island states and recommended 'diversifying the tourism product, enhancing its quality and increasingly targeting the upper segment of the tourist market' (UNESCO, 1996b: 19). Such a recommendation conforms to similar conclusions of the burgeoning literature on sustainable tourism (see, for example, Hunter, 1995; Middleton and Hawkins, 1998; Collins, 1999; various issues of the *Journal of Sustainable Tourism*). The jury is still out as to whether alternative tourism forms, including ecotourism, is an oxymoron or whether it is possible to 'consume places' like eating cake and having it too. Nevertheless, many places share Cyprus' and Malta's desire to replace the less-well heeled members of their golden hordes with fewer, higher-spending guests (see discussion in various chapters in this volume). The following sections review the policy's drawbacks and benefits, for the two islands as they enter the third millennium, concluding that it may be inappropriate, given the context of the global tourist industry.

Tourism in Malta

Tourism constitutes a large and important sector of the Maltese economy, directly contributing around 15 per cent of the Maltese GDP and generating an estimated 40 per cent of the country's economic activity. It is among the largest sources of jobs, employing approximately 17 per cent of the labour force, and constitutes about 25 per cent of the country's foreign exchange earnings. Since 1992 more than 1 million tourists have arrived on the Maltese islands annually, with the largest market share being from the UK (see Table 12.1). In recent years government policy has been aimed at reducing dependence on this market, to diversify the sources, and increase the share of 'upmarket' visitors. Thus, the more affluent markets of Germany, Scandinavia and the USA have been targeted, while there has been less emphasis (and less government subsidy) on the traditional package holidaymaker from the British middle and working classes. Thus, the UK share decreased from 60 per cent in 1988 to 39 per cent in 1997, while the German share in the same

Table 12.1 Tourist arrivals on Malta by nationality

Country	No. 1988	1988 (%)	No. 1997	1997 (%)
Australia	5,189	0.66	8,952	0.81
Austria	5,085	0.65	17,913	1.61
Belgium	6,238	0.80	25,567	2.31
Canada	4,555	0.58	6,060	0.55
Denmark	16,425	2.10	15,769	1.24
Finland	3,797	0.48	5,672	0.51
France	23,927	3.05	62,457	5.62
Germany	77,644	9.91	193,020	17.37
Greece	706	0.09	5,964	0.54
Irish Republic	7,908	1.01	11,717	1.05
Italy	50,678	6.47	90,190	8.12
Japan	1,033	0.13	3,879	0.35
Libya	37,133	4.74	39,289	0.54
Netherlands	17,831	2.27	52,238	4.70
Norway	1,640	0.21	7,478	0.58
Spain	801	0.10	4,937	0.44
Sweden	4,468	0.57	11,329	1.02
Switzerland	14,014	1.79	17,924	1.61
UK	476,578	60.80	436,899	39.32
USA	8,734	1.11	14,924	1.34
Others	19,462	2.48	79,983	7.20
TOTAL	783,846	100	1,111,161	100

Source: National Tourist Organization, Malta (1999)

period increased from 10 per cent to over 17 per cent. At the same time, government policy has concentrated investment in the construction of luxury accommodation and attempted to slow down or stop the construction of cheaper hotels and holiday flats. Policy-makers assume the island's carrying capacity for visitors may have been reached and that in order for the economy to continue growing, higher 'yield' per visitor is sought. The policy is aimed at attracting more affluent, 'cultural' tourists while maintaining (or even reducing) the numbers of sun/sea seekers.

In exploring the economic, environmental and social implications of this policy we argue that for Malta at the turn of the millennium such an emphasis is counterproductive. Five-star guests are more expensive to cater to and can have greater environmental and possibly social costs than two-star tourists. While they may spend more money per day, the elite tourists also require more imports, resulting in a higher leakage of foreign exchange. Luxury tourists are also more expensive to attract, and may have greater detrimental effects on Maltese society than their more plebian counterparts. The policy of upgrading the tourist 'product' (by, for example, investing in luxury hotels and other amenities, restoring and improving access to archaeological and historic sites, building golf courses) to attract upmarket guests assumes that the cultural/heritage tourist (a main niche market targeted by Malta) spends more than his/her sea/sun/sand counterpart. However, this assumption may not be correct. The policy confuses 'high culture' visitors with high spenders, whereas the two may not be synonymous. As a group, probably the most affluent visitors to Malta are the yacht owners using Malta as a port of call while sailing the Mediterranean. Although these individuals contribute revenue through port charges and purchases, they are highly unlikely to use luxury accommodation onshore (Wilkinson, 1999). Hard evidence to support these arguments proved elusive since there is little available Maltese data on differential spending patterns, energy and water use or conservation measures by tourist segment. The paucity of such data, however, also suggests that when the policy was promulgated in the mid-1990s it was not backed by a rigorous cost/benefit analysis.

As noted earlier, Malta is the second most densely populated state in the world and has experienced rapid urban sprawl. The built-up area expanded from 5 to 18 per cent over 30 years. Just as in Cyprus, the standard of living has also increased with car and second-home ownership at high levels, especially compared to many other Mediterranean islands and mainland states. As is the case in many Mediterranean insular environments (see other chapters in this volume) water is scarce, with over 60 per cent obtained from desalinated seawater (Smith, 1997). While the largest demand for water is for domestic consumption, the fact that the peak tourist season coincides with the summer months with least water availability means that tourism places particular demands on this scarce resource. Virtually all energy is derived from imports, though some small-scale solar energy is used. Hence the energy used for desalinization is imported (including oil from Libya).

Culturally, Malta is a traditional, Catholic country where social change, though occurring, has been slower than in Northern Europe. Independent from Britain since 1963, strong ties with that country remain and are manifested in such things as language (most Maltese are bilingual in Malti and English and increasingly tri-lingual with Italian learned from television!), support for British football teams, and the thousands of British tourists who visit each year. Undoubtedly, part of Malta's attraction for British visitors is that it presents no linguistic or culinary challenges. The local food is not highly spiced or too 'exotic', while fish and chip shops and pubs abound. The Leyland buses (now being replaced) are the same as those that plied English roads half a century ago. Until recently, a significant proportion of British visitors were World War II veterans who had visited the islands during the war. Most of these veterans are now dead or too old to travel, but their children still visit and the war is a focus of several popular tourist sites, including a multi-media show.

The policies instituted during the 1990s aimed at attracting more affluent visitors from more diverse market areas. Many other small island states, including Cyprus, have also increasingly emphasized ecotourism or nature tourism as alternatives to conventional mass tourism. 'Underlying this trend is greater environmental awareness globally, greater health consciousness, and a growing preference by travelers to experience unspoiled environmental surroundings' (UNESCO, 1996b: 9). Noting the need for an integrated approach to environmental care in the tourist industry, the 1st Conference on Sustainable Island Development called for specific tools to develop sustainable tourism including the need to 'promote the creation of ecotourism quality labels by the islands themselves' (1997: 4). Similarly, Insula's report on *Tourism and Sustainable Development: The Island Experience* calls for the use of ecotourism as an important strategy for environmental conservation (Gortazar and Cipriano, 1999).

In Malta, however, promoting ecotourism is difficult given that the country has little 'unspoiled' environment left and the few rural parts (such as the smaller island of Gozo) need to be retained in agriculture. Malta currently produces only about 20 per cent of its food needs so the possibilities of integrating domestic agricultural products with tourism demand are already extremely limited. The rapid pace of urbanization and an increase in consumption have overtaken the development of what could be called a public environmental ethic. Litter abounds and recycling efforts are limited. The Malta Ecological Foundation notes that 'unfortunately a morning walk at one of our beaches is often a reflection of the lack of altruism of the Maltese ... We expect everyone to show he [*sic*] is civilized and while enjoying bar-b-qued pork, avoid behaving like one' [*sic*] (1999a). Although some progress has been made in the use of recycling, plastics continue to be sent to the scarce landfill sites. Unfortunately, hunters have decimated the potentially rich bird life. Indeed, various governmental attempts to regulate this traditional pastime have met with only limited success. A survey of 841 residents found 70 per cent were opposed to the abolition of hunting and fewer than half felt hunting regulations were not severe enough (Malta Ecological Foundation, 1999b). Malta does have some capacity for the lucrative sea diving tourism trade, but the Mediterranean has less fertility, less coral, and fewer colourful fish than the competing Caribbean. In the mid-1990s only 14 per cent of all sewage was treated before disposal into the sea and although the government has committed itself to treat all sewage by the year 2003, it will take some time before the marine ecosystem recovers. In brief, it would be a great stretch of the imagination to conceive of Malta as an ecotourist destination.

Malta does, however, have considerable heritage and cultural tourism assets, ranging from Copper Age temples to state-of-the-art media productions. The numerous small villages replete with baroque churches and frequent fiestas, the walled medieval towns of Mdina, Valletta, and Victoria (Rabat), and the traditional stone farmhouses set in terraced fields present a delightful landscape to explore (Balm, 1995). Malta is rightfully marketing these indigenous attractions as well as less home-grown events such as the Malta Jazz Festival and has been successful in either placing or winning coverage in travel and mainstream media in English (e.g., Armsden, 1998; Gordon, 1998; Grossman, 1998; Whitman, 1998). What is harder to assess is the extent to which visitors drawn to Malta for its cultural treasures stay in upmarket accommodation and spend more than the mass travellers who visit mainly for the sun.

In 1999 there were ten five-star hotels in Malta reflecting a 100 per cent increase over the five luxury hotels just three years previously. Planning applications and construction were pending on others. The Planning Department (established in 1992) did not accept applications for the construction of new hotels with fewer than five stars during the second half of the 1990s, although remodelling and expansion of lesser-quality hotels were possible. Five-star hotels are mostly (though not all) large, require significant land area, are conspicuously sited, and include some foreign ownership and/or management, such as Radisson and Westin multinational chains, though the two five-star Corinthia hotels are said by the US government to be controlled by the Libyan government! (Rocks, 1998).

Moreover, the construction of new projects generates significant controversy. In spring 1996 the proposed Munxar project, for which only an application to the Planning Authority existed, generated organized protest and opposition from the Labour Party, Din L-Art Helwa (a cultural organization), the Religion page of the *Sunday Times of Malta*, and numerous letters to the paper's editor. The project was proposed for 120 tumoli (approximately 15 hectares) on a scenic and ecologically important peninsula on the eastern coast. It was to include 150 holiday bungalows, restaurants, shops, tennis courts and a swimming pool. After initial protests, a revised plan scrapped a proposed hotel and offered free access to the pool for residents of nearby Marsascala. However, a committee of local residents continued to oppose the project and the Italian developer is reported to have branded them 'communists' who 'do not understand what environment means' (*The Malta Independent*, 1996: 5). The developer ultimately withdrew the application, but the future of the site remains undetermined.

A luxury project near Xlendi, a magnificent cliff-top site in Gozo, also aroused controversy while still at the 'rumour' stage. The largest project ever proposed for Malta, the redevelopment of Manoel Island, formerly the site of a fort, an isolation hospital and various port-related establishments, began in the late 1990s but is likely to take a decade to complete. The new development is to incorporate first-class hotel accommodation and a luxury yacht marina. The controversy surrounding this project has already led to a change in government. As *The Economist* somewhat condescendingly reported:

Only on a small, sun-drenched Mediterranean island would a government be swept out of office over the weighty matter of a new yacht marina. That, at least, was the affair that caused a member of Malta's ruling Labour Party to vote against his government and force an early general election ... which his party then lost. (1998: 58)

Other luxury projects that have aroused considerable controversy include the San Gorg hotel that incorporated an eighteenth-century historic tower into its construction, thus removing this piece of the island's heritage from the public domain. Another building is the Excelsior, a cement monster built adjacent to the medieval bastions of Valletta and a lamentable aesthetic intrusion into the landscape of this UNESCO World Heritage site. The five-star scene is not, however, totally bleak. A single-storey hotel in Gozo, the Ta Cenc, is more respectful of its surroundings, though its swimming pools and luxuriant landscaping are nevertheless discordant in a scenic cliff top with garrigue vegetation. The newly restored Xara Palace, which re-opened in 1999, is housed in a seventeenth-century building in the bastions of Mdina, has only 17 rooms and no pool (Xara Palace web site 1999)!

Almost invariably, luxury accommodation consumes more energy and water, as well as land. Five-star hotels are centrally heated and air conditioned, while their downmarket equivalents usually have small electric heaters and fans with openable windows. Luxury hotels typically have large public spaces such as atria, dining rooms, and lounges that must be air conditioned and lit. Their exterior landscaping, parking lots and façades are illuminated at night. More water is used per capita in luxury hotels since baths are larger, there are more swimming pools (some of which are freshwater and/or heated), whirlpools, health clubs, more frequent linen changes, more irrigated landscaping, and more automatic dish and laundry washing machines. While the industry standard for hot water storage in high-grade hotels is about 10 gallons a head, it is only 7 gallons for budget hotels (Lawson, 1995). Luxury hotels use more machinery (and energy) than hand labour for cleaning, maintenance, and landscaping. They are more likely to incorporate elevators, to provide refrigerated minibars in guestrooms, and to heat swimming pools. Their rooms are larger. In Malta, most of the furnishings and fixtures for hotels are imported, thus a well-equipped five-star room will likely add to the balance of payments deficit more than a relatively spartan budget hotel room furnished with used and recycled equipment.

While data on energy use by sectors of the tourist industry in Malta are not available, some comparison can be made with Hawaii. Similar to Malta, Hawaii relies heavily on imported petroleum supplying 92 per cent of the state's energy, a percentage equivalent to Malta. Also, like Malta, tourism is Hawaii's leading export earner. A recent study found that tourists account for about 40 per cent of total energy demand in Hawaii (though the equivalent proportion is almost certainly lower in Malta) (Tabatchnaia-Tamirisa *et al.,*

1997). What is interesting concerning the upmarket policy, however, is that the Hawaii study demonstrated that as the mix of tourists to Hawaii changed, foreign visitors (of whom Japanese constituted 60 per cent), who are more upmarket than domestic tourists (from other parts of the USA), consumed more energy. 'Indirect use of electricity per dollar of visitor expenditures is about 24 per cent higher for foreign tourists than for domestic tourists' (ibid.: 397). In 1987 domestic tourists constituted about 68 per cent and foreign tourists 32 per cent of total visitors to Hawaii, but foreign tourists generated about 60 per cent of total energy and fuel demand by visitors to the islands. Since the proportion of foreign visitors is increasing, energy demands will also increase. An equivalent situation is likely in Malta if the policy of attracting upmarket tourists is ultimately successfully implemented.

Similarly, data on water use in Malta by different sectors of the tourist industry were not available, but comparisons with Majorca, a competing Mediterranean island destination which has also sought to move away from British working-class package tourists to a more upmarket visitor, are instructive. Majorca also has depleted water resources so a 'country Mallorcan, always having known how scarce water was, would not ordinarily use more than 140 litres a day. A city dweller uses 250 litres a day and an average tourist 440. The luxury-minded tourist can use up to 880 litres a day' (Boers and Bosch, 1994: 58). The same source reports that the average tourist produces 50 per cent more rubbish than a Majorcan resident, a significant factor in small islands with limited landfill capacity. Majorca's visitor mix contrasts with Malta's as 60 per cent are German and only 20 per cent British, however, Majorca 'is rapidly changing its image. It is not a place for retired people anymore. It is the "in" place for thirty to sixty-year-olds looking for an upscale vacation' replete with golf and 'neighbours' such as Claudia Schiffer and Richard Branson (Guttman, 1999: 33).

Obviously, hoteliers are aware of energy and water costs and thus seek to conserve both by incorporating appropriate technology or retrofitting such features as automatic light and air conditioning shut-off when the guest is out of the room. In fact, research indicates that five-star hotel chains are more likely to adopt conservation practices than are more modest accommodation, although their overall energy and water usage per guest remains higher (Buckley and Aranjo, 1997). Nevertheless, in Malta government policies are not particularly conducive to conservation. In a country which produces over half its water through reverse osmosis – effectively 'importing' water since the energy to produce the water is imported – both energy and water costs are significantly subsidised. The true costs of heavy energy and water use are borne, then, by the taxpayer at large, rather than by hoteliers or their guests. There is even public subsidy of imports of high energy-utilizing equipment – an amendment of the Aid to Industry Ordinance in 1995 exempted from import duty equipment such as air conditioners, computerized telephones and other items used by hotels for upgrading (*The Times of Malta*, 1995).

Despite the potential for solar energy on the island, less than 5 per cent of energy is from renewable sources and the Malta Ecological Foundation's efforts to obtain subsidies and tax relief for solar power are ongoing (Malta Ecological Foundation, 1999c).

The environmental costs of upmarket tourism are not confined to hotels. The heliport extension in Gozo and a proposed second golf course in Malta aim at improving amenities for affluent visitors, but both carry serious environmental threats (Markwick, 2000). Heavier visitation of archaeological sites and ecologically fragile areas may result in more damage. Boissevain (1996) and Black (1996), among others, have written of the stress placed on the social fabric of Maltese villages by tourists although they have also noted that the concentration of the great bulk of visitors in established centres around Sliema and St Pauls Bay confines their impact spatially. They also argue that seasonality preserves winters as a time of relative peace and renewal for locals.

Hotels and other guest accommodation suffer from rapid obsolescence as fashions and tastes change and new technologies are introduced. However, luxury accommodation has an even shorter life span than its budget counterpart because the latest convenience and this year's hues are *de rigueur*. When the Xara Palace had two stars in the mid-1990s it could (and did!) use patched blankets or mismatched glasses. Now it offers antique furniture period pieces and original paintings as well as gastronomic treasures served with elegant crystal and silverware (Xara Palace web site 1999). Sometimes, as in the case of the Hilton, the entire building becomes obsolete and is torn down and rebuilt. The Malta Hilton's life span was only three decades and its replacement, on a larger scale, controversial. While some of the equipment from the hotel was reused elsewhere, much was discarded and investment in the original building was lost. Hence, upmarket tourists require considerable capital investment.

Occupancy rates in Malta are a perennial concern and, thus, part of the motivation behind targeting the affluent German and Scandinavian markets was to increase visitor numbers in off-peak seasons. In 1991 the average occupancy rate in Malta was only 56 per cent, meaning that nearly half the accommodation was empty for half the time. While hotels, especially those in the luxury category, have higher occupancy rates, even five-star hotels only reach 75 per cent so that a quarter of their rooms remain vacant on average (Briguglio and Vella, 1995). In 1997 Malta received over 10,000 visitors per month in April, May, July, August, September, and October, but only 3,600 in January and 5,000 in February (Malta Tourism Authority, 1999). While one of the authors has argued elsewhere that there are benefits to seasonality in tourism (Holcomb, 1995), clearly it also has economic costs. However, it can be argued that the cost of low occupancy is greater for a five-star than a two-star hotel. The five-star stays open year round while the two-star may close for a period during the low season. The facilities of the five-star hotel must be maintained, despite their low utilization. The pool is heated even if nobody swims in it. The minibars with their perishable stock stay switched on despite the lack of guests seeking refreshment.

One of the presumed economic benefits of emphasizing luxury accommodation is that it provides more employment. While this is true, it is also the case that Malta (and Cyprus) enjoys very low rates of unemployment, hence the cost of maintaining year-round employees in under-utilized hotels may not be the best use of labour. The waiter who wanders around the mostly empty cocktail lounge seeking a thirsty customer could be better employed learning telematics or selling banking services. To compete in the international marketplace of the future Malta will need more information processors and fewer waitresses. Cyprus' growing success in financial and other high value-added services could serve as an example to emulate (Murdoch, 1998).

When considering the upmarket tourist market, several points can be made. In the marketing world the best customer is the repeat customer because he or she requires less expensive marketing campaigns. Malta's newspapers frequently have letters from people who have been to the islands twenty or thirty times. Upmarket tourists, by contrast, are much less likely to be repeaters (see also chapter by Tom Selänniemi in this volume). If they are 'culture vultures' they may enjoy the one or two weeks visiting Malta's heritage and cultural attractions, but next year they will want to see something new in Greece, or Egypt, or Thailand. Similarly, if they are 'trophy tourists,' they are likely to want to 'do' a new destination next. Affluent travellers are influenced less by the costs of distance than are package tourists. Malta must compete with global destinations (many of them exotic) for five-star guests. Marketing to the affluent market is not only more expensive than seeking mass tourists but, with few repeaters, new customers must be continuously sought.

In the late 1990s fewer than five out of every hundred tourists visiting Malta stayed in five-star hotels. It is hard to estimate the economic impact of this small segment of visitors. It can be argued that although they may spend more, a greater proportion of what they buy and consume is imported and relatively little supports local enterprises. Hotel gift shops typically display Cartier watches and imported jewellery. The locally made glassware and lace is low-priced by comparison, and generates equivalently small profits. Nor is there much elasticity of demand for such products. There is a lack of locally produced high-priced artefacts or souvenirs of potential interest to affluent visitors. In brief, there is not a lot on which to spend money! Domestic wines and *fenkata* (rabbit stew), however delicious, do not generate high profit margins. Paul Theroux echoes the point in his account of a Mediterranean cruise. On leaving the islands he asked a fellow traveller ' "What did you think of Malta?" ... "If you wanted to buy a brass doorknocker" he said, "I guess you'd come to Malta. There are thousands of them for sale there, right? Apart from the doorknockers, it wasn't much."' (Theroux, 1995: 321).[1]

In summary, the Maltese policy of emphasizing luxury tourism appears environmentally and economically flawed. Recent efforts to upgrade the quality of service (rather than accommodation) and the goal of renovating and upgrading existing accommodation, rather than constructing new hotels, are preferable to continued investment in new luxury construction. However, the campaign by the Tourist Secretariat to impress upon the Maltese people that tourism benefits everyone and that all should be responsible for the 'tourist product' is more debatable. Illustrated newspaper advertisements argued that 'Malta's Image is Our Daily Living. Our island is beautiful, let us keep it that way', 'Money and Effort are Spent Marketing our Country. You can be our best advert', and 'It's not just Hotels that make Tourism. We all have our part to play'. The Tourism Parliamentary Secretary had hoped to run the campaign exclusively in Maltese 'since it was targeted at fostering hospitality in the locals and tourists need not be aware that this was taking place' (*The Sunday Times of Malta*, 1996: 2). The Maltese Government is not alone in running such campaigns – both Bahamians and Singaporeans are among those exhorted by their governments to smile at strangers. But such efforts may increase residents' sense of living in an ephemeral tourist milieu and being, as Disneyland calls its employees, cast members.

Finally, it can be argued that the class structure of many of the mass visitors on Malta is not unlike those of its residents; most visitors are middle- and working-class people who appreciate local facilities and services and may indeed be envious of Maltese social cohesion and family supports. Many of the young people who come from Northern Europe to learn English in the sun, the young families for whom even a two-star holiday village provides a touch of luxury, and the retirees may not be the biggest of spenders. Nevertheless, many of these visitors often stay longer, return more frequently and some of them may even appreciate heritage and respect traditions. If, by contrast, the island attracts a larger share of the 'rich and famous' perhaps its sons and daughters will have to learn to be more obsequious and, in what has been called the demonstration effect, may desire the trappings and lifestyle of affluent foreigners. What may be right for some other small island states may not be right for Malta.

Tourism in Cyprus

Just as in Malta, since independence the growth of tourism on the island of Cyprus has been phenomenal. Following the *de facto* division of the island in 1974, the industry has developed particularly rapidly on the southern coast of the Greek Cypriot-controlled Republic of Cyprus. By 1994, the number of tourists on this part of the island exceeded 2 million for the first time, and by 1998 2.2 million arrivals were recorded (Cyprus Tourism Organization,

1998). During the same year the total tourist accommodation capacity that had grown on average by 5.19 per cent per annum between 1989 and 1998 amounted to 86,151 beds with another 2,816 beds under construction. Over 90 per cent of the tourist accommodation facilities were concentrated in the coastal resorts of Larnaca, Limassol, Paphos, and the Paralimni-Ayia Napa region. In 1998, an estimated 40,000 persons were directly employed in the hotel industry alone, while tourism receipts of CY£878 million (US$1.6 billion) amounted to just under 40 per cent of the region's receipts from the export of goods and services. By contrast, tourism's growth and economic contribution on the Turkish-controlled northern part of the island have been far less impressive due to the region's political and economic isolation (Ioannides, 2001). In 1994 only 350,000 arrivals were recorded (17.5 per cent the number of arrivals witnessed in the south), the majority of whom were short-term visitors from Turkey (*North Cyprus Home Page*, 1997). Tourism contributed US$172.9 million to the region's economy (4 per cent of the GDP). Moreover, there were just under 8,000 beds in this part of the island compared to 76,000 in the south (Lockhart, 1994).

The rapid growth of tourism in the Republic of Cyprus has had both positive and negative impacts. Over 25 per cent of the Republic's labour force were either directly or indirectly dependent on tourism-related employment while the rapid construction of hotels and other tourist establishments during the last two decades has fuelled a boom in the construction industry (Vassiliou, 1995). In no small manner, tourism has played a role in enhancing the Republic's standard of living to a point where it now is one of the most affluent societies of the Mediterranean rim (Ioannides, 2001). Yet another, indirect effect arising from tourism is that it has served to promote recognition of Cypriot products such as wines and cheeses, thus creating new markets for these commodities in northern European countries and further afield.

However, it is the negative repercussions, particularly the environmental impacts, associated with the sector's rapid growth that have caused alarm among policy-makers. Such impacts have been discussed at length elsewhere (Ioannides, 1995; Ioannides and Apostolopoulos, 1999; Jensen, 1989; Vassiliou, 1995). Suffice it to say that the largely uncontrolled growth of tourism on the island's southern coast has led to a condition where 'excessive strip development along coastal areas has raised concerns that the carrying capacity of several coastal areas may already have been exceeded' (World Bank 1992: 27) (Plate 12.1). Among the most serious environmental effects of tourism-related development are the threat to local flora and fauna particularly from inadequate waste disposal systems (Panayiotou, 1989), aesthetic pollution (Jensen, 1989), coastal erosion, and severe water shortages (Mansfeld and Kliot, 1996). Unlike its neighbour, Northern Cyprus has been spared some of the worst environmental damages by virtue of the industry's slower pace of development. Nevertheless, there is evidence that

Plate 12.1   Limassol, Cyprus – coastal development of tourist-related establishments

Turkish Cypriot authorities have not heeded the lessons from the south and have already embarked on strategies that could prove costly for the environment in the near future. Although there is a planning and zoning framework in northern Cyprus, Mansfeld and Kliot (1996) argue that regulations are often not enforced and, thus, it is possible that the region could eventually witness the same type of uncontrolled development seen in the south.

Concerns over tourism's negative environmental impacts have prompted authorities in the Republic of Cyprus to adopt various measures to protect the destination's future competitiveness. The 1990 Town and Country Planning Law, for instance, requires local authorities to designate tourism development zones according to prescribed criteria in the island-wide strategic plan. Similar to measures adopted in Malta and other Mediterranean islands, the New Tourist Policy of the Cyprus Tourism Organization (CTO, 1990) calls for the promotion of a high quality, diversified tourism product. When it was first adopted, the policy aimed to curb the rapid growth of organized inclusive tours, impose an upper ceiling on tourist arrivals (particularly those arriving on charter flights) and implement strict controls for policing the development of informal tourist facilities. Among the programmes proposed to diversify the tourism product were the promotion of yachting and sailing facilities, conventions and cultural events, agrotourism, ecotourism, hill-resort tourism, and golfing holidays. In order to attract higher spending individuals, the Council of Ministers (1990) enacted legislation emphasizing the development of luxury class hotels (four and five stars) and all-inclusive holiday centres.

Interestingly, many of these policies have not been successfully implemented for a variety of reasons. For instance, construction moratoria in the early 1990s did not affect the multitude of building permits that had been previously issued for hotels and hotel apartments (World Bank, 1992) nor did they apply to ancillary tourist facilities or private homes in resorts (Lockhart, 1994). Thus, in the last few years the speculative construction of hotels, second homes, retail establishments, and informal tourist facilities has continued unabated. It also appears that politicians have not always been willing to embrace planning restrictions, fearing a loss of popularity at the polls. In the early 1990s, 'environmental groups accused a government Minister of voting to relax zoning restrictions to permit the construction of a 352-bed [luxury] hotel on an untouched nature reserve' (Bosselman *et al.*, 1999: 135) (Plate 12.2). Moreover, while alternative tourism forms such as agrotourism have become increasingly popular on the island, it has been impossible to set limits on mass tourism because of the over-supply of tourist accommodation. The Cyprus Hoteliers' Association, in particular, has lobbied fiercely in recent years to protect the accommodation industry from waning occupancy rates, forcing authorities to make an unofficial U-turn on their policy to limit mass tourism. In fact, the number of charter flight arrivals in Cyprus has increased over the last few years, despite the CTO's official pursuit of quality tourism. During 1998 more than a million package tourists

Plate 12.2 Controversial construction of luxury hotel in the Akamas Peninsula

arrived in the Republic of Cyprus on cheap charter flights from various parts of Europe including Britain (more than half), Russia, Scandinavian countries, and Germany (CTO officer, personal communication, 1999).

The Greek Cypriot government's inability over the last nine years to strictly control the growth of tourist facilities and enforce many aspects of the New Tourism Policy has not deterred the CTO from seeking to develop a 'sustainable tourism' strategy for the next decade (2000–10). This strategy, which was due to be completed by the end of 1999, aims to continue pursuing quantitative limits on the number of mass arrivals while attracting higher-spending individuals as opposed to budget travellers. The CTO and government officials are particularly concerned that the average revenue per visitor has consistently declined since 1990 despite the goals of the original policy (CTO officer, personal communication, 1999) (Table 12.2). While the details of the new strategy have not been disclosed, it is clear the authorities continue to believe they must reposition Cyprus in the travel markets away from its traditional sun, sea and sand image and seek to extend the tourist season. Workshops have been held in which the industry's various stakeholders were briefed on the merits of balanced growth. However, how this goal will eventually be achieved, given the island's recent history of uncontrolled tourism development, is not yet clear.

There is no doubt that mass tourism in the Republic of Cyprus in its present uncoordinated form needs to be curbed. Yet, just as in the case of Malta, it appears that the authorities' belief in 'luxury' tourism as a solution is misplaced. True, Cyprus has more options to diversify its tourism product than Malta and has, as discussed earlier, embarked on various programmes including attempts to bolster tourism in the interior of the island through rural tourism or ecotourism initiatives. For instance, a number of villages in the Akamas peninsula are being renovated and promoted as rural tourist

Table 12.2 Tourist arrivals and expenditure patterns in Cyprus 1990–98 (constant 1998 prices)

Year	Arrivals	Average revenue/ visit (CY£)	Total revenue (CY£m)
1990	1,561,479	504.57	788
1991	1,385,129	450.02	623
1992	1,991,000	428.31	853
1993	1,841,000	443.16	816
1994	2,069,000	438.36	907
1995	2,100,000	420.92	884
1996	1,917,000	431.02	826
1997	2,088,000	412.74	862
1998	2,222,706	393.23	874

Source: Evi Soteriou, CTO tourist officer, personal communication.

Plate 12.3 Restoration of a village home for agrotourism in the Akamas Peninsula

destinations (Foundation for the Revival of Laona, 1993) (Plate 12.3). This project is aimed primarily at promoting growth in a historically declining area with few options for economic survival. Preliminary observations indicate the programme has successfully created locally run agro-businesses in this region and has stemmed (at least in some villages) the out-migration of the population (Ioannides, 1995). Given, however, that only an estimated 10,000 visitors per year (many of them Cypriots from other parts of the island) will visit these villages once the project is completed, it is likely that the economic benefits of agrotourism will be relatively small and highly localized (Karouzis, 1999). On the plus side, the agrotourism project has encouraged other villages in the island's interior to explore their potential as tourist destinations. Importantly, a number of localities have embarked on projects to preserve their traditional architecture and revive their arts and crafts industry.

Programmes promoting ecotourism to remote parts of the island have had more dubious effects especially since there does not appear to be a coordinated plan relating to this segment of the industry. A number of companies located in the mass tourist resorts have jumped on the 'eco' fad as a marketing gimmick and begun selling 'eco-safaris'. Ironically, it is mainly the mass tourists desiring a short break from the sea who make up these companies' clientele. Nowadays, it is not unusual to encounter endless convoys of Land Rovers or Jeeps disturbing the peace in remote parts of the island. The operators of these companies seem to feel that as long as they shuttle tourists to undeveloped spots to view nature or historical ruins and as long as the transportation is by (usually camouflaged) off-road vehicles they can legitimately use the 'eco-tourism' label. Ironically, these off-road vehicles are probably creating more pollution collectively than is normally produced by a single, more conventional, 70-seater sightseeing coach. Most of these companies do not, as may be expected of ecotourism outfits, employ trained guides in the natural sciences or archaeology and only a handful of them encourage their clients to explore their surroundings (e.g., go on a nature hike) once they reach their destination. Also, most eco-operators transport their own food and beverages meaning that little or no money is spent in the settlements they travel through. Thus, it appears that in the case of Cyprus ecotourism is anything but environmentally sensitive especially as it opens up previously remote (and often ecologically sensitive areas) to hundreds of tourists per day (Plate 12.4). In fact, the coastal part of the Akamas peninsula has already suffered irreversible damage due to the popularity it has received as an alternative destination on the island (Ioannides, 1995).

Many of the same criticisms regarding luxury-oriented tourism in the case of Malta apply to Cyprus. There are now 18 five-star large-scale hotels on the island (most of them with more than 400 bed spaces). Almost every four- and five-star hotel has a swimming pool (many of them are heated) and every

Plate 12.4   The downside of ecotourism? Litter beneath an environmental protection sign at Lara Bay

single one is centrally air conditioned. Most establishments are surrounded by lavish gardens and manicured lawns placing an enormous burden on the island's meagre water resources. In view of the island's chronic water shortages (made worse by a series of severe droughts in the last decade), the construction of two, and plans for a further three, 18-hole golf courses reflects a misguided policy. Even though the authorities claim the courses use treated sewage for their irrigation needs, the introduction of golf reflects poor judgement in a country where water distribution to households has to be rationed on a regular basis. In large part because of the increase of tourism in recent years, the island has had to construct a desalination plant while a second one has already been planned despite the enormous costs involved in operating such facilities.

In sum, it appears that the Republic of Cyprus' blind faith in an upmarket tourism product in order to rectify the impacts of mass tourism has a number of flaws. Given current trends it appears highly unlikely that the authorities will be able to rid the island's principal resorts from their mass tourism image any time soon. The alternative products that have been developed or are in the pipeline will probably not attract enough 'quality' visitors, especially ones who are going to spend a lot of money. As Karouzis (1999) argues, Cyprus still has to overcome many problems like incomplete sewage treatment facilities, lack of sidewalks in many areas, inadequate airport facilities, indifferent service by shopkeepers, and poorly maintained archaeological sites before it can really be promoted as a quality destination. Otherwise, one needs to ask why luxury tourists would visit Cyprus as a destination in the first place, especially since there are so many other competing upmarket destinations in the Mediterranean and elsewhere offering vastly superior products. Surely, rather than pursuing luxury tourists, a more realistic objective for the Cypriot authorities is to seek to enhance the sustainability of the existing mass tourism product (de Kadt, 1990), while continuing attempts to diversify the economy through sectors such as offshore banking, software production, and medical services (Murdoch, 1998). Drastic efforts to improve the quality of the built environment while protecting the island's natural and historical attributes, particularly in coastal areas, should be the government's principal priority relating to tourism. The case of Majorca, which has seen a revival (and re-imaging) of its tourist industry accompanied by the adoption of a rigorous planning framework (see contribution by Bardolet in this volume), should serve as a useful example for the Republic of Cyprus, Northern Cyprus, and Malta.

Conclusion: Upping the Ante or the Downside of Upmarket

Certain islands have long histories as luxury tourist destinations. Examples include Bali, the Seychelles, and Bermuda. Cyprus and Malta, by contrast, have emerged as mass tourist destinations displaying a number of serious environmental and sociocultural problems associated with the sector's rapid and uncontrolled growth. In turn, these problems have meant that in recent years the two destinations have begun losing their respective competitive advantage as mass tourist destinations. In both cases, this has resulted in slower annual growth rates of arrivals and revenues with the average expenditure per tourist demonstrating a consistent decline. Currently, both Malta and the Republic of Cyprus display characteristics placing them in the consolidation or even stagnation point of their respective resort life-cycles. The authorities' response on these two islands has been to propose the development of an upmarket tourism product in order to attract well-to-do tourists. The prevailing argument is that tourism's negative impacts can be diminished if the destinations can replace a high number of budget-minded mass tourists with a more manageable number of big-spending individuals.

While there is a certain rationale behind this argument, it appears that in the case of Cyprus and Malta quality tourism cannot provide a feasible solution to their respective woes. Though both islands have attempted to diversify their product (e.g., through cultural tourism), it is unlikely that such programmes can attract enough quality tourists, especially ones willing to spend large sums of money. After all, many budget-minded tourists (e.g., backpackers) are often attracted to these islands for their historical/ archaeological attractions. These cultural tourists can hardly be described as big spenders. Certain mass tourists, by contrast, may end up spending considerable sums on food, drinks and nightclubs. More importantly, it is obvious that many of the upmarket projects proposed for the islands reflect considerable folly on the part of policy-makers. Air-conditioned mega-hotels with heated swimming pools and lush gardens, 18-hole golf courses, and (at least in the case of Cyprus) operations offering escorted ecotours to a few remaining remote spots can hardly be described as environmentally sensitive in areas experiencing severe water shortages and rapidly diminishing natural landscapes.

Generally, the efforts to enhance these islands' competitiveness as tourist destinations mirror the inability or unwillingness of policy-makers to distinguish between sustainable tourism and the need to promote tourism within an overall balanced growth framework (Butler, 1997; Wall, 1997). Thus, policies on both islands indicate the prevailing obsession with tourism's perpetuation without acknowledging that a balance should be found between this sector and all 'other existing and potential activities' (Wall, 1997: 44–5). It is precisely the authorities' failure to tie in tourism strategies within a comprehensive development framework accounting for all economic and land use activities that has hindered these destinations' attempts to achieve balanced growth. Surely, then, a more realistic agenda for the future overall development of these destinations must pay attention to tourism's interplay with other sectors (e.g., transportation, infrastructure, employment, housing, the environment). Authorities should explore ways to enhance the contribution of the industry towards achieving overall balanced growth on the islands. Ensuring that the prevailing mass tourism product is revamped within the guidelines of a comprehensive sustainable development agenda, while enhancing economic diversification efforts in other sectors such as financial and telecommunications industries would constitute a step in the right direction.

Finally, it is important for Cyprus and Malta to cooperate with countries bordering the Mediterranean and other small island nations throughout the globe in terms of promoting environmental protection in insular regions. Since almost all the small island nations worldwide are heavily dependent on petroleum for their energy needs, it is imperative that they seek cheaper and more efficient sources (e.g., renewable sources such as solar energy). Energy-intensive activities such as desalination of seawater should be limited. Moreover, following the lead of the Maldives, small islands such as Cyprus and Malta should contribute to efforts to reduce the threat of global warming. As the Foreign Minister of the Maldives recently mentioned at the Symposium on Sustainable Energy Options for Small Island States in New York (Jameel, 1998), while 'no state would be immune from the hazards of climate change' it is islands and 'low-lying areas that would be most affected'.

Note

1. It could be noted that Theroux was equally dismissive of most other Mediterranean destinations.

References

Armsden, A. (1998) Treasure Island. *Geographical*, 70(7): 56–9.

Balm, R. (1995) *Malta*. Blacksburg, VA: McDonald and Woodward.

Black, A. (1996) Negotiating the tourist gaze: the example of Malta. In J. Boissevain (ed.), *Coping with Tourists: European Reactions to Mass Tourism*. Oxford: Berghahn Books (112–42).

Boers, H. and Bosch, M. (1994) *The Earth as a Holiday Resort: An Introduction to Tourism and the Environment*. Utrecht: Netherlands Institute of Tourism and Transport Studies.

Boissevain, J. (1996) 'But we live here!' Perspectives on cultural tourism in Malta. In L. Briguglio, R. Butler, D. Harrison and W.L. Filho (eds), *Sustainable Tourism in Islands and Small States: Case Studies*. London: Pinter (220–40).

Bosselman, F.P., Peterson, C.A. and McCarthy, C. (1999) *Managing Tourism Growth: Issues and Applications*. Washington, DC: Island Press.

Briguglio, L. and Vella, L. (1995) The competitiveness of the Maltese Islands in Mediterranean international tourism. In M. Conlin and T. Baum (eds), *Island Tourism: Management Principles and Practice*. Chichester: John Wiley (133–47).

Brydone, P. (1792) *A Tour through Sicily and Malta*. London: J. Johnson.

Buckley, R.C. and Aranjo, G.F. (1997) Environmental management performance in tourism accommodation. *Annals of Tourism Research*, 24(2): 465–9.

Butler, R.W. (1997) Modelling tourism development. In S. Wahab and J.J. Pigram (eds), *Tourism Development and Growth: The Challenge of Sustainability*. London: Routledge (109–25).

Butler, R.W. (1980) The concept of a tourist area cycle of evolution: implications for management of resources. *Canadian Geographer*, 24(1): 5–12.

Collins, A. (1999) Tourism development and natural capital. *Annals of Tourism Research*, 26(1): 98–109.

Cypriot Council of Ministers (1990) *Control Measures Relating to Tourism Development and the Supply of New Bed Spaces*. Decision no. 34,544. Nicosia, Cyprus: Secretariat of Council of Ministers.

Cyprus Tourism Organization (1990) *New Tourism Policy*. Nicosia, Cyprus: Cyprus Tourism Organization.

Cyprus Tourism Organization (1998) *Annual Report*. Nicosia, Cyprus: Cyprus Tourism Organization.

de Kadt, E. (1990) *Making the Alternative Sustainable: Lessons from Development for Tourism*. Brighton: Institute of Development Studies.

1st European Conference on Sustainable Island Development (1997) European island agenda: operational fields. http://www.insula.org/field.htm.

Economist, The (1998) Malta changes its mind, again. 12 September, 348(8085): 58.

European Union (1998a) *Agenda 2000 Enlargement: Regular Report 1998 from the Commission on Cyprus's Progress towards Accession*. Bulletin of the EU Supplement 15/98. Brussels: European Union.

European Union (1998b) *Agenda 2000 Enlargement: Progress made by the Candidate Countries towards Accession*. Bulletin of the EU Supplement 4/98. Brussels: European Union.

Foundation for the Revival of Laona (1993) *Paphos, Laona Project: Interim Report Phase IV (1993–94)*. Limassol, Cyprus: Laona Foundation.

Gordon, M. (1998) Malta: haven for the non-heroic traveler. *Travel and Leisure*, 28(8): 76–85.

Gortazar, L. and Cipriano, M. (1999) *Tourism and Sustainable Development: From Theory to Practice – The Island Experience*. Tenerife, Canary Islands: Insula – International Scientific Council for Island Development http://www.insula.org/pdf/tursus.pdf.

Government of Republic of Cyprus (1990) *Town and Country Planning Law*. Nicosia, Cyprus: Government Publications.

Grossman, C.L. (1998) Malta's feminine mystique: ancient fertility goddesses attract more visitors to Mediterranean temples. *USA Today*, 11 September: 5D.

Guttman, R. (1999) Island of calm boasts lively activities. *Europe*, 384: 32–3.

Holcomb, B. (1995) Time out or going native: benefits of seasonality in tourism. Unpublished paper presented at the Annual Meeting of the Association of American Geographers, Chicago, March.

Hunter, C.J. (1995) On the need to reconceptualize sustainable tourism development. *Journal of Sustainable Tourism*, 3: 155–65.

Ioannides, D. (1995) A flawed implementation of sustainable tourism: the experience of Akamas, Cyprus. *Tourism Management*, 16(8): 583–92.

Ioannides, D. (2001) The dynamics and effects of tourism evolution in the divided island of Cyprus. In Y. Apostolopoulos, P. Loukissas and L. Leontidou (eds), *Mediterranean Tourism: Facets of Socioeconomic Development and Cultural Change*. London: Routledge.

Ioannides, D. and Apostolopoulos, Y. (1999) Political instability, war, and tourism in Cyprus: effects, management, and prospects for recovery. *Journal of Travel Research*, 38(1): 51–6.

Jameel, F. (1998) Keynote Address. Symposium on Sustainable Energy Options for Small Island States, New York.
http://www.climate.org/conferences/SmallIslandStatesRock10.../

Jensen, L. (1989) Cyprus: boom in tourism, battle on the environment. *World Development*, 2: 10–12.

Karouzis, G. (1999) *Contemporary Geography of Cyprus (vol. 3): Economic Geography of Cyprus*. Nicosia, Cyprus: Centre of Studies, Research, and Publications.

Lawson, F. (1995) *Hotels and Resorts: Planning, Design and Refurbishment*. Oxford: Butterworth-Heinemann.

Lockhart, D.G. (1994) Tourism in Northern Cyprus: patterns, policies, and prospects. *Tourism Management*, 15(5): 370–9.

MacGill, T. (1839) *A Handbook, or Guide, for Strangers Visiting Malta*. Malta: Luigi Tonna.

Malta Ecological Foundation (1999a) BBQs – Are you a Pig?
http://www.geocities.com/rainforest/8076/

Malta Ecological Foundation (1999b) Shoot only photos.
http://www.geocities.com/rainforest/8076/

Malta Ecological Foundation (1999c) Use solar energy.
http://www.geocities.com/rainforest/8076/

Malta Independent, The (1996) Amended plans fail to impress Munxar Protection Committee, 25 February: 5.

Malta Tourism Authority (1999) *Tourism Statistics*.
http://www.tourism.org.mt/Statistics/

Mansfeld, Y. and Kliot, N. (1996) The tourism industry in the partitioned island of Cyprus. In A. Pizam and Y. Mansfeld (eds), *Tourism, Crime and International Security Issues*. London: Wiley (187–202).

Markwick, M.C. (2000) Golf tourism development, stakeholders, differing discourses and alternative agendas: the case of Malta. *Tourism Management*, 21: 515–24.

Middleton, V.T.C. and Hawkins, R. (1998) *Sustainable Tourism*. Oxford: Butterworth-Heinemann.

Murdoch, A. (1998) Service centre Cyprus. *Management Today*, January: 74–80.

North Cyprus Home Page (1997) General information.
http://www.emu.edu.tr/trnc/index.html (29 June 1997).

Panayiotou, T. (1989) Tourism and environmental impact assessment: towards a new tourism policy for Cyprus. Unpublished paper.

Rocks, D. (1998) Sale of hotel chain in Czech Republic sparks diplomatic fight involving U.S. *Wall Street Journal*. 1 April.

Smith, B. (1997) Water: a critical resource. In R. King, L. Proudfoot and B. Smith (eds), *The Mediterranean: Environment and Society*. London: Arnold (227–51).

Sunday Times of Malta, The (1996) New campaign highlights value of tourism to all. 24 March: 2.

Tabatchnaia-Tamirisa, N. *et al.* (1997) Energy and tourism in Hawaii. *Annals of Tourism Research*, 24(2): 390–401.

Theroux, P. (1995) *The Pillars of Hercules: A Grand Tour of the Mediterranean*. London: Hamish Hamilton.

Times of Malta, The (1995) Assistance to small hotels. 19 October: 1.

UNESCO Commission on Sustainable Development: Addendum (1996b) *Sustainable Tourism Development in Small Island Developing States*. New York: UNESCO.

United Nations Development Program (1999) *Human Development Report 1999*. New York: Oxford University Press.

United Nations Economic and Social Council (UNESCO) Commission on Sustainable Development (1996a) *Progress in the Implementation of the Programme of Action for the Sustainable Development of Small Island States*. New York: UNESCO.

Vassiliou, G. (1995) Tourism and sustainable development: lessons from the Cyprus experience. In UNU World Institute for Development Economics Research. *Small Islands, Big Issues: Crucial Issues in the Sustainable Development of Small Developing Islands*. Helsinki: The United Nations University (38–62).

Wall, G. (1997) Sustainable development – unsustainable development. In S. Wahab and J.J. Pigram (eds), *Tourism Development and Growth: The Challenge of Sustainability*. London: Routledge (33–49).

Whitman, W. (1998) Mediterranean hot spot. *National Geographic Traveler*, 15(6): EA2.

Wilkinson, P.F. (1999) Caribbean cruise tourism: delusion? illusion? *Tourism Geographies*, 1(3): 261–82.

World Bank (1992) *Republic of Cyprus: Environmental Review and Recommendations*. Washington, DC: International Bank for Reconstruction and Development.

Xara Palace Web Page (1999) http://www.xarapalace.com.mt

Epilogue
New Directions for
Mediterranean Tourist Islands

13

Tourist Migration, Public Health, and Sustainable Development in the Insular Mediterranean

Yorghos Apostolopoulos and Sevil Sonmez

Introduction

Human migration has been the pathway of epidemics throughout recorded history and continues to shape the emergence, frequency, and diffusion of infections in geographic regions and populations (Wilson, 1995). Ironically, while the sustainability of tourism (the world's largest peacetime migration) and consequently of tourist regions requires the control of the spread of infectious diseases and epidemics, travel actually creates the conditions that facilitate their very emergence. Paradoxically, the association between tourism and potential health risks does not only pose a detriment to tourism viability, but it also constitutes an anathema for a sector that is devoted to the promotion of pleasure.

The Mediterranean remains the leading tourist destination despite gradual shifts to other less 'spoiled' regions such as Southeast Asia and the Pacific. The lucrative tourism sector has transformed the socio-economic, cultural, and physical spheres of the coastal and insular Mediterranean so much so that it has become entirely reliant upon the industry. At the same time, massive growth with extreme temporal and spatial concentration has brought about adverse ramifications for the region's environment. As a result of intense consumer, legislative and commercial pressures, the Mediterranean tourist industry and local governments have realized the importance of environmental impact assessment and ecological audit as management and planning tools to be used in mitigating negative impacts (Apostolopoulos, Loukissas and Leontidou, 2001).

As with any other form of population mobility, the tourist influx to Mediterranean islands demonstrates extraordinary public health repercussions not only for the ecosystems of the receiving societies but also for those of traveller-generating regions. Potential problems are also likely to manifest themselves as severe legal consequences for the tourism sector – particularly law suits against travel intermediaries held liable for affected travellers. Considering tourism's vulnerability to internal and external shocks (i.e., recession, geopolitical conflicts, natural disasters, epidemic disease), the welfare of the littoral Mediterranean may be underpinned and ultimately constrained by neglect of the critical importance of social and geographic ecology. The epidemiological and public health ramifications of transient tourist populations exposed to unprecedented health hazards necessitate the widespread use of environmental risk management.

This chapter examines the tourism sector of the insular Mediterranean in the midst of a prolonged crisis of the conventional (mass charter) tourism model, intense globalization and restructuring trends, growing consumer demand for high-quality travel health information, industry concerns by consumer legislators and the risks of medical litigation, as well as an upsurge of infectious diseases (Apostolopoulos and Sonmez, 2000b). Within this broad framework, the chapter critically reviews the multifaceted dimensions of the health hazards of international travel, assesses tourist health in the littoral Mediterranean, and appraises its consequences on the sustainability of the tourism sector. Finally, with regard to the planning and development of a sustainable tourism sector in Mediterranean islands, the chapter stresses the critical significance of travel health promotion as well as the imperative need for emergency mitigation planning, ongoing disease prevention, and hazard mapping and surveillance, bolstered by collaborative medical and inter-disciplinary social scientific research.

Travel, Health Risks, and Sustainable Development

Human mobility and health hazards

Historically, population movement (temporary or permanent) has been stimulated by necessity (i.e., to flee from famine and over-population, or to seek safety and better living conditions), pleasure, or business. Travellers (as individuals or groups) have grown to comprise an enormously hetero-geneous group numbering nearly one billion a year (Gushulak, 1999), including refugees, missionaries, merchant marines, students, immigrants, truck drivers, seafarers, fishermen, pilots, temporary workers, pilgrims, Peace Corps workers, commercial sex workers, military personnel, diplomats and representatives of international organizations, natural disaster victims, pleasure travellers, and adventure-seeking tourists, to name just a few. Approximately 2 million people migrate and permanently resettle outside their country of origin, over 12 million individuals are forced out of their countries, over 20 million get displaced within their own nations, nearly 1 million individuals seek asylum annually, and over 90 million people, mostly from developing countries, work either legally or illegally in other countries (United Nations High Commission for Refugees, 1998; Gushulak, 1999). Further, tourist destinations have been flooded by 625 million international tourists, not to mention the worldwide boom in domestic tourism (estimated to be ten-fold greater than international) (WTO, 2000). Business travel, in its various forms, has grown exponentially to parallel the globalization of the world economy (Shaw and Williams, 1997).

These unprecedented migratory flows (often constituting displacement of people) disperse people to different climatic zones and previously isolated geographic areas. In addition, immense strides in transportation developments and alterations in the underlying natural history of certain diseases collectively exert enormous pressure on ecosystems and subsequently create ideal conditions for the emergence of health hazards and the spread of infectious diseases (Gushulak, 1999). The earth's climatic and geographic evolution can create conditions that favour new or different diseases as well as the re-emergence of past infectious disease threats (Wilson, 1995). The genesis of diseases is attributable to microbial adaptation and change, human demography and behaviour, environmental change, technology and economic development, breakdown in public health measures and surveillance, and international travel and commerce (Wilson *et al.*, 1994). When people migrate, they transport their genetic make-up, their accumulated immunologic experience, their technology, their methods for treating disease, their cultural and behavioural traditions and patterns, their social class, and their resources to previously uninfected regions (Apostolopoulos and Sonmez, 2001).

Throughout history, epidemics and diseases can be traced to population mobility. In the fifth-century BC city–state of Athens, outbreaks of a pneumonia-causing influenza epidemic were associated with travellers from Ethiopia, Egypt, and the Persian Empire (Cossar, 1997). In the twelfth and thirteenth centuries, outbreaks of plague in Venice were linked to the arrival of ships from the east (Reid and Cossar, 1993). Columbus' sailors allegedly brought syphilis back to Europe having acquired it through intercourse with native women during their first trip to America in 1492 (Mulhall, 1996). The subsequent explosion of syphilis in Europe was presumably transported not only by the returning military and sailors, but also by camp followers, traders, pilgrims, and other mobile populations (Mabey and Mayaud, 1997).

In the fourteenth to the sixteenth centuries, explorers from crowded urban centres of Europe brought measles, influenza, mumps, smallpox, tuberculosis, and other infectious diseases to the New World, inflicting disaster upon the native populations of the Americas who had no previous exposure to such infections (Black, 1992). Further, the 1817–1822 and 1826–1832 cholera pandemics that spread across Asia, Africa, Europe, and America are a convincing example of effective dissemination of one pathogen around the world, courtesy of travellers (Cossar, 1997).

More recently, a returning pilgrim from Mecca caused a massive smallpox outbreak in the Former Yugoslavia in the early 1970s (Wilson, 1995). A cholera epidemic in Africa in the 1990s spread along fishing and trading routes while markets, funerals, and refugee camps facilitated the spread of the infection (Glass *et al.*, 1991). The sudden large-scale movement of approximately one million Rwandan refugees into Zaire in 1994 resulted in the death of nearly 50,000 during the first month, as epidemics of cholera and dysentery swept through refugee camps (Goma Epidemiology Group, 1994). The mobility patterns of migrant workers in southern Africa and the migration of Rwandan refugees to Tanzania have profoundly influenced the epidemiology of sexually transmitted diseases (STDs) and particularly the human immunodeficiency virus/acquired immunodeficiency virus syndrome (HIV/AIDS) epidemic in Sub-Saharan Africa (Bartholet, 2000). Because the prevalence rate of venereal disease is much higher among seafarers and long-distance truck drivers compared with other male populations, the epidemiology of much of the HIV epidemic in Africa can be traced along major highways (Stratford *et al.*, 2000). The foregoing exemplify the historic relationship between population mobility and public health.

Insular mass tourism and sustainability?

Early human mobility (e.g., need-based movement of hunter-gatherers, nomadic trade) has led the way for 'exploration' during the Renaissance, to the age of travel of the bourgeoisie, to tourism of the proletariat movement (Fussell, 1989) and finally to the present age of mass tourism, which has become the predominant travel form of the post-World War II era. Increasing interventionism of international financial organizations in the policy-making decisions of national governments during the past 50 years has precipitated the adoption of tourism as a quick development tool, particularly by developing nations, a trend which is paralleled in insular destinations (Apostolopoulos, Loukissas and Leontidou, 2001). The simultaneous growth of the middle class and technological revolution have helped usher in the massive explosion of tourism during the second half of the twentieth century which, in turn, has had dramatic impacts on the life chances and welfare of developed and developing regions alike.

Conservative estimates project that the annual movement of 625 million international tourists will grow at 4.2 per cent, surpassing 1.6 billion by 2020 (WTO, 2000). Tourism holds a leading position in the world economy and constitutes a sector with immense long-term growth potential aided by continuous worldwide expansion of the services sector. The tourist industry, despite setbacks of the 1990s (i.e., collapse and subsequent instability of Eastern Europe; Persian Gulf War; civil war in the Former Yugoslavia; and financial turmoils in Southeast Asia, Japan, Russia, and Latin America and their subsequent sociopolitical ramifications) and a fluid post-Cold War international state of affairs, has evolved into the world's pre-eminent economic sector. It is estimated that, by the end of 2000, tourism will have generated over $3.7 trillion in gross output (contributing over 12 per cent to world GDP) and over 193 million jobs (over 8.3 per cent of global employment) (World Travel and Tourism Council/Travel Business Round-table, 1999).

Although tourism has long been advocated as an effective development tool, the neoliberal philosophy of 'outward-oriented growth strategies' (Brohman, 1996) has helped to promote tourism (among other new growth and non-traditional export sectors) as a panacea, particularly during the past two decades. Because sweeping globalization trends in international trade have not bypassed the tourist industry, the hegemony of tourist transnationals has weakened the negotiating power (and ultimate benefits) of developing nations by manipulating tourist flows, controlling managerial and marketing expertise, and regulating immense financial resources, a pattern that also occurs at insular destinations (Apostolopoulos and Gayle, 2001). Unprecedented tourist flux and investment during the past five decades have rendered considerable short-term positive change for developed nations, while simultaneously inflicting long-term negative effects on peripheral and semiperipheral regions which are heavily dependent on tourism (Apostolopoulos, 1996). These negative effects, particularly in insular regions, include spatial and socio-economic polarization, uneven development, ecological degradation, domination of regional political economies, inequality and economic dependency, leakages of earnings, lack of articulation with other domestic sectors, management repatriation, rising alienation among locals, and structural under-development (Apostolopoulos and Gayle, 2001). Such negative externalities of tourism have eclipsed the potential for equitable social, sectoral, and regional distribution of the costs and benefits of growth at islands, where tourism was expected to demonstrate the greatest positive impact.

Increasingly, globalization guides the creation of tourist destinations in developing regions (where most insular destinations are) as well as the notions of sustainability – albeit disproportionately for developing nations. At the same time, concerns for the health of the planet have fuelled the emergence of globalized environmental politics. In the current frenzy of globalization, governments, scholars, cultures, interest groups, and business people from industrialized nations impose their notion of the global economy, culture, politics, and environment on their less developed insular counterparts. Considering the colonizing nature of these views, the need for development that will not undermine the local communities' ecological and social systems is imperative. In this context, the conventional model of mass tourism must undergo an overhaul in order to assure significant economic, social, and cultural transformations in the geography of production and consumption; to encourage qualitative shifts from mass to more flexible systems of production and organization; to address diversity in traveller preferences; and to facilitate the proliferation of alternative destinations and growth of 'green tourism'. The foregoing actions, which include neoteristic approaches in the search for new tourist markets and in the development of new tourist products as well as improvements in management and marketing approaches, involve structural changes in the composition, articulation, and spatial distribution of tourist consumption patterns *vis-à-vis* tourist markets and products (Apostolopoulos, Sonmez and Timothy, 2001). Such actions should further involve interregional differentiation, diverse regional tourism production, and maximized economic benefits (in both the informal and formal sectors) over an entire region. All of these could be accomplished by initiating effective interlinks between tourism and other economic sectors, by equity and encouragement of local involvement, by environmental considerations in policy-making and tourist product development, and by continuity and adjustability of a region's tourism development within its wider environment (Apostolopoulos, Loukissas and Leontidou, 2001).

Health risks of tourist migration and sustainability

Although pleasure and business travel constitute only a fraction of total population movement, they play a pivotal role in the emergence and spread of infectious diseases. This type of travel activity sets the stage for intermingling diverse genetic pools and cultures. The public health consequences of such travel affect not only the traveller, but also the population visited, the geographic region generating the travellers, and both ecosystems in ways previously unknown and unanticipated (Apostolopoulos and Sonmez, 2000b). The global leisure revolution, ongoing improvements in transport media, and movement between diverse climatic zones (exemplified by global warming and climate change) have exacerbated the vulnerability of humans to infectious diseases. Beyond the illnesses induced by travel itself (i.e., motion sickness, altitude effects, injuries, jet lag), the exposure to unfamiliar infectious agents and risky behaviours (i.e., substance abuse, sexual experimentation), which are heightened by the vacation setting and culture, have the potential to cause enormous health strains on the parties involved (Apostolopoulos and Sonmez, 2000a). Epidemiological studies have supported the fact that infections imported to a country via returning international travellers include malaria, HIV/AIDS, alimentary symptoms (diarrhoea and vomiting), cholera, dysentery, hepatitis, rabies, various STDs, tuberculosis, and typhoid (Steffen, 1997). Several of these are difficult to diagnose immediately due to lengthy incubation periods. Usually, travel advisories counsel travellers about potential health hazards at tourist destinations and offer precautionary methods to take while in the region.

In several cases, organized journeys have been cancelled as a result of epidemic outbreaks (i.e., the 1994 pneumonic plague in India) (Grabowski and Chatterjee, 1997).

Health risks differ by types of travel. Most at-risk travellers include package holidaymakers, inexperienced travellers, travellers to African countries posing significant health threats, summer travellers, smokers, youth travellers, individuals travelling alone (i.e., business travellers, military personnel, sailors, immigrants), single travellers, individuals who practise unprotected or casual sex, those with multiple sex partners, and those who abuse substances (Cossar, 1997). Diarrhoea, malaria, acute febrile respiratory track infection, hepatitis A and B, gonorrhoea, animal bites with rabies risk, dengue fever, typhoid, HIV infection, poliomyelitis, legionella infection, and cholera have been reported more frequently in less developed regions, although they also were found elsewhere (Steffen, 1997). As a result, many contemporary tourists have taken on the role formerly attributed primarily to armies – in spreading STDs (De Schryver and Meheus, 1989).

Lifestyle has a bearing on the emergence and spread of epidemics via travel (Apostolopoulos and Sonmez, 2000a); however, the very space of the tourist resort provides a conducive setting where personal and social moral codes are suspended, behavioural norms and constraints are removed, and inhibitions evaporate (Ford and Eiser, 1996; Maticka-Tyndale *et al.*, 1998). In addition, prior experience with risky behaviours, social norms of acceptable behaviour, peer influences, and situational expectations play pivotal roles in travellers' propensity for health-risk activities (Apostolopoulos *et al.*, 2000a, b, c, d). Subsequently, the disinhibiting nature of the vacation setting perpetuates higher risk-taking. Package holidaymakers, in particular, find their 'liminal' zone – where strict social conventions and constraints are relaxed under the exigencies of travel and anonymity, and freedom from community scrutiny prevails – while on vacation (Shields, 1992). Tourist destinations operate as 'action spaces', which are dedicated to pleasure, fun, thrills, and excitement, and which allow tourists to taste adventure and risk they might not experience in their daily lives. The 'holiday romance syndrome' aptly describes the conditions for heightened behavioural risks (of contracting STDs, HIV, and HBV), which result from the overlap of high alcohol consumption, drug experimentation, intravenous drug use, and casual sex (Apostolopoulos and Sonmez, 2000a). Tourist destinations often function as environments for 'role reversals' where primarily single, unaccompanied travellers (Wickens, 1997) are more likely to have sexual encounters (often unprotected), along with opportunities for excessive drinking and drug experimentation (Apostolopoulos *et al.*, 2000a, b, c, d).

The foregoing risky behaviour can be interpreted under the spectrum of broad approaches to leisure motivation such as the 'compensatory leisure hypothesis' *vis-à-vis* the 'spillover leisure hypothesis' (Pearce, 1982). The former argues that people seek types of stimulation in their leisure environments that are the opposite of those in their work environments, whereas the latter supports the theory that individuals seek the same types of stimulation in both environments. Tourist motives can be viewed as an interplay between these two approaches. However, the debate can be extended further to whether health-risk behaviour during one's vacation can be viewed as a representation of personal values and attitudes, or should be regarded in terms of situational factors of the vacation environment. The school of thought, which purports that general value systems influence behaviour across various environmental settings (i.e., work, vacation), has also led to the empirically supported argument that casual or permissive sexual attitudes in the vacation environment are not simply a function of the situation (Eiser and Ford, 1995).

Prostitution's link to international travel and tourism, where travelling sex workers and tourists seeking commercial sex opportunities converge, constitutes an explosive health hazard (Apostolopoulos, Sonmez and Timothy, 2001; Broring, 1997; Mulhall, 1996). Sex tourism and tourism-oriented prostitution have become increasingly important topics partly due to the proliferation of STDs and partly due to the growing reliance of some nations on income generated by tourism and tourism-related activities (Apostolopoulos, Sonmez and Timothy, 2001). Sex tourism varies from organized package tours that include exotic sexual opportunities (i.e., tours to Cuba, Thailand, Philippines) to incidental 'romantic' encounters between the tourist and the 'native'. Despite variations, these forms of tourism not only incorporate men and women as either tourists, clients, or sex workers, but, distressingly, children as sex workers (Kempadoo, 1999).

Skyrocketing costs of travel-related health problems in developed tourist generating countries (Reid and Cossar, 1993) along with enormous problems faced by host destinations (irrespective of development level) demand a serious and effective approach to these problems. Traveller-induced transmission of infectious diseases to locals, vandalism and recreational crime resulting from intoxication, environmental damage/pollution, and adverse impacts on locals' quality of life (i.e., crime, safety, health, prostitution) constitute a social phenomenon worthy of study and action. Not surprisingly, any perceived association between public health hazards and tourist destinations can quickly undermine those destinations' sustainability. In the age of increasing STDs and AIDS, tourism has become a controversial business, whereas HIV has heightened xenophobia (as tourists are presumed transmitters of infectious disease). Thus, tourism-dependent nations face a serious dilemma: to downplay the threat of AIDS or to protect public health by acknowledging risks (Lewis and Bailey, 1992/1993).

The negative effects of associating a destination with health risks can reach new levels among international tour operators and insurance companies. This detrimental association can burden the destination with a negative image, can affect prospective travellers' destination choices, and impair locals' quality of life. As a result, the receiving destination's sustainability can be jeopardized and prospects for overall sustainable development can be threatened. With these in mind, tourism development should aim for equitably distributed economic growth with minimal sociocultural and ecological consequences for the present – without compromising the ability of future generations to meet their own needs. Effective translation of the concept of sustainable development into action has been elusive. Barriers such as fragmented governmental tourism policies isolated from national development (multi-sectoral) policies, varying and often conflicting stakeholders' perspectives on tourism development, conflicting and often short-sighted governmental and non-governmental perspectives on tourism, and different levels of tourism and overall development create challenges for tourism proponents in their efforts to offer clearly defined approaches to achieving sustainable tourism development objectives (Apostolopoulos and Sonmez, 2000b). Bringing together diverse groups – such as tourism developers, tour operators, government officials and community leaders – for a consensus on how to achieve economic growth, social equity, and environmental protection without compromising the sector and alarming the community at large with public health concerns is a serious challenge. The destination's phase in its life-cycle (exploration, involvement, development, consolidation, stagnation, rejuvenation, or decline) (Butler, 1980) is likely to influence stakeholders' views as well. Spatial and temporal contingencies influence stakeholders' perspectives and the resulting policy directions.

Tourist Health in Europe's 'Pleasure Periphery'

Mass tourism in the insular Mediterranean

At the dawn of the twenty-first century, the Mediterranean region remains the world's leading tourist destination, accounting for approximately 40 per cent of all international tourist arrivals and 30 per cent of all tourism revenues, employing over 5 million people, and representing 13 per cent of Mediterranean countries' exports and 23 per cent of trade in services (Apostolopoulos, Loukissas and Leontidou, 2001). Aggregate numbers of tourist arrivals in the 21 Mediterranean countries, which rose from 86 million in 1975, to 125 million in 1985 to over 200 million in 1990, are expected to surpass 250 million by the end of 2000 (Jenner and Smith, 1993). The Mediterranean's over 40-year dominance of the global tourist market has begun to fade, however, as the region loses market share to other geographic areas.

The region's mainland coasts have long been enormously popular, but the tourist explosion of recent decades and its analogous increase in reputation have been observed in numerous islands. The increasing popularity of these islands is linked as much to traveller expectations for authentic and less commercialized experiences as to their physical attributes. Unlike the Pacific and Caribbean insular regions (natural competitors with Mediterranean islands), where islands are mostly politically autonomous or remote outposts of metropolitan countries, all but two Mediterranean islands belong to sovereign states. Literally thousands of islands are disbursed throughout the Mediterranean basin.[1]

The Mediterranean islands have always been viewed as part of the European periphery, exhibiting symptoms akin to those in small developing economies (i.e., Aegean, Aeolian, or Adriatic islands). Historically, these tourist destinations have represented the poorest locales of their respective countries and have experienced challenges of scarce human and natural resources, economic underdevelopment, and inadequate infrastructure and institutions. Their natural dependence on external agents has been further exacerbated by the adoption of a monocrop economic sector, based on mass charter tourism, to serve as the cornerstone of their development plans. As a result, Europe's political and economic periphery has gradually been transformed into its 'pleasure periphery', catering to sun-seeking package tourists, particularly from northern European countries (Apostolopoulos, Loukissas and Leontidou, 2001).

Despite the fact that most Mediterranean islands are newcomers to the transnational tourism arena, they have experienced phenomenal growth, as a result of aggressive funding from national governments and European Union-sponsored development programmes aimed at the south (Apostolopoulos, Loukissas and Leontidou, 2001). Because of this increased development, some Mediterranean islands face problems that threaten their sustained growth and long-term welfare, such as accessibility, geomorphology, adverse sociocultural ramifications, marked alterations in fragile marine and terrestrial ecosystems, ineffective public policies, spatial and socioeconomic polarization, and tour operator hegemony (Apostolopoulos and Gayle, 2001). The unprecedented growth in tourist activity has resulted in a surplus of accommodation and its subsequent consequences, in inflationary pressures causing dramatic rises in costs of living, in labour and other resource shortages, and in a lack of integrating tourism with other sectors (Apostolopoulos, Loukissas and Leontidou, 2001). Mediterranean islands are also vulnerable to substitutability (with not only other coastal Mediterranean destinations, but also other insular regions such as the Caribbean and South Pacific) and an over-dependence on tourists who originate from a limited number of countries (i.e., France, Germany, Britain and Scandinavia).

The role played by rapid tourism development in the improvement of locals' living standards, through invisible contributions, employment opportunities, and infrastructural developments, certainly cannot be underestimated; however, the foregoing challenges need immediate attention. The entire tourism system of the Mediterranean islands illustrates the imperative need for restructuring, reorganizing, and modernizing that would occur within the framework of a tourism philosophy that focuses on sustained and widespread long-term development. This change is of primary importance, especially because several Mediterranean islands have already reached the 'consolidation' phase (in some cases 'stagnation') of their life-cycles. Therefore, it is crucial to 're-draw' tourist destinations based on a comprehensive sustainable development model. Efforts to enhance Mediterranean islands' competitiveness as tourist destinations demonstrate policymakers' surprising inability to differentiate between developing sustainable tourism and developing tourism within a broader sustainable development framework.

Tourist health in the Mediterranean

Just as Thomas Cook's innovative use of rail and water transportation media transformed the tourist industry by developing organized excursions in the nineteenth century, the introduction of jet aircrafts in 1957 and jumbo jets in 1970 revolutionized tourist movements and precipitated the tourist explosion of the late twentieth century, which has, in turn, created circumstances to foster potential disease and epidemic spread. Health risks for travellers naturally vary by geographic region; those in the insular Mediterranean are both qualitatively and quantitatively distinct from those in subtropical and tropical destinations (i.e., Caribbean, South Pacific, Southeast Asia).

Mediterranean island groups are either territories of developed European Union nations or developed island states (with the exemption of the Dalmatian islands of Croatia) with high health standards and low health risks, where geomorphology and climate do not constitute significant health hazards (Centers for Disease Control and Prevention, 2000). Although health hazards for travellers in the littoral Mediterranean are not primarily determined by geographic location, endemic diseases, or associated epidemics (often associated with tropical areas) – and the Mediterranean islands constitute overall 'safe havens' for travellers – as with all geographic regions, irrespective of tourism's presence, the Mediterranean islands have endemic diseases and infectious agents that are confined either by geography or to specific population groups. These include hepatitis A or hepatitis B (immune globulin) caused by viruses, bacteria, or parasites contaminating water or food and leading to severe diarrhoea; cholera, typhoid and enteroviral diseases caused by salmonella and escherichia coli found in raw seafood (Saliba, 1990).

The Mediterranean Sea, no doubt, constitutes the main attraction for the millions of travellers who visit the region's islands. In addition to accepted benefits (i.e., solar vitamin D activation, swimming, water-based recreation), various health hazards are also linked to coastal activities. Experts have pointed to the detrimental effects of excessive exposure to the sun (i.e., subsequent dangers of sunburn, skin cancers, weakened human immunity mechanisms caused by short-wavelength UV rays); poor recreational water quality (i.e., gastrointestinal and respiratory symptoms, skin irritation, external ear infection, gynaecological infections); water sports accidents (i.e., drowning, sailing accidents, aquatic biotoxins risks including poisonous fish and jellyfish); seafood safety, with particular emphasis on shellfish, due to marine pollution (i.e., food-borne infections and intoxications); inadequate medical care on cruise ships and at accommodation establishments (i.e., motion sickness, man-made hazards, sanitary hazards) (Page *et al.*, 1994; WHO, 1994; Wilks and Atherton, 1994).

Mediterranean islands are associated with travellers' risky behavioural patterns involving casual/unprotected sexual activity and substance abuse during vacation. Not unusual for coastal tourist destinations (regardless of tourist arrival figures), the Mediterranean islands attract tourists from various sociodemographic groups who seek primarily adventure and fun. Therefore, the well-documented and alarming association between tourist migration, alcohol and drug intoxication, risky sexual behaviour, and other infectious diseases should not come as a surprise. Tourists vacationing at Mediterranean islands engage in these risky activities in the context of pronounced transformations of norms and behaviour resulting from the atmosphere of 'disinhibition' attributed to the vacation setting. Various hedonistic and risky behaviours, on the part of both locals and tourists, have been observed at Mediterranean vacation settings: vacationers (or locals) routinely seeking out sexual liaisons with strangers and indulging in sexual activities on the beach (Wickens, 1997); Greeks practising their infamous 'national sport' of *kamaki* (aggressive pursuit of women with sexual goals analogous to 'harpooning') and 'ravers' pursuing sexual pleasure through unprotected sex often with multiple partners (Wickens, 1997); the prevalence of 'sun, sex, and sangria' tourists in Malta (Clark and Clift, 1996; Page *et al.*, 1994); destinations (i.e., Ibiza and Mykonos) catering to a gay travel market that are conducive to risky sexual practices (Clift and Forrest, 1999a, b); and excessive drinking leading to hazardous driving, recreational crime, and vandalism (Apostolopoulos and Sonmez, 1999). Still, there is an inexplicable paucity of relevant epidemiological and socio-behavioural studies on the health risks faced by mass tourists in an area that is the oldest and most advanced tourist region in the world and where high volumes of tourist arrivals occur in extremely small areas.

Other worrisome health hazards emerge from the tourist-based commercial sex industry, which is fuelled by the eagerness of certain travellers to seek out commercial sex opportunities while on vacation and which provides prostitutes with ample opportunities to transmit STDs to travellers. The commercial sex industry also targets military base personnel (Enloe, 1989) of which there are many in the insular Mediterranean (i.e., British or American military bases in Malta, Cyprus, Crete; Turkish military in northern Cyprus, as well as national military installations), seafarers, seasonal workers, and business travellers. The acute importance of regulation and health surveillance of the commercial sex industry, particularly as it intersects with travellers, is self-evident.

The public health ramifications of social behaviour at Mediterranean islands clearly impart responsibility to all parties involved in tourism, hospitality, and public health (WHO, 1994). International health and development organizations, individual countries' health ministries, the tourist industry, and the scientific community should be held accountable for epidemiological surveillance of both environmental and behavioural hazards and for disseminating pertinent information to the travelling public as well as host communities. Public health organizations need to establish regulations to maintain healthy tourist areas, to mitigate health hazards in risky areas, to provide efficient medical services, to conduct ongoing hygienic surveillance of food and drink, and to oversee raw sewage disposal (re-use rather than discard) – among numerous other necessary tasks. Directors of tourism bureaux and local governments should establish proper building codes and health education, cruise ship owners and operators should establish and monitor hygiene standards, conduct ongoing staff training and make available medical advice. Further, the particularly serious responsibility of the travelling public should not be overlooked. These individuals need to evaluate risks, obtain pre-travel health advice and education, and monitor their health behaviour (WHO, 1994).

Socio-medical Research and Sustainable Tourism in the Insular Mediterranean

The multi-factorial globalization process and its subsequent impacts on demographics, economics, communication, transportation, and relocated work opportunities have dramatically transformed global mobility patterns (International Organization for Migration, 2000). Further, there are clear indications that as human mobility intensifies over the coming years, it will launch immense public health ramifications. Tourists as well as host populations are increasingly exposed to new health problems as the circulation of pathogens and vectors increases due to intersecting epidemiological and sociocultural boundaries (Cossar, 1997). Discrepancies in the level of knowledge and types of beliefs, attitudes towards diseases and health, and expectations for and access to health services or information are likely to exist between travellers' home communities and the destinations they visit. Assessing and monitoring factors that affect health and health services for international tourists are crucial for anticipating and proposing changes and adaptations to tourists' health needs. A clear understanding of the related causes and risk factors is critical for targeting adapted preventive interventions, especially since tourist health is practically treated as a hidden dimension of tourist migration and is consequently neglected.

In situations where numerous environmental hazards need to be controlled and few resources are available, considerations of preventive measures intended to improve tourist health and well-being must focus on the seriousness and magnitude of the problem, feasibility of intervention, analysis of hazard control, and a community's readiness to adopt the intervention or behavioural change (Philipp *et al.*, 1999). Tourist health promotion presents a definite challenge for the tourist industry – particularly for travel agents and tour operators who may not wish to share public health risks associated with proposed travel activity/destinations, public health officials, such as the WHO (with expansive global responsibilities), national governments (and their responsibility to advise and caution), and tourist industry representatives (to provide travellers with complete and necessary information to help protect their health and avoid hazards).

Health promotion, advice, services, and protection of tourists

Although many infectious diseases are now preventable through vaccines, there are several obstacles to efficient vaccinations for travellers, including lack of awareness among travellers and lack of knowledge among travel health practitioners. In the case of non-vaccine preventable infections, it is imperative for travellers to be provided with useful advice about prophylaxis, where appropriate, and risk avoidance, when not.

Tourist health promotion remains a relatively uncharted area for the vast majority of those involved in the tourism sector and public health. Health promotion includes prevention, education and protection (Tannahill, 1985). These, in turn, generate preventive services (immunization); preventive health education (influencing lifestyle); preventive health protection (controlling legal or fiscal issues); health education for preventive health protection (stimulating a social environment conducive to success of preventive health protection); positive health education (influencing traveller behaviour and helping to develop positive health attributes); positive health protection (applying 'health public policy' to the prevention of ill-health and disease; and health education aimed at positive health protection (raising public awareness and support for health protection measures) (Downie *et al.*, 1993). These principles should ideally be part and parcel of a comprehensive intersectoral agenda for travel health accepted by various stakeholders (tourist industry, national governments, public health organizations, etc.).

Prevention and intervention measures can be classified as pre- and post-travel measures and on-site interventions. Pre-travel measures can provide travellers not only with the necessary immunizations and medications for their protection, but also practical advice and information tailored to the risks that they might face. In the case of Mediterranean islands, pre-travel measures to reduce health risks might involve advice on behavioural modifications, since they constitute a highly difficult yet critical preventive measure for that area. Obstacles, such as lack of awareness in travel health professionals, misconceptions about infections, financial obstacles for countries, and the risk of toxicity and adverse reactions to immunizations, need to be eliminated for successful implementation of preventive measures. In addition to these measures, the usefulness of purchasing medical insurance to cover medical emergencies while abroad needs to be stressed to travellers.

On-site (at the vacation destination) multi-faceted interactive strategies can aim to increase tourist awareness of various health risks. For travellers to the Mediterranean islands, special emphasis should be placed on HIV and sexual health risks and on the problems associated with intravenous drug use and alcohol abuse while on holiday. The clear reticence to stress HIV risks at tourist resorts is rooted, first, in the underlying desire to avoid discouraging potential tourists from visiting particular destinations and, second, in the uncertainty about whether local tourism-oriented HIV prevention strategies are feasible (Ford *et al.*, 1996). Such programmes, however, have the potential to sensitize the public to the dangers of unprotected sexual intercourse in areas with highly mobile populations. Thus, resources should be focused on the subsets of the travelling and local population who are most vulnerable to sexual health risks (i.e., gay locals and tourists, youth travellers, commercial sex tourists and workers, as well as travellers originating from African or eastern European countries). The European project AIDS and Mobility clearly exemplifies a successful HIV/AIDS intervention programme focusing on tourists in the Greek islands along with other mobile groups (Broring, 1997).

Post-travel measures focus on travellers as they return to their places of origin following an insular Mediterranean journey or on outbound Mediterranean tourists returning from travel abroad. Travellers with particular health concerns about having been exposed to sexually transmitted diseases (viral, bacterial, or protozoa caused) or other infections should be encouraged to seek immediate diagnosis and treatment, particularly because they may endanger their own community by going untreated.

To ensure successful and effective implementation of these health promotion measures, seven key principles are proposed (Tones, 1992):

1. Class, ethnicity, gender, and racial equity should oversee provision of health advice and care.
2. Empowering and involving host communities and travellers in their health decisions.
3. Health promotion for travellers should be disseminated as part of an overall public policy that recognizes the link between travel and health.
4. Traveller health services should expand their objectives to encompass broader health issues rather than simply focusing on medical intervention.

5. Intersectoral collaboration for effective health promotion should involve a variety of institutions and organizations (i.e., public health departments, medical centres, health promotion units, travel agents, tour operators, tourism bureaux, local authorities).
6. Educating individuals about empowering personal and social skills that can be used in making responsible health and lifestyle choices.
7. Establishing an international network integrating research findings, health practice advice, and health promotion campaigns.

These principles provide a useful framework for clarifying and enhancing the aims and objectives of travel health promotion.

Planning and developing a sustainable tourism sector

Unprecedented growth of international tourism, globalization trends, global population growth, and increasing global health problems call for drastic public health responses as well as effective tourism management. The global tourist industry may trigger much needed investment in environmental health programmes in order to protect the health of mobile and stationary populations.

Sustainable tourism requires a solid understanding not only of economics and international relations, but also of geo-ecology which underpins and ultimately constrains actual and potential tourism development in the insular Mediterranean. While environmental impact assessments and environmental audits have been routinely utilized as management and planning tools, the epidemiological and public health ramifications of transient tourist populations exposed to unparalleled disease hazards definitely necessitates the widespread use of environmental risk assessment. In this context, sustainable tourism on Mediterranean islands will require an emergency mitigation programme for disease prevention and geomedical surveillance of tourist sending and receiving areas – tasks which cannot be accomplished solely by the medical community.

In the relevant tourism development literature, the issue of health hazards and imported disease at best occupy a distant place behind topics of environmental impacts, socio-economic change, economic restructuring, environment safeguarding, and preserving societies and cultures under the aegis of a new 'ecotourism'. Although the literature addresses the topic almost as an afterthought, the travel industry's responsibility to protect its customers should not be downplayed. Keeping in mind both medical and geomedical information, the medical community should be involved in these changes because of legal liabilities as well as the economic and medical benefits to their own communities.

Those who are responsible for planning and operating sustainable tourist industries would benefit greatly from research in hazard mapping and disease ecology (at both tourist sending and receiving areas), which ultimately ought to become essential components of such activities. In order to safeguard the health of tourists while ensuring tourism sustainability at destinations, especially at potentially 'hazardous' areas, a well-coordinated interdisciplinary approach is needed. In this context, the importance of the contributions of applied medical sociology and geography to the proper development and management of the tourist sector at coastal and insular Mediterranean destinations cannot be overstressed. Other essential tools towards the same end include the employment of traditional cartography and geographical information systems in producing maps that highlight high, medium and low health-risk areas. These techniques, together with wider environmental risk assessment, should eventually become an integral part of the feasibility planning stages of tourism development projects and continue as part of ongoing monitoring, given the mercurial nature of disease and environmental change.

In the era of rapid technological developments, contemporary tourism development requires not only professionalism and planning, but also greater appreciation for the utilization of innovative tools as they have been applied to other, more traditional sectors. The growing awareness of the dangers of HIV/AIDS and other STDs make this even more imperative, especially since such serious health risks can create irreversible problems for the '4S' tourist market of the insular Mediterranean (Fsadni and Selwyn, 1996).

Conclusion

The future is projected to see increasing numbers and varieties of travellers who are moving from disparate areas of origin (and related epidemiological conditions) to an ever-expanding number of destinations. The factors stimulating the mobility or relocation of populations, the nature of the journey itself, and the demographic composition of each subgroup of travellers can essentially determine the health characteristics of populations. Between the trip origin and destination, travellers often cross bio-geological boundaries that demarcate the incidence and prevalence of illness and disease. The health-related consequences associated with travel across these prevalence demarcations may have potential significance. The migration of large numbers of individuals with the sequela of chronic disease can influence the micro-epidemiology of disease in the area of resettlement. Additionally, travellers returning after a prolonged absence may be at unappreciated risk of illness or disease acquisition. As a result, it is anticipated that the study and management of disease and health in mobile populations will be increasingly needed in the foreseeable future.

Tourism is important to the economies of both developing and developed countries. Therefore, the promotion of travel health represents a crucial strategy because subsequent public policies, if properly initiated, could make significant contributions to the maintenance and growth of international economies. While travel health promotion may have the correct intentions, its shortcomings are often due to unplanned and uncoordinated activities within the amorphous, acephalous, and fragmented tourist industry, to the narrowed focus of much contemporary medical education, and to widespread ignorance of medical (disease) geography, and to the associated risks of disease importation and spread from tourist migration.

A significant number of people are affected by the issues raised in this chapter. Many actual and potential tourist destinations are concerned with safety and security problems caused by social unrest, delinquency, terrorism, natural disasters, and health hazards. The medical profession is burdened with the responsibility of prevention through pre-travel immunizations and advice as well as curative interventions when the system fails; however, the true costs are faced by governments and individuals. Ultimate solutions require fresh thinking about disease prevention on a global scale, which will require critical collaboration between researchers (e.g., medical geography, medical sociology, social sciences) and the tourist industry.

Because of increasing global tourism, the World Health Organization and World Tourism Organization have been urged to cooperate on a strategic initiative to provide guidelines for future action (Schulte, 1999). The emphasis of the initiative rests on the importance of working with primary stakeholders involved in and influenced by global tourism patterns. The result has been the 'healthy travel and tourism' campaign, whose primary objectives are to impact tourism constructively in order to ensure avoidance of health problems, to promote health among both travellers and host communities, and to establish healthy tourism networks among private sector representatives (such as tour operators and travel agencies) and the destination authorities in order to define action priorities. The global public health ramifications of travel can only be mitigated by the synergistic efforts of the aforementioned international organizations.

Note

1. The Mediterranean Basin includes the larger islands of Crete (Greece), Sicily and Sardinia (Italy), and Corsica (France), the smaller Aegean and Ionian islands of the Greek Archipelago (over 2,500 islands and islets), the Adriatic islands of Croatia (1,185 islands, islets, and reefs), the Aeolian islands (Lipari, Vulcano, Stromboli, Salina, Panarea, Basiluzzo, Filicudi, Alicudo) and the Archipelago of Tuscany of Italy, the Balearic islands of Spain (16 islands, of which the best known are Majorca, Minorca, Cabrera, Ibiza, and Formentera), and the island-microstates of Cyprus and Malta (Gozo and Comino belong to the same group).

References

Apostolopoulos, Y. (1996) *The Effects of Tourism Expansion in the Greek Islands: Regional Tourism Planning and Policy Lessons for Sustainable Development*. Athens: Papazissis.

Apostolopoulos, Y. and Gayle, D.J. (eds) (2001) *Island Tourism and Sustainable Development: Experiences of Caribbean, Pacific, and Mediterranean Islands*. Westport: Praeger.

Apostolopoulos, Y., Loukissas, P., and Leontidou, L. (eds) (2000) *Mediterranean Tourism: Facets of Socioeconomic Development and Cultural Change*. London and New York: Routledge.

Apostolopoulos, Y. and Sonmez, S. (1999) From farmers and shepherds to shopkeepers and hoteliers: constituency-differentiated experiences of endogenous tourism in the Greek island of Zakynthos. *International Journal of Tourism Research* 1: 413–27.

Apostolopoulos, Y. and Sonmez, S. (2000a) The epidemiology of tourist migration: a structural model for health risks of young vacation travelers. *Social Science & Medicine* (under review).

Apostolopoulos, Y. and Sonmez, S. (2000b) Tourist migration, public health, and sustainable development: theoretical and applied perspectives. *World Development* (under review).

Apostolopoulos, Y. and Sonmez, S. (2000c) New directions in Mediterranean tourism: restructuring and cooperative marketing in the era of globalization. *Thunderbird International Business Review* 42: 1–13.

Apostolopoulos, Y. and Sonmez, S. (2001) Disease mapping and risk assessment for public health and sustainable tourism development in insular regions. In Y. Apostolopoulos and D.J. Gayle (eds), *Island Tourism and Sustainable Development: Experiences of Caribbean, Pacific, and Mediterranean Islands*. Westport: Praeger.

Apostolopoulos, Y., Sonmez, S., Mattila, A. and Yu, L.C. (2000a) Casual sex and substance abuse on spring break: theoretical and empirical considerations. In progress, to be submitted to the *Journal of Applied Social Psychology*.

Apostolopoulos, Y., Sonmez, S., Mattila, A., and Yu, L.C. (2000b) Risk and protective factors associated with casual sex on spring break: a case of situational disinhibition? In progress, to be submitted to the *Journal of Health and Social Behavior*.

Apostolopoulos, Y., Sonmez, S., Mattila, A. and Yu, L.C. (2000c) Risk and protective factors associated with substance abuse on spring break: gender comparisons. In progress, to be submitted to the *American Journal of Public Health*.

Apostolopoulos, Y., Sonmez, S., Mattila, A. and Yu, L.C. (2000d) Alcohol abuse and HIV risk behaviors of American spring-break travelers. In progress, to be submitted to the *International Journal of STD & AIDS*.

Apostolopoulos, Y., Sonmez, S. and Timothy, D.J. (2001) *Women as Producers and Consumers of Tourism in Developing Regions*. Westport: Praeger.

Bartholet, J. (2000) The plague years. *Newsweek*, 17 January: 32–8.

Black, J. (1992) *The British Abroad: The Grand Tour in the Eighteenth Century*. New York: St Martin's Press.

Brohman, J. (1996) New directions in tourism for third world development. *Annals of Tourism Research*, 23: 48–70.

Broring, G. (1997) Prostitution, intravenous drug use, and travel: European HIV/AIDS prevention initiatives. In S. Clift and P. Grabowski (eds), *Tourism and Health*. London: Pinter.

Butler, R. (1980) The concept of a tourist area cycle of evolution: implications for management of resources. *The Canadian Geographer*, 24: 5–12.

Centers for Disease Control and Prevention (2000) *Health Information for International Travel.* Atlanta: US Department of Health and Human Services.

Clark, N. and Clift, S. (1996) Dimensions of holiday experiences and their health implications. In S. Clift and S.J. Page (eds), *Health and the International Tourist.* London and New York: Routledge.

Clift, S. and Forrest, S. (1999a) Gay men and tourism: destinations and motivations. *Tourism Management*, 20: 615–25.

Clift, S. and Forrest, S. (1999b) Factors associated with gay men's sexual behaviors and risk on holiday. *AIDS Care*, 11: 281–98.

Cossar, J.H. (1997) Health and travel: historical perspectives, emerging problems. In S. Clift and P. Grabowski (eds), *Tourism and Health.* London: Pinter.

De Schryver, A. and Meheus, A. (1989) International travel and sexually transmitted diseases. *World Health Statistics Quarterly*, 42: 90–9.

Downie, R., Fyfe, C. and Tannahill, A. (1993) *Health Promotion: Models and Values.* Oxford: Oxford University Press.

Eiser, J.R. and Ford, N. (1995) Sexual relationships on holiday: a case of situational disinhibition? *Journal of Social and Personal Relationships*, 12: 323–39.

Enloe, C. (1989) *Bananas, Beaches, and Bases: Making Feminist Sense of International Politics.* Berkeley, CA: University of California Press.

Ford, N. and Eiser, J.R. (1996) Risk and liminality: the HIV-related socio-sexual interaction of young tourists. In S. Clift and S.J. Page (eds), *Health and the International Tourist.* London and New York: Routledge.

Ford, N., Inman, M. and Mathie, E. (1996) Interaction to enhance mindfulness: positive strategies to increase tourists' awareness of HIV and sexual health risks on holiday. In S. Clift and S.J. Page (eds), *Health and the International Tourist.* London and New York: Routledge.

Fsadni, C. and Selwyn, T. (eds) (1996) *Sustainable Tourism in Mediterranean Islands and Small Cities.* Malta: Med-Campus.

Fussell, P. (1989) *Abroad, British Literary Traveling Between the Wars.* New York: Oxford University Press.

Glass, R.I., Claeson, M., Blake, P.A., Waldman, R.J. and Pierce, N.R. (1991) Cholera in Africa: lessons on transmission and control for Latin America. *Lancet*, 338: 791–5.

Goma Epidemiology Group (1994) Public health impact of Rwandan refugee crisis: what happened in Goma, Zaire. *Lancet*, 345: 339–44.

Grabowski, P. and Chatterjee, S. (1997) The Indian plague scare of 1994: a case study. In S. Clift and P. Grabowski (eds), *Tourism and Health.* London: Pinter.

Gushulak, B. (1999) Travel health in a broader context: issues of migration health for the next century. In W. Pasini (ed.), *Mobility and Health: From Hominoid Migration to Mass Tourism.* Rimini: Tipolito La Pieve.

International Organization for Migration (2000) Migration health in the year 2000 – whither the future? *Migration and Health Newsletter* 1/2000.

Jenner, P. and Smith, S. (1993) *Tourism in the Mediterranean.* London: Economist Intelligence Unit.

Kempadoo, K. (ed.) (1999) *Sun, Sex, and Gold: Tourism and Sex Work in the Caribbean.* Lanham: Rowman and Littlefield.

Lewis, N.D. and Bailey, J. (1992/93) HIV, international travel, and tourism: global issues and Pacific perspectives. *Asia-Pacific Journal of Public Health*, 6: 159–67.

Mabey, D. and Mayaud, P. (1997) Sexually transmitted diseases in mobile populations. *Genitourin Medicine*, 73: 18–22.

Maticka-Tyndale, E., Herold, E.S. and Mewhinney, D. (1998) Casual sex on spring break: intentions and behaviors of Canadian students. *Journal of Sex Research* 35: 254–64.

Mulhall, B.P. (1996) Sex and travel: studies of sexual behavior, disease, and health promotion in international travelers – a global review. *International Journal of STD and AIDS*, 7: 455–65.

Page, S.J., Clift, S. and Clark, N. (1994) Tourist health: the precautions, behavior, and health problems of British tourists in Malta. In A.V. Seaton (ed.), *Tourism: The State of the Art*. New York: Wiley.

Pearce, P.L. (1982) *The Social Psychology of Tourist Behavior*. Oxford: Pergamon Press.

Philipp, R., Pond, K., Rees, G. and Bartram, J. (1999) The association of tourist health with aesthetic quality and environmental values. In W. Pasini (ed.), *Mobility and Health: From Hominoid Migration to Mass Tourism*. Rimini: Tipolito La Pieve.

Reid, D. and Cossar, J.H. (1993) Epidemiology of travel. *British Medical Bulletin*, 49: 7–68.

Saliba, L.J. (1990) Making the Mediterranean safer. *World Health Forum*, 11: 274–81.

Schulte, V. (1999) Healthy travel and tourism: a new initiative of the World Health Organization and the World Tourism Organization. In W. Pasini (ed.), *Mobility and Health: From Hominoid Migration to Mass Tourism*. Rimini: Tipolito La Pieve.

Shaw, G. and Williams, A.M. (1997) *Critical Issues in Tourism: A Geographical Perspective*. Oxford: Blackwell.

Shields, R. (1992) *Places of the Margin: Alternative Geographies of Modernity*. London: Routledge.

Steffen, R. (1997) The epidemiology of travel-related health problems. In S. Clift and P. Grabowski (eds), *Tourism and Health*. London: Pinter.

Stratford, D., Ellerbrock, T.V., Akins, J.K. and Hall, H. (2000) Highway cowboys, old hands, and Christian truckers: risk behavior for human immunodeficiency virus infection among long-haul truckers in Florida. *Social Science and Medicine*, 50: 737–49.

Tannahill, A. (1985) What is health promotion? *Health Education Journal*, 44: 167–8.

Tones, K. (1992) Empowerment and the promotion of health. *Journal of the Institute of Health Education*, 30: 133–7.

United Nations High Commission for Refugees (1998) www.unhcr.ch/un&re/numbers/numbers.htm

Wickens, E. (1997) Licensed for thrills: risk-taking and tourism. In S. Clift and P. Grabowski (eds), *Tourism and Health*. London: Pinter.

Wilks, J. and Atherton, T. (1994) Health and safety in Australian marine tourism: social, medical, and legal appraisal. *Journal of Tourism Studies*, 5: 2–16.

Wilson, M.E. (1995) Travel and the emergence of infectious diseases. *Emerging Infectious Diseases*, 1: 39–46.

Wilson, M.E., Levins R. and Spielman A. (1994) *A Disease in Evolution: Global Changes and Emergence of Infectious Disease*. New York: New York Academy of Sciences.

World Health Organization (1994) *Public Health and Coastal Tourism*. Geneva: WHO.

World Tourism Organization (2000) *Yearbook of Tourism Statistics*. Madrid: WTO.

World Travel and Tourism Council/Travel Business Roundtable (1999) *Travel and Tourism: A White Paper*. Brussels: WTTC and TBR.

14

Tourism and Sustainability in the Mediterranean: Issues and Implications from Hydra

Richard Butler and Eleni Stiakaki

Introduction

The Mediterranean, and the land within and surrounding it, represent the largest tourist destination in the world in terms of visitor numbers. The region attracts, as it has done for many years, around a quarter or more of international arrivals (WTO, 1998). Numbers of arrivals exceed one hundred million a year, and in many localities there are sizeable pockets of extremely intensive tourist development and very high densities of tourists.

Sustainability is not a term that springs instantly to mind in the context of Mediterranean tourism. The area is, like most tourist areas, dynamic in terms of the nature and level of tourism it experiences. While major markets and popular destinations have a measure of durability, overall length of stay in Mediterranean resorts is declining. There is also a shift away from conventional hotel accommodation, and a rise in specialized forms of tourism, if not a decline in conventional sun and sand tourism (Montanari, 1995; Priestley *et al.*, 1996). Perhaps more significantly, the continued overall appeal of the Mediterranean masks the rise and fall in popularity of individual destinations, regions, and even countries. The Mediterranean finds itself facing intense competition from other parts of the world and competing from a position of relative declining strength. The region still possesses locational advantages in terms of proximity and easy access from its traditional major markets in industrial Europe, and a potentially new large market from the former communist countries of Eastern Europe. Nevertheless, other, more distant parts of the world offer similar attractions at often comparable cost, with newer infrastructure, lower densities of development, fewer tourists, and the added appeal of the exotic.

The Mediterranean, perhaps more than any other tourist region of the world is suffering from its own success, a success that has continued for a long time. Jenner and Smith comment 'the Mediterranean has been "spoilt". This includes a mixture of perceptions – that the area is too crowded, that the local culture has become diluted, that the sea is polluted by sewage, or that long airport delays have to be endured' (1993: 8–9). If for no other reason than to remain competitive, Mediterranean tourism needs to become more sustainable, although whether it can achieve this in any significant sense remains to be seen.

The issues raised by the consideration of sustainability and sustainable development of tourism in the Mediterranean are little different from those resulting from a consideration of these topics in other tourist destinations. In the context of the Mediterranean, however, the relatively long history of tourism development, combined with the magnitude of tourism in the region makes many of the problems particularly complex and significant. This short discussion cannot examine these issues in depth. Instead, it provides a context for discussion and raises what are regarded as key themes and issues, which are felt to be at the core of the problems faced by many of the Mediterranean countries when attempting to deal with the issues of sustainable development in a tourism context. The problems of capacity and crowding and, by implication, the issue of excessive tourist numbers, are key elements in any discussion of sustainability, and are examined by way of the example of tourism pressures on the Greek island of Hydra.

Sustainability and the Tourism Product

One might argue that to a major segment of the large tourism market, 'The Mediterranean' symbolizes a product with a rather generalized and at times stereotypical image, rather than a specific geographical or political region. This image can be taken to include sun and sand destinations, coastal resorts, the Mediterranean or one of its adjoining seas and waterways, historic communities, charter flights and other traditional elements of 'mass' tourism. Elements of confusion inevitably occur with such an image and complicate discussions of sustainability and other aspects of tourism. The range of tourism products offered in the Mediterranean region is extremely wide, and while most visitors may fit the stereotype of mass tourism, clearly, a wide variety of forms of tourism have developed and are being developed in this region. Some of these other forms, such as visits focused upon the historical and cultural heritage of the region, gambling at the casinos of Monte Carlo and elsewhere, and cruises, have a history as long or longer than modern tourism in the region (Pearce, 1978). Other forms of tourism such as those focusing on sports and activities, natural history, or education are much more recent in development. These forms of tourism vary widely in their responsiveness to sustainable development principles and practices as noted below.

The literature on sustainable development is replete with discussions on the difficulties of defining and operationalizing the term. Even within a single country it is clear that there is a very wide range of opinion on what the term means and how it might be applied. Within the range of countries included in the Mediterranean region one can expect even wider variations and ideas of the term. The Brundtland Commission's (WCED, 1987) oft-quoted definition of sustainable development as meeting the needs of the present while safeguarding the needs of future generations is almost meaningless in real terms. Moreover, when applied in the context of tourism, which was not even mentioned in the report, this definition leaves more than a little measure of uncertainty. Any review of sustainability in the tourism context, or the ill-named and equally undefined sustainable tourism makes clear the fact that there is no clearly agreed definition of the term (Butler, 1999). While innumerable recent developments have termed themselves, or have been hailed as sustainable, in reality such claims are probably as unrealistic as they are unverifiable. We have not yet been able to define or measure the needs, if they are such, of the present generation with respect to tourism, let alone come anywhere close to defining the requirements of future generations in this area. In this sense, the Mediterranean is only slightly different from any other area, except that it has the added difficulty of being comprised of a considerable number of individual states (the number varies depending on definition, but is over twenty). Considerable physical variety and a large number of traditions and beliefs about the environment and human use of that environment also characterize the region.

As noted above, the use of the Mediterranean as a tourist destination has a long history and the patterns of the present day have evolved in an unplanned and often highly competitive manner. This is only to be expected in an area with no overall responsible authority, in which many governments are present, often at odds, if not conflict with one another. The Grand Tour of 200 years ago (Towner, 1985) laid the pattern of much tourism activity in parts of the northern Mediterranean, and established it as one of the major tourist destinations in the civilized world. In more recent times, from the early development of elite tourism in southern France and northern Italy, one can clearly trace the spread of tourism through the region. It has essentially followed a distance-related expansion (relative to markets in north central Europe) in terms of large numbers of visitors, or mass tourism, although certain centres such as Venice, parts of Spain and of course Egypt have equally long histories of tourism development for specific limited markets. Spain, in the 1960s, began a new form of intensive tourism development, based on low prices and chartered jet aircraft, catering to the lower income mass market rather than the more affluent market that had been attracted to France and Italy previously. After Spain came Malta, Cyprus, the Adriatic coast, Greece and then North Africa and Turkey.

In most of these destinations some form of small-scale, often what might be termed elite tourism, had already existed as demonstrated by a few normally large and often luxurious hotels. The result now is that tourism in the Mediterranean displays the full range of the stages of tourism development, along with all that this implies, including a variety of attitudes towards tourism, varying expectations and appreciation of the sector's contributions, and many different forms of impacts.

The Difficulties of Achieving Sustainability

Sustainability in any context rarely just happens and in the context of tourism is extremely unlikely to occur by chance unless circumstances mitigate heavily against large-scale tourism development (Butler, 1996). In the Mediterranean, this clearly is not the case, since the area has experienced rapid and extensive tourism development. Moreover, in the absence of major changes in exogenous factors, the region is likely to continue to witness further development, although such development is unlikely to be evenly spread or follow existing patterns (Jenner and Smith, 1993). If we accept even the very basic concepts of the resort cycle model (Butler, 1980), then it is likely that destinations will be developed continuously until they reach a point at which further development is impossible because of environmental, economic, social or political factors. In most cases, this translates into being developed until the destinations' capacity has been exceeded and their appeal and marketability have begun to decline. In recent decades we have seen this pattern experienced in Spain, France, Malta and Cyprus (Ioannides, 1992). Without recent political troubles such a pattern may have emerged as well in parts of the former Yugoslavia. It is fair to say that, to date, no destination in the Mediterranean has achieved a state of sustainability in tourism. Additionally, few places have seriously begun to move towards such a state, to the degree where they have been prepared to contemplate reducing numbers of tourists in order to improve quality of experience and reduce impacts on the destination environments.

The reasons for this are fairly clear and have been stated by a number of writers in a variety of forms (for example, see Andronikou, 1987; Montanari and Williams, 1995; Priestley *et al.*, 1996), but essentially can be reduced to a few simple statements. To achieve sustainability specific conditions must be met. Before this can occur, however, there must be a change in mindset from expecting or demanding continued growth to one of operating within a destination's capacity limits. This in turn requires an acceptance that tourism may not be able to continue to operate as it has done in the past and that the level of tourism may have to be limited if not actually reduced. In reality, this should not be such an unpalatable pill to swallow, because past experience in the Mediterranean and elsewhere suggests that if such changes are not instituted, then numbers and receipts will probably decline inevitably and perhaps irreparably anyway.

The conditions to be met include the determination of limits to development (these include both social and environmental limits). They also necessitate the identification of the most appropriate and acceptable forms of tourism that will come closest to meeting economic requirements while remaining within the aforesaid limits. Moreover, they require the establishment of institutional arrangements to ensure that limits are not exceeded, and a willingness to ensure that these arrangements are implemented over the long term. In short, this necessitates good planning and management of tourism development, hardly a revolutionary concept in theory but perhaps a very real revolution in application, particularly given the experience in many Mediterranean countries to date.

The Mediterranean countries are in an appropriate position to want a move towards sustainability. This is because a good number of them now see the problems resulting from the rapid construction of relatively poorly planned and managed developments of a few decades ago, and are experiencing pressures from competing destinations, new marketing concepts and ever more rapidly changing tastes of tourists. It is a sad commentary on all involved in tourism that demands for sustainable development have arrived so late and frequently come from those who previously had allowed or encouraged tourism to have been developed in an as unsustainable form as possible. Unfortunately for areas such as the Mediterranean, it is much easier for destinations just entering tourism to introduce and operate sustainable development principles than it is for established and mature destinations to retroactively apply such principles. Introducing any form of what may be regarded as restrictive controls is much easier to accomplish before there is any development when such regulations can be applied universally from the start, than applying such controls in an established tourism area. What frequently happens in established tourist destinations is that while new development may be subject to controls aiming at making such developments more sustainable, existing developments continue to operate in their normal unsustainable manner. Adding more sustainable developments to already existing unsustainable ones does not help greatly in achieving overall sustainability. In discussing the introduction of more rigorous planning laws in Cyprus in the last decade, Godfrey concluded that the new smaller-scale developments 'will do little to mitigate the effects of the estimated two million visitor arrivals'. He went on to comment that the new legislation 'may have little effect on controlling the impact of tourism. While, on paper, the introduction of stronger development control policies recognizes the failure of past actions, this alone may not bring about a more sustainable industry' (1996: 73).

Cyprus was not alone in claiming to have 'adequate controls at the national level' (Andronikou, cited in Godfrey, 1996: 74), but as Godfrey points out, legislation and policies designed to exclude mass tourism are only the framework, and much depends on how local authorities define and enforce such overall objectives. The fact is that in many countries, not only those in the Mediterranean basin, final decisions on development are made at the local level, where individual freedom and the desire for economic development are often paramount. This frequently means that the community involvement in tourism called for by many commentators (Murphy, 1985) may in fact result in intensive local development in opposition to stated goals at higher levels. It is true to say that local autonomy and the right to develop are probably stronger in many Mediterranean countries than elsewhere. Unfortunately, this tradition of individual development rights represents a major problem to the successful introduction of controls and regulations to limit development in pursuit of sustainable development principles.

One essential point that must be borne in mind when discussing sustainable development is that while the maxim 'think globally, act locally' has some merit, acting locally in isolation is likely to have very little effect in achieving sustainability at any scale. No tourist development can achieve true sustainability; rather, at best it can only approach such a state (Butler, 1997; Wall, 1997). Tourist development in isolation, however, is unlikely to function effectively for it has to be linked to at least the domestic market and almost certainly in this day and age to the international market to have any chance of success. In the same way, no destination can achieve complete sustainability, and nor can it exist divorced from its market and its surroundings. Sustainable development cannot and will not be attained at the local scale in isolation, and neither will it be achieved at the sectional level. Tourism alone cannot attain sustainability, as sustainable forms of tourism can only be approached if tourism is integrated environmentally, socially, and economically with other forms of economic activity. The public sector at all levels must integrate with the private sector if controls and regulations are to be successful in moving towards sustainability. The territorial strategy described by Vera and Rippin (1996) in the Valencia region of Spain as part of the Plan Futures would appear a significant development in the right direction in that regard (see also chapter by Bardolet in this volume).

The Case of Hydra

Although the problems with many of the major large-scale tourism developments and destinations are well known, there are numerous examples of unsustainable development at much smaller and more local scales in various parts of the Mediterranean. In many respects these small destinations display the same set of problems and difficulties as the major destinations. In fact, in relative terms with respect to the human and physical environments involved, these problems may be more significant in certain smaller destinations because these may not yet have gone beyond the point of no return as far as some aspects of sustainability may be concerned. The island of Hydra is an interesting example that reveals the difficulties of trying to achieve suitable tourism growth and development in line with the principles of sustainable development when facing particular problems of excessive pressures on the destination's carrying capacity.

Issues of Sustainability and Tourism Pressure in Hydra

Tourism development on Hydra

Hydra is one of 167 inhabited Greek islands, and because of its relatively close proximity (some 60 km) to Piraeus, the port of Athens, experiences considerable tourist pressure during the summer months. The island is small, covering a surface area of only 50 km^2 and maximum dimensions of 23 and 5 km in length and breadth respectively. Unlike some of the other Greek islands, the population is relatively low, being only 2,800. The island has an extremely rich history and was declared a 'Heritage Site' in 1993 and an 'Archaeological Site' in 1996 by the Greek Ministry of Culture. The laws protecting the architectural heritage of the island mean that construction is severely restricted, and specific controls exerted in cases where permission for development is granted. Motor vehicles have been prohibited on the island since 1971 (Stiakaki, 1998).

Tourism, currently the principal economic activity and the only real source of economic development, began to appear in Hydra in the 1950s. Previously, the economy, like that of many similar Mediterranean islands, was based primarily on marine resources, particularly fish and sponges. As with many small islands in peripheral areas, Hydra has suffered from emigration for many years (Filho, 1996; Buhalis, 1998). The focal area of the island is the town and port of Hydra, the only formal access to the island. The town is built in an amphitheatrical fashion around its bay, stretching up the surrounding hills, and characterized by narrow streets and densely packed houses, many of outstanding architectural merit.

A few small hotels existed before 1950, but the scale of tourism changed drastically in the early years of that decade. An English cruise boat visited the island in 1951. A year later, two larger hotels (although still modest by modern-day standards) began operating and 8,872 tourists were recorded during the summer (*Future of Hydra*, 1952). The single event that placed Hydra firmly on the tourist map was the filming on the island of the movie *The Child and the Dolphin*, starring Sophia Loren. During the same decade Melina Merkouri starred in the movie *Fedra* which was also filmed on Hydra. This further enhanced the island's popularity. In the 1960s several larger hotels were built and the island became known as the 'Capri of Greece'. In 1961, over 48,000 tourists visited Hydra, up from 32,355 the year before (*Future of Hydra*, 1960). By the end of the 1960s, visitor numbers were around

100,000 and cruise boats had begun to visit the island regularly. The first two in service carried 400 visitors each and remained on the island for a short time (approximately one hour), a practice that has become common in subsequent years.

At present there are approximately 600 official beds on Hydra. Nevertheless, a more realistic figure of available accommodation is close to 1,200, if unregistered facilities are taken into account (Stiakaki, 1998; see Chapter 8 by Buhalis and Diamantis, in this volume). The predominant feature of tourism today, however, is not guests staying overnight, but day visitors arriving by cruise boats. On most days in the summer there are at least three boats visiting Hydra from Piraeus, with a capacity of around 2,300 passengers. These passengers normally stay on the island for 2 to 3 hours. In addition to these regular cruise services, larger cruise ships travelling for several days through the Aegean also stop on the island. Hydra is also visited by smaller boats (each with a passenger capacity of 200) from other Greek islands and many private yachts and small water taxis from the neighbouring small islands. The town of Hydra is the focus of attention of visitors, because of its location as gateway to the island but also because of its impressive setting, its architectural heritage and its array of shops and restaurants. Hydra shares many similarities in its development history with other Greek islands. For example, Coccossis and Parpairis (1996) and Stott (1996) make parallel remarks about the development of tourism in Mykonos. These authors note that tourism development on Mykonos has been based on heritage and climate plus a limited range of other resources. This development has halted and even reversed the chronic decline in population that had occurred until recently. While Mykonos now has far more available accommodation and is visited by many more tourists than Hydra, some of the same problems are present on both these destinations, as well as many other Mediterranean islands.

Sustainability and crowding issues in Hydra

While the overnight visitors have a predictable pressure on the local community, it is the day visitors who appear to create the greatest barrier to achieving sustainability. On average, overnight visitors arriving on commercial vessels tend to stay slightly over two nights, mostly during weekends. Figures for visitors who stay overnight on their own boats are unavailable. During the 1990s, the numbers of overnight visitors have fluctuated between 5,000 and 9,000 annually, while total nights spent have been between 13,000 and 23,000. In a population of around 2,800 permanent residents, these numbers do not represent a very high ratio of visitors to locals, even at peak times during July and August compared to the situation in some other Greek islands. Nevertheless, there are problems related to water supply and sewage disposal. Water is brought to the island daily by boat while sewage is untreated and allowed to flow freely into the harbour. These permanent problems are exacerbated by the concentration of most arrivals during the summer months. In addition to the overnight visitors mentioned above an unknown number of day visitors also arrive on the island, a reasonable estimate being in excess of 4,000 on any peak summer day (Stiakaki, 1998).

The key problems faced by Hydra are related to the high concentration of tourists in a relatively small area. The island's topography and the layout of the town itself are major factors behind this concentration. Ironically, the absence of motor transport further contributes to this problem. Since tourists must walk (or rent a donkey) and given the relatively short amount of time most of them have on the island, they cannot travel far from the harbour. Overnight visitors are also mostly confined to the town, especially during weekends, which is when most of them visit. Of key interest within the context of this chapter was the distribution of these tourists within the town, along with their activity profile and their perceptions of crowding and congestion. This information was necessary in order to identify mitigating strategies that might eventually relieve some of the pressure and make the destination more sustainable in terms of preventing over-use and abuse of the island's heritage.

Data

As noted above, Hydra has an impressive architectural heritage, and this, combined with its climate and culture and its proximity to Piraeus, plus its film-derived fame, has resulted in increasing tourist pressure particularly during the peak months of July and August. During these two months, crowding and capacity problems reach critical levels especially on the island's main arrival point, the harbour within the old town, a problem that is exacerbated because of the area's configuration and scale. However, until recently no detailed examination of the pattern of visitor behaviour, or of the perceptions of visitors with respect to congestion and possible decline in quality of experience, had been conducted. The field study on which this chapter is based took place during the summer months of 1998 (Stiakaki, 1998) and consisted of three elements. These were respectively: interviews with tourists arriving by all boats except cruise vessels, a specific survey of passengers travelling on cruise ships, and observation of visitor behaviour in the port and old town of Hydra.

Two hundred interviews were conducted during July 1998 with tourists travelling on ferries and local commercial vessels as they were waiting to board their vessels for departure at the end of their visit to Hydra. A further 50 interviews were conducted with owners of private yachts and boats in the harbour. The second element consisted of short surveys with cruise vessel passengers as visitors were departing Hydra. The sample size for this survey was 260 visitors. The emphasis in this short survey was on visitor movement around the town. The third element was a covert non-participant observation of cruise ship visitors to Hydra, conducted on all days of the week between 9.00 a.m. and 8.00 p.m. over two-hour periods. Fifteen specific groups were followed and observed. The focus of the ensuing discussion is on the visitation patterns within the town of Hydra as this is of primary interest in the context of capacity and sustainability of tourism on the island. It is based primarily on data from the observations and a limited amount of information gathered from the interviews and surveys.

Day visitors

The observational data were obtained in order to determine peak times during the day and peak days during the week. These data were cross-referenced with available statistics on arrivals in the harbour. Not surprisingly, peak days were Saturday and Sunday, while peak hours were between noon and 5.00 p.m. Congestion was observed in the port area and the area of the old town immediately adjacent to the port but was not identified in other parts of the town. The town was divided into six zones, each of which had its own entrance, and data collected on use patterns for each of these zones (Table 14.1).

The figures in Table 14.1 show the numbers of tourists entering each zone during the time periods identified and indicate clearly the concentration of visitors in the two zones (East Bay and West Town 2). The first zone represents a popular walk in the harbour and the area where people go if they wish to swim near the town. The next busiest zone is the first part of the town where people enter after leaving the cruise boat disembarkation point. Considering that the total population of the island is only around 2,800, the presence of over 700 people per hour within the East Bay during peak times gives some indication of the impact the town of Hydra experiences. The pattern of visitor flows around the town, discussed more fully elsewhere (Stiakaki, 1998), reflects very clearly that most day visitors have only a

Table 14.1 Visitor numbers in Hydra Port area zones

Zone/numbers	Time 12.00–13.00	Time 13.00–14.00	Total
East Bay	754	704	1,458
East town	230	270	500
Central	200	230	430
West town 1	160	150	310
West town 2	631	403	1,034
West harbour	350	200	550

Source: Based on Hydra survey

limited time to spend in the town and, thus, do not venture far from the harbour. Generally, the data indicate that with increasing distance away from the disembarkation points in the harbour the density of visitors falls.

The activity patterns of cruise visitors were examined in further detail through a survey of departing visitors. These individuals were given a map of the town on which they had to identify the places they had visited. All 260 individuals in the sample had walked the port road from the disembarkation point to the central marina, which is the 'bottleneck' of the pedestrian routes. The pattern of movement of cruise visitors matched closely the pattern of all visitors shown in Table 14.1. Over half the cruise arrivals entered the 'East Bay' while the second most popular area was the 'West town 2' zone. Almost half (45 per cent) also entered other zones away from the harbour. Approximately 70 per cent entered more than one zone. The covert non-participant observation of 15 groups revealed a similar pattern of visitation, with all groups walking the port road. Just like the cruise visitors, individuals in these groups entered the two most popular zones: 55 per cent entered the 'East Bay' and 45 per cent the 'West town 2'.

Some general conclusions can be drawn from the movement patterns of day visitors. There is a fairly common pattern of distribution of arrivals with the majority visiting two of the town's six zones. All visitors surveyed and observed used the port road and entered the harbour area of the town, a flow that is almost inevitable given their arrival by boat at one or the other side of the bay.

Several other factors also influence the spatial distribution of visitors on Hydra. In the summer the temperatures are high, and to most tourists a long walk in hot sun is unappealing. Considering many of the cruise boat passengers are not young (over half being over 40 and more than a quarter over 50) they are not expected to traverse long distances on foot although, it must be noted, there was no statistical relationship between age and visitation patterns. Moreover, the town's attractions are not immediately visible and not all are well sign-posted. Thus, some visitors are generally reluctant to venture too far from the harbour because they may fear getting lost in the small streets and missing certain key features and/or being late for their departure. As 85 per cent of cruise visitors are first time visitors to Hydra, they are not familiar with the geography of the town and, as revealed by the interviews, most of them had received no information about Hydra before their visit. Indeed, the majority of those interviewed were even uncertain about the specific identity of the island they were on at the time of the interview. Finally, many of the obvious tourist attractions such as the shops and cafés are concentrated around the harbour and, thus, delay tourists who might otherwise have ventured further afield if they had more time. The concentration pattern of day visitors on Hydra supports Russo's (1999) assertion that excursionists are blamed most often for causing carrying capacity problems in destinations.

Overnight visitors

Overnight visitors were expected to have a greater knowledge of Hydra and, of course, to have more time at their disposal than the excursionists. These overnight tourists fell into two distinct groups, those staying in land accommodation and those spending their holiday on their own boats (Stiakaki, 1998). Both groups shared certain similarities. The majority of overnight visitors in each set were Greek (70 per cent and 60 per cent, respectively). However, while as many as 30 per cent of the yacht-based visitors were either English or American, these nationalities were rarely represented among land-based tourists. The most common age category in each group was 30–40 years old, although the yacht visitors were overall somewhat older than the land-based tourists. Forty-five per cent of land-based visitors were on their first visit to Hydra compared to 55 per cent of yacht visitors. As might be expected, Greeks represented a higher proportion of return visitors in both groups. Length of stay was significantly different, with two-thirds of land-based visitors staying two days, and a further 30 per cent staying three days or more, while of the yacht-based visitors, 80 per cent stayed just one day, with the remainder staying two or three days at most. Although both groups cited proximity to Athens and scenery as popular reasons behind their visits, heritage, culture and architecture received a surprisingly low ranking. The majority (70 per cent) of land-based visitors had no prior information on Hydra, although a slight majority (52 per cent) of yacht-based visitors did.

Of the land-based visitors, 18 per cent stayed in the town of Hydra for the duration of their visit, spending most of that time in the port area. The accommodation they used was also close to the harbour. Those staying three or four days and even some of the shorter stay visitors travelled to different parts of the island, most frequently to swim. All visitors spent some time in the town and the port area. While the overall majority felt that Hydra as a whole was not overcrowded (76 per cent), an even larger proportion (84 per cent) felt that the port area of the town was congested. They also made negative comments concerning the litter and the sewage in the port.

The yacht-based visitors displayed somewhat different patterns of movement. During their stay on Hydra, most of them (70 per cent) sailed around the island and even visited other islands. Even so, while on Hydra, they spent most of their time in the port area, since this is where their boat was moored and where supplies were available. Compared to other groups, only a small proportion of yacht-based tourists had ventured away from the harbour. There was no consistency in their pattern of movement around the town or in features visited. The majority of these visitors (52 per cent) felt the port area was overcrowded, although a few (12 per cent) stated that the rest of the town was congested. Finally, they were dissatisfied with the marina size, particularly because of congestion, and also expressed negative opinions about the sewage and smell in the port.

Implications

Issues relating to capacity and crowding are fundamental to the concept of sustainability, because over-use eventually causes the deterioration of resources. This affects the quality of destinations and, consequently, the overall visitor experience. The actual geography of any destination can play a major role in the pattern of tourist activities and their subsequent impacts upon resources and attractions. In this respect, Hydra is typical of many island destinations, particularly in the Mediterranean, where history and geography have combined to limit the nature and extent of development and the distribution of attractions. The data summarized in the previous sections reveal there is considerable congestion in specific areas, most notably the port area of the town of Hydra. While most visitors surveyed said they would return to Hydra, more than two-thirds indicated their belief that the port area was congested and expressed concerns about its overall environmental quality. Based on Shelby *et al.*'s (1989)[2] argument, this situation indicates that the area has already exceeded its capacity.

The length of the visit and overall awareness about Hydra according to prior information also influence visitor use patterns and, hence, may result in congestion in specific areas. For example, many of the island's attractions such as its architectural heritage are not fully appreciated and are not the principal reason for visitation among stay-over visitors. Lack of knowledge about such attractions means that few tourists venture away from the island's harbour area and its various tourist-oriented establishments (e.g., cafés, restaurants, and shops). Most day visitors, in particular, have negligible information about the island and, thus, remain concentrated in the port area and those parts of the town immediately adjacent to it. It is evident that these day visitors represent a greater problem in terms of congestion than their overnight counterparts. This is because they have a short time at their disposal and because, compared to overnight visitors, a large proportion of them is comprised of first-time arrivals. Also, unlike the yacht-based tourists who can sail around the island or to other islands even, the short-term visitors have limited mobility meaning they cannot travel considerable distances. Finally, the concentration of a large number of short-term visitors on a small part of Hydra is particularly problematic considering their stay is for only a few hours (Stankey and Manning, 1986).

While, at least for the moment, it is not the expressed desire of local residents or of tourism agencies to reduce the number of visitors to Hydra, the issue of congestion and decline of environmental quality and, hence, the island's overall appeal cannot be ignored. The concentration of visitors and popular attractions in a very limited area is a common feature on many small islands, not just in Greece, but throughout the Mediterranean. The promotion of Hydra's unique heritage has been relatively ignored and while in one sense this has possibly helped reduce pressure on specific elements, it has meant that visitors have not been exposed to or had much, if any, information about some of the island's best features. There is, therefore, something of a dissonance between the reality of the island's heritage attractions and the main purpose for which it is visited. In other words, what is a rare and unique heritage site is actually visited for features that are common throughout most of the Greek islands, such as the climate, scenery and its harbour. This situation is exacerbated by the island's proximity to Athens, the focal area of international tourist arrivals in Greece.

A necessary element for readjusting a destination's tourism product is information. Generally speaking, visitors have a desire to maximize their enjoyment. Thus, they will try to fit their use of a particular destination into their expectations and desires. If Hydra is not portrayed and promoted as a heritage destination at least to a greater extent than at present, then certain visitors will miss out on the opportunity to maximize their enjoyment by not being aware of all of the island's attractions. Moreover, a number of tourists with a genuine interest in heritage sites may avoid the island altogether if they are not aware of all it has to offer. By the same token, those tourists who currently arrive on the island for its beaches and other related recreational attractions may be somewhat disappointed by the overall quality compared to other Greek islands.

Information can be presented in many ways (Hall and McArthur, 1996). Unfortunately, Hydra presently does a poor job at disseminating information. Improvements to enhance the information about the island could include the establishment of a tourist information centre in the port area while maps and signs could be strategically located throughout the town. Moreover, leaflets and other materials could be provided on the cruise boats and ferries for visitors to receive before arrival, including information about possible walks around the island. Physical adjustments such as one-way streets are much more difficult to enforce for pedestrian movement, but well-signposted walks and routes can encourage coordinated movement of pedestrians and thus alleviate crowding in specific areas.

Shifts in policy are necessary if the heritage of Hydra is to be protected effectively and promoted efficiently. There is little evidence, however, that this is likely to take place in the short term. Simple legal tools for protecting heritage sites do not always ensure preservation and do little to encourage interpretation or appropriate uses. Perhaps an increased focus on attracting a greater proportion of foreign visitors would be appropriate in the case of Hydra. If some of the Greek visitors, especially those desiring recreational attractions (e.g., quality sandy beaches) can be persuaded to visit other islands better suited to their needs, then a smaller number of higher spending foreign visitors could be drawn to Hydra to experience its heritage. After all, currently foreign yacht-based tourists are best informed about Hydra and its heritage and also spend less time in the island's most congested areas. Moreover, the day-visitor market could be more focused on those individuals seeking heritage experiences rather than those pursuing recreational activities they can obtain elsewhere. Hydra could then look to a future tourist industry based more on its unique resources, namely its heritage. Eventually, this would create a more sustainable future, than is presently the case.

Conclusion

The lessons to be learned from the examination of tourism-related problems in Hydra are ones that have some validity throughout the Mediterranean. In short, the issues that need to be addressed relate to two main elements, namely over-use and misuse of the environment.

There is little doubt that, for much of the peak season, Hydra, like many Mediterranean island destinations, is congested and overcrowded. The problem is manifested in the form of too many visitors at one point in time, in a destination facing difficulties of access and distribution of visitors. This is a common predicament in many destinations in the region. First, seasonality compounds this problem since visitors are concentrated within the short summer period. Second, the morphology of Hydra, like that of many Mediterranean settlements, does not encourage visitors to spread over the whole island. Instead, it forces them into one small part of the island, the main town and, in turn, into one or two specific areas of that town. These problems will remain unless both the temporal and spatial patterns of visitation can be made less concentrated. This, however, is relatively unlikely as the attraction of the area in general lies in its summer temperatures and its cultural legacy. In the long term, climatic change and global warming may reduce visitation in the two peak months, but little is likely to change the spatial pattern of the attractions or the distribution of visitors to Hydra.

In the context of what is labelled misuse, the authors are mindful of the fact that many of the visitors to Hydra were unaware of its architectural and archaeological heritage and obviously viewed it primarily as a location for a day trip by boat. This use of what is often sensitive heritage areas and facilities for uninformed casual visitors who could and, perhaps should, use less significant areas is common throughout the Mediterranean and elsewhere. The provision of additional and improved information about Hydra to potential visitors would at least allow them to benefit from the island's heritage opportunities. It also might persuade some of the tourists that other destinations better able to handle large numbers of visitors and offering a wider range of facilities such as bathing beaches and amusements would be more appropriate for visitation, thus reducing the pressure on locations like Hydra. Matching the needs and preferences of the visitor with the facilities and attractions of the destination is one essential step towards achieving appropriate and hence more sustainable use of resources and destinations.

The Mediterranean is too important a tourist destination to disappear from the world tourism map. Even a continuation of the decline in relative attractiveness in certain over-developed areas of the region is likely to be balanced by the development of new markets and redevelopment of older destinations such as Benidorm and Majorca (Vera and Rippin, 1996; see also the contribution by Bardolet in this volume). Nevertheless, competition will continue to be strong if there are continued increases in long-haul air travel and the development of other new destinations. One cannot be optimistic about the likelihood of many of the Mediterranean destinations achieving, or even shifting significantly, towards sustainability in the short to medium-term future. Nevertheless, there is little doubt that governments are moving, and will continue to promise to move, towards sustainable development, and that at the local level and individual scale many new developments will be more in line with sustainable development principles than most existing developments. Some national and regional level authorities may actually establish and even enforce regulations pertaining to sustainable development principles. Renewal and regeneration of some existing tourism developments are already taking place as noted above on the Costa Brava and other destinations, and redevelopment and possible revisioning and repositioning of other destinations in the region can be expected to follow.

Despite this, major difficulties remain. There is no overall agency responsible for the Mediterranean, and the effects of this void can be seen only too clearly in the quality of the sea itself. Tourism is far from being the only problem facing the Mediterranean, and as long ago as 1975 the severe environmental problems of the Mediterranean were recognized and the MAP (Mediterranean Action Plan formulated by countries bordering the Mediterranean under the UN Environmental Programme) launched (Montanari, 1995). Nevertheless, water and air quality problems still exist, and may be exacerbated if industrial relocation from northern to southern Europe continues. In addition to water quality, another severe problem for tourism and the region generally is water quantity. Tourism cannot solve its own problems alone and it certainly cannot solve the problems of the Mediterranean as a whole by striving to achieve sustainability single-handedly. Rather, the countries of the region must adopt a co-operative approach towards sustainable development if tourism itself is to have any hopes of moving significantly towards sustainability.

Note

1. Shelby *et al.*'s argument was that if more than two-thirds of visitors indicated that they felt crowded or congested, then the capacity of the location could be considered exceeded.

References

Andronikou, A. (1987) *Development of Tourism in Cyprus: Harmonization of Tourism with the Environment*. Nicosia: Cosmos.

Buhalis, D. (1998) *Tourism in Greece: Strategic Analysis and Challenges*. Aix-en-Provence: CISET.

Butler, R.W. (1980) The concept of a tourist area cycle of evolution: implications for management of resources. *Canadian Geographer*, 24(1): 5–12.

Butler, R.W. (1996) Problems and possibilities of sustainable tourism: the case of the Shetland islands. In L. Briguglio, R.W. Butler, D. Harrison and W. Filho (eds), *Sustainability in Islands and Small States: Case Studies*. London: Pinter (11–31).

Butler, R.W. (1997) Modelling tourism development: evolution, growth and decline. In S. Wahab and J.J. Pigram (eds), *Tourism, Development and Growth: The Challenge of Sustainability*. London: Routledge (109–28).

Butler, R.W. (1999) Sustainable tourism: a state of the art review. *Tourism Geographies*, 1(1): 7–25.

Coccossis, H. and Parpairis, A. (1996) Tourism and carrying capacity in coastal areas: Mykonos, Greece. In G.K. Priestley, J.A. Edwards and H. Coccossis (eds), *Sustainable Tourism? European Experiences*. Wallingford: CAB International (153–75).

Filho, W.L. (1996) Putting principles into practices: sustainable tourism in small island states. In L. Briguglio, B. Archer, J. Jafari and G. Wall (eds), *Sustainable Tourism in Islands and Small States: Issues and Policies*. London: Pinter (61–8).

Future of Hydra (1952 and 1960) (Annual publication of the history of Hydra and statistics). Hydra, Greece.

Godfrey, K. (1996) Towards sustainability? Tourism in the Republic of Cyprus. In L.C. Harrison and W. Husbands (eds), *Practising Responsible Tourism: International Case Studies in Tourism Planning, Policy, and Development*. Chichester: Wiley (58–80).

Hall, C.M. and McArthur, S. (1996) *Heritage Management in Australia and New Zealand: The Human Dimension*. Melbourne: Oxford University Press.

Ioannides, D. (1992) Tourism development agents: the Cypriot resort cycle. *Annals of Tourism Research*, 19(4): 711–31.

Jenner, P. and Smith, C. (1993) *Tourism in the Mediterranean Area*. London: The Economist Intelligence Unit.

Montanari, A. (1995) The Mediterranean region: Europe's summer leisure space. In A. Montanari and A.M. Williams (eds), *European Tourism: Regions, Spaces and Restructuring*. Chichester: John Wiley and Sons (41–66).

Montanari, A. and Williams, A.M. (1995) *European Tourism: Regions, Spaces and Restructuring*. Chichester: John Wiley and Sons.

Murphy, P.E. (1985) *Tourism: A Community Approach*. New York: Methuen.

Pearce, D.G. (1978) Form and function in French resorts. *Annals of Tourism Research*, 5(1): 142–56.

Priestley, G.K., Edwards, J.A. and Coccossis, H. (1996) *Sustainable Tourism? European Experiences*. Wallingford: CAB International.

Russo, A.P. (1999) The vicious circle of tourism development in heritage destinations: Why does it occur and how can it be prevented? Associação Portuguesa para Desenvolvimento Regional (ed.), *Tourism Sustainability and Territorial Organization*. Coimbra: APDR (255–76).

Shelby, B., Vaske, J.J. and Haberlein, T.A. (1989) Comparative analysis of crowding in multiple locations: results of fifteen years of research. *Leisure Sciences*, 11(4): 269–91.

Stankey, G. and Manning, R.E. (1986) Carrying capacity of recreational settings. In

Literature Review: President's Commission on American Outdoors. Washington, DC: US Government Printing Office (45–57).

Stiakaki, E. (1998) Carrying capacity and capacity management of heritage sites: case study of Hydra, Greece. MSc thesis, University of Surrey, Guildford.

Stott, M. (1996) Tourism development and the need for community action in Mykonos, Greece. In L. Briguglio, R.W. Butler, D.C. Harrison and W.L. Filho (eds), *Sustainable Tourism in Islands and Small States: Case Studies*. London: Pinter (281–306).

Towner, J. (1985) The Grand Tour: a key phase in tourism. *Annals of Tourism Research*, 12(3): 297–334.

Vera, F. and Rippin, R. (1996) Decline of a Mediterranean tourist area and restructuring strategies: the Valencian Region. In G.K. Priestley, J.A. Edwards and H. Coccossis (eds), *Sustainable Tourism? European Experiences*. Wallingford: CAB International (120–36).

Wall, G. (1997) Sustainable tourism: unsustainable development. In S. Wahab and J.J. Pigram (eds), *Tourism, Development and Growth: The Challenge of Sustainability*. London: Routledge (33–49).

World Commission on Environment and Development (WCED) (1987) *Our Common Future*. Oxford: Oxford University Press.

World Tourism Organization (WTO) (1998) *Digest of Statistics*. Madrid: World Tourism Organization.

Index